# CONSULTATION, COLLABORATION, AND TEAMWORK FOR STUDENTS WITH SPECIAL NEEDS

**Peggy Dettmer**
*Kansas State University*

**Linda P. Thurston**
*Kansas State University*

**Norma Dyck**
*Kansas State University*

**Allyn and Bacon**
Boston • London • Toronto • Sydney • Tokyo • Singapore

*Series Editor:* Ray Short
*Series Editorial Assistant:* Christine M. Shaw
*Production Editor:* Christopher Rawlings
*Cover Administrator:* Linda Dickinson
*Composition Buyer:* Linda Cox
*Cover Designer:* Suzanne Harbison
*Manufacturing Buyer:* Louise Richardson

Copyright © 1993 by Allyn & Bacon
A Division of Simon & Schuster, Inc.
160 Gould Street
Needham Heights, Massachusetts 02194

**Library of Congress Cataloging-in-Publication Data**

Dettmer, Peggy.
    Consultation, collaboration, and teamwork for students with special needs
Peggy Dettmer, Linda P. Thurston, Norma Dyck.
        p.    cm.
    Includes index.
    ISBN 0-205-13930-2
    1. Special Education—United States. 2. Educational consultants—
–United States. 3. Teaching teams—United States. I. Thurston,
Linda P. II. Dyck, Norma. III. Title.
LC4031.D48 1992
371.9′0973—dc20                                                       92–21643
                                                                            CIP

*The figures and tables in this text were designed and illustrated by Leonard Katzer, a doctoral student at Kansas State University. These images were created electronically using a Macintosh© SE/30 computer and Apple LaserWriter© printers. Programs used include Adobe Illustrator©, MacDraw©, Microsoft Works©, Cricket Paint©, and Cricket Draw©. These product names are trademarks or registered trademarks of their respective holders.*

Printed in the United States of America

10  9  8  7  6  5  4  3  2  1      97  96  95  94  93  92

# CONTENTS

# PREFACE

The time for consultation, collaboration, and teamwork in schools is overdue. Society's problems are immense and complex. Educated citizens are needed now more than perhaps ever before in the history of civilization. The public rightfully demands excellent education, effective teachers, and competent school graduates. To keep up with these demands, sweeping educational reforms are periodically proposed, attempted, discarded, rethought, and reinstated. Complex goals are generated. Innovative plans are ripped from administrative and legislative drawing boards to be put to use before the pages are dry, much less well-researched.

In the midst of all of the criticism and directives flung at the educational system and its teachers, the sage words of Henry David Thoreau to "Simplify, simplify" have much appeal. Can it be that we have overlooked some of the most pristine and economical ways of educating children and youth as we close out one remarkable millennium in civilization's history and usher in the next? An increasing number of educators think that consultation, collaboration, and teamwork in schools are among the most promising tools for effective education in the 21st century.

This book is designed to serve as a bridge between theory and practice. It contains background information and field-tested recommendations to help teachers, parents, administrators, and support personnel work together within their school context. Several of the chapters stress the importance of word analysis and semantics to develop deeper insights into the subtleties of consultation, collaboration, and teamwork.

The book is organized into three sections featuring school context, processes, content, and an epilogue for looking toward the future, as they relate to school consultation, collaboration, and teamwork. Part One is the *Context* section. Chapter 1 describes school consultation and delineates benefits and problems related to the use of consultation and collaboration in educational settings. Chapter 2 presents key elements in planning, implementing, evaluating, and preparing for consultation and collaboration roles. Chapter 3 provides a brief history, theoretical bases, and research bases of school consultation. It summarizes systems, perspectives, approaches, prototypes, modes, and models for implementing school consultation and collaboration, and recommends synthesizing the components into workable methods for each school context.

Chapter 4 focuses upon the constructive use of individual differences among adults, one of the most powerful but neglected factors affecting school consultation, collaboration, and teamwork. Cultural, ethnic, and language differences that affect consultation are addressed, along with differentiated needs for consultation in the context of rural and urban settings.

In Part Two, the *Process* section, Chapters 5 through 8 introduce process skills and problem-solving tools that are needed for effective consultation and collaboration. Verbal and non-verbal communication skills, plans for dealing with resistance and resolving conflicts, steps in problem-solving, and conference and interview techniques are discussed. Time management, organization and record-keeping techniques, components of ethical consultation, and evaluation of consultation outcomes are outlined.

Part Three, the *Content* section that includes chapters 9 through 12, contains recommendations for structuring learning environments and facilitating student achievement, parent involvement, and staff development through consultation, collaboration, and support from teams of educators. The Epilogue looks toward the future in stressing the development of support systems and advocacy techniques which encourage school consultation practices for a changing world's educational and social needs. This final section proposes that the ideal outcome from consultation, collaboration, and teamwork is the existence of learning environments where education is special for all students, and teachers are successful in their complex, demanding profession.

# ACKNOWLEDGMENTS

Authors often dedicate their work to family members and others who helped them with forgiving natures and firm support throughout the arduous writing process. However, we choose to acknowledge a different kind of contribution by dedicating this product to our graduate students of the past fifteen years at Kansas State University.

Paradoxically, these students both hindered and helped us with the writing. When we needed to write, they hindered because they were always there--taking classes, seeking information, requesting inservice, making the effort to engage in collaborative consultation that would assist them in their own challenging and demanding roles. On the other hand, they helped us greatly by allowing us to "discover what we knew," and they verified that it was indeed important knowledge for bringing about better teaching and learning. Many times they contributed the seed of an idea, a key phrase, a caution, a necessary filter of skepticism, or a vote of confidence for our efforts. We began to sense that we were on the right track.

Whenever it is possible and appropriate to do so, we credit individual students for their contributions, just as we cite other sources of material. However, within a collegial, collaborative process it is not easy to tell just where the contribution of one person occurs, another contribution interfaces, and then yet another takes over from there. As we addressed this dilemma, we realized once again the complexity and the beauty of collaborative consultation. We knew that our students' perceptions and suggestions were shared unselfishly without need for recognition or praise, in the spirit of professionalism and progress. This is what collaborative consultation is all about. We trust that the material in the book will serve as a tangible example of the usefulness of consultation, collaboration, and teamwork in meeting the special needs of students and educators.

For all of our students in teacher preparation programs who gave us purpose and influenced us in the preparation of this, we are very grateful. Any oversights, omissions, or errors are ours, of course, but the essence of our philosophy comes from them and the school children and adolescents they represent. So we dedicate the final product to these professional colleagues in their past, present, and future educational roles. The energy, enthusiasm, and expertise they provide have been truly inspirational.

# 1

# DESCRIPTION OF SCHOOL CONSULTATION, COLLABORATION, AND TEAMWORK

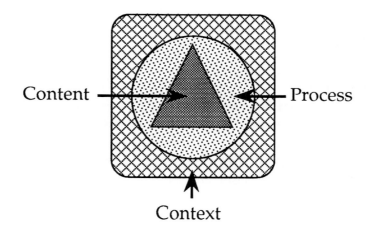

## To Think About

What does the term *consultant* bring to mind? An expert? A specialist? Someone who assesses another person's situation and makes recommendations toward solving a problem?

Life presents many situations in which people must act on important matters without having all the information and expertise they would like. In today's increasingly interdependent, specialized world it is unlikely that any one person has all the knowledge and skill needed for every circumstance. People engage services of consultants to analyze situations and generate possible alternatives for resolving them.

Many people have used consultation services at one time or another in their lives, often paying dearly for them. The demand for consultation services is escalating in fields as varied as business, medicine, law, industry, fashion, construction, decorating, and finance. Sometimes consultants even have their own consultants! However, such services are underutilized in education. Until recently, consultation and collaboration have been overlooked as key elements in a strong educational system. Little time and virtually no structure have been provided to encourage interaction among educators in collaborative or consultative sessions.

Preparation for the complex roles of consultant and collaborator has not been a significant component of most teacher education programs. Now, however, the increasing complexity of school environments and intensified efforts toward school reform and restructuring are catalysts for working together in schools. Teaching is more than ever a multidimensional responsibility. Teachers are involved with all facets of student development— cognitive, affective, physical, and social. Effective teaching depends on extensive interaction among educators and teamwork with parents and resource personnel in home, school, and community settings.

## Focusing Questions

1. What school conditions today call for greater emphasis on working together?
2. How do educational reform and restructuring movements signal the need for consultation, collaboration, and team effort in education?
3. What are useful definitions of consultation, collaboration, and teamwork that can be applied to the educational setting?
4. Who will serve as consultant, consultee, and client in school consultation?
5. What benefits can be expected for students, parents, and school personnel through consultation and collaboration?
6. What obstacles hinder the practices of consultation and collaboration among educators?
7. What process skills and content skills are needed for consultation and collaboration within diverse school contexts?

## Key Terms

| | |
|---|---|
| *America* 2000 | consultation |
| at-risk students | consultant |
| autonomy | consulting teacher |
| client | consultee |
| collaboration | content skills |
| communication | cooperation |

coordination
iatrogenic effect
inclusion
least restrictive environment
mainstreaming
multiplier effects
positive ripple effects
preschool handicapped
process skills
Public Law 94-142

Public Law 99-457
Public Law 101-476
Regular Education Initiative (REI)
school reform
synergy
school context
school restructuring
teamwork
transition from preschool to school
transition from school to the adult
world

**Scenario**

The setting is the faculty room of a typical high school where two teachers are sharing school news and professional concerns.

*ENGLISH TEACHER:* I'm getting another special education student next week—severe learning disabilities, the cumulative folder says. I guess this is more fallout from Public Law 94-142, along with the behavior-disordered student I've been coping with all semester.

*MATH TEACHER:* (grinning) Must be because you're doing such a great job with that one. (serious tone) But I know what you mean. Our special education teachers aren't taking these kids out of our classes as much as they did when I started teaching.

*ENGLISH TEACHER:* They say a person designated as a consulting teacher is coming to our next departmental meeting to talk about helping the students with special needs. We're going to be asked to consult and collaborate—along with all the other things we do.

*MATH TEACHER:* Don't those two words cancel each other out? *Consult* and *collaborate*, that is. I believe you English teachers call that an oxymoron.

As I see it, I might consult my tax accountant for some expert advice, but isn't collaboration where everyone works together to come up with a plan for something? As for teamwork, the coaches could probably tell us how difficult that concept is to develop and implement among a group of adults who all think differently about things.

*ENGLISH TEACHER:* Frankly, I'm not interested in word games or coaching strategies right now. I'm more concerned about finding out where the time is going to come from to do all this. And I want to know who will be responsible for the progress reports and grades for these students.

*MATH TEACHER:* Right. I've had some reservations about mainstreaming all along. So, I hope we get some good answers for your concerns.

## Teacher Responsibilities in Schools

*Here is Edward Bear, coming downstairs now, bump, bump, bump, on the back of his head, behind Christopher Robin. It is, as far as he knows, the only way of coming downstairs, but sometimes he feels that there really is another way, if only he could stop bumping for a moment and think of it. . . .* ( A. A. Milne, *Winnie-the-Pooh*, p. 3)

Teaching has never been easy, and it becomes more challenging every year. The public is demanding fiscal responsibility and competent school personnel. The media present diatribes against declining test scores and urge higher student achievement. Rising costs of education are a major concern of policymakers, school administrators, and taxpayers. In the face of public criticism and declining teacher morale, burnout and attrition increase. Some teaching positions are vacated because teachers can not or will not absorb the pressures any longer. Other positions are unfilled because career options with greater potential for salary and advancement are available. Administrators are faced with filling more and more teacher vacancies every school term, increasing the loads of teachers who remain, or discontinuing certain services.

Some disenchanted educators remain in the profession to simply "fizzle out," "rust out," or "coast out." They go through the motions of their profession in lackluster fashion, just getting by until retirement age arrives or a better opportunity comes along. These situations are particularly penalizing for students with special needs who are the most vulnerable to ineffective, inconsistent teaching.

### *Autonomy in the Classroom*

Teachers tend to function autonomously in their classrooms (Goodlad, 1984). After the attendance forms, lunch counts, and other required procedures are completed, they close their doors and *teach*. They are expected to handle all kinds of school situations with minimal assistance. After all, didn't the teacher of eight grades in a one-room schoolhouse get along without special help?

Goodlad (1984) describes teachers as autonomous within the context of isolation. Autonomy minimizes the impact of outside influences (Rosenfield, 1985). Because teachers seldom have the privilege of rich professional dialogue, they are isolated from sources of ideas beyond their own experiences. The chunking of a school day insulates them. Many go through the entire school day without speaking to an adult in a meaningful way (Eisner, 1988).

Few structured arrangements exist to assist teachers in performing their complex roles. This is particularly problematic at the high school level where teachers teach five classes, prepare two or more lessons each day, and face as many as 150 students during a school day that is sliced into fifty-minute periods (Cuban, 1986). Although schools are in a certain sense very social places, and classrooms are multidimensional centers of activity, an individual teacher may feel stranded on a crowded island that is devoid of adult interaction and stimulation. In a poll of over one thousand teachers conducted by *Learning* magazine and reported by the Education Commission of the United States, 78 percent of the respondents said that isolation from their colleagues is a major or moderate problem (Turner, 1987).

On one hand, teachers wish for more small-group meetings on mutual interests, regular grade level meetings, chances to observe other teachers, and richer opportunities for in-service training. On the other hand, many teachers are not comfortable initiating collaborative efforts and engaging in interactions with other teachers. Some state candidly that they did not choose a teaching career to work extensively with adults. Others feel that calling on a colleague or using a school consultant will be perceived as a sign of professional weakness and incompetency.

Teachers have few incentives for getting together to collaborate or team teach. They rarely have an opportunity to visit other school settings to obtain new ideas and revitalize their enthusiasm. When they do have the time and opportunity to interact with colleagues, it is likely to be during in-service or staff development sessions. Unfortunately, these activities too often are highly structured sessions, inappropriately designed or poorly managed. Many are scheduled at the end of a hectic day, when teachers are tired and want to turn their attention toward home or community responsibilities.

Now and then, teachers are visited in their classrooms by supervisors, administrators, student teachers, and even parents. However, these occasions tend to create feelings of stress and aloneness rather than support and collegiality. Well-intentioned efforts to team teach too often result in turn teaching—"You teach this part of the lesson and then take a break while I handle the next part."

Wildman and Niles (1987) stress that professionals cannot be forced to be collegial. Teachers who are accustomed to being in charge and making virtually all the day-to-day decisions in their classrooms cannot be ordered to go out and consult and collaborate with each other to any meaningful degree. They need structure, training, and practice in order to perform these sophisticated, demanding functions effectively. The typical teacher preparation program provides little or no instruction in collaborating with professional peers.

It is becoming increasingly evident that teachers cannot serve all needs of their students effectively without extensive communication, cooperation, and coordination among school personnel, support personnel, and parents. A growing body of school consultation literature and research forecasts wider use of consultation services and greater interest in collaboration and teamwork in the future. Current books, periodicals, conferences, staff development sessions, and media messages are convincing educators that consulting, collaborating, and teamwork can combine the best that school personnel and parents have to contribute toward helping students learn. Educational reform movements have strengthened these convictions.

## Demands within School Reform Movements

During the 1970s and 1980s, educators witnessed an explosion of reports, proposals, and legislative mandates calling for educational reform. *A Nation at Risk,* the report submitted by the National Commission on Excellence in Education in 1983, and as many as thirty other major reform reports of the 1980s directed the nation's attention to the status and conditions of its schools. After these reports were publicized, public pressure mounted to improve schools.

The first wave of educational reform sought to strengthen the rigor of American public education (Michaels, 1988). It stressed accountability, lengthening of school days and years, and increased investments of time, money, and effort in education. The second wave focused on the individual school as the unit of decision making. It featured the development of collegial, participatory environments among students and staff, with particular emphasis on personalizing school environments and designing curricula for deeper understanding (Michaels, 1988). One component of this second wave of reform was school restructuring. Many states have initiated some form of school restructuring; however, few schools truly are restructured. Where restructuring efforts have occurred, they tend to be idiosyncratic in that they are carried out by a small group of teachers, creating only marginal, easily eroded changes (Timar, 1989).

Effective restructuring calls for rethinking. In order to do that, educators must take their eyes off the rearview mirror of first-wave reform and look carefully at the twenty-first century (Michaels, 1988). Futrell (1989) charges that the decade of the 1980s turned out to be one of educational debate, not educational reform. When the redefinition of education was beginning, a primary outcome was just argument. But educators now are learning the kinds of questions to ask. Many of the questions and subsequent thinking signal the need for an extensive use of consultation, collaboration, and teamwork by the entire school staff with parents as partners. Futrell suggests that schools can be restructured only through cooperation and collaboration among many factions.

### *The Regular Education Initiative (REI)*

A significant ripple that has helped create waves of educational reform is the Regular Education Initiative (REI), calling for a merger of general education and special education efforts. Demands for cost containment and growing concerns over labeling of students have fueled interest in a merger of general education with special education. The primary impetus for the merger was the mainstreaming movement brought about by Public Law 94-142. When Public Law 94-142 mandated placement for students with handicaps into a least restrictive learning environment, classroom teachers were given the responsibility for student success. However, in order to fulfill this new responsibility, they were promised help from special education personnel.

The least restrictive environment mandate created changes in the way general education teachers and special education teachers are to interact in order to serve students with exceptional learning needs. Students with handicaps are to be educated with nonhandicapped peers in regular school settings as much as possible. Special education teachers and general classroom teachers are to modify educational settings and teaching methods for exceptional students with handicaps. Such modifications facilitate inclusion of students with handicaps in the least restrictive environment, and minimize social and educational exclusion from their age peers.

Thus the Regular Education Initiative, referred to by some educators as the General Education Initiative (GEI), encourages major changes in the way education is delivered. All students, with the exception of the severely handicapped, can be served primarily in a regular education setting. The rationale for the REI is that:

the changes will serve many students not currently eligible for special education services;

the stigma of placement in special education programs that separate them from peers will be eliminated;

early intervention and prevention will be provided before more serious learning deficiencies occur; and

cooperative school-parent relationships will be enhanced (Will, 1986).

The more extreme position regarding the REI is that special and regular education should merge into a unified system structured to meet needs of all students, because all students are unique individuals with special needs and require differentiated individual attention. Therefore, practices that are effective for exceptional students should be used with all students (Stainback and Stainback, 1984).

Many educators have emphasized that the Regular Education Initiative is not an initiative of regular educators, but a change in both general and special education that has been proposed by special educators. This assumption has been the subject of considerable debate (Hallahan, et al., 1988). A number of special education personnel contend that regular educators are not interested in making the proposed changes required by the REI. So, without significant changes in educational programs, the children who were failed by a traditional educational system will once again fail to be served in the merged system.

Public Law 94-142 was amended in 1990 by Public Law 101-476. The title was changed to Individuals with Disabilities Education Act (IDEA). Key elements of the amendment that affect school consultation and collaboration include:

all references to handicapped children were changed to children with disabilities;

new categories of autism and traumatic brain injury (TBI) were added, to be served with increased collaboration among all special education teachers, classroom teachers, and related services personnel; and

more emphasis was placed on requirements to provide transition services for students sixteen years of age and older.

Even as the REI debate continues, resource teacher roles are uniquely positioned to collaborate and team with general classroom teachers. By sharing responsibility for students with special learning needs, all educators can contribute not only to remediation of problems, but prevention as well. Current research and practices suggest that the help for teachers promised by the mainstream movement can be delivered effectively and efficiently by consultants and consulting teachers. As early as 1981, Lilly and Givens-Ogle stressed that teacher consultation practices were critical for cultivating the relationships between regular education and special education teachers that can facilitate student success within the least restrictive environment (Haight, 1984; Huefner, 1988). Special education skills are the very ones classroom teachers need to acquire, and current referral models can be replaced with a collaborative model to help more students succeed in school. However, as things stand now, jobs and professional identities are dependent on separate systems of special education and regular education.

The impact of the Regular Education Initiative on collaborative consultation will be a negative one if the two thrusts are perceived as synonymous, but positive if REI clarifies and refines the concepts and practices of consultation (Friend, 1988). While the Regular Education Initiative is not a panacea, it can be—if rigorous, open and democratized—a vehicle for generating collaborative thinking, problem solving, and action for many school dilemmas (Davis, 1989). Indeed, as Davis articulates, it should be looked on as a rare opportunity to assess the readiness of public education not only for accommodating, but for respecting and valuing, individual student differences. Education in its "reformed state" might bypass entirely the special education for mildly handicapped students now in operation and provide a new system for teachers and children. It also might forestall the increasing trend to place large numbers of children with relatively minor learning and behavior problems into special education pull-out programs. Many believe that special educators must envision themselves as contributing members of the general education community, working toward integration of special education and general education (Lilly, 1987).

### At-Risk Students

An important result of the Regular Education Initiative was reexamination of the criteria for student eligibility for special education services. Many states developed more restrictive requirements, causing a number of students in pull-out special education programs to be returned to general classrooms without special services. Classroom teachers often refer to these and other students who are experiencing school failure for various reasons as *at-risk* students. Reynolds (1989) defines at-risk students as those who fall into various categories for which the base rate for experiencing educational difficulties is relatively high.

Some school reformers promote the concept of shared responsibility between regular educators and special educators to provide more coordinated and inclusive educational arrangements for all students, including those at risk. In the meantime, people are not waiting for special educators to come and save them (Conoley, 1985). School doors open each morning, bells ring, students congregate, and classes begin. In those classes many students have special learning and behavior needs. Up to one-third of all school-age children can be described as experiencing difficulty in school, and if the significant learning needs of gifted students were added, this figure would increase substantially. As many as ten percent of the students enrolled in public schools are eligible for special education services, while another ten to twenty percent have mild to moderate learning problems that interfere with their school progress (Idol, West, and Lloyd, 1988; Will, 1986). Although the public envisions "handicapped children" as crippled, deaf, blind, or retarded (Schenkat, 1988), up to 90 percent of the children served in special education programs are very mildly handicapped (Shepard, 1987), being more accurately described as slow learners, second language students, misbehavers in school, frequent absentees, transients, or simply average learners in significantly above-average populations. Even so, educational programs for these students generally make up 50 to 70 percent of special education budgets. Paradoxically, 68 percent of handicapped students receive most of their education in regular classes (Friend and McNutt, 1984).

## Early Childhood Education for the Handicapped

Concern for preschoolers from poverty-level environments and other conditions of disadvantage gained momentum in the 1960s. The passage of Public Law 99-457 expanded attention to handicapped preschoolers; public schools are now required to provide special services for children age three and above who have disabilities. Public Law 99-457 has gone far beyond classroom concerns to include family, social workers, speech and language pathologists, medical personnel, and other professionals. The law authorizes funding for state grants and experimental, demonstration, and outreach programs that are multidisciplinary in nature. An increase in programs for preschool children with disabilities calls for increased collaboration among professionals, parents, and other caregivers. Collaboration, consultation, and teamwork are at the heart of these programs.

Early intervention programs for infants and toddlers with disabilities have proliferated following the early childhood legislation. Parents and other caregivers outside the school now play an even more integral part in the education and well-being of children with disabilities. Because most children in early intervention programs have severe disabilities, services of specialists from several disciplines are essential. Moreover, parents also are fully involved in the therapy, through "home-based" programs. In these programs therapists go into the homes to provide stimulation for the children, and guidance and instruction for the parents. In order to meet the children's special needs, staff and parents must collaborate with all available resources, including health and medical personnel, social services personnel, public school personnel, and community resources such as preschool and day-care centers.

*Transition from Preschool Settings to Kindergarten Programs*  While formal programs for young children, such as Head Start and Follow Through, have been successful in and of themselves, P.L. 99-457 reaches far beyond classroom interventions. Transition from preschool settings to kindergarten school programs requires strong, continuous efforts toward collaboration and teamwork.

Preschool teachers will want to identify essential skills needed in the local kindergarten, in order to prepare the children for that setting (Beckhoff and Bender, 1989; Salisbury and Vincent, 1990; McCormick and Kawate, 1982). Their contributions to elementary school programs are invaluable for getting new kindergarten students off to a successful start. Collaboration and teamwork among all parties involved with very young children are essential.

## Transition from School to the Adult World

At the opposite end of the continuum from early childhood needs are those of students leaving school to enter the world of work and adult living. Heightened awareness of this important transition period for young people with handicaps grew in the 1980s. One of the realities was that no one parent, teacher, or counselor can adequately provide the necessary assistance. It requires a team effort provided by all parties involved in the interest of the students.

The emphasis on college preparatory curriculum that grew out of school reform was appropriate for perhaps only 40 percent of the students (Daggett, 1989; Edgar, 1990; Goodlad, 1984; Pugach and Sapon-Shevin, 1987). Without concerted team effort, students with disabilities do not make a successful transition to adult life. More than fifty percent remain unemployed or underemployed.

The transition movement of the 1980s was preceded by two similar movements in the 1960s and the 1970s (Halpern, 1992). During the 1960s a work-study program emerged as an approach to preparing students with mild disabilities for adjustment into their communities. Two flaws of this movement were the funding mechanism that supported it and the requirement that rehabilitation agencies could not pay for services that were the responsibility of other agencies (Halpern, 1992). The 1970s career education movement was an expansion of the work-study movement. However, it eventually was disowned as a federal initiative, leaving the door open for the emergence of the transition movement during the 1980s.

The goal of transition programs during the 1980s was to assist students with disabilities in obtaining education services that enabled them to lead meaningful and productive lives. In order for the transition process to be successful, all parties and agencies were required to work together systematically to plan for it (Clark and Knowlton, 1988; Rusch and Menchetti, 1988). Collaborative consultation was helpful in providing this support (Sileo, Rude, and Luckner, 1988). The 1990s will be important years for making transition approaches work in the local communities (Halpern, 1992). Educational and social reform movements will increase awareness of this population of teenage students at risk.

## *Agenda of* America 2000

In April of 1991 President Bush and Secretary of Education Lamar Alexander presented a four-part educational strategy called *America 2000*. The plan outlines several education goals for the nation to achieve by the year 2000, including ideas and proposals for new national tests, new national standards, federal encouragement of choice, new federally appointed agencies for research, and a nationwide emphasis on English, mathematics, science, history, and geography (Howe II, 1991). The six goals (Bush, 1991; Halpern, 1992) are that:

Every American child must begin school prepared to learn.

The high-school graduation rate in the United States must increase to no less than 90 percent.

All students in grades 4, 8, and 12 will be tested for progress in key subjects.

American students will rank first in the world in science and math achievement.

Every adult will be a skilled, literate worker and citizen.

Every school will be drug-free and provide a climate in which learning can occur.

Some educators describe the *America 2000* plan as vigorous, optimistic, and upbeat in its intent to mobilize public opinion and focus national energy on education without creating bureaucratic structures (Doyle, 1991; Sewall, 1991). Others criticize it as a call for cosmetic change that will not restructure schools from the ground up, as they need to be.

Howe II (1991) contends that there are three major omissions from *America 2000* target areas—school finance, growing poverty among children and youth, and cultural and racial diversity in American society. The plan also seems to ignore the 10 percent or more of exceptional children who have special learning and behavior needs. Furthermore, considering the need for a diversity of schools and educational approaches, and a wide range of alternatives to meet society's demands for practical education, the proposed instruction and testing may be educationally damaging for the 98 percent not destined to become academic scholars (Clinchy, 1991). Some educators suggest that standardized testing may have already harmed low-achieving students and should be replaced by alternative forms of assessment based on projects, exhibits, and portfolios of student work, not accountability systems stipulated in *America 2000* (Lieberman, 1991). If these educators are correct in targeting diverse schools, approaches, and assessments as mandates for education by the year 2000, then consultation, collaboration, and teamwork are sure to be key components of meaningful school reform for the future.

## Summary of School Reform Movements

Friend and Cook (1990) group the avalanche of school reform recommendations into three categories. The first calls for curricular changes, such as increasing academic standards, lengthening the school day and year, and adding math, science, computer, and foreign language requirements to the curriculum. The second category focuses on governance of schools, with reformers arguing for teacher empowerment within the school organization and site-based management of the schools. The third category addresses the school structure, producing recommendations that traditional classroom groups and grade levels become reorganized. Strategies for enhancing the at-risk learner's ability to succeed and use of career ladders and other expanded career paths for teachers are proposed.

The recent waves of reform movement have brought about keen interest in staff development, new program models, and organizational changes. Teachers, administrators, and support personnel face significant changes in the ways they function. These changes will be comprehensive and schoolwide. Cosmetic alteration of programs and policies will not be sufficient to address the complex issues and concerns.

A key element for ensuring school success in the wake of the reforms will be the ability of the school staff to collaborate (Friend and Cook, 1990). Yet despite the increasing interest in collaborative formats, implementation of such formats has been sporadic. Phillips and McCullough (1990) cite the inconsistent use of the term collaborative consultation, the lack of overarching theoretical orientations, and myriad concepts of consultation as causes of the variable success. The literature on effective schools challenges educators to cultivate collegiality when planning and learning new skills (Lieberman, 1986). A collaboration ethic is needed, with general and special educators as co-consultants pooling interdisciplinary content, processes, and expertise (Phillips and McCullough, 1990).

Key educational leaders are proposing that unless major structural changes are made in the field of special education, the field is destined to become more of a problem and less of a solution in providing for students' special needs (Reynolds, Wang, and Walberg, 1987). Urgently needed are coordinated educational services in regular school settings for all students, including those with special needs; time-limited waivers for school districts to experiment with the more coordinated programs; and alternatives to the current three categories of systems for helping students who have special needs.

## What School Consultation Is

According to many who study and write about education policy and trends, there is little doubt that collaboration will affect teachers and administrators, their counterparts in other public agencies, and policymakers at all levels. In recent years, no education legislation has passed in Congress, or for that matter, has been considered, that does not foster collaboration (Lewis, 1992).

Now that reform movements have fueled interest in more interaction and collaboration among educators and parents, it is time to follow through with plans and actions. Just what is school consultation? How can collaboration be a significant part of consultation? In what ways can consultation and collaboration promote teamwork among educators and parents for the special needs of students?

## Defining Consultation, Collaboration, and Teamwork

A definition of *consultation* for school settings must be general enough to apply to a wide range of school structures and circumstances, yet flexible enough for adaptation to local needs. *Webster's Third New International Dictionary, unabridged* (1976), and *Webster's New Collegiate Dictionary* (8th ed.) (1981), provide a wealth of synonyms for words related to consultation. There are also many useful synonyms for other words integral to school consultation, such as collaboration, communication, cooperation, coordination, and teamwork or teaming. When studied as a group, it is readily apparent that the words complement each other to form a foundation for understanding and using concepts of complex human interaction. Examples are quoted from one of the above-mentioned works:

> *consult:* Advise, confer, confab, huddle, parley, powwow, counsel, deliberate, consider, examine, refer to, review, apply for information, take counsel, discuss, seek the opinion of, and/or have prudent regard to.

> *consultation:* A council, conference, or formal deliberation.

> *consulting:* Deliberating together, asking advice or opinion of, or conferring.

> *consultant:* One who gives professional advice or services in a field of special knowledge and training, or simply one who consults another.

> *consulting teacher:* One with major teaching responsibilities who also works with other school personnel in order to serve special needs of students.

*consultee*: Described in social science literature as the mediator between consultant and client (Tharp, 1975).

*client:* Individual, group, agency, department, community, or sometimes even a nation, that benefits from the services of a consultant.

*collaborate*: Labor together or work jointly, especially in an intellectual endeavor.

*communication*: The act of transmitting, giving, or exchanging information, or the art of expressing ideas.

*cooperation*: The act of uniting, banding, combining, concurring, or conjoining.

*coordination*: Bringing elements into a common action, movement, or condition.

*teamwork, teaming*: Joining forces or efforts, with each individual contributing a clearly defined portion of the effort, but also subordinating personal prominence to the efficiency of the whole.

## Descriptions of School Consultation, Collaboration, and Teamwork

The verbs consult, collaborate, communicate, cooperate, coordinate, and team are rich words for describing professional activities that can enhance student growth as well as increase teacher satisfaction. These words and the variants that were presented earlier appear in the educational literature in many combinations.

In order to fit a variety of school contexts and educational needs, school consultation is defined in this book as follows:

*School consultation is activity in which professional educators and parents colla- borate within the school context by communicating, cooperating, and coordinating their efforts as a team to serve the learning and behavioral needs of students.*

The school consultant is defined as:

*A school consultant is a facilitator of communication, cooperation, and coor- dination who consults, collaborates, and engages in teamwork with other educators to identify learning and behavioral needs, and plan, implement, and evaluate edu- cational programs to meet those needs.*

In the scenario at the beginning of this chapter, the client is the new student who has a learning disability. The learning disabilities consultant will serve the student indirectly, for the most part, by collaborating with the classroom teacher, who will be the consultee and provider of direct service to the student. Some direct service might be provided to the student by the learning disabilities consultant, but for the most part, the direct service will be the responsibility of the classroom teacher.

*Collaborating* is assisting or cooperating with. Its antonyms include struggling and resisting. One intriguing dictionary definition of collaborating is "cooperating with the enemy." For educational purposes, the "enemy" might be viewed as the learning problem needing service, or the behavior requiring modification, or lack of tolerance toward a problem. Communication, cooperation, and coordination are vital aspects of the collaborative process.

Teamwork in school settings is receiving increased attention among school professionals. In the fall of 1990 a CBS television documentary hosted by Charles Kuralt showcased teamwork among teachers. The premise was that schools with strong team activities are more successful than schools whose teachers and staff function autonomously. Many team-oriented schools are exemplary models of teacher empowerment and shared decision making (*The Holmes Group Forum*, 1990). However, teamwork frequently is not yet as efficient as it can and should be (Reynolds and Birch, 1988).

Successful teaching calls for collegiality and partnerships among professionals and parents as well. A collaborative ethic has been inoperative or virtually nonexistent in schools during the 1970s and 1980s. Schools will need precise guidelines for developing systems of consultation dyads, cooperative teaching, teacher assistance teams, and prereferral interventions (Phillips and McCullough, 1990).

## When Educators Consult, Collaborate, and Team

Educators—including special education teachers, classroom teachers, school administrators, related services and support personnel, as well as parents—consult, collaborate and work as team members when they:

- Discuss students' needs.
- Listen to colleagues' concerns about the teaching situation.
- Help identify and define educational problems.
- Facilitate problem solving in the school setting.
- Promote classroom alternatives as first interventions for students with special learning and behavior needs.
- Serve as a medium for student referrals.
- Demonstrate instructional techniques.
- Provide direct assistance to classroom teachers who have students with special learning and behavior needs.
- Lead or participate in staff development activities.
- Assist teachers in designing and implementing behavior-change programs.
- Share materials and ideas with colleagues.
- Participate in team teaching or demonstration teaching.
- Engage in assessment and evaluation activities.

- Serve on curriculum committees, textbook committees, and school advisory councils.
- Follow up on educational issues and concerns with colleagues.

Many teaching activities formerly were carried out by a single teacher in the classroom or in a special education resource setting. However, many of the teacher responsibilities that are conducted autonomously might be fulfilled more productively through collaborative efforts and teamwork. An important question to ask is, "Would student needs, particularly those of students at risk because of serious learning or behavior problems, be served more effectively and efficiently if educators regularly pooled their talents, energies, and resources to address these needs?"

## *Differentiating Consultation, Collaboration, and Teamwork*

Consultation, collaboration, and teamwork are characterized as interactions among people working together to address a problem or to achieve common goals. All three processes, as they occur in the school context, involve interaction among professionals and parents. However, subtle distinctions exist. In school consultation, the consultant contributes specialized expertise toward an educational problem, and the consultee delivers direct service utilizing that expertise. When consultants and consultees collaborate, they assume equal ownership of the problem and solutions. When they engage in teamwork, leader and follower roles usually develop.

Friend and Cook (1992) distinguish between consultation and collaboration by describing collaboration as a style or an approach to interactions that occur during the consultation process. They propose that a collaborative approach can be used at some stages of consultation and not others, and with some consultees, but not others. It is their observation that successful consultants use different styles of interaction under different circumstances and within different situations involving consultation.

Characteristics that consultation, collaboration, and teamwork have in common include:

- engaging in interactive process; and
- using specialized content to achieve shared goals.

Collaboration and teamwork provide consultants and consultees the opportunity to engage in a strengths model of interaction, with each person using and building on the strengths of the others. Several examples which follow will demonstrate similarities and differences among consultation, collaboration, and teamwork.

***Problem Solving with Consultation*** A preschool teacher is concerned about a child in the group who is not fluent in speech. So the teacher asks the speech pathologist to help determine whether or not this is a matter of concern, and if so, what to do about it. The speech pathologist consults with the teacher, getting more information about the observed behavior, and makes additional observations. The consultant then uses expertise in speech pathology to address the teacher's questions.

In another instance, a speech pathologist provides individual therapy for a preschool child who has articulation errors or fluency disorders. The speech pathologist wants to know how these speech patterns are affecting the child's social development as well as performance in preacademic skills such as letter naming and sound discrimination. The speech pathologist asks the teacher to serve as a consultant regarding this issue, and the preschool teacher provides the information requested.

***Problem Solving with Collaboration*** The preschool teacher and the speech pathologist are both concerned about a child's generalization of speech skills learned in speech therapy sessions. The two teachers meet to discuss their mutual concern. Both parties discuss their observations and engage in problem-solving activities to identify the problem clearly and select possible solutions. Both parties agree to make some changes in their respective settings to solve the problem. If the solutions do not work, both are committed to try other possibilities.

In another situation, a teacher of students with behavioral disorders, along with the school counselor, three classroom teachers, and a student's parents, meet to discuss the behavior of that student. The individuals involved in the meeting engage in problem solving to formulate a plan for addressing the problem. Each individual has a role to play in implementing the plan.

***Problem Solving with Teamwork*** A team of professionals is providing services for severely and profoundly disabled infants and toddlers. Each professional has an area of expertise and responsibility, but the social worker has the leadership role. This is because the social worker is responsible for most parent contacts and often goes into homes to provide additional training and assistance. The nurse takes responsibility for monitoring the physical well-being of each child and keeps in close contact with other medical personnel as well as parents. The speech pathologist works with the children to develop speech and language skills. The occupational therapist is responsible for teaching the children certain self-help skills. The physical therapist follows through with the medical doctor's prescribed physical therapy. Special education teachers provide language stimulation and modeling, coordinate schedules, and facilitate communication between team members. The team meets twice weekly to discuss individual cases.

In a middle school, seventh-grade teachers work as a team to plan curriculum goals, share instructional techniques and materials, and solve mutual problems. The language arts teachers take responsibility for monitoring the curriculum. The math teachers make suggestions that apply to their discipline. The learning disabilities teacher is a member of the team because so many learning-disabled students are mainstreamed. The team meets early every Friday morning. One member has been selected by the team to serve as team leader.

## What Collaborative School Consultation Is Not

School consultation is not therapy, nor is it counseling for the consultee (Brown, et al., 1979). The focus must be on educational issues relevant to the needs of the client, not the personal concerns of the consultee. West and Idol (1987), and Morsink, Thomas, and Correa (1991) differentiate counseling from consultation by describing counseling as focused on individuals and consultation as focused on issues.

Collaboration among professional colleagues is not talk or discussion for its own sake. It does not suggest taking on the authority of school administrators, and it should not be a substitute for the individual teacher's accountability (Smith, 1987).

The consultant role is not always the responsibility of the educational specialist. For example, while reading specialists, bilingual specialists, computer specialists, augmentative communication specialists, or low-vision specialists are often consultants, they become consultees when they seek expertise and information from a classroom teacher, school psychologist, administrator, parent, or resource person in the community. On some occasions a general classroom teacher is consultant for a special education teacher, contributing information about a student's problems within a social context not available to the special education teacher. In another instance, a parent might act as consultant for a principal, the consultee, to help a teacher, the client, in a classroom situation.

A student could be consultant to a teacher consultee in a situation where the parents are defined as clients because they are accentuating the student's school problems. The student might contribute to problem identification and interventions, with the teacher providing direct service to parents.

While the client of a consultation is typically an individual, clients also can be a group or team of individuals, such as a family or an in-class group of students. On occasion the client might even be an entire staff, school system, or community. So consultant, consultee, and client roles are interchangeable according to student need and educational circumstance (see Figure 1–1).

Some authors stress that the term *collaborative consultation* creates possibilities for a new mix of consultation and collaboration practices, with each participant alternating between the consultant/expert role and the consultee/recipient role as warranted by differing knowledge and expertise (Thousand et al., 1992). Thus the solution-finding responsibility is jointly and equally shared.

Shift each column to make the appropriate combinations.

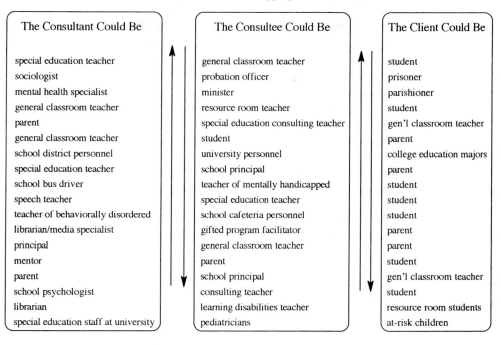

| The Consultant Could Be | The Consultee Could Be | The Client Could Be |
|---|---|---|
| special education teacher | general classroom teacher | student |
| sociologist | probation officer | prisoner |
| mental health specialist | minister | parishioner |
| general classroom teacher | resource room teacher | student |
| parent | special education consulting teacher | gen'l classroom teacher |
| general classroom teacher | student | parent |
| school district personnel | university personnel | college education majors |
| special education teacher | school principal | parent |
| school bus driver | teacher of mentally handicapped | student |
| speech teacher | special education teacher | student |
| teacher of behaviorally disordered | school cafeteria personnel | student |
| librarian/media specialist | gifted program facilitator | parent |
| principal | general classroom teacher | parent |
| mentor | parent | student |
| parent | school principal | gen'l classroom teacher |
| school psychologist | consulting teacher | student |
| librarian | learning disabilities teacher | resource room students |
| special education staff at university | pediatricians | at-risk children |

**FIGURE 1–1  Interchangeable Roles in Consultation and Collaboration**

# Benefits of School Consultation

Consultation can help classroom teachers deal more effectively and efficiently with a wide range of individual student needs. Miller and Sabatino (1978) report that students served in consulting teacher programs make academic gains comparable with students in resource rooms, while the teacher-pupil interactions cultivate improved teaching behaviors. Some of the mystique surrounding special education is reduced when classroom teachers become familiar with special education techniques and come to appreciate and understand special education roles.

## Meeting the Intent of P.L. 94-142

As stated earlier, Public Law 94-142 stipulates that classroom teachers are responsible for the learning programs of students mainstreamed into their classes, but they are to receive assistance. Consulting teachers help classroom teachers develop repertoires of materials and instructional strategies. Many special education teachers find these practices more productive than racing from one student to another in the resource room as all students work on individual assignments. As one learning disabilities teacher succinctly put it, "In my resource room, by the time I get to the last student, I find that the first student is stuck and has made no progress. So I frantically run through the whole cycle again. Tennis shoes are a must for my job!"

A consulting teacher who assumes an instructional role for a time in the general classroom frees the classroom teacher to study student progress, set up arrangements for special projects, or work intensively with a small group of students. The special education teacher might serve as team teacher, support facilitator, or consultant (Stainback, Stainback, and Forest 1989). Effective special education consultants find ways of helping teachers to become confident and successful with special needs students. When general classroom and special education teachers collaborate, each has ownership and involvement in serving special needs. This promotes a sense of responsibility among all teachers for appropriate service to all children (Lieberman, 1984).

## *Minimizing the Effects of Labeling*

Serving student needs resourcefully in heterogeneous settings will minimize the stigmatizing effects of labels such as "handicapped," "exceptional," or "disabled." It also can help reduce referrals to remedial programs. In a study to determine effects of consultation on teacher referral patterns over a seven-year period, Ritter (1978) notes that providing consultation service resulted, over time, in decreasing referrals by teachers. Fewer referrals for special education services mean reduced expenditure for costly and time-consuming psychological assessments and special education interventions. Educators can focus more on teaching and facilitating, and less on testing and measuring.

When introduced to the concept of school consultation, some special education personnel are concerned that after a time they will work themselves out of a job. They fear their positions will be abolished if teachers become fully capable of serving the needs of mildly handicapped, gifted, and at-risk students in the classroom. However, this possibility is extremely remote. Research since 1980 demonstrates that when consultation service is increased, there is more demand for the benefits generated by the service (Friend, 1988). A successful consultation process becomes a supportive tool that teachers increasingly value and use.

Consultation services contribute to the total school program as a bridge between the parallel systems of special education and general education (Greenburg, 1987); they are an effective way of alleviating confusion over goals and relationships of general and special education (Will, 1984). When consultants and consultees collaborate in the educational setting, students are beneficiaries and schools are more nearly the kinds of places the public wishes them to be.

## Assistance for Administrators

Administrators benefit from collaborative consultation when classroom teachers are efficient in working with a wide range of student needs. Consulting teachers can help ease the load special education programs impose on a building administrator and teaching staff. Furthermore, a principal might visit and observe in classrooms as a team participant, collaborating on ways of helping every student succeed in the school and reinforcing teacher success with all students. This is, for many administrators, a welcome change from the typical classroom visitations for teacher evaluation.

## Containment of School Costs

The consultation approach is a cost-effective use of school personnel when it enhances teacher skills for preventing learning problems that might otherwise escalate into more serious needs (Idol, 1986; Heron and Kimball, 1988). Students with borderline special needs can be served in classrooms with little or no additional expenditure of time and money.

Special education resources can become developmental capital for needed educational reforms. Through consultation and collaboration, single-case outcomes can be replicated with an entire class or throughout a school. Coordination of diversified school programs, funds, and services is a resource-saving effort that can be carried out by well-prepared school consultants.

Another important and frequently overlooked benefit is the maintenance of continuity in learning programs as students progress through their school experiences. This, too, is a savings in time, energy, and resources of the educational staff and often the parents as well.

## Catalyst for In-service and Staff Development

Consulting teachers serve their school colleagues as catalysts and implementers of in-service and staff development. They can identify areas in which faculty need awareness and information sessions and workshops to learn specific teaching techniques (McKenzie et al., 1970). This is such a promising aspect of the consulting teacher role that in-service and staff development techniques are detailed separately in Chapter 12.

## Impetus for Staff Harmony and School Cohesion

A collaborative consultation approach is a natural system for nurturing harmonious staff interactions. More opportunities are available that allow special education and general education teachers to become part of the complete educational process. The sharing of ideas can add to creativity, open-endedness, and flexibility in developing educational programs for students with special needs. In addition, more emphasis and coordination can be given to cross-school and long-range planning, with an increased use of outside resources for student needs. School consultation and collaboration also promote nonthreatening systems for evaluating teacher effectiveness.

## Parent Satisfaction and Involvement

Parents or guardians of the exceptional student often become extremely frustrated with the labeling, the fragmented curriculum, and the isolation from peers endured by their children. Therefore, they respond enthusiastically when they observe several educators functioning as a team for the student. Their attitudes toward school improve and they become more involved in planning and carrying through with the interventions (Idol, 1988). They are more eager to share their ideas and help monitor their child's learning. They are particularly supportive when consulting services allow students in special education programs to remain in their neighborhood schools.

## Multiplier Effects from School Consultation

Multiplier effects provide compelling arguments for the practice of school consultation. They create benefits beyond the immediate case involving an individual student and that student's teachers.

Direct services for consultees are one level of positive effects (see Figure 1–2). At this level, the consultation and collaboration are most likely to have been initiated for one client's need. (Note that a client can be an institution such as class, school, family, or community, as well as a single student.) But consultation benefits often extend beyond the level of immediate need for Level 1 direct service to consultees. At Level 2, consultees use information and points of view generated during the collaboration to be more effective in similar but unrelated cases. Both consultant and consultee repertoires of knowledge and skills are enhanced so that they can function more effectively in the future (Brown et al., 1979). When consultation outcomes extend beyond single consultant/consultee situations of Levels 1 and 2, the entire school system can be positively affected by Level 3 outcomes. Organizational change and increased family involvement are potential results of Level 3 outcomes.

Level 1 effects result from the following types of school situations:

- The consultant engages in problem solving with a high school teacher to determine ways of helping a severely learning-disabled student master minimum competencies required for graduation.
- The audiologist helps the classroom teacher arrange the classroom environment to enable a hearing-impaired student to function comfortably in the regular classroom setting.

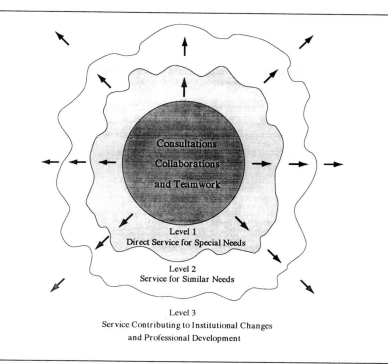

Consultations
Collaborations
and Teamwork

Level 1
Direct Service for Special Needs

Level 2
Service for Similar Needs

Level 3
Service Contributing to Institutional Changes
and Professional Development

**FIGURE 1–2 Positive Ripple Effects of Consultation, Collaboration, and Teamwork**

Level 2 effects include these examples:

- The classroom teacher becomes more familiar with the concept of hyperactivity in children, subsequently regarding fewer children as attention-deficit disordered with hyperactivity, and adjusting the classroom curriculum to more appropriately address very active children's needs.
- The classroom teacher becomes comfortable with enrichment activities provided for gifted students through collaboration with the gifted program facilitator, and makes enriching activities available to a larger group of very able children in the classroom.

Level 3 effects involve these kinds of outcomes:

- The efforts toward collaboration and teamwork result in a staff development plan called "Teachers Helping Teachers," during which teachers in a school system provide training for interested colleagues in their areas of expertise.
- The school district's emphasis on consultation, collaboration, and teamwork pleases parents who find that their children are receiving more integrated,

personalized instruction for their learning needs. The parents become more active and interested in the school's programs.

As discussed earlier, consulting teachers sometimes are concerned that if Level 2 and 3 outcomes enable classroom teachers to handle more serious learning needs without their involvement, their positions may be eliminated if funds are reduced. It is important that the consulting role is not regarded as an add-on position to be dispensed with when money and personnel are in short supply, but rather as an indispensable component of each school's present and future context.

The use of specialized intervention techniques for many more students than those identified, categorized, and remediated in special education programs is a major benefit of consultation. Multiple benefits of collaborative consultation often described as positive ripple effects, can extend well beyond the immediate classroom, because consulting teachers are in a unique position to facilitate interaction among many target groups. These effects from mutual planning and problem solving ripple out across grade levels, subject areas, and schools, and are powerful instruments for initiating positive changes in the educational system.

## Obstacles Hindering Consultation, Collaboration, and Teamwork

In spite of the anticipated benefits of school consultation, proponents of a collaborative school consultation approach face several major obstacles in initiating the concept within their school context. These problems must be recognized and addressed if consultation methods are to succeed. Most certainly, school consultation must not create an iatrogenic effect—a term borrowed from the medical profession to describe a treatment that is more debilitating to the patient than the illness it is designed to treat. An iatrogenic effect from a school service would have educators placing students in a less desirable state than they were before receiving the service.

The literature base for school consultation includes some material on theory and models, methodology, training and practice issues, and guidelines and competencies (Heron and Kimball, 1988). However, little information is available on practical applications. Most of the material has been theoretical, focusing upon *why* consultation should occur rather than on *how* it can be conducted.

Huefner (1988) identifies risks as well as opportunities in a discussion of consultation practices. Johnson, Pugach, and Hammittee (1988) categorize obstacles as pragmatic barriers, such as unclear definitions of the consultation process, and conceptual barriers, including a consultant's lack of credibility in the eyes of some classroom teachers.

During a national symposium on school consultation held in Austin, Texas in 1987, participants focused on driving forces and restraining forces that affect school consultation. They summarized restraining forces as:

- lack of integration for consultation theories and models;
- lack of consultation research, both basic and applied;
- nonsupportive attitudes toward consultation services;
- inability to put consultation theory into practice;
- scarcity of human and material resources to operationalize consultation models;
- lack of preservice and in-service training in consultation;
- organizational resistance to consultation; and
- lack of interdisciplinary collaboration among educators.

Some of the obstacles to school consultation and collaboration loom as formidable barriers. These need to be dismantled before school consultation can take place. Examples of major barriers are issues of ownership, job security, role equality and respect, valuing of adult differences, and willingness to change. Other obstacles appear as hurdles to be vaulted or pushed aside. An example of a hurdle might be teacher autonomy. Obstacles that are most amenable to adjustment will crop up as stumbling blocks to be noted, and then corrected or avoided. In fact, it can be argued that some stumbling blocks are beneficial if they cause people to pause and reflect on existing conditions and possible methods for improvement. In these cases they serve as stepping stones to opportunity. Examples of stumbling blocks are the need for time, clarification of roles, and maintaining equitable caseloads.

Training programs in school consultation are needed to cultivate awareness of consultation as an educational tool and to develop effective attitudes and skills among those who will be consultants and consultees. Communication, cooperation, and coordination among administrative and teaching staff for collaborative consultation must be achieved to establish role expectations and to provide the time and facilities necessary for success. Educators at all school levels, including institutions of higher education, must be involved in preparation for consultation, delineation of roles, implementation of a consultation framework, and assessment and support of consultation and collaboration.

The most significant obstacles to school consultation can be categorized into four groups (see Figure 1–3):

- lack of role definition;
- absence of a framework within which to consult;
- failure to document and evaluate both formal and informal consultations and collaborations; and
- little or no training in consultation skills.

Effective school consultation calls for distinct and equal roles for all participants, and clear expectations regarding those roles. Suitable frameworks, including time, facilities, and structure for the consultation, must be arranged.

*Lack of Understanding about Roles*

> Needed:
>> Role clarification
>> Role parity
>> Appropriate role expectations

*Lack of Framework for Consultation and Collaboration*

> Needed:
>> Methods for consultation and collaboration
>> Resources (time, facilities, supplies)
>> Management (organization, record keeping)

*Lack of Assessment and Support of Consultation*

> Needed:
>> Evaluation
>> Involvement
>> Acceptance

*Lack of Preparation for the Roles*

> Needed:
>> Preservice awareness
>> Certification and degree programs
>> In-service and staff development

**FIGURE  1–3  Obstacles to School Consultation and Collaboration**

Training in consultation and collaboration roles is needed at the preservice, in-service, and advance-degree levels. In addition, documentation and evaluation of the consultation and collaboration efforts are critical components in establishing role clarity and parity.

## Consultation Process and Content in the School Context

School consultation combines process skills and content knowledge within the school context of each educational setting (see Figure 1–4). Schools have characteristics of hierarchy, subsystems, and rules (Hansen, Himes, and Meier, 1990). The school context is composed of many ecological factors which greatly affect consultation practices, such as community and political structures, cultural and ethnic diversity, the financial climate, personality structures of personnel, and student characteristics. These systems continuously exert pressures on the schools (Gallessich, 1973), and are not always within the control of school personnel, particularly teachers. Lack of organizational sensitivity to school contexts can be disastrous.

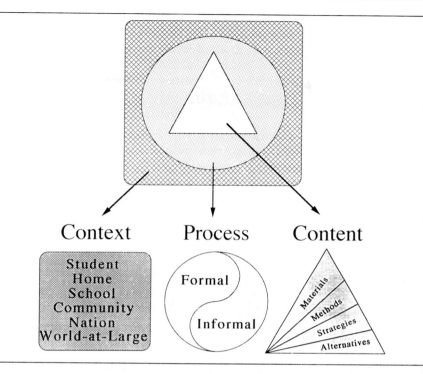

**FIGURE 1–4  Components of School Consultation**

The context of the school setting can be categorized as: student, home, school, community, nation, and world at large. (See Table 1–1.)

Each of these areas affects the ease and efficiency with which consultation can occur. Critical contexts of the educational system in regard to consultation and collaboration include public attitudes, geographic features of the school environment, staff support, financial structure, parent involvement, political action, and legal issues. Characteristics of each school's context must be assessed objectively, understood, and appreciated by the school consultant.

Process skills include but are not limited to communication, coordination, and cooperation. They can occur in formal or informal settings (refer again to Table 1–1). With these skills, the consultant and consultee listen to each other and interact, seek to identify the problem, share information and ideas, resolve conflicts, conduct observations, develop courses of action, coordinate activities, follow through on results, and assess the outcomes for further planning and implementation. Process skills are described by Idol (1990) as the artful base of consultation.

Content skills include selection of materials and resources, proficiency with a variety of teaching methods and strategies, and awareness of learning options and alternatives (refer again to Table 1–1). It is too often the unfortunate case

**TABLE 1–1 Examples of School Consultation Components**

| Context | | |
|---|---|---|
| Student | Needs, styles, accomplishments, handicaps, interests, achievement levels, social skills, talents, peer status, gender, age, physical development, ability level... |
| Home | Family constellation, siblings, socio-economic status, cultural identity, family stability, parent involvement, cooperation, support... |
| School | School philosophy, climate, setting, staff, morale, instructional leadership, staff development, follow-up, modeling and coaching, facilities, support... |
| Community | Economic level, stability, resources, media, awareness levels, partnerships, law and order, neighborhood unity, educational level... |
| Nation | Public support, citizenship, democracy, educational standards... |
| World | Peace, diversity, self-sufficiency, models, political conditions, equity, resources... |

| Process | | |
|---|---|---|
| Formal | Meetings, structured problem-solving sessions, training activities, scheduled communications, planned innovations... |
| Informal | Conversations, shared responsibilities, compensations for personality differences, idea swapping, spontaneous innovation... |

| Content | | |
|---|---|---|
| Materials | Books, worksheets, programmed instruction, kits, study aids, computer-based applications, tests, media, learning machines, laboratory equipment, instruments, artifacts... |
| Methods | Cooperative learning, peer tutoring, grouping arrangements, direct instruction, independent study, computer assisted instruction, self directed learning... |
| Strategies | Test taking practice, behavior management, sensory augmentation, reinforcement schedules, flexible pacing, curriculum compacting... |
| Alternatives | Course options, testing alternatives, test-out and dual credit or half credit, revision of requirements, modification of materials... |

that consultees jump ahead to content, "buying" a quick remedy for the immediate situation rather than identifying the problem and collaborating on viable plans to resolve the problem. The content or knowledge base a consultant brings to the consulting process is described by Idol (1990) as the scientific base of consultation.

Effective school consultation is the result of an interaction of process skills and content methodology within the immediate school context. Contexts of a school setting are a "given" in the assessment of the educational scene. Schools without content would be unnecessary. Processes are the most malleable and promising of the parameters that delineate school consultation, but processes such as communication, problem solving, conflict resolution, time and resource management, and constructive use of adult differences tend to be either neglected or poorly carried out in too many school situations.

Can there be content-free processes for consultation? No, because process is composed of content (Tharp, 1975). This is one of the greatest strengths of consultation. Process can serve content to provide services for students in each school context.

Scientific bases and artful bases must be merged to produce school consultants and consulting teachers who can practice the scientific art of classroom consultation (Idol, 1990). Collaboration performed in conjunction with consultation requires harmonious, efficient teamwork. Consultants and consultees meet to assess the student's situation, develop courses of action to help the student, carry out the actions, and follow through on the results. Each party contributes points of view, information, and suggestions for resolution of the situation.

Thus, consultation with collaboration is not an oxymoron, but *synergy*—"a behavior of whole systems unpredicted by the behavior of their parts taken separately" (Fuller, 1975). Each part contributes expertise both directly and indirectly, without superior-inferior conditions, to develop educational plans within a climate of equality.

## Consultation as Synergy of Context, Process, and Content

Process skills and content methodology are ineffectual unless grounded in the specifics of each school context. For example, a process-based educational approach that is exclusively process specific will be perceived as "talk, talk, talk—never mind about what" (Britt, 1985) without firm roots in the consultees' content skills. Content-based consultation alone will rarely move beyond Level l effects. But a synergistic combination of process skills, content methodology, and school context considerations can set the stage for effective consultation, collaboration, and teamwork to help students with special needs succeed in school.

## Tips for Collaborating and Consulting

1. Keep up to date on educational issues and concerns.
2. Be aware of school reform movements.
3. Be knowledgeable about special education legislation and litigation.
4. Survey the school context for ways to consult.
5. Attend to attitudes and norms within the school context.
6. Refrain from criticizing the school system. Instead, work within the system to cause needed changes.
7. Do not wait to be approached for consultation and collaboration.
8. Try not to press for your own solutions to schools' needs, educators' needs, or students' needs. Strive instead for collaborative efforts to problem solve.
9. Do not carry tales from one setting to another.
10. Refrain from assuming that colleagues are waiting around to be "saved."

## Chapter Review

1. Educators have not developed positive attitudes toward consultation and collaboration. Teachers tend to function autonomously in their classrooms without requesting help from outside resources, and administrators provide few incentives for consultation and collaboration among their school personnel. Teacher preparation programs have not featured consultation and collaboration skills.

2. School reform movements that highlight the need for consultation and collaboration include the Regular Education Initiative and restructuring efforts, curriculum modifications for at-risk students, transition from preschool into school, and transition from school into the adult world.

3. School consultation can be described as professional activity in which teachers, parents, school administrators, resource personnel, and others significant in the life of the student communicate, cooperate, and coordinate efforts to develop courses of action for meeting the student's unique educational needs.

4. A consultant, consultee (or mediator), and client (or target) in one school-related situation may function in any of the other capacities under different circumstances. For example, a special education teacher might be a consultant for one situation, yet in another situation function as the consultee. The student is usually, but not always, the client, or target, for the direct and indirect services provided by consultee and consultant.

5. As a result of school consultation and collaboration many opportunities are available for schools, parents, and students, including service for a wider range of the student population who are at risk or have special learning needs; development of teacher competency for solving varied learning problems; increased ownership and involvement of teachers in helping all students

succeed; reduced labeling and stigmatizing of students; and increased parent involvement in children's learning activities.

**6.**   Although collaborative school consultation produces many benefits for schools, educators, and students, there are obstacles to overcome in using this educational tool. These obstacles include lack of understanding about the consultant role; lack of a framework for consultations to occur; absence of documentation and evaluation of consultations, collaborations, and team efforts; and the need for training in process and content skills of consultation.

**7.**   Consultation is a synergy of school context, process skills, and skills in content methodology.

## Activities

**1.**   Using material in this chapter, a dictionary, interviews, recollections from teaching experiences, discussion with colleagues or classmates, and any other pertinent references, formulate a description and philosophy about school consultation which reflects your viewpoint at this time.

**2.**   Brainstorm with a group to list current issues and major problems in education. (See Chapter 5 for a discussion of brainstorming if you are not familiar with the technique.) After generating as many ideas as possible, note those that seem most amenable to solutions afforded by consultation, collaboration, and teamwork.

**3.**   What questions or concerns about consultation and collaboration are uppermost in your mind at the end of this chapter?

**4.**   List all the responsibilities a teacher typically performs during the course of a school year. Use your recollections of student days, college coursework, student teaching, and any teaching experience you have had. You will probably develop a lengthy list of a wide range of duties and activities, and it most likely will include potential opportunities for using consultation and collaboration tools in order to be more effective and efficient in the teaching role.

If you team up with other teachers in various grade levels, content areas, and specialized roles to do this exercise, the combined lists could become a colorful and impressive mosaic of teaching responsibilities. The process itself will be an example of teamwork, with each person adding information from his or her own perspective and experiences. And so—collaborative consultation!

**5.**   Using your list generated in Activity 4, find areas of teacher responsibility in which consultation and collaboration efforts might take place appropriately and helpfully for students with special needs. For example, under the managerial responsibility of ordering books and supplies, teams of teachers might collaborate to pool library money and plan orders of materials that address special needs of students for remediation and enrichment. In this way, shared decision making in selecting resources could lead to shared planning and implementation of programs that use the resources collaboratively.

**6.** If you could make schools more productive for society and education more rewarding for students and teachers, what would you do? How might school consultation and collaboration fit into your plans? What would it take to put your plan into practice?

# For Further Reading

Hansen, J. C., Himes, B. S., and Meier, S. (1990). *Consultation: Concepts and Practices.* Englewood Cliffs, NJ: Prentice Hall.

Hoy, W. K. (1990). Organizational climate and culture: A conceptual analysis of the school work place. *Journal of Educational and Psychological Consultation, 1* (2): 149–168.

Idol, L., Paolucci–Whitcomb, P., and Nevin, A. (1986). *Collaborative consultation.* Austin, TX: PRO–ED.

Morsink, C. V., Thomas, C. C., and Correa, V. I. (1991). *Interactive Teaming: Consultation and Collaboration in Special Programs.* New York: Macmillan.

Reynolds, M. C., and Birch, J. W. (1988). *Adaptive Mainstreaming: A Primer for Teachers and Principals* (3rd ed.). New York: Longman.

Stainback, S., Stainback, W., and Forest, M. (1989). *Educating All Students in the Mainstream of Regular Education.* Baltimore, MD: Brookes.

# References

Beckhoff, A. G., and Bender,W. N. (1989). Programming for mainstream kindergarten success in preschool: Teachers' perceptions of necessary prerequisite skills. *Journal of Early Intervention, 13*(3): 269-280.

Britt, S. (1985). Our high priests of process. *Newsweek,* November 18.

Brown, D., Wyne, M. D., Blackburn, J. E., and Powell, W. C. (1979). *Consultation: Strategy for Improving Education.* Boston: Allyn and Bacon.

Bush, G. (1991). *America 2000: An Education Strategy.* Washington, D.C.: U.S. Department of Education.

Clark, G. M., and Knowlton, H. E. (1988). A closer look at transition issues for the 1990's: A response to Rusch and Menchetti. *Exceptional Children, 54*(4): 365-367.

Clinchy, E. (1991). Helping parents make the school system work for them. Buffalo Public Schools Parent Center. *Equity and Choice, 7* (2–3), 83–88.

Conoley, J. C. (March, 1985). Personal correspondence.

Cuban, L. (1986). Persistent instruction: Another look at constancy in the classroom. *Phi Delta Kappan, 68*(1): 7-11.

Daggett, W. R. (1989). The changing nature of work—A challenge to education. Unpublished speech delivered to the Kansas Legislative and Educational Leaders, Topeka, KS.

Davis, W. E. (1989). The regular education initiative debate: Its promises and problems. *Exceptional Children, 55*(5): 440-447.

Doyle, D. P. (1991). America 2000. *Phi Delta Kappan, 73* (3), 184–191.

Edgar, G. 1990. Is it time to change our view of the world? *Beyond Behavior, 1*(1): 9-13.

Eisner, E. W. (1988). The ecology of school improvement. *Educational Leadership, 45*(5): 24-29.

Friend, M. (1988). Putting consultation into context: Historical and contemporary perspectives. *Remedial and Special Education, 9*(6): 7-13.

Friend, M., and Cook, L. (1990). Collaboration as a predictor for success in school reform.

*Journal of Educational and Psychological Consultation, 1*(1): 69-86.

Friend, M., and McNutt, G. (1984). Resource room programs: Where are we now? *Exceptional Children, 51*, 150–155.

Fuller, R. B. (1975). *Explorations in the Geometry of Thinking Synergetics.* New York: Macmillan, p. 3.

Futrell, M. (1989). Mission not accomplished: Education reform in retrospect. *Phi Delta Kappan, 71* (1), 9–14.

Gallessich, J. (1973). Organizational factors influencing consultation in schools. *Journal of School Psychology, 11:* 57-65.

Goodlad, J. (1984). *A Place Called School: Prospects for the Future.* New York: McGraw-Hill.

Greenburg, D. E. (1987). *A special educator's perspective on interfacing special and general education: A review for administrators.* Clearinghouse on Handicapped and Gifted Children. Reston, VA: The Council for Exceptional Children.

Haight, S. L. (1984). Special education teacher consultant: Idealism versus realism. *Exceptional Children, 50*(6), 507-515.

Hallahan, D. P., Kauffman, J. M., Lloyd, J. W., and McKinney, J. D. (eds.) (1988). The regular education initiative. *Journal of Learning Disabilities, 21*(1): special issue.

Halpern, A. S. (1992). Transition: Old wine in new bottles. *Exceptional Children, 58*(3), 202-211.

Hansen, J. C., Himes, B. S., and Meier, S. (1990). *Consultation: Concepts and Practices.* Englewood Cliffs, NJ: Prentice Hall.

Heron, T. E. and Kimball, W. H. (1988). Gaining perspective with the educational consultation research base: Ecological considerations and further recommendations. *Remedial and Special Education, 9*(6): 21-28, 47.

*Holmes Group Forum.* (1990). Back to school basics. *The Holmes Group Forum, 5* (1), 1, 3.

Howe II, H. (1991). America 2000: Bumpy ride on four trains. *Phi Delta Kappan, 73* (3), 192–203.

Hoy, W. K. (1990). Organizational climate and culture: A conceptual analysis of the school work place. *Journal of Educational and Psychological Consultation, 1* (2): 149–168.

Huefner, D. (1988). The consulting teacher model: Risks and opportunities. *Exceptional children, 54* (5), 403–414.

Idol, L. (1986). *Collaborative school consultation: Recommendations for state departments of education.* The Task Force on School Consultation, Teacher Education Division, Council for Exceptional Children.

Idol, L. (1988). A rationale and guidelines for establishing special education consultation programs. *Remedial and Special Education, 9*(6), 48-58.

Idol, L. (1990). The scientific art of classroom consultation. *Journal of Educational and Psychological Consultation, 1*(1), 3-22.

Idol, L., Paolucci–Whitcomb, P., and Nevin, A. (1986). *Collaborative consultation.* Austin, TX: PRO–ED.

Idol, L., West, J. F., and Lloyd, S. R. (1988). Organizing and implementing specialized reading programs: A collaborative approach involving classroom, remedial, and special education teachers. *Remedial and Special Education, 9*(2), 54-61.

Johnson, L. J., Pugach, M. C., and Hammittee, D. J. (1988). Barriers to effective special education consultation. *Remedial and Special Education, 9*(6): 41-47.

Lewis, A. C. (1992). All together now: Building collaboration. *Phi Delta Kappan, 73*(5): 348-349.

Lieberman, A. (1991). Accountability as a reform strategy. *Phi Delta Kappan, 73*(3): 219-220.

Lieberman, L. (1984). *Preventing Special Education . . . for Those Who Don't Need It.* Newtonville, MA: GloWorm.

Lieberman, L. (1986). *Special Educator's Guide . . . to Special Education.* Newtonville, MA: GloWorm.

Lilly, M. S. (1987). Lack of focus on special education in literature on educational reform. *Exceptional Children, 53*(4): 325-26.

Lilly, M. S. and Givens-Ogle, L. B. (1981). Teacher consultation: Present, past, and future. *Behavioral Disorders, 6*(2): 73-77.

McCormick, L., and Kawate. J. (1982). Kindergarten survival skills: new directions for preschool special education. *Education and Training of the Mentally Retarded, 17*(3): 247-252.

McKenzie, H. S., Egner, A. N., Knight, M. F., Perelman, P. F., Schneider, B. M., and Garvin, J. S. (1970). Training consulting teachers to assist elementary teachers in management and education of handicapped children. *Exceptional Children, 37*(2): 137-143.

Michaels, K. (1988). Caution: Second-wave reform taking place. *Educational Leadership, 45*(5): 3.

Miller, T. L., and Sabatino, D. (1978). An evaluation of the teacher consultant model as an approach to mainstreaming. *Exceptional Children, 45*: 86-91.

Milne. A. A. (1926). *Winnie-the-Pooh.* New York: Dutton.

Morsink, C, V., Thomas, C. C., and Correa, V. I. (1991). *Interactive Teaming: Consultation and Collaboration in Special Programs.* New York: Macmillan.

Phillips, V., and McCullough, L. (1990). Consultation-based programming: Instituting the collaborative ethic in schools. *Exceptional Children, 56*(4): 291-304.

Pugach, M., and Sapon-Shevin, M. (1987). New agendas for special education policy: What the national reports haven't said. *Exceptional Children, 53*(4): 295-299.

Reynolds, M. C. (1989). An historical perspective: The delivery of special education to mildly disabled and at-risk students *Remedial and Special Education, 10*(6): 7-11.

Reynolds, M., and Birch, J. (1988). *Adaptive Mainstreaming: A Primer for Teachers and Principals.* New York: Longman.

Reynolds, M. C., Wang, M. C., and Walberg, H. J. (1987). The necessary restructuring of special and regular education. *Exceptional Children, 53*(5): 391-398.

Ritter, D. R. (1978). Effects of a school consultation program upon referral patterns of teachers. *Psychology in the Schools, 15*(2): 239-243.

Rosenfield, S. (1985). Teacher acceptance of behavioral principles: An issue of values. *Teacher Education and Special Education, 8*(3): 153-158.

Rusch, F. R., and Menchetti, B. M. (1988). Transition in the 1990s: A reply to Knowlton and Clark. *Exeptional Children, 54* (4), 363–364.

Salisbury, C. L., and Vincent, L. J. (1990). Criterion of the next environment and best practices: Mainstreaming and integration 10 years later. *Topics in Early Childhood Special Education, 10*(2), 78-89.

Schenkat, R. (1988). The promise of restructuring for special education. *Education Week,* November 16.

Sewall, G. T. (1991), America 2000: An appraisal. *Phi Delta Kappan, 73* (3), 204–209.

Shepard, L. A. (1987). The new push for excellence: Widening the schism between regular and special education. *Exceptional Children, 53*(4): 327-329.

Sileo, T., Rude, H., and Luckner, J. (1988). Collaborative consultation: A model for transition planning for handicapped youth. *Education and Training in Mental Retardation, 23*(4): 333-339.

Smith, S. C. (1987). The collaborative school takes shape. *Educational Leadership, 45*(3), 4-6.

Stainback, S., Stainback, W., and Forest, M. (1989). *Educating All Students in the Mainstream of Regular Education.* Baltimore, MD: Brookes.

Stainback, W., and Stainback, S. (1984). A rationale for the merger of special and regular education. *Exceptional Children, 51*(2): 102-111.

Tharp, R. (1975). The triadic model of consultation. In C. Parker (ed.), *Psychological Consultation in the Schools: Helping Teachers Meet Special Needs.* Reston, VA: The Council for Exceptional Children.

Thousand, J. S., Villa, R. A., Paolucci-Whitcomb, P., and Nevin, A. (1992). In W. Stainback and S. Stainback (eds)., *Controversial Issues Confronting Special Education: Divergent Perspectives.* Boston: Allyn and Bacon.

Timar, T. (1989). The politics of school restructuring. *Phi Delta Kappan, 71*(4): 265-275.

Turner, R. R. (April, 1987). Here's what teachers say. *Learning 16:* 55-57.

*Webster's New Collegiate Dictionary* (8th ed.). (1981). Springfield, MA: Merriam-Webster.

*Webster's Third New International Dictionary, unabridged:* The Great Library of the English Language. (1976). Springfield, MA: Merriam-Webster.

West, J. F., and Idol, L. (1987). School consultation (Part I): An interdisciplinary perspective on theory, models, and research. *Journal of Learning Disabilities,* 20(7): 385-408.

Wildman, T. M., and Niles, J. A. Essentials of professional growth. *Educational Leadership,* 44(5): 4-10.

Will, M. (1984). Let us pause and reflect—but not too long. *Exceptional Children)* 51: 11-16.

Will, M. (1986). Education children with learning problems: A shared responsibility. *Exceptional Children,* 52(5): 411-415.

# 2

# ROLES AND RESPONSIBILITIES IN CONSULTATION, COLLABORATION, AND TEAMWORK

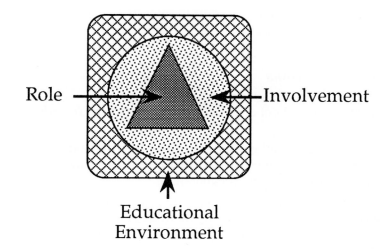

Role ⟶ ⟵ Involvement

Educational
Environment

## To Think About

Major concerns educators have about school consultation center around roles, framework, evaluation, and preparation of consultants and collaborators. The concerns are reflected in questions such as:

- Who am I in this role?
- How do I carry out responsibilities of the role?
- How do I know whether or not I am succeeding?
- How do I prepare for the role?

The consultant role creates concomitant roles—the consultee who confers with the consultant, and the client who benefits from the consultation and collaboration. These participatory roles must be understood and managed if school consultation is to be a useful tool. More educators would be encouraged to support school consultation if they knew the parameters of the role and could develop a basic profile of their responsibilities.

In order for school consultation to succeed, central administrators and policymakers must authenticate the need for consultant and consultee roles. Building-level administrators need to stress the significance of the consultant role and endorse consultant parity among their staff. Teachers should support consulting teachers with cooperation and not impede consultation and collaboration through apathy or resistance. Related services and support personnel can enhance the functions of consulting types and need to be integrated into the school consultation context. Parents will need to have information about the service, with assurance that this type of service is appropriate for their child's needs. Ultimately, community members must be aware of the long-range purposes and probable benefits of indirect special services before they can be expected to support and pay for them.

## Focusing Questions

1. What are the school consultant's major concerns regarding the consultant role?

2. How does a school consultant clarify the role and cultivate appropriate expectations of others toward that role? What other roles are created by school consultation and collaboration?

3. How do consultants go about initiating and implementing consultation services? How will they know the consultation service is meeting student needs and having positive ripple effects within the school context? How can they prepare for their roles in consultation?

4. What competencies characterize effective consultants and consultees?

## Key Terms

| | |
|---|---|
| caseload | preservice teachers |
| consultant competencies | role clarification |
| evaluation | role delineation |
| onedownsmanship | role parity |

---

**Scenario**

The following scene takes place in a school district conference room, where five special education teachers are talking before their special education director arrives for a planning meeting.

*LEARNING DISABILITIES TEACHER*: I understand we're here to decide how we're going to inform staff and parents about the consulting service methods we'll be implementing soon. But I think we'd better figure out first just what it is we *will* be doing.

*BEHAVIORAL DISORDERS TEACHER*: Definitely. I have a really basic question. What do I do the first day, and the first week, as a consulting teacher? I know you had some consultant training for your former job in another state, but this is new to the rest of us.

*GIFTED EDUCATION TEACHER*: Good question. And I've been thinking about all those personalities and teaching styles and subject areas we will be consulting with. They won't all like or want the same things.

*LEARNING DISABILITIES TEACHER*: I doubt this is something we can pick up and put into place overnight or by next week. From what little I've had a chance to read on school consultation, the secret for success lies in using good process skills.

*GIFTED EDUCATION TEACHER*: Yes, but at the same time we have to take into consideration the content that each student needs to learn. So I'm a bit apprehensive about this new role, but I'm looking forward to having it available, too.

*BEHAVIORAL DISORDERS TEACHER*: Yes, I've suspected for some time now that our present methods of dealing with learning and behavior problems are not as effective and efficient as they should be. I agree that we must be optimistic about the benefits the service could provide.

## Initiating School Consultation Practices

Educational reforms, social concerns, and economic issues may have convinced educators that consultation, collaboration, and teamwork are promising practices for helping students with special needs, but conversion of paper plans and philosophies to real-world roles and responsibilities is not simple. The questions put forth in the school-district conference room reflect real-world concerns that must be addressed thoughtfully:

- Where do I begin as a school consultant?
- What do I do the first day on the job?
- Let me see a sample schedule for the first week.
- Where am I to be headed by the end of the year?

Other questions and concerns likely to surface include:

- Will I be able to work with students at all? That is why I chose teaching as a career.
- Where's my room? Will I get office space and supplies?
- Can I fit at least a small group of students into that space for some group work?
- I need training for consultation, but where do I get it?
- How will I be evaluated in this position, and by whom?
- If consulting prepares consultees for direct delivery of services for special needs, will I be working myself out of a job?

Participants in consultation and collaboration must be able to voice their concerns, confusions, and feelings of inadequacy as they sort out the requirements of new roles. School administrators have a responsibility to initiate and encourage intensive discussion of questions and issues among school personnel who are asked to embark significantly different service delivery approaches.

School consultation per se is not a new concept. The literature base includes material on theory and models, methodology, training and practice issues, and guidelines and competencies (Heron and Kimball, 1988). However, most of it is theoretical, focusing on *why* consultation should occur, rather than *how* it can be conducted. Too little information is available on practical applications. Professional dialogues and practical materials are needed in order to cultivate positive attitudes and effective skills among consultants and consultees. Communication, cooperation, and coordination of administrative and teaching responsibilities will help establish role expectations and create a framework for implementing effective school consultation.

## Identifying Consultation Roles

As discussed in Chapter 1, individuals who serve as consultant (specialist), consultee (mediator), and client (target) in one consultative situation may exchange roles under different circumstances. For example, a special education teacher might be a consultant for one situation and consultee in another. The student is typically the client, or target, for the direct and indirect services of consultee and consultant, but in some cases the student could be a consultee or consultant. Consultation may be initiated by a special education teacher, school administrator, supervisor, or support service professional who has determined that a student's learning or behavior problem requires attention from a collaborative team. It also might be initiated by a teacher, parent, or student acting in a consultee role. In either case, both parties—consultant and consultee—share responsibility for working out a plan to help the client (Heron and Harris, 1982).

Roles and responsibilities may vary among individuals from situation to situation, but with appropriate role delineation, a collaborative spirit can prevail. Collaboration to achieve a common goal generally produces more beneficial results than isolated efforts by an individual. The whole of the combined efforts then is greater than the sum of its parts (Slavin, 1988). It is the basic idea that two heads are better than one, and several heads are better yet. The consultation process takes advantage of every individual's strengths and talents and directs them to the client's advantage.

Practitioners who are experienced consultants state their concerns precisely and succinctly. Problems they identify are:

losing touch with the students;
uncertainty about what and how to communicate with resistant consultees;
being perceived as a teacher's aide, "gofer,"
quick-fix expert, or jack-of-all-trades;
turning consultation into a tutorial for students;
territoriality of professional colleagues;
rigid curriculum and assessment procedures;
facing unrealistic expectations;
not having enough information and materials to share;
being considered a show-off, or a bossy expert;
professional politeness, but not acceptance;
management of time and resources;
lack of training;
being assigned an overload caseload;
too many "hats" to wear in the role;
indecision about designing and setting up consultation methods;
and, most of all, a reluctance to change.

## Key Elements for Effective School Consultation

Four major categories of roles and responsibilities for school consultation are displayed in Figure 2–1:

- role delineation in consultation;
- framework for consultation and collaboration;
- evaluation consultation; and
- preparation for consultation and collaboration.

Within the four categories, twelve key elements must be addressed in order to build excellent school consultation philosophies and practices. Timing of the focus on key elements is critical. In many school contexts, educators begin "too late in the day" to implement consultation, collaboration, and teamwork. When involvement and acceptance are the first priorities (see the "4 P.M. and 5 P.M." positions in clocklike Figure 2–1), failure of school consultation is all but assured. Instead, educators in all educational contexts—administrators, university instructors, teachers, and support staff—must begin "very early in the

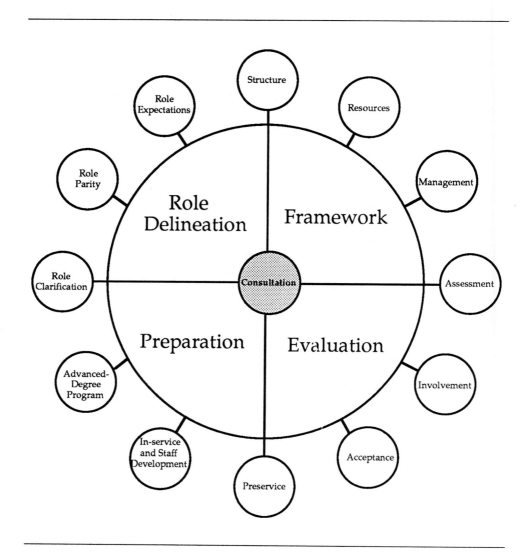

**FIGURE 2-1  Key Elements for Effective School Consultation**

morning" (see the "6 A.M." position in Figure 2–1) to prepare for school consultation at preservice, graduate, and in-service levels.

## Role Delineation in School Consultation

A school role, such as counselor, general classroom teacher, hearing-impaired student, or behavior-disordered child, does not designate a consultation role. The role in consultation is determined by the circumstance that targets the need. A consultant might be a parent who provides information to the school administrator, a learning disabilities teacher who helps a coach assess a student athlete's learning problem, or a mentor who provides gifted-program facilitator material for class use by a gifted student. This concept supports the contemporary approach to special services. Student needs, not student labels, determine the service and delivery method.

A consultee teams up with and collaborates with the consultant to help students succeed in school. As the need or problem is identified, the client or target role is established. In this way the consultant role allows direct service to the consultee so that the consultee can serve the client's need.

*Role Clarification*   The most important element in implementation of consultation is the clarification of roles. Until educators become familiar with the concepts of consultation and collaboration and ways they can participate as partners and team members, doubt and confusion may exist. School personnel sometimes are not sure why they have consulting teachers or what these people are supposed to be doing. A facilitator for gifted programs who had been consultant in a large urban high school for several years kept hearing variations on the same concern—"Just how do you spend your day with only 30 students assigned to you? After all they *are* fast learners." So the facilitator developed a job matrix to categorize the planning, implementation, and evaluation aspects and expectations of the role and shared it with teaching colleagues and administrators (Hay, 1984).

Classroom teachers may blame their heavy caseloads of students on seemingly lighter caseloads of consulting teachers. One high school English teacher told a newly appointed consulting teacher, "If you were back in your classroom teaching English instead of 'facilitating' for a few gifted students, my student load wouldn't be so big." Paradoxically, consulting teachers often have excessively high caseloads when travel time among schools is taken into account. If the caseload is too great, the effectiveness of consulting service will be diminished severely, for there will be little time for the coordination and communication so critical to consultation success.

Achieving coherent instructional plans for students' learning and behavioral needs requires extensive knowledge of role responsibilities among all involved (Allington and Broikou, 1988). A classroom teacher and a reading specialist each have information to share in addressing a struggling reader's strengths and deficits, yet both may know relatively little about each other's curriculum, teaching style, or expectations for the student. They must coordinate their efforts, or those efforts may be counterproductive. In one unfortunate case, a reading specialist was instructing a fifth-grader with reading problems to slow down and read more deliberately, while the learning disabilities specialist was encouraging him to read much more rapidly and was planning to refer him for the gifted program. Communication, cooperation, and coordination are first steps in helping such students with their special learning needs. The overall factor is clarification of each role in order to communicate and coordinate efforts.

Consultees may question a consultant's ability to address their particular situation, especially if the consultant is young and inexperienced. As one classroom teacher put it concerning the special education consulting teacher, "I'd never ask for *her* help. What does she know about a full classroom of students? She's never had more than five or six at a time, and she never has taught in a regular classroom." Keller (1981) describes with irony some of the more common perceptions of resource teacher roles: the "invisible woman" who seldom ventures out of her room; the "fifth wheel" who is not taken seriously; the "new fellow on the block" who is perceived as an expensive extra of no visible help to others; the "sweet young thing" just out of graduate school with limited classroom experience; and "Mr. or Ms. Wizard" who is supposed to work magic and transform children. While not all resource or consulting teachers suffer from such characterizations, misperceptions like these can occur.

---

**Applications for Developing Role Clarification**
*Where to Start and How to Begin*

**1.** Read, study, think, interview others, and complete coursework if possible, to gain information and skills for the role.

**2.** Formulate a personal philosophy of and commitment to school consultation, collaboration, and teamwork.

**3.** Meet with central administrators of your school(s) to listen to their perceptions of this role.

**4.** If an advisory council is available, engage the members in discussion about consultation and collaboration roles. This council should involve general and special education teachers, support personnel, administrators, parents, and other community leaders.

**5.** Meet with all building administrators to whom you are assigned, to practice responsive listening (see Chap 6 for techniques) and learn their viewpoints. This is a *very important* step.

**6.** After meeting with each principal, reorganize your own thoughts and ideas, and gather more information if necessary.

**7.** Develop a tentative role description and goals based on administrators' views as well as your own perspective.

**8.** Return to central administration, trying out your role description and goals, and then revise if necessary.

**9.** Return to building administrators to share the revised package and obtain their approval and support. Again, this is *very* important.

**10.** After honing your document to a concise format, put it up for discussion, explaining it to teaching staff and non-teaching staff. Refine it further, based on their comments.

**11.** Meet with parent groups to inform them about school consultation service and solicit their opinions.

**12.** Keep stressing the opportunities and benefits inherent in collaboration and teamwork enterprises.

**13.** Work out a master schedule for your role, and distribute it to administrators whose attendance centers will be affected.

**14.** Have an open house in your work area, with refreshments if possible, and distribute handouts that tell your goals and schedule.

**15.** Post your schedule for access by teachers, support staff, and secretaries.

**16.** Conduct needs-sensing and needs-assessment surveys to find out what school personnel and parents want to happen. If appropriate, ask students, too (see Chapter 12 for techniques).

**17.** Request time during in-service or staff development meetings to discuss the program.

**18.** Begin to work first with receptive, enthusiastic teachers as consultees.

**19.** Begin right away to log consultations and related activities, for accountability and evaluation.

**20.** Solicit and welcome input from all.

*Role Parity* Along with role ambiguity and misunderstanding, consultants may feel an absence of role parity. This makes it seem as if they do not belong to any one school or department. They may complain of isolation from general classroom teachers and from specialist colleagues as well. It is all too obvious to many consulting teachers that classroom teachers are not waiting with open arms for the consultants to come and save them. Life, and school, will go on every day for students and their teachers with or without support staff assistance.

Substitutes may not be provided for absent consulting teachers. Indeed, consultants may be pulled out of their own roles to substitute for absent classroom teachers or perform other tasks that come up suddenly. Consulting teachers have been asked to guide visitors on a school tour, to drive the school bus, and to perform secretarial tasks. This diminishes the contribution of the consulting role. Such a myopic approach to the consulting teacher method could transform it into a tutor or teacher aide program.

On the other hand, colleagues might place unreasonable expectations on the role of the consultant, rather like the Mr. or Ms. Wizard situation mentioned earlier, expecting instant success and miraculous student progress in a very short while. When success with students is slower than the consultees had hoped, or does not come at all, their attitudes may range from guarded skepticism to open disapproval of the consultation approach. A consultant cannot be a panacea for every student's difficulties. Recognizing and acknowledging this certainty will help counteract yet another barrier—the misconceived notion that consulting teachers will threaten job security by replacing resource room staff and other support and ancillary personnel.

Stress and burnout, additional barriers to effective consulting models, can accompany lack of role clarity and role parity. Consultants and consulting teachers may feel like "second-class" colleagues, not accepted or appreciated as a vital part of the staff. Some who travel extensively among schools in their cars have been dubbed "windshield" personnel. The problem is magnified by the misconception that consultants have no ownership in student welfare and development. Students served indirectly by the consultant are not viewed as "belonging" to the consultant. Therefore, recognition and reinforcement of the consultant's effort in helping students succeed in school is important for credibility and morale.

---

**Applications for Building Role Parity**
*Becoming Part of the School Team*

1. Get involved in each building where you are scheduled. Accept responsibility for lunch, bus, playground duty. Offer to help during book fairs, school carnivals, ball games, as much as time and energy will allow.

2. Don't be seen around the building doing nothing, or *seeming* to be doing nothing. Spending time in the library to locate resources for a consultee or student may be perceived by the skeptic as recreational reading. This is not intended to discourage the activity, but to urge that the purpose of the activity be made clear to those who might like to suspect the worst.

3. Invite colleagues and parents to your room. Have student work displayed and occasionally serve refreshments. One consultant for behavioral disorders was disappointed that no teachers ever came to her room. So she began a four o'clock exercise class there for fifteen minutes daily. As her room soon became the hub of after-school activity, colleagues also became much more knowledgeable about her students' progress in the resource room and their needs in the classroom.

4. Avoid hierarchical relationships by practicing the communicative art of "onedownsmanship" (Conoley and Conoley, 1982). This is the opposite of the oneupmanship demeanor of the expert and role superior.

5. If you have any choice in the matter, locate your work space in the mainstream of the school. Of course, consultee and client rights to privacy and confidentiality must be protected, but when consulting teachers are located at the far ends of hallways, they are easily isolated and ignored. One consulting teacher expressed his frustration in feeling cut off from the life of the school. His room was in a most out-of-the-way location. "I am viewed as that teacher over there they occasionally send kids to," he said, "so I have tried to make myself visible and available before and after school."

**6.** Promote the value of consultation in education just as it is valued in medical, legal, and other professions. The "second opinion" is sought widely in these other important areas of life, but a teacher often is expected to handle problems by relying solely on his or her own resources.

**7.** Eat lunch with other staff members, and interact just enough, but not too much, in the teacher workroom. (see Chapter 12 for more about the "teachers' lounge").

**8.** Ask teachers for their advice on educational issues, and encourage them to demonstrate for you some of their favorite techniques. However, do not share their favorites with others unless permission is given.

**9.** Dress for the school and the occasion. Variables such as high or low status, titles, and clothes have a significant impact on consultation effectiveness (Kratochwill and Van Someren, 1985). One consulting teacher confided that she was having trouble being accepted by a particular school's staff. She approached the problem straight on and asked what she was doing wrong. The reply surprised her. "You don't come here to *work* like the rest of us. You come in a suit and heels, all dressed up, to advise, observe, and supervise." She quickly altered her style of dress and was rewarded with changed attitudes at that school. In sharing her story with another consultant, the second replied, "Yes, I learned to do that. I have two schools, and luckily for me, the colleagues who like to dress up are at my morning school. At noon I whip off the earrings and scarf and slip on tennis shoes. Then I fit in at both places. It paid off for me."

**10.** The golden question to ask of any colleague is this: "What can I do for you and your students *that you don't have the time and materials to do?*" Compare that question with any comment which might imply, "What can I do that you don't have the expertise to do?" After asking what you can do to help the busy, over-worked, classroom-bound teacher, suggest that you both talk about the need and how you can help. This is the starting point for the collaborative ethic and team effort.

*Role Expectations*  Educators may expect too much, or too little, from the consulting role. They may wish to see results too soon, or neglect to monitor results and then let ineffective service drag on too long. They may expect to work, and wish to work, only with students and not with adults. "I was trained to work with kids, and that's what I enjoy," confided one consultant whose role was to become a provider of indirect service only. Unrealistic and unreasonable expectations should be set aside in the early planning stages of school consultation methods. Consultants must set reasonable goals for themselves and not try to do too much.

Consultees may exploit consulting service by expecting the consultant to "fix" the student; then, if this does not happen, they downgrade consultation as a failure and collaboration as a flop. The team approach may be awkward for an educator at first, not only for a consultant, but for the consultee as well. Some times the most difficult part of a support role is backing out once the consultee experiences success in meeting the client's needs (Stainback and Stainback, 1985). When the consultee no longer intensively needs support and assistance, the consultant should adopt the philosophy, "It *would* be wonderful to solve all the problems so that I eventually work myself out of a job," although, as discussed earlier, this is extremely unlikely to happen. The more successful the consultation services become, the more the teachers and administrators seem to value them for their immediate contribution and long-range positive ripple effects.

Consultation often is not the immediate choice of service delivery for students with severe learning and behavior problems. For example, many behavior-disordered students need complex interventions. Braaten, et al. (1988) emphasize that teachers of behavior-disordered students need additional instructional resources, including staff, to handle dangerously disruptive behavior. They stress the rights of other students for a safe and supportive learning environment. Severely disruptive behavior can result in peer rejection and intolerance from teachers.

Those who promote a consultation and collaboration approach for helping students with special needs should not be surprised to encounter cautiousness and reserve toward consultation service by those who work with behavior-disordered students. Braaten et al. (1988) suggest that data do not support the contention that special education service for behavior disorders can be reduced by interventions such as cooperative learning, peer tutoring, and involvement of consulting teachers in general educational settings. They argue that some students with behavioral disorders simply require special educational environments. On the other hand, special education teachers who adopt a consulting teacher approach often find that colleagues become more understanding and accepting of their students and more willing to include them in the school mainstream.

When one teacher of students with behavior disorders implemented a consulting model, she structured her responsibilities into three categories: students who spend the day in the mainstream, students who spend part of each day in the resource room, and students with less troublesome behaviors who are not staffed into the behavioral disorders program. She outlined her goals as follows:

*For students in the mainstream:*

- daily contact with their teachers to provide support and handle problems immediately;
- maintenance of behavior management systems for the student until the teacher feels they are no longer necessary (see Chaps 9 and 10 for behavior management techniques);
- parent contact to complement the teacher's contact;

- coordination of planning with the principal, social worker, special subject teachers, parents, and community agencies;
- direct service to student as needed, to help with assignments, and interpersonal relationships; and
- observation to monitor progress.

### *For students who attend the resource room:*

- daily contact the with classroom teacher;
- monitoring system for behavior, designed with the classroom teacher to be responsive to the classroom management style and to the needs of the student;
- planned direct service in the resource room;
- crisis intervention;
- parent contact, along with that by classroom teacher; and
- observations.

### *For students with less problematic behaviors:*

- demonstration of intervention measures such as  charting for classroom teachers;
- sharing materials for specific academic needs;
- information on school and community resources;
- observations; and
- participation in staffings.

This teacher commented that it was surprising to see on paper just how many aspects of consultation apply to the special education teacher, especially one who serves behaviorally disordered children. In today's world of immense risk for children—fetal alcohol syndrome, prenatal effects of crack and other drugs, violence in society, fragmentation of the family, poverty, and much more—the need for the kinds of interventions this teacher has set up is profound. As stressed earlier, it would be foolhardy and myopic to suggest that consultants and consulting teachers will work themselves out of their jobs any time in the foreseeable future.

The involvement of as many school personnel as possible, through needs assessments, interviews, staff development, and both formal and informal communications, will minimize unwarranted expectations for consulting roles. Building on successful collaborations with more receptive and cooperative colleagues will generate confidence in the consultant and respect for the program.

Educators sometimes avoid collaborating because they feel the need to remain separate and visible. In too many instances, jobs and professional identities depend on separate systems (Shepard, 1987). The result is entrenchment and expectations for role separatism. Unless school personnel are informed about consultation and are involved in implementing the plan, they may underestimate not only the problems that could occur, but more importantly, the power of this educational service when it is conducted appropriately.

**Applications for Fulfilling Role Expectations**
*Living up to Expectations*

**1.** Provide colleagues with information that helps them see the fallacy of the "quick fix" for complex learning and behavior problems. Practical information written in practical terms for practitioners will be most effective.

**2.** Promote an exchange-of-roles day in which consultants teach the class and teachers observe, plan modifications, and consult with others.

**3.** Review goals with consultees, revise the objectives, and document successes, no matter now small they might seem.

**4.** Discourage any tendency of colleagues to regard the consultants as supervisors, evaluators, or therapists. Pugach and Johnson (1989) identify a major problem in achieving parity within collaborative models as the tendency among specialists to take on the expert role and disregard experienced classroom teachers as resources for students' special needs. They report that one candid specialist said in reference to classroom teachers, "Why doesn't anyone ask about all the things I have learned from them?"

**5.** Refrain from making any recommendations that conflict with administrative policy or teacher values.

**6.** When a consultee wishes to have a student removed from the classroom, *right now*, just pretend not to hear; instead, suggest something that the consultee, or you and the consultee together, might try.

**7.** Know content areas well for the students and subjects about which you consult. Also, be knowledgeable about regulations and recommendations governing special education, education for at-risk students, and school reform movements.

**8.** Develop a newsletter for school personnel and parents. Inform readers, without breach of privacy or confidentiality, about program activities, educational issues, materials, and home-school partnerships, taking care not to identify individuals.

**9.** Seek out and provide resources for teachers and parents.

**10.** Continue to read, study, attend conferences, and take courses in consultation and related professional development.

**11.** Teach students in or out of classrooms where feasible.

**12.** Demonstration teach for teachers who request. (Make the offer if no requests are forthcoming.)

**13.** Observe in classrooms, always following up with the teacher soon afterward. (See Chapter 7 for observation techniques.)

**14.** Maintain contact with parents.

**15.** Observe students outside the classroom (playground, lunch, extracurricular events) to get a different perspective.

**16.** Make attractive bulletin boards that complement the goals of consultation and collaboration, stressing teamwork and partnerships.

**17.** With a colleague or two or three, brainstorm periodically for ways to improve services and enhance collaborative efforts among educators.

**18.** Reach out to more reluctant colleagues, asking for their views, and offering materials, information, and assistance that fit into their plans.

**19.** Encourage collaborative staff development activities and partnerships such as "Teachers Helping Teachers."

**20.** Find texts and basal readers that work best in collaborative efforts.

**21.** Design curriculum materials and modifications to meet collaborator and student needs.

**22.** Seek grant money and seed money that benefits many teachers and students.

**23.** Evaluate the program regularly and thoroughly.

**24.** Reassess your plans, time allocation, resources, program results, and revise if necessary.

**25.** Share results of successful programs at regional, state, and national conferences.

**26.** Engage in research efforts for new information about consultation and collaboration practices.

**27.** Carry out advocacy and public relations efforts for excellent education.

## Framework for School Consultation

The framework element for school consultation, collaboration, and teamwork calls for developing structures for consultation, providing time and facilities in which to meet, and managing details, so consultation is as convenient and nonintrusive as possible.

*Structure for Consultation and Collaboration*   Consultants need a structure within which to carry out their roles and responsibilities. Chapter 3 will set the stage for developing structures (note the plural) in which to conduct consultation, collaboration, and teamwork. However, for now, it is one thing to design a hypothetical method of consultation, quite another to design multiple methods for different circumstances, and an even greater challenge to select and put into motion the right method for each situation. This intricate task is easier if preceded by role clarification and assurance of role parity and appropriate role expectations.

The consultant will want to formulate several methods for consultation and collaboration in a variety of grade levels, subject areas, special needs categories, and school, community, and family contexts. The structure should attend to the context of the system (such as school, neighborhood, family, athletic, or business arena). It also should include perspectives such as models, which will be discussed in Chapter 3. Consultants need not hesitate to design their own consultation method through trial and error, in order to fit a model to school needs. Polling teachers to find out how they would use a consultant for their students is a good way to begin. Studying and observing structures from other school systems also are helpful.

*Time and Facilities for Consultation and Collaboration*   One of the most overwhelming obstacles to school consultation is lack of time for consultation to occur. Lack of time is a major deterrent to success of collaborative consultation (Johnson, Pugach and Hammittee, 1988; Idol-Maestas and Ritter, 1985; Speece and Mandell, 1980; McGlothlin and Kelly, 1982). Idol (1986) recommends that resource teachers have at least one-third of their school time available for consultations. However, in a study by Neel (1981), forty-eight percent of the special education teachers queried reported that they have no time scheduled for consultation and are expected to provide consultation services beyond regularly scheduled teaching hours. Most often they must use their own planning time for consultation, which is not an ideal way to enhance attitudes toward the consultation approach. Many special education teachers and classroom teachers report that their school day is simply not designed to accommodate collaboration (Stainback and Stainback, 1985; Idol-Maestas, 1983).

Even when the consultant can arrange and coordinate a schedule for meeting with consultees and following up on outcomes, it can be next to impossible to arrange significant blocks of consultee time for productive collaboration. Working out such a plan is one of the most formidable tasks facing a consultant, particularly one who also has direct teaching responsibilities at specific times.

In spite of the difficulties involving allocation of time and the significance of providing scheduled time for successful consultation, the discussion of time has not been first in this chapter. Just as the factor of cost should not be addressed first in designing a new product or procedure, neither should time constraints be allowed to impede planning for consultation and collaboration. The problem must be reckoned with, of course. But if allowed to take precedence over other considerations, time can dictate thought patterns and restrict the free flow of innovative ideas. "We haven't the time," is as debilitating for a school staff as "We haven't the money," is for a family or a business. In normal circumstances people find the time, just as they find the money, for things that really are necessary. This is not to minimize the time-related difficulties of curtailed staff or mushrooming caseloads, any more than to discount the money-related pain of poverty and need. However, resolution of the dilemma lies in the visions and plans for the use of that time.

Administrators must assume responsibility for scheduling the time needed by consultants and consultees to collaborate. If they lend their authority to this endeavor, school personnel will be more willing to brainstorm ways of getting together. Schenkat (1988) points out that if working conditions in schools were restructured to allow greater flexibility in scheduling, teachers could find the time to collaborate with colleagues and create solutions for learning and behavior problems of students with mild handicaps. This would help build bridges between special education and general education, while expanding services to all students who are at risk of failing in the school environment.

When consulting teachers initiate consultation and collaboration, it is very likely that these activities will have to come out of their own time—before school, after school, during lunch hours, perhaps even on weekends. Even so, they must move as soon as possible to more appropriate times during the school workday. This is not only for their well-being, but to emphasize that consultation and collaboration are not add-on services that will be supplied as an extreme role overload by a zealous, dedicated few.

When time *is* arranged for a consultation, a facility must be available in which to conduct the consultation. The area should be pleasant, quiet, and relatively private for free exchange of confidences. Such a place is at a premium in a busy school building.

*Management of Consultation*   School consultation is a cost-efficient way of serving students with special needs (Heron and Kimball, 1988). But there is a danger of letting fiscal issues, rather than student needs, dictate the service delivery method. Assigning large caseloads to consulting teachers might save money in the short run, but could cost more eventually if student performance does not improve (Huefner, 1988). Therefore, the caseload issue must be addressed with extreme caution.

Problems related to caseload are complex. For example, the average time needed to complete one Individual Education Program (IEP) has been assessed as 6.5 hours (Heron and Kimball, 1988; Price and Goodman, 1980). A consulting teacher with an overwhelming caseload of students and time-consuming responsibilities, such as developing IEPs, will have no time to consult and collaborate. Although direct service can be a strategy for easing into indirect service, care must be taken to keep the load manageable. If a consulting teacher's caseload is too great, direct service is inadequate, possibilities for indirect services are minimal, and the program is self-defeating.

In discussing the Resource/Consulting Teacher model (to be discussed more fully in Chapter 3), Idol-Maestas (1983) recommends that teachers spend 20 to 40 percent of their school day in consulting-related activities, such as discussing educational problems, presenting ideas for use in regular classrooms, attending in-service sessions, observing, performing curriculum-based assessment, demonstrating instructional techniques (Wiederholt, Hammill, and Brown, 1983), and coordinating the program.

A consultant must be organized and efficient. Greenburg (1987) notes a number of studies indicating that although resource teachers may be committed to direct contact as their major activity, considerable portions of their time are required for record keeping, paperwork, and teacher-consultant responsibilities (McGlothlin, 1981; Miller and Sabatino, 1978; Evans, 1980). Consulting teachers manage and monitor consultee use of materials as varied as books, tests, kits, tapes, films, and media equipment. They help teachers develop systems of observation, monitoring, and assessment, along with performing these activities themselves. Their paperwork, scheduling, and communication systems must be efficient and effective. Techniques for managing these activities will be addressed in Chapter 7.

---

**Applications for Structuring Consultation**
*Finding Time and Facilities for Consultation*

1. Rotate school visits and vary schedules for preparation periods.

2. Rearrange commitments so you are not always in the same building at the same time on the same days.

3. Arrange peer tutoring so you and the classroom teacher can have time to collaborate.

4. Invite colleagues to your work area and have aides or paraprofessionals take over as you monitor.

5. Encourage administrators to fill in for consultants and consultees by teaching a lesson, managing a study period, or reading stories to students. This also has a positive ripple effect of allowing them to interact with students and experience the classroom from the teacher's perspective.

6. Team teaching among classroom teachers lends itself to collaborative arrangements.

7. A permanent "floating substitute" can travel among grades to free up consultees as well as consultants (West and Idol, 1990).

8. Volunteers, including parents, grandparents, and retired teachers (West and Idol, 1990), can provide enriching activities to students as well as release time for collaboration among teachers.

9. Record all consultative activities, and encourage consultees to do so as well. Careful documentation of consultations and results can be used to underscore the benefits of these activities and to negotiate for consistent, significant consultation time.

10. Arrange for the physical and psychological comfort of all.

11. Place furniture in arrangements that convey equality, not hierarchy.

12. Provide room to spread out materials, and equipment for viewing film or hearing tapes if necessary.

13. Refreshments, especially at the end of the day, are energizing and help establish camaraderie. (Note the change in atmosphere during an airplane flight after beverages and snacks are served.)

14. Space for stashing coats, briefcases, and books is appreciated.

15. If collaborators are new to the building, provide them in advance with maps of the neighborhood, building arrangement, and room location, with parking areas visibly marked.

Recommended caseload numbers will vary, depending on school context, travel time required, grade level, exceptionalities and special needs served, and structure of the consulting method. The numbers must be kept manageable to fulfill the intent and promise of consultation and collaboration. The key lies in documenting carefully all consultation activities *and* making note of those that should have happened but were precluded by time constraints. Through meetings with administrators, interactions with colleagues during staff development, and conferences with parents, consultants can negotiate for reasonable caseload assignments and blocks of time for consultation, collaboration, and teamwork.

## Evaluation and Support of Consultation

The third of four key elements in school consultation features evaluation and support. Educators need to document the effectiveness of consultation and collaboration, in order to ensure continuing support for these kinds of educational services. School personnel are understandably skeptical of indirect service if it does not demonstrate its usefulness. They may be involved initially because they have been told to, or because they have been coerced into giving indirect service a try, but their interest will wane if positive results are not forthcoming. There will be out-and-out resistance if they suspect indirect service is a detriment to children and education.

*Assessment of the Consultation*   Assessment of consultation is a requirement for continuing to obtain consultation time and facilities. Involvement and acceptance by school personnel will increase when effectiveness of consulting as a professional practice in education is demonstrated. In keeping with the philosophy of collaboration, consultation evaluation should be designed cooperatively by personnel from varying roles.

McGaghie (1991) expresses strong dissatisfaction with most professional evaluations because:

- They typically cover a narrow range of practice situations.
- They are biased toward assessment of acquired knowledge.
- They devote little attention to direct assessment of practical skills.
- Little attention is given to assessment of  professional or personal qualities.
- Measurement problems exist.

All of these points are cogent criticisms to keep in mind when evaluating consultation and collaboration. McGaghie stresses that the key to professional assessment lies in ascertaining the nature of the professional role, not just mastery of information that experts think beginners should acquire. True job-proficiency assessment cannot be relegated to paper-pencil exams. The necessary competencies are not easily quantified, and there is no single answer for all professional problems and needs.

**Applications for Evaluation of Consultation**
*Finding Out How It Is Going*

**1.** Teacher involvement in consultation and collaboration must not be perceived as a sign of weakness or inadequacy. Instead, consultees should be commended for taking advantage of services provided to help both educators and students succeed.

**2.** Involvement in consultation and collaboration should be valued as a strength in the performance evaluations of school personnel by administrators and supervisors.

**3.** Involve school personnel in developing and implementing consultation practices and assessing their outcomes. Figure 2–2 is a form that can be used by the consultee to determine benefits of the service. The instrument should include space for open-ended response, and may be confidential if the consultee chooses.

**4.** Conduct self-assessment of consultation and collaboration. Self-assessment is a painful but necessary practice for the progressive consultant. The Consultation Log provided in Chapter 7 includes a brief self-assessment.

**5.** Videotaping, having a colleague observe and report, and often just reflecting on your habits are all potentially helpful ways of growing professionally. Reflection leads to insights about yourself, prompting changes in self-concept, changes in perception of an event or person, or plans for changing some behavior (Canning, 1991). One speech/language pathologist analyzed her emerging consultation skills this way:

*In my early perception of consulting I viewed myself as the expert. Experience has taught me I am not. Expert language usually is understood by very few. Knowing how to frame good questions is an invaluable tool. I used to think I knew what was best for the child. Experience again has shown me this is not so—we must all get our respective "what's bests" on the table and mediate. I felt that I needed to have all the workable solutions to the problem at hand, but this was assuming too much. I thought everyone likes and respects the "expert" and wants his or her help. I now perceive my task as one of earning the right to become part of the planning for any child. This means I must be as knowledgeable as possible, not only in my own field, but about the total environment (physical and mental) of each child. I am still learning that effective intervention takes time and careful planning.*

**6.** Other self-assessment questions the consultant can ask include:

1. What solutions have I offered for discussion?
2. What documentation have I gathered to support my opinions?
3. Can I list the questions I want to ask the consultee?
4. Can I listen and work cooperatively on the problem?
5. Can I be honest about my feelings toward the child, the problem, and the personnel involved?
6. Will I follow through on the plan?
7. Will I document the efficacy of the plan?
8. Will I try new methods and strategies?
9. Will I persist in the plan?
10. Will I give feedback to the consultee about the situation?
11. Am I willing to ask for help or advice?

Please evaluate your use of the consulting teacher service provided in the _____ program by providing the following information. Indicate your views by responding with 1, 2, 3, 4, or 5 in the following manner:

1=Not at all      2=A little      3=Somewhat      4=Considerably      5=Much

1.  The consulting teacher provides useful information.                      _____
2.  The consulting teacher understands my school environment and
    teaching situation.                                                      _____

3.  The consulting teacher listens to my ideas.                             _____
4.  The consulting teacher helps me identify useful resources that
    help my students' special needs.                                        _____

5.  The consulting teacher explains ideas clearly.                          _____

6.  The consulting teacher fits easily into the school setting.             _____
7.  The consulting teacher increases my confidence in the special
    programs.                                                               _____

8.  I value consulting and collaborating with the consulting teacher.       _____

9.  I have requested collaboration time with the consulting teacher.        _____
10. I plan to continue seeking opportunities to consult and
    collaborate with the consulting teacher.                                _____

Other
comments: _____

---

**FIGURE 2–2   Consultee Assessment of Consultation and Collaboration**

McGaghie (1991) cites the assessment system for becoming a chartered accountant in Canada as an exemplary one. A major part of that exam is a set of short and long business accounting problems or cases. The candidate is expected to "frame" each problem, identify its elements, figure out which parts require immediate versus delayed attention, formulate a problem solution, exercise judgment in developing alternatives, propose practical solutions, communicate effectively with users, and respond to users' needs. These exercises target the kinds of expertise school consultants should demonstrate. Persons responsible for assessing consultation and collaboration competency would do well to pattern their evaluation procedures on this kind of exam. Desirable attributes of the professional are determined by many forces, with the key to assessment being the nature of the role a professional will fill, not just the information that "experts" think beginners should master.

Only two kinds of evaluation measures are readily available in the published research on education-based consultation (Tindal and Taylor-Pendergast, 1989): rating scales of judgments that represent a variety of skills and activities, and estimates of engaged time that note the activities required or demanded. Administrators, advisory council members, and policymakers will need to study carefully the few procedures that are available for assessment, and beyond that, use their skills to design more helpful and practical assessment techniques that fit their school context and consultant role responsibilities.

The context of the school setting must be assessed as well. For example, a consultant may have excellent communication skills and a wealth of content with which to consult and collaborate, but if no time is provided for interaction, there will be few positive results. Chapter 8 focuses on assessment and evaluation for consultation and collaboration practices.

Consultants will want to evaluate at every stage of the process, to keep heading in the right direction (see Chapter 8 on formative evaluation). Evaluation should include a variety of data collection methods to provide the kinds of information needed by target groups. When assessment is completed, consultation and collaboration practices must not be judged inadequate for the wrong reasons or due to erroneous assumptions. If time has not been allocated for the interactions, if staff have not had preparation and encouragement, and if administrator support is lacking, those elements should be targeted for improvement before consultation is disparaged or discouraged for the wrong reasons.

**Involvement in Consultation and Collaboration**    Friend and Cook (1990) emphasize that collaborative programs must address "voluntariness" before detailed planning can occur. Others have stressed that participation in collaboration must be voluntary on the part of the consultee. However, for some school personnel, that desirable condition may never appear. In these instances, administrator influence and appealing tactics by the consultant may help. Sometimes a bandwagon effect can exert power in getting everyone on for the ride. Broadcasting the successes and promoting the benefits of consultations and collaborations that have occurred may get the bandwagon rolling and the reluctants on board.

Most important, however, is involving people right from the start in needs assessments, planning efforts, evaluations, staff development presentations, and personal contacts, to instill ownership and even arouse a little curiosity. Techniques and incentives for promotion of consultation, collaboration, and teamwork will be discussed in Chapter 12.

**Acceptance of School Consultation**    Effective collaboration takes practice. Consultation creates change. Teamwork means giving up part of the ownership. These realities make acceptance of school consultation more difficult and extensive, and enthusiastic involvement by all school personnel somewhat unrealistic. Consultation, in the minds of many general educators, is associated

**Applications for Gaining Acceptance**
*Being Accepted as One of the School Team*

   1. As a consultant, portray yourself as assistant to the teacher.

   2. Become more visible, visiting each classroom and making positive comments about what is going on there.

   3. Always have an ear open to opportunities to help out, and spin off helping situations to become more established as a consulting teacher.

   4. Be realistic and understanding about the demands that are placed on classroom teachers, administrators, and parents in fulfilling *their* roles.

   5. Be realistic about what consultants can do.

   6. Keep school personnel wanting more consultation services, making them so valuable that if they were taken away from the schools, your role and those services would be missed.

   7. "Advertise" consultation successes.

   8. Keep providing benefits for teachers. "What can I do for you and your students that you do not have time or resources to do?" is the operative question.

   9. Identify ways for parents, as consultees, to contribute and have ownership in programs for their children.

   10. Create and nurture many opportunities for special education programs and related services to interface with general education programs.

   11. Institute communication networks among staff, parents, and advocacy groups.

   12. Demonstrate strategies, methods, and materials to any who will listen.

   13. Identify successful, exemplary consultation and collaboration practices, *especially* when they occur in your school district!

   14. Share newest trends and techniques in a nonpatronizing way.

   15. Work with a group of collaborating colleagues to write a guide on the use of consultation and collaboration. Present it to new faculty members and periodically in staff development for refresher courses.

   16. Send notes of appreciation to consultees regularly.

   17. Do not expect a uniformly high level of acceptance and involvement from all, but keep aiming for it.

with special education. If teachers resent having more responsibility for special education students, they may blame school consultation and consultants for this condition. Consultees and support personnel need a precedence for accepting and adapting to this model. Most of all, they need administrator support and encouragement. Consultants must find every opportunity to cultivate these conditions.

## Preparation for School Consultation Roles

Preparation programs for mastering the skills of school consultation and collaboration are a necessity. Opportunities and incentives must be provided for three populations:

1. Preservice students should prepare to be consultees and potential consultants.
2. Degree-program graduate students in consultation should prepare to be consultants and to train consultants and consultees.
3. In-service teachers should prepare for roles as consultees and advocates for integrating consultation and collaboration into their school contexts.

Skills of the consultant and consultee are enhanced through training activities, coaching, and feedback in process and content skill areas.

*Preservice Preparation*   Teacher preparation programs often do not include process skills such as communication and conflict resolution in teaching methods. Not so many years ago, studies revealed that consultation training in college and university programs was very much the exception rather than the rule (Lilly and Givens-Ogle, 1981). Some progress has been made since that time in teacher preparation programs, but much more is needed (West and Brown, 1987).

Phillips, et al. (1990) suggest that collaboration and consultation skills can be cultivated by teacher educators at the preservice level. They recommend that teacher preparation programs provide introductory education courses in which general and special education preservice teachers participate jointly in practicum experiences that serve a diverse range of children's needs. However, this approach would require concerted effort by college and university personnel, for many of them have not been trained to perform collaboration and consultation functions themselves, let alone facilitate development of these behaviors in their students.

Some veteran educators will be nervous about having "novice teachers" address consultation practices before they have experienced student teaching and real-world teaching. Nevertheless, the seeds of awareness, which may bear fruit in important ways for students with special needs, can and should be planted early. After all, for most new teachers, there is not much time or experience gained between that last day of teacher training and the first day they are all alone in their classrooms with real students of their own.

*Graduate Certification and Degree Programs*   Formal training in consultation lags behind the increasing demands for service (Curtis and Zins, 1988). White and Pryzwansky (1982) assert that resource teachers in schools are not prepared to deliver consultation and are keenly aware of their insufficiencies in that regard. The number of preparation programs is increasing (Dickens and Jones,

---

**Applications for Preservice Preparation**
*Building Awareness of Consultation and Collaboration*

**1.** At several points in every teacher preparation program, textual and class information should feature examples of teachers working together—problem solving, team teaching, and learning in staff development activities.

**2.** Student teachers need to observe experienced teachers teaming and collaborating, and to sit in on consultations.

**3.** Videotapes and simulations of consultation episodes can be used at the undergraduate level.

**4.** Interactive video, with opportunities to select actions and observe the outcomes of those actions, is a promising tool for providing undergraduate training in a safe and correctable professional environment.

---

1990; Gersten, et al. 1991; Thurston and Kimsey, 1989), but universities have far to go to meet the training needs.

Some states require training in consultation skills for teacher certification. Inclusion of school consultation and collaboration skill development in standards for accreditation of teacher education programs would be one way to encourage emphasis on school consultation and collaboration at the graduate and preservice level. School administrators should recruit prospective consultants who welcome the opportunity for working with adults as well as students.

Training programs for school consultants should center around elements featured in this book, to develop competencies such as communication and problem solving that enable them to be effective within the school context. While each training program can be expected to be unique, a basic program must prepare future school consultants for effectiveness in four areas:

- delineating their roles;
- creating a framework that allows them to fulfill their roles;
- evaluating their effectiveness; and
- helping prepare colleagues for collaborative consultation even as they extend their own learning.

*In-service and Staff Development*    Training institutions may eventually include consultation in special education programs, but White and Pryzwansky (1982) note that school personnel now teaching are largely unprepared to deliver consultation service. Their lack of preparation for consultation is compounded by a dearth of empirical studies that might provide evidence for or against various components of consultation training. However, movements such as school reform, restructuring, and mainstreaming have stimulated efforts such as those reported by Rule, et al. (1990). In their study, Rule and colleagues identified the need for administrative support, technical assistance, and follow-up assistance, as well as in-service training.

At the in-service and staff development level, consultation and collaboration programs can be tailored to each school context. Unfortunately, too many in-service activities and staff development programs are rightly criticized as irrelevant, poorly conducted, redundant, boring, confusing, and a host of other denigrating terms. But they do not need to be that way. Staff development should be looked on by consultants as a golden opportunity for promoting consultation, collaboration, and teamwork. It can help teachers be more successful in their complex roles. This important topic is the focus of Chapter 12.

## Consultant Competencies

A consultant wears many hats. Consultants are context systems analysts, process specialists, and content information banks, as well as role models and educational leaders. Consulting and collaborating require flexibility, adaptability, resilience, and tolerance for delayed reinforcement—or none at all. A person in these roles is called on to diagnose, problem identify, problem solve, prescribe, evaluate, and follow-up, but all as part of a team that does not always understand or want to understand each other. Therefore, effective school consultants are knowledgeable not only about special education and general education curriculum and methods; they also recognize and value adult differences among colleagues. They understand how schools function, and demonstrate a panoramic view of the educational scene. They are careful to interact with diplomacy, because in many instances they will be innovators.

Successful school consultants relate well to teacher colleagues and staff members, administrators, students, and parents. They have good communication skills, a patient and understanding demeanor, and assertiveness when it is needed. The consultant links people with resources, refers people to other sources when necessary, and teaches when it is the most appropriate service for student needs. A consultant is self-confident, but if running low on resources and ideas, the consultant may even find a consultant for himself or herself!

Perhaps most of all, the consultant is a change agent. As one very experienced consulting teacher put it, "You have to be abrasive enough to create change, but pleasant enough to be asked back so you can do it some more" (Bradley, 1987).

To summarize a host of characteristics and competencies needed for school consultation, the consultant is:

| | | |
|---|---|---|
| communicator | observer | instructional specialist |
| planner | ombudsman | researcher |
| coordinator | manager | staff developer |
| advisor | thinker | student |
| spokesperson | arbitrator | supervisor |
| advocate | problem finder | listener |
| resource gatherer | problem solver | presenter |
| mediator | leader | teacher |
| assessor | visionary | life-long learner |

The ideal consultant encourages other educators, including parents, to help students with special needs succeed in school. Most of all, consultation, collaboration, and teamwork among educators in schools and at home can nurture the potential and productivity of all students.

## Tips for Consulting and Collaborating

**1.** Leave the door open, both figuratively and literally, for future partnerships and collaborations.

**2.** Know when to stay in the consultation, and when it is time to get out.

**3.** Have a specific way, time, and place consultees can interact with consultants.

**4.** Be sure the consulting teacher's work plan for the student does not overlap or contradict the consultee's plan.

**5.** Be knowledgeable about related services and support that are available both in school and in the community.

**6.** Use resource personnel to a greater extent.

**7.** Value consultation and collaboration as tools for improving long-range planning and coordination among educators.

**8.** Attend extracurricular functions of assigned schools as much as possible, and offer to help if feasible.

**9.** Carry your share of the load in contributing to social funds, work schedules, and other professional obligations and courtesies.

**10.** Do not share problems or concerns with classroom teachers unless they can have significant input or you have a suggestion for them that might help.

**11.** Stop by and see building administrators when in the building, leaving a brief note if they are unavailable.

**12.** Log all visits and consultations.

**13.** Have lunch, workroom breaks, and informal visits with building staff often.

**14.** Initiate a suggestion-box approach to demonstrate your interest in your colleagues' input and suggestions.

**15.** Have a visible, accessible work space.

**16.** Attend monthly grade-level/departmental meetings to interact with colleagues and to learn of their needs and concerns.

**17.** Ask for help when you have a problem, because this has a humanizing, rapport-building effect.

**18.** Find ways to inform, support, and interact with principals, promoting the idea that each is a "prince-and-a-pal" or "princess-and-a-pal."

**19.** Provide adequate privacy when talking with consultees.

**20.** "Dress for success" in each setting, matching your level of dress with the context in order to establish parity.

**21.** If serving two or more schools or districts, refrain from carrying stories (either good or bad) from one setting to another.

22.  Visit every teacher in the building regularly.
23.  Be available—and available—and available.

## Chapter Review

1.  Several questions reflect the immediate concerns of consultants and consulting teachers: What do I do? How do I begin? What is my schedule for a week? How do I know I am succeeding? How do I prepare for this kind of role?

2.  The consultant role creates concomitant roles of consultee and client. These roles are interchangeable.

3.  Key elements in the success of school consultation and collaboration are role delineation, a framework for these activities, evaluation and support of the efforts, and preparation for consultation and collaboration.

4.  Consultant competencies include skills of communication, organization, diplomacy, knowledgeability, self-confidence, and a genuine interest in working with adults as well as with children and youth.

## Activities

1.  If you were to pick up the newspaper and see a want ad for a consulting teacher to assist students with learning and behavior problems in any of the following schools, what would you expect the job description to include?

- elementary school in suburban area
- large consolidated middle school in rural area
- high school in inner-city area

2.  A person's design for a workday puts a certain framework around the day and gives meaning to the rhythms of activity that help define his or her role. Using one of the situations in Activity 1, visualize an ideal day in a consultant's life. Think of the setting, the schedule, the goals and activities for that day, and how the impact of that day's events might be assessed.

3.  What characteristics and competencies should each of the consultants in Activities 1 and 2 possess?

4.  Develop a file of humor and satire about consultation. As a start, consider these, which have been around for awhile.

> "The consultant is one who drives over from the central office and borrows your watch to tell you what time it is."
>
> "A consultant is someone from two counties away wearing a suit and carrying a briefcase."
>
> "A consultant just pulls in, pops off, and pulls out."

How can humor and satire be used to the consultant's advantage in interactions with consultees? If you have the creative urge, make up a joke or cartoon about consulting or collaboration that could be used to defuse resistance and build rapport toward school consultation.

**5.** Interview three school professionals (elementary, middle school, and high school levels if possible) and two parents to find out their views of school consultation and collaboration and consulting teachers. You can approach this in one of two ways, by giving interviewees a definition of these terms if they ask, or by asking them instead to share their own perceptions. Compare the interview results, and draw inferences. Note indications of willingness to collaborate or a glimmer of awakening interest in consultation, and determine how these positive signs might be followed up productively.

**6.** Begin an "obstacle remover" chart for each of the four key element areas depicted in Figure 2–1 (role delineation, framework, evaluation and support, and preparation).

## For Further Reading

Brown, D., Pryzwansky, W. B., and Schulte, A. C. (1991). *Psychological Consultation: Introduction to Theory and Practice.* Needham Heights, MA: Allyn and Bacon. Chapters 6 and 7, on roles of consultants and consultees.

Conoley, J. C., and Conoley, C. W. (1982). *School consultation: A Guide to Practice and Training.* New York: Pergamon Press.

Hansen, J. C., Himes, B. S., and Meier, S. (1990). *Consultation: Concepts and Practices.* Englewood Cliffs, NJ: Prentice Hall. Chapter 3, on consulting with educational institutions.

Hay, C. (1984). One more time: What do I do all day? *Gifted Child Quarterly,* 28(1): 17–20.

Heron, T. E., and Harris, K. C. (1982). *The Educational Consultant: Helping Professionals, Parents, and Mainstreamed Students.* Austin, TX: PRO-ED. Chapter 2, on the consultant role.

Morsink, C. V., Thomas, C. C., and Correa, V. I. (1991). *Interactive Teaming: Consultation and Collaboration in School Programs.* New York: Macmillan. Chapter 4, on understanding roles and perspectives of team members.

## References

Allington, R. L., and Broikou, K. A. (1988). Development of shared knowledge: A new role for classroom and specialist teachers. *The Reading Teacher, 41* (8), 806–811.

Braaten, S., Kauffman, J. M., Braaten, B., Polsgrove, L., and Nelson, C. M. (1988). The regular education initiative: Patent medicine for behavioral disorders. *Exceptional Children,* 55(1): 21–27.

Bradley, M. O. (1987). Personal communication.

Brown, D., Pryzwansky, W. B., and Schulte, A. C. (1991). *Psychological Consultation: Introduction to Theory and Practice.* Needham Heights, MA: Allyn and Bacon. Chapters 6 and 7, on roles of consultants and consultees.

Canning, C. (1991). What teachers say about reflection. *Educational Leadership,* 48(6): 18–21.

Conoley, J. C., and Conoley, C. W. (1982). *School consultation: A Guide to Practice and Training.* New York: Pergamon Press.

Curtis, M. J., and Zins, J. E. (1988). Effects of training in consultation and instructor feedback on acquisition of consultation skills. *Journal of School Psychology,* 26: 185–190.

Dickens, V. J., and Jones, C. J. (1990). Regular/special education consultation: A teacher education training strategy for implementation. *Teacher Education and Special Education,* 13(3-4): 235–239.

Evans, S. (1980). The consultant role of the resource teacher. *Exceptional Children, 4* 6(5): 402–404.

Friend, M., and Cook, L. (1990). Collaboration as a predictor for success in school reform.

*Journal of Educational and Psychological Consultation, 1*(1): 69–86.

Gersten, R., Darch, C., Davis, G., and George, N. (1991). Apprenticeship and intensive training of consulting teachers: A naturalistic study. *Exceptional Children, 57*(3): 226–237.

Greenburg, D. E. (1987). *A special educator's perspective on interfacing special and general education: A review for administrators.* Clearinghouse on Handicapped and Gifted Children. Reston, VA: The Council for Exceptional Children.

Hay, C. A. (1984). One more time: What do I do all day? *Gifted Child Quarterly, 28*(1): 17–20.

Heron, T. E., and Harris, K. C. (1982). *The Educational Consultant: Helping Professionals, Parents, and Mainstreamed Students.* Boston: Allyn and Bacon.

Heron, T. E., and Kimball, W. H. (1988). Gaining perspective with the educational consultation research base: Ecological considerations and further recommendations. *Remedial and Special Education, 9*(6): 21–28, 47.

Huefner, D. S. (1988). The consulting teacher model: Risks and opportunities. *Exceptional children, 54*(5): 403–414.

Idol, L. (1986). *Collaborative School Consultation* (Report of the National Task Force on School Consultation). Reston, VA: Teacher Education Division, The Council for Exceptional Children.

Idol-Maestas, L. (1983). *Special Educator's Consultation Handbook.* Rockville, MD: Aspen.

Idol-Maestas, L., and Ritter, S. (1985). A follow-up study of resource/consulting teachers: Factors that facilitate and inhibit teacher consultation. *Teacher Education and Special Education, 8*(3): 121–131.

Johnson, L. J., Pugach, M. C., and Hammittee, D. J. (1988). Barriers to effective special education consultation. *Remedial and Special Education, 9*(6): 41–47.

Jones, P. (1981). *A practical guide to federal special education law: Understanding and implementing PL 94-142.* New York: Holt, Rinehart, & Winston.

Keller, H. R. (1981). Behavioral consultation. In J. C. Conoley (ed.), *Consultation in the Schools,* pp. 59–100. New York: Academic Press.

Kolb, D. A. (1976). *Learning-style inventory: Technical manual.* Boston: McBer.

Kratochwill, T. R., and Van Someren, K. R. (1985). Barriers to treatment success in behavioral consultation: Current limitations and future directions. *Journal of School Psychology, 23:* 225–239.

Lilly, M., and Givens-Ogle, L. (1981). Teacher consultation: Present, past, and future. *Behavioral Disorders, 6* (2): 73–77.

Miller, T. L., and Sabatino, D. (1978). An evaluation of the teacher consultant model as an approach to mainstreaming. *Exceptional Children, 45:* 86–91.

Morsink, C. V., Thomas, C. C., and Correa, V. I. (1991). Interactive teaming: Consultation and collaboration in school programs. New York: macmillan.

McGaghie, W. C. (1991). Professional competence evaluation. *Educational Researcher, 20* (1): 3–9.

McGlothlin, J. E. (1981). The school consultation committee: An approach to implementing a teacher consultation model. *Behavioral Disorders, 6*(2): 101–107.

McGlothlin, J., and Kelly, D. (1982). Issues facing the resource teacher. *Learning Disabilities Quarterly, 5:* 58–64.

Neel, R. S. (1981). How to put the consultant to work in consulting teaching. *Behavioral Disorders, 6*(2): 78–81.

Pelletier, J. (1982). Consultation model for students with behavior disorders. Unpublished manuscript, Kansas States University, Special Education Department, Manhattan, KS.

Phillips, W. L., Allred, K., Brulle, A. R., and Shank, K. S. (1990). The regular education initiative: The will and skill of regular educators. *Teacher Education and Special Education, 13*(3–4): 182–186.

Price, M., and Goodman, L. (1980). Individualized education programs: A cost study. *Exceptional Children, 46*(6): 446–454.

Pugach, M. C., and Johnson, L. J. (1989). The challenge of implementing collaboration between general and special education. *Exceptional Children, 56*(3): 232–235.

Rule, S., Fodor-Davis, J., Morgan, R., Salzberg, C. L., and Chen, J. (1990). An inservice training model to encourage collaborative consultation. *Teacher Education and Special Education, 13*(3–4), 225–227.

Schenkat, R. (1988). The promise of restructuring for special education. *Education Week,* November 16.

Shepard, L. A. (1987). The new push for excellence: Widening the schism between regular and special education. *Exceptional Children, 53*(4): 327–329.

Slavin, R. (1988). *The School Administrator, 45*: 9–13.

Speece, D. L., and Mandell, C. J. (1980). Resource room support services for regular teachers. *Learning Disability Quarterly, 3*: 49–53.

Stainback, S., and Stainback, W. (1985). The merger of special and regular education: Can it be done? A response to Lieberman and Mesinger. *Exceptional Children, 51*(6): 517–521.

Thurston, L. P., and Kimsey, I. (1989). Rural special education teachers as consultants: Roles and responsibilities. *Educational Considerations, 17*(1): 40–43.

Tindal, G. A., and Taylor-Pendergast, S. J. (1989). A taxonomy for objectively analyzing the consultation process. *Remedial and Special Education, 10*(2): 6–16.

West, J. F., and Brown, P. A. (1987). State departments of education policies on consultation in special education: The state of the states. *Remedial and Special Education, 8*(3): 45–51.

West, J. F., and Idol, L. (1990). Collaborative consultation in the education of mildly handicapped and at-risk students. *Remedial and Special Education, 11*(1): 22–31.

White, G. W., and Pryzwansky, W. B. (1982). Consultation outcome as a result of in-service resource teacher training. *Psychology in the Schools, 19*: 495–502.

Wiederholt, J., Hammill, D., and Brown, V. (1983). *The Resource Teacher.* Austin, TX: PRO-ED.

# 3

# BACKGROUND, THEORY, AND STRUCTURAL ELEMENTS OF SCHOOL CONSULTATION

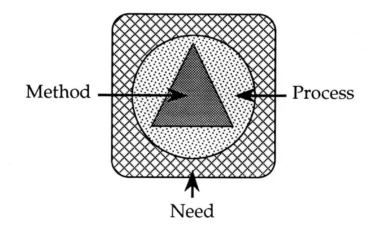

## *To Think About*

Consultation, collaboration, and teamwork probably began around cave fires ages ago. As men and women listened to the ideas of others in the group and voiced their own opinions, they honed skills of communication and collaboration. These skills have become more and more essential for survival and progress in an increasingly complex, interconnected world.

All members of every society must interact effectively and work together cooperatively if the world is to survive. In this age of global interdependence, educators play a major role by helping young people learn to communicate, cooperate, and collaborate effectively. Schools must provide the structure that will serve students' needs and help them develop the interpersonal competencies required for survival in the world they will inherit.

## Focusing Questions

1.  What is the historical background of school consultation, collaboration, and teamwork?
2.  Is there a theoretical base for school consultation?
3.  What research is needed to determine the best practices in school consultation?
4.  What structural elements are components for developing appropriate consultation methods to fit school contexts and student needs?
5.  What models of consultation, collaboration, and teamwork have evolved in education and related fields?
6.  How should educators incorporate existing models and other structural elements into useful school consultation methods?

## Key Terms

approach
collaborative consultation model
method
mode
model
perspective
prototype
Resource/Consulting Teacher
    Program model

School Consultation Committee model
semantics
Stephens/systems model
synthesis
system
thought experiment
triadic model
Vermont Consulting Teacher Program
    model

---

**Scenario**

The setting is a school administration office where the superintendent, the principal, and the special education director are having an early-morning conference.

*SPECIAL EDUCATION DIRECTOR:* I've assigned five people on our special education staff to begin serving as consulting teachers in the schools we targeted at our last meeting.

*PRINCIPAL:* I understand the high school is to be one of those schools. I'm all for trying a new approach, but at this point I'm not sure my staff understands how this method of service is going to affect them.

*SUPERINTENDENT:* Are you saying we need to spend a little more time at the drawing board and get the kinks out of our plan before flinging it at the teachers?

*PRINCIPAL:* Yes, and I think the parents also will want to know what will be happening.

> *SPECIAL EDUCATION DIRECTOR*: I've been compiling a file of theoretical background, research studies, program descriptions, even cartoons and satire, involving consultation and collaboration approaches. Let me get copies of the most helpful material to you and the principals of the other targeted schools. Perhaps we should plan in-service sessions for teachers and awareness sessions for parents before we proceed.
>
> *SUPERINTENDENT*: That sounds good. Draft an outline and we'll discuss it at next week's meeting. I'll get the word out to the other principals to be here.

## A Brief History of School Consultation

School consultation probably originated in mental health and management fields (Reynolds and Birch, 1988). Friend (1988) cites the work of Caplan (1970) in training staff members to counsel troubled adolescents in Israel at the close of World War II. Building on Caplan's work, mental health services escalated and moved into school settings, where consultation services of school psychologists generated promising results. Gallessich (1974) and Pryzwansky (1974) discuss the role of consultation in school psychology as it was broadened to encourage collaborative relationships. Such relationships were nurtured to help teachers, administrators, and parents deal with future problems as well as immediate situations.

### School Consultation before 1970

Gallessich (1973) notes a professional dialogue emerged during the 1950s that stimulated the development of strategies for implementing consultative services in schools. By the mid-1960s, the term *school consultation* was listed in *Psychological Abstracts* (Friend, 1988). School counselors began to promote the concept of proactive service, so that by the early 1970s, consultation was being recommended as an integral part of contemporary counseling service. This interest in collaborative relationships on the part of counselors and psychologists reflected a desire to influence those individuals, groups, and systems that most profoundly affect students (Brown et al., 1979).

Since the late 1950s, the consulting teacher plan for delivery of special services has received frequent attention in the special education literature. There are early examples of consulting in the areas of speech and language therapy, and programs for the hearing impaired and visually impaired. Emphasis on teacher consultation for learning-disabled and behavior-disordered students surfaces in the literature as early as the mid-1960s. At that time, for the most part, consultants were not special educators, but clinical psychologists and psychiatric social workers.

The behavioral movement, which was gaining momentum in the late 1960s and early 1970s, fueled interest in alternative models for intervention and efficient use of time and other resources. This interest sparked development of a text by Tharp and Wetzel (1969) in which they presented a triadic consultation model using behavioral principles in school settings. This triadic model is the basic pattern on which many subsequent models and methods for consultation are constructed.

By 1970 the special education literature contained references to a method of training consulting teachers to serve handicapped students at the elementary level (McKenzie et al., 1970). The Vermont Consulting Teacher Program model, using a consulting teacher to serve students with mental handicaps, was put into place in 1970 (Haight, 1984).

## *School Consultation after 1970*

The decade of the 1970s was a busy time in the field of special education. Intensive special education advocacy, federal policy making for exceptional students, and technological advancements affected special education practices for handicapped students (Nazzaro, 1977). By the mid-1970s, consultation began to be regarded as a significant factor in serving students with special needs. Special education became a major catalyst for promoting consultation and collaboration in schools (Friend, 1988).

Haight (1984) cites several sources for learning more about special-education teacher consultation as it has occurred since 1970: Chandler (1980); Coleman et al. (1975); Evans (1980); Knight et al. (1981); McKenzie et al. (1970); McLoughlin and Kass (1978); Miller and Sabatino (1978); Neel (1981); and Nelson and Stevens (1981). Much of this literature on consultation focuses on indirect service to students by working with consultees, direct service as resource consulting teachers, and various combinations of direct and indirect service.

By the mid-1980s, consultation was becoming one of the most significant educational trends for serving students with special needs. In keeping with this trend, a questionnaire was sent by West and Brown (1987) to directors of special education in the fifty states. Thirty-five state directors responded. Twenty-six of the respondents stated that service delivery models in their states include consultation as an expected role of the special educator. The twenty-six states reported a total of ten different professional titles for consultation as a job responsibility of special educators. About three-fourths of the respondents acknowledged the need for service delivery models that include consultation. However, only seven stated that specific consultation competency requirements are included in their policies.

As interest in school consultation escalated in the 1980s, the National Task Force on Collaborative School Consultation, sponsored by the Teacher Education Division of the Council for Exceptional Children, sent a publication to state departments of education containing recommendations for teacher consultation services in a special-education services continuum (Heron and Kimball, 1988). Guidelines were presented for: development of consultative assistance options; definition of a consulting teacher role, with pupil-teacher ratio recommended;

and requirements for preservice, in-service, and certification preparation programs for personnel development. The report included a list of education professionals skilled in school consultation and a list of publications featuring school consultation.

In 1987, personnel from the Research and Training Project on School Consultation at the University of Texas sponsored the Austin Symposium on School Consultation. The theme for the symposium was "Interdisciplinary Perspectives on Theory, Research, Training, and Practice of School Consultation." Major presenters, panel members, and participants met under the leadership of Frederick West and Lorna Idol for three days of discussion and planning. One outcome of the symposium was a paper developed by the group on *Driving and Restraining Forces and Issues Impacting the Future of School Consultation.*

By 1990 a new journal focusing on school consultation, the *Journal of Educational and Psychological Consultation,* appeared in the literature. A preconvention workshop on school consultation and collaboration programs and practices, sponsored by the Teacher Education Division (TED) of the Council for Exceptional Children (CEC), was a featured event at the 1990 annual CEC conference in Toronto. Blueprints and contexts for collaborative program planning and practices were presented by Marilyn Friend and Lynne Cook.

Discussion of consultation practices in the field of education for gifted students has been minimal, although this promises to be one of the most viable fields for extensive use of collaborative consultation. Dettmer (1989), Dettmer and Lane (1989) and Idol-Maestas and Celentano (1986) recommend consultation practices to assist with learning needs of gifted and talented students. Dyck and Dettmer (1989) suggest methods for facilitating learning programs for gifted learning-disabled students within a consulting teacher plan.

All in all, social movements and school reforms of the 1980s and early 1990s fueled the interest in school consultation, collaboration, and teamwork that had begun in the 1960s and 1970s. The result has been an increasing number of journals, periodicals, studies, pilot programs, federal and state grants, and training projects, as well as some teacher preparation programs, for the application of consultation and collaboration practices in schools.

## Theoretical Bases of School Consultation

Is school consultation a theory-based practice or an atheoretical practice related to a problem-solving knowledge base? Differing points of view exist in regard to this issue. Studies of consultation center around the analysis of existing structures, or models, as some educators refer to them. Bergan (1977) addresses consultation through operant learning theory, while Brown and Schulte (1987) present a model based on social learning theory.

West and Idol (1987) propose that school consultation can be regarded as theory-based if it is identified across more than one literature source focusing on the relationship between consultant and consultee. On the other hand, if identified by methods for solving consultation problems, then it should be regarded as knowledge-based in the area of problem solving. They suggest that ten models of consultation can be delineated, of which six have clearly identifiable theory or theories. These six include mental health, behavioral, process, advocacy, and two types of organizational consultation. West and Idol further note that a seventh model, the collaborative consultation model, has the essential elements for building theory because it contains a set of generic principles required for building collaborative relationships between consultants and consultees.

Initial work by West, Idol, and Cannon (1987) examines principles of collaborative relationship empirically for the purpose of building sound theories of successful communication and collaboration practices. Brown, Pryzwansky, and Schulte (1991) assert that consultation is not a conceptual wasteland, but stress that there is work to be done in strengthening the theoretical base.

## Research Bases of School Consultation

As school consultation theory building continues and the concepts of consultation, collaboration, teamwork, and school partnerships capture the attention of education policymakers and practitioners, researchers seek new information to guide planning and programming efforts in these areas. West and Idol (1987) stress the importance of defining clearly the constructs and principles for consultation and collaboration, in order to expedite basic research for testing a match between model and theory. In this way there is a clear line of progression from theory development to model building to basic research to field-based application.

Heron and Kimball (1988) note that the emerging research base in school consultation addresses several areas:

- theory and models (West and Idol, 1987);
- methodology (Gresham and Kendell, 1987);
- training and practice (Friend, 1984; Idol and West, 1987);
- professional preferences for the consultation service (Babcock and Pryzwansky, 1983; Medway and Forman, 1980);
- guidelines (Salend and Salend, 1984); and
- competencies for consultants (West and Cannon, 1988).

### *Categories of School Consultation Research*

Gresham and Kendell (1987) organize research in school consultation around three areas of investigation: (1) outcome research, (2) process research, and (3) practitioner use. They suggest training as a possible fourth area. Outcome research focuses on changes in consultee classroom behavior, knowledge, and attitudes, as well as changes in client classroom behavior and frequency of consultation use (Bergan, 1977; Gutkin and Curtis, 1982; Pryzwansky, 1986.) Outcomes also involve growth in student achievement after consultation with parents (Jackson, Cleveland, and Merenda, 1975) and comparisons of problem severity in schools with and without consultants (Gutkin, Singer, and Brown, 1980). Process research examines the amount of teacher time required for consultation (Witt and Elliott, 1985), the ability to identify the relevant problem (Bergan and Tombari, 1976), and use of communication skills (Gutkin, 1986), as well as the need for "common-sense" language, not jargon (Witt et al., 1984). Research in practitioner use of consultation includes studies of preferences for job functions (Gutkin and Curtis, 1982) and perceived importance of consultation to school psychologist services (Curtis and Zins, 1981). One study analyzed the most frequent reasons consultees give for not attempting a consultation plan (Happe, 1982).

As recently as 1987, Gresham and Kendell argued that research methodology in school consultation is elementary at best. They characterize most consultation research as descriptive, which may be useful for identifying key variables in consultation processes and outcomes, but not for determining interactions between variables or directions of influence on the outcomes of consultation. Gresham and Kendell (1987) stress that consultation research must assess the integrity of consultation plans, since consultees are not implementing many plans as designed (Witt and Elliott, 1985).

West and Idol (1987) organize dimensions of school consultation research into four groups:

- Input variables, focusing on factors such as consultant and consultee ages, teaching experience, personality characteristics, and readiness for consultation.
- Process variables, including model, style, technique, and stages in the consultation. One example is Pryzwansky's finding (1989) that experienced problem solvers are more capable of conceptualizing the presentation of problems in consultation than are novices. Another is the study by Gertsen, et al. (1991) showing that extensive consultation training is costly in the short run, but produces immense benefits in technical knowledge, competence, and communicative sensitivity.
- Situational variables, identified by West and Idol as time, location, school organization, and learning environment. These variables precipitated studies such as the one identifying lack of time as the most common constraint on fulfilling consultation roles (Voltz and Elliott, Jr., 1990).
- Outcome variables, including teacher behaviors and attitudes, student behaviors and attitudes, and organizational or systems change. Examples are provided in a study analyzing tendencies toward inertia in education regarding change (Friend and Bauwens, 1988), and a study by Pedron and Evans (1990) recognizing change in teacher attitudes toward adopting and implementing a consulting teacher model.

Studies of consultation effectiveness from related professions have produced promising data on consultee-client and systems-level changes that result from consultation interventions (West and Idol, 1987).

As West and Idol point out, research efforts in this complex, multidimensional field of school consultation are impeded by lack of psychometrically reliable and valid instrumentation and controls. The requirements for control during research studies violate the need for flexible responses during the delivery of consultation services. In addition, research should be designed to move beyond studies for simply justifying consultation roles and focus on studies for determining the efficacy of consultation and collaboration in practice.

Comments by Gresham and Kendell (1987) are equally direct. They find little empirical evidence to show that what people are calling consultation actually *is* consultation. Therefore, they urge researchers to define the research variables more explicitly, control them more carefully, and measure them more accurately.

## Structures for School Consultation

Overlapping philosophies of consultation have evolved from a blending of consultation knowledge and practices from several fields. This overlap creates a tangle of philosophy and terminology that is problematic for educators endeavoring to develop viable school consultation structures and explain them to the public.

The practice of school consultation is by definition situation specific, and to make matters more problematic, the concepts of consultation, collaboration, and teaming are still so ambiguous that busy teachers and administrators tend to become frustrated by the lack of consensus and direction. On the other hand, patterns for teaching, learning, and administrating in schools are already in place. Therefore, when faced with choice between the uncertainty and confusion that often surround new practices such as school consultation, collaboration, and working in teams, or adhering to existing practices, educators tend to open their classroom doors in the morning and conduct school as usual.

It is time to sort out and refine the myriad consultation terms, theories, research findings, and practices into structures that are useful and well received in the school setting. After considering all existing structures that have been proposed, discussed, and on occasion researched, educators will need to select and refine the methods that work best for their school context.

### Semantics of Consultation

When focusing on complex educational issues and school concepts, it is tempting for educators to slip into "educationese," (convoluted and redundant phrases), "jargon," (in-house expressions that approximate educational slang), and "alphabet soup" (acronyms that seem like uncracked codes to lay people).

For theories and applications for school consultation to become an accepted, integral part of school programs, it is advantageous to draw on semantics as a way of crystallizing concepts.

Semantics, the study of meanings, is a helpful tool with which to begin simplifying and sorting out the tangle of concepts. Meanings of words vary from user to user and from context to context. This semantic principle is obvious in regard to abstract words such as *education, democracy,* and *society,* but more elusive when deciding on the meaning of a word so simple as *chair* (Sondel, 1958). For example, to a dentist, chair might mean an appliance that is used at work. To a college professor, it might mean a coveted position, while to a convicted murder it might mean potential extermination (Sondel, 1958).

> *Words make the trip through the nervous system of a human being before they can be referred outward to the real thing—chair, or whatever it is. Don't assume that everyone responds to your words in precisely the same way you do. Make the context in which you use the words clear, and do this through the use of words that refer to specific things. (Sondel, 1958, p. 55)*

Using semantics as a tool, the existing maze of philosophy and terminology about consultation in a number of fields can be organized into six basic elements with which to structure viable methods of school consultation.

## Structural Elements for School Consultation

Consultation terms and procedures involve components of six elements—system, perspective, approach, prototype, mode, and model (see Figure 3–1). These six elements are defined as:

- system—the unity of many parts which serve a common purpose;
- perspective—a thought from a particular standpoint;
- approach—a preliminary step toward a purpose;
- prototype—a pattern;
- mode—a form or manner of doing; and
- model—an example.

Characteristics of these six elements can be combined to create a suitable school consultation method for each local context and learning situation.

For brevity and graphic clarity, the six elements are designated in this book by the upper-case form of their first letter—for example, system = S. (When two elements begin with identical letters, another prominent letter in the word is used.) Thus the six categories are designated as S (system), P (perspective), A (approach), R (prototype), E (mode), and M=(model). In this book the position will be that a good method of school consultation attends to elements from each of the six categories but is designed to be appropriate for the school context in which it will be implemented.

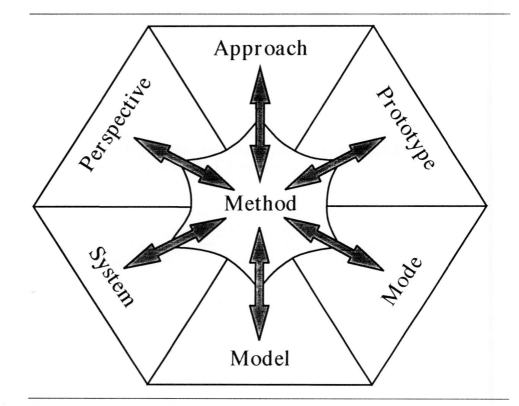

**FIGURE 3–1   A Structure for Consulting**

*Systems for School Consultation*    The first structural element to be discussed is system. The word *system* (S) is a powerhouse of semantic utility, requiring considerable dictionary space for its many definitions and possible uses. For this study of consultation, *system* means a complex unity composed of many diverse parts that serve a common purpose. The most natural system within which to conduct school consultation and collaboration is, obviously, the school. However, as pointed out in Chapter 1, and to be elaborated on in later chapters, educators are involved not only in the academic or cognitive part of student development, but also in physical, emotional, social, and life-orientation aspects. Educators include not only teachers, but parents, related services and support personnel, other caregivers, and the community in general.

Systems (S) in which educators function to serve special needs of students include: home and family, community, medical and dental professions, mental health, social work, counseling, and advocacy and support groups. Other systems with which consultants and collaborators may be involved from time to time in addressing very specialized needs are: therapy, industry, technology, mass communications, cultural enrichment, and special interest areas such as talent development.

***Perspectives on Consultation***    A *perspective* (P) is an aspect or object of thought from a particular standpoint. Consultation perspectives that have evolved in education and related fields include:

- purchase;
- doctor-patient; and
- process.

These categories are sometimes referred to as approaches, and at other times as models. However, in order to organize the terminology, they are differentiated here as perspectives.

A purchase perspective is one in which the consumer shops for a needed or wanted item. The consumer, in this case the consultee, "buys" services that will help that consultee serve the client's need. For example, the teacher of a developmentally delayed student might ask personnel at the instructional media center for a list of low-vocabulary, high-interest reading material with which to help the student have immediate success in reading. The purchase perspective makes several assumptions (Neel, 1981); (1) that the consultee describes the need precisely; (2) the consultee is in the right "store" to get something for that need; (3) the consultant has enough "inventory" (strategies and resources) to fill the request; and (4) the consultee can assume the costs of time, energy, or modification of classroom procedures.

As a consumer, the consultee is free to accept or reject the strategy or resource, using it enthusiastically, putting off trying it, or ignoring it as a "bad buy." Even if the strategy is effective for that case, the consultee may need to go again to the consultant for similar needs of other clients. For this perspective to work, many things have to go right, so the consultee must think through the consequences of the purchase technique (Schein, 1969). Little change can be expected in consultee skill as a result of such consumer-type interaction. Thus the overall costs are high and the benefits are limited to specific situations.

A doctor-patient perspective casts the consultant in the role of diagnostician and prescriber. The consultee knows there is a problem but is not in a position to correct it. Consultees are responsible for revealing helpful information to the consultant. Again, this perspective makes several assumptions: (1) the consultee describes the problem to the consultant accurately and completely; (2) the consultant can explain the diagnosis clearly and convince the consultee of its worth; (3) the diagnosis is not premature; and (4) the prescribed remedy is not *iatrogenic* in outcome—meaning, as discussed in Chapter 1, that it creates more problems for student, educators, or school context than the initial condition did. For example, an iatrogenic effect caused when gifted students leave classrooms to attend gifted program activities might be resentment and antagonism toward those gifted students by their peers and perhaps even by their classroom teachers.

A classroom teacher might use a doctor-patient perspective by calling on a special education teacher and describing the student's learning or behavior problem. The consultant's role would be to observe, review existing data, perhaps talk to other specialists, and make diagnostic and prescriptive decisions. With the doctor-patient perspective, as in the medical field, there is generally little follow-up activity on the consultant's part, and the consultee does not always follow through with conscientious attention to the consultant's recommendations.

In a process perspective, the consultant helps the client perceive, understand, and act on the problem (Neel, 1981; Schein, 1969). Consultant service does not replace the consultee's direct service to the client. In contrast to the purchase and doctor-patient perspectives, the consultant neither diagnoses nor prescribes a solution. As Neel puts it, the consultee becomes the consultant's client for that particular problem.

Schein (1978) sorts process consultation into two types—a catalyst type in which the consultant does not know a solution but is skilled toward helping the consultee figure one out, and the facilitator type where the consultant contributes ideas toward the solution. In both catalyst and facilitator types of process consultation, the consultant helps the consultee clarify the problem and develop solutions. Skills and resources used to solve the immediate problem might be used later for other problems. Assumptions are: (1) the consultee can diagnose the problem; (2) the consultant is able to develop a helping relationship; (3) the consultant can provide new and challenging alternatives for the consultee (who is the consultant's immediate client) to consider; and (4) decision making about the alternatives will remain the responsibility and privilege of the consultee.

In the process perspective for consultation, the consultee who needs help with a student or school situation collaborates with a consultant to identify the problem, explore possible alternatives, and develop a plan of action. The consultee then implements the plan.

All three perspectives have strengths; therefore, each is likely to be employed at one time or another in schools (Vasa, 1982). One factor influencing the adoption of a particular perspective is the nature of the problem (West, 1985). For example, in a noncrisis situation, the consultee may value the process perspective. But in crisis situations the consultee may need a quick solution, even if temporary, for the problem. In such cases the purchase or doctor-patient perspectives would be preferred. Situations that immediately affect the physical and psychological well-being of students and school personnel require immediate attention and cannot wait for process consultation. However, when process consultation is employed regularly, many of the skills and resources that are developed for solving a particular problem can be used again and again in situations involving similar problems. This makes process consultation both time efficient and cost effective for schools.

*Approaches to School Consultation* An *approach* (A) is a preliminary step toward a purpose. School consultation approaches may be formal or informal. Formal consultations occur in planned meetings such as staffings, conferences for developing Individual Education Plans (IEPs), arranged meetings between school personnel, and organized staff development activities. They also include scheduled conferences with parents, related services personnel, and community resource personnel.

In contrast, informal consultations often occur "on the run." These interactions have been called "vertical consultations" because people tend to engage in them while standing on playgrounds, in parking lots, at ball games, even in grocery stores. They also are dubbed "one-legged consultations" when they occur in hallways with a leg propped against the wall (McDonald, 1989; Hall and Hord, 1987). Conversations also take place frequently in the teacher workroom. This aspect will be addressed more fully in Chapter 12 as a form of informal staff development.

It is very important to designate these informal interactions as consultations because they do require expenditures of time and energy on the part of both consultant(s) and consultee(s). Highlighting them as consultations will help establish the concept of school consultation and promote efforts toward constructing a suitable framework for the support of consultation and collaboration. Informal consultations should be encouraged because they can initiate more planful, productive consultation and collaboration. They often become catalysts for meaningful in-service and staff development activities. In some cases they may cultivate team efforts that would have been overlooked or neglected in the daily hustle and bustle of school life.

*Prototypes for School Consultation* A *prototype* (R) is a pattern. Categorical descriptions include mental health consultation, behavioral consultation, advocacy consultation, and sometimes process consultation. In the continuing effort in this book to sort out and organize consultation terminology, these categories are termed prototypes.

Mental health consultation is a prototype with a long history (Conoley and Conoley, 1988). The concept originated in the 1960s with the work of psychiatrist Gerald Caplan. Caplan conceived of consultation as a relationship between two professional people in which responsibility for the client rests on the consultee (Hansen, Himes, and Meier, 1990). Caplan (1970) proposed that consultee difficulties in dealing with a client's problems usually are caused by any one, or all, of four "lack-ofs":

- Lack of knowledge about the problem and its conditions;
- Lack of skill to address the problem in appropriate ways;
- Lack of self-confidence in dealing with the problem;
- Lack of professional objectivity in approaching the problem.

In mental health consultation the consultant not only helps resolve the problem at hand, but enhances the consultee's ability to handle future situations more effectively. Caplan's most important intervention goal is to reduce the consultee's loss of professional objectivity whereby the consultee identifies subjectively with the client, or tries to fit the client into a category and assume an inevitable outcome (Conoley and Conoley, 1982). When the mental health prototype is used for consultation, consultee change may very well precede client change. Therefore, assessment of success should focus on consultee attitudes and behaviors more than on client changes (Conoley and Conoley, 1988). This is an important, desirable effect for school consultants and collaborators to consider.

Another prototype frequently used is behavioral consultation. This problem solving procedure is also intended to improve the performance of both consultee and client. Since behavioral consultation is based on social learning theory, skills and knowledge contribute more to consultee success than unconscious themes such as objectivity or self-confidence (Bergan, 1977). Behavioral consultation probably is more familiar to educators and thus is more easily introduced into the school context than is mental health consultation. The consultant is required to define the problem, isolate environmental variables that support that problem, and plan interventions to reduce the problem. Conoley and Conoley (1988) regard behavioral consultation as the easiest prototype to evaluate, since problem delineation and specific goal setting occur within the process. Evaluation results can be used to modify plans and to promote consultation services among other potential consultees.

A third kind of consultation prototype is advocacy consultation. The client is the community, not the established organization (Gallessich, 1974), with the consultant serving the "client" directly as trainer and catalyst, and indirectly as advocate (Raymond, McIntosh, and Moore, 1986). This concept is considered by some as highly political, with one group trying to overcome another for a greater share of the finite resources. Advocacy consultants stress that power, influence, and politics are the motivating influences behind human behavior (Conoley and Conoley, 1982). At some place in the consulting relationship, these consultants face the realization that facilitation of school context goals is contrary to their values. Advocacy consultants need specific consulting skills for organizing people and publicizing events to serve special needs appropriately.

Process consultation is sometimes included as a fourth prototype, along with mental health, behavioral, and advocacy consultation. However, in this book it is treated as a perspective, not a prototype.

*Modes of School Consultation*    A *mode* (E) is a particular form or manner of doing something. Modes for school consultation can be regarded as direct delivery of service to clients or indirect delivery of service to consultees. A direct service delivery mode allows a consultant to work directly with a special needs student. For example, a learning disabilities consulting teacher or a speech pathologist specialist might use a technique with the student, while a parent or classroom teacher consultee observes and assists with the technique.

As early as 1962, Reynolds described a hierarchical configuration for special education services that differentiated indirect service in least restrictive settings from direct service in more restrictive settings. The hierarchy (Reynolds, 1962) began at Level 1, the least restrictive level for students, in which special needs were handled in the regular classroom. Then attention to more severe needs was given at Level 2 in the regular classroom with consultation. Level 3, the regular classroom with supplementary teaching or treatment, was more restrictive, followed by Level 4, the regular classroom with resource room service, Level 5 for a part-time special class, and so on to Level 10, or placement in a hospital or treatment center. Within this hierarchical configuration, the intensity of special needs at any given time for an individual student determines the level of service needed to offer an appropriate program. The less severe the need, the closer that placement can be made to the general classroom setting.

Direct service to students usually is carried out subsequent to a referral (Bergan, 1977). The consultant may conduct observations and discuss the learning or behavioral need directly with the student (Bergan, 1977; Heron and Harris, 1987). The consultant becomes an advocate and the student has an opportunity to participate in decisions made pertinent to that need. Another example of direct service is teaching coping skills to students for their use at home or at school (Graubard, Rosenberg, and Miller, 1971; Heron and Harris, 1982).

Some states have limited consulting teachers to spending a specific portion of their time in direct service to special education students. Other stipulations require that the direct service teaching time must occur in the presence of the classroom teacher, and that general classroom students should participate in the activities if at all appropriate. This service is not to be equated with team teaching, a concept that is discussed in Chapter 9.

In contrast to direct service, the indirect service delivery mode calls for "backstage" involvement among consultants and consultees to serve client needs. The consultant and consultee interact and problem solve together. In doing so, the consultant provides direct service to the consultee, who then provides related direct service to the client.

While school consultation typically is regarded as indirect service to students through direct work with their teachers or parents (Lilly and Givens-Ogle, 1981), variants of service delivery are possible in particular circumstances. It is in this arena that some of the most significant changes have occurred since the enactment of Public Law 94-142. Attention continues to be focused on appropriate use of both indirect and direct service delivery modes in the wake of both the Regular Education Initiative and movements to restructure school programs. Indirect service has conceptual merits and pragmatic potential for multiplying the impact of professional services (Pryzwansky, 1986). This is an important consideration in times of shrinking fiscal and staff resources.

*Models for School Consultation*   Models (M) are patterns, examples for imitation, representations in miniature, descriptions, analogies, or displays. A model is not the real thing, but an approximation of it. It functions as an example through which to study, mimic, replicate, approximate, or manipulate intricate things. Models are most useful for examining objects or ideas when they are too big (such as a model of the solar system) or too small (a DNA molecule) to copy. They also help to understand things that cannot be replicated because they are too costly (a supersonic jet plane), too complex (the United Nations system), or too time intensive (travel to outer space). These qualities make the model a useful structure on which to pattern complex human processes such as school consultation and collaborative interactions.

Six of the more familiar models adopted or modified for school consultation are:

- the triadic model;
- the Stephens/systems model;
- the Vermont Consulting Teacher Program model;
- the School Consultation Committee model;
- the Resource/Consulting Teacher Program model; and
- the collaborative consultation model.

**The Triadic Model.**   The triadic model, developed by Tharp and Wetzel (1969), is a classic consultation model from which many school consultation models have evolved. It includes three roles—consultant, consultee (or mediator), and client (or target). In this most basic of the existing consultation models, services are not offered directly, but through an intermediary (Tharp, 1975). The service flows from the consultant to the target through the mediator. The consultant role is typically, although not always, performed by an educational specialist such as a learning disabilities teacher or a school psychologist. The consultee is typically, but not always, the classroom teacher. The client or target is usually the student with the learning or behavioral need. An educational need may be a handicapping condition or a talent requiring special services in order for the student to approach his or her learning potential.

When studying the triadic model, or any other consultation model, it is important to recall the discussion in Chapter 1 about school consultation roles. Roles are interchangeable among individuals, depending on the school context and the educational need. For example, on occasion a learning disabilities consulting teacher might be a consultee who seeks information and expertise from a general classroom teacher-consultant. At another time, a student might be the consultant for a resource room teacher, the consultee, with the parents as the clients, or targets, for intervention intended to help their child. Tharp gives the following example:

> *Ms. Jones the second-grade teacher may serve as mediator between Brown, the psychologist, and John, the problem child. At the same time, she may be the target of*

*her principal's training program and the consultant to her aide-mediator in the service of Susie's reading problem. The triadic model, then, describes relative position in the chain of social influence. (Tharp, 1975, p. 138)*

In later years, Tharp elaborated on the linear aspect of the triadic model to include influences of others on consultant, mediator, and target, and the interactions that those influences facilitate (Tharp, 1975).

Tharp identifies several advantages of the triadic model (Tharp, 1975), including the clarity it provides in delineating social roles and responsibilities, and the availability of evaluation data from two sources—mediator behavior and target behavior. However, it may not be the most effective model for every school context and each content area with the process skills and resources that are available. Advantages and "amber light" suggestions for using a triadic model of school consultation are included in Table 3–1. (An amber traffic light indicates "slow down, proceed slowly, or stop" if red light appears. In similar fashion, the "amber lights" suggested for each model indicate that readers will want to proceed with special care in the areas that might present problems when using the model.)

**Stephens/systems Model.**  The systems model constructed by Stephens (1977) is an extension of his directive teaching approach (Heron and Harris, 1982). It includes five phases:

- assessment, observation, data collection;
- specification of objectives, problem identification;
- planning, finding ways of resolving the problem;
- implementation of the plan, measurement of progress; and
- evaluation, data analysis.

Baseline data are collected on target behaviors. Then interventions are planned, and additional data are collected to compare intervention effects. If the plan of treatment is not effective, further assessment is conducted. The consultant helps the consultee devise criterion-referenced assessments or coding devices (Heron and Harris, 1987). This helps consultees become an integral part of the program and acquire skills to use after the consultant leaves. Advantages of using the systems model, as well as amber light points to be considered, are included in Table 3–1.

**The Resource/Consulting Teacher Program Model.**  The Resource/Consulting Teacher Program model (R/CT) has been implemented at the University of Illinois and in both rural and large urban areas (Idol, Paolucci-Whitcomb, and Nevin, 1986). It is based on the triadic model, with numerous opportunities for interaction among teachers, students, and parents. The resource/consulting teacher offers direct service to students through tutorials or small-group instruction and indirect service to students through consultation with classroom teachers for a portion of the school day. Students who are not staffed into special education programs can be served along with exceptional students mainstreamed into general classrooms. Parents are sometimes included in the consultation.

In the R/CT model, emphasis is placed on training students in the curricula used within each mainstreamed student's general classroom (Idol-Maestas, 1983). Close cooperation and collaboration between the R/CT and the classroom teacher are required so that teacher expectations and reinforcement are the same for both the resource room and regular class setting (Idol-Maestas, 1981). Advantages and concerns regarding the R/CT model are included in Table 3–1.

**The School Consultation Committee Model.**   McGlothlin (1981) provides an alternative approach for school consultation in the form of a School Consultation Committee model. The committee typically includes a special education teacher, a primary classroom teacher, an upper-grade classroom teacher, the building principal, and persons involved in ancillary and consultant roles. After a one-day training session conducted by an outside consultant, the committee meets as frequently as needed to screen referrals, assess problems and develop plans, and evaluate the results of those plans. The consultant remains available to help the committee as needed (McGlothlin, 1981).

The School Consultation Committee is a familiar approach for school personnel who have had experience on preassessment teams and other referral groups. Advantages and concerns in using this model are given in Table 3–1.

**The Vermont Consulting Teacher Program Model.**   The Vermont Consulting Teacher Program model is a collaborative effort of local school districts, the Vermont State Department of Education, and University of Vermont personnel for providing consultative services statewide to teachers who have children with handicaps in their classrooms (Heron and Harris, 1987). This model, another adaptation of the triadic model, includes four phases after student referral:

- entry-level data collection and diagnosis;
- specification of instructional objectives;
- development and implementation of a plan; and
- evaluation and follow-through.

There are three forms of instruction within the model: (1) university coursework for teachers, (2) specialized workshops as an alternative to the coursework format, and (3) consultation through working partnerships between consulting teacher and classroom teacher (Knight et al., 1981). Through the coursework, teachers learn principles of measurement, behavior analysis, and instructional design. These principles are then applied to the teaching and learning processes in the classroom. A key feature is that the consulting teacher

## TABLE 3–1

### The Triadic Model

| Advantages | Possible Concerns |
|---|---|
| A way to get started with consultee | Little/no carry-over to other situations and problems |
| Quick and direct | Needed again for same or similar situations |
| Informal and simple, keeps problems in perspective | Only one other point of view expressed |
| Objectivity on the part of the consultant | Expert consultation skills needed by consultant |
| Student anonymity if needed | May not have necessary data available |
| Appropriate in crisis situations | Little or no follow-up |
| Time-efficient | Tendency to blame lack of progress on consultant |
| May be all that is needed | |
| Can lead to more intensive consultation/ collaboration | |

### Stephens/Systems Model

| Advantages | Possible Concerns |
|---|---|
| Each step in concrete terms | Extensive paperwork |
| Follows familiar IEP development system | Assumes spirit of cooperation exists |
| Collaborative | Time-consuming |
| Changes easily made | Might become process-for-process sake |
| Formative and developmental | May seem "much ado about little" |
| Strong record-keeping | Assumes training in data-keeping and observation |
| Avoids the "expert" role | Multiple Steps overwhelming to busy teachers |
| Has an evaluation component | Delayed results |
| Much accountability | |
| Provides whole picture of need, plan, and results | |

### Resource/Consulting Teaching Model

| Advantages | Possible Concerns |
|---|---|
| Provides direct and indirect service | Energy-draining |
| Parent involvement | Time often not available |
| "In-House" approach to problems | Scheduling difficult |
| Opportunity for student involvement | High caseloads for consulting teacher |
| Compatible with non-categorical/interrelated methods | Indirect service not weighted as heavily as direct |
| Ownership my many roles in problem-solving | Training needed in effective interation |
| More closely approximates classroom setting | Delayed, or no, reinforcement for consultant |
| Spreads the responsibility around | Administrator support and cooperation essential |
| Opportunity to belong as a teacher/consultant | |
| Opportunity for regular contact between consultant/consultee | |

*(Continued)*

**TABLE 3–1** *(Continued)*

## School Consultation Committee Model

| *Advantages* | *Possible Concerns* |
| --- | --- |
| Administrator involved | Only one day of training for special assignment |
| Miltiple sources of input | |
| Skill gains from other teachers | Time-consuming |
| Familiar to those using preassessment/building team | Possible resentment toward specialized expertise |
| Time provided for professional interaction | Potential for too much power from some committee members |
| Many points of view | |
| Good for major problem-solving | Solution might be postponed |
| Focuses on situations of the school context | Confidentiality harder to ensure |
| Involves a number of general education staff | Indirect, not direct service to student |
| Can minimize problems before they get too serious | Could diffuse responsibility so no one feels responsible |

## Vermont Consulting Teacher Model

| *Advantages* | *Possible Concerns* |
| --- | --- |
| Active participation by parents and teachers | Time, travel, scheduling |
| Teachers learning from the training | Possible chain-of-command problems |
| New, even experimental, procedures possible | Teachers may resent "imported expert" |
| Student performance, not label, determining placement | Job security dependent on number of students identified |
| Supports mainstreaming ad parent involvement requirements | Time needed for task analysis for participating role |
| Collaborative efforts with major institutions | Time required for personnel to reach general consensus |
| Different professional perspectives | Perhaps not feasible in larger states |
| Ongoing program evaluation | Requires specification of minimum achievement levels in certain time frame |

## The Collaborative Model

| *Advantages* | *Possible Concerns* |
| --- | --- |
| Fits current reform movements | Little or no training in collaboration |
| Professional growth for all through shared expertise | Lack of time to interact |
| Many ideas generated | Working with adults not preference of some educators |
| Maximizes opportunity for constructive use of individual differences among adults | Requires solid administrator support |
| Allows administrrator to assume facilitative role | Takes time to see results |
| Parent satisfaction | |

must individualize the program to meet the specific needs of the classroom teacher (Heron and Harris, 1987). Parent involvement is an integral component of the model. Advantages and concerns related to the model are listed in Table 3–1.

**The Collaborative Consultation Model.** The collaborative consultation concept is emerging as a model in which the consultant and consultee are equal partners in consultation—identifying problems, planning intervention strategies, and implementing recommendations through collaboration (Idol, Paolucci-Whitcomb, and Nevin, 1986; Raymond, McIntosh, and Moore, 1986). Pryzwansky (1974) provided the basic structure of the collaborative approach by emphasizing the need for mutual consent on the part of both consultant and consultee, mutual commitment to the objectives, and shared responsibility for implementation and evaluation of the plan. The consultant, mediator, and target have reciprocally reinforcing effects on one another, which encourages more collaborative consultation at a later date (Idol-Maestas, 1983).

Research studies support the value of cooperative ventures such as those created by collaborative consultation (Idol, Paolucci-Whitcomb, and Nevin, 1986). Johnson and Johnson (1980) note that cooperative interaction among faculty and administrators can be as powerful a tool for adults as cooperative learning can be for children. However, Morsink, Thomas, and Correa (1991) warn that while collaborative consultation can result in shared expertise among professionals, implementation to date has focused primarily on a triadic relationship between general and special educators. Advantages, as well as potential concerns, for the collaborative model are given in Table 3–1.

## Synthesizing Structural Elements into Methods of Consultation

Any plan for school consultation should take into account the school's needs with regard to consultation by including facets of all the components that have been introduced:

S. System (school systems, other social systems);
P. Perspective (purchase, doctor-patient, process);
A. Approach (formal, informal);
R. pRototype (mental health, behavioral, advocacy);
E. modE (direct, indirect); and
M. Model (triadic, Stephens/systems, Resource/ Consulting Teacher Program, School Consultation Committee, Vermont Consulting Teacher Program, collaborative consultation).

The most relevant factors of these six key components can be synthesized into an appropriate method for serving a student or educator's special needs as they occur. Once again, refer to Figure 3–1. Note that the Method area in the middle draws from each of the six descriptive elements to provide components for developing consultations for special needs.

Educators will recognize the need for having all six elements—systems, perspectives, approaches, prototypes, modes, and models—understood and available for potential combination into appropriate methods for serving special needs of students within every school context. *Locally developed methods* for addressing *special learning needs* are the most effective school consultation practices educators can employ.

## Thought Experiments to Reflect on School Consultation, Collaboration, and Teamwork

A helpful activity for thinking about complex functions is the thought experiment. Thought experiments, practiced by eminent scientists such as Einstein, take place in the mind, not in the laboratory or classroom. The idea is to manipulate variables and concepts mentally, "seeing" them from all angles and deferring judgment until all conceivable avenues have been explored. A thought problem is an opportunity to reflect on something intently before presenting it for discussion and critique by others. Much of the time this type of activity precedes intricate processes such as consultation.

The following thought problem has several parts, one for each of the models described earlier. This exercise encourages you to be *very* "Einsteinian" as you reflect on school consultation, and manipulate and embellish your images of the models.

First, study again the brief descriptions of consultation models. Then select one of the models and mentally manipulate its components to create a graphic way of illustrating a consultation method that could be useful in your school context. Einstein used trains, clocks, kites, rushing streams, and even swirling tea leaves to reflect on phenomena and conceptualize his ideas. You may find it helpful to use building blocks, toy people, pictures, or other special effects as you manipulate the elements of your ideas. Here are some possibilities for starters:

1.    How might you depict the interactions intended for the triadic model? One enterprising student of consultation drew a bow, with arrow poised for flight toward a target. The bow represents the consultant, the arrow is consultee, and the target is the client. The bull's-eye is the problem or need (see Figure 3–2). Another thinker/illustrator created a restaurant scene, with the consultant as behind-the-scenes cook, the consultee as the counter cook-and server, and the client as the diner. A third person devised the heads graphic in Figure 3–3. How do you visualize a triadic model of consultation?

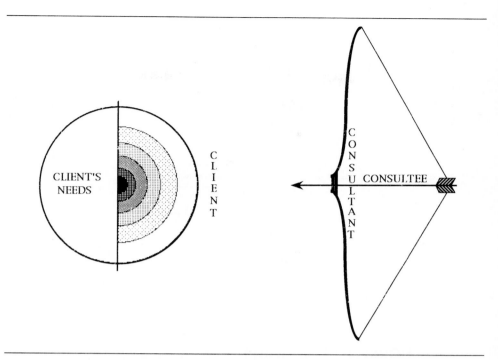

**FIGURE 3–2   Interpretation of Triadic Consultation**

by LaVetta Rolfs

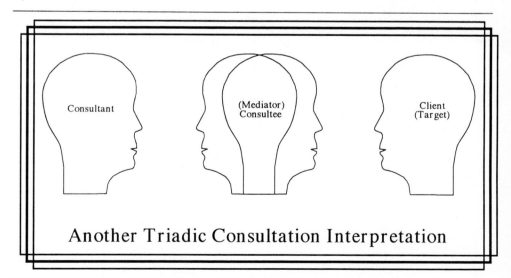

## Another Triadic Consultation Interpretation

**FIGURE 3–3   Another Triadic Consultation Interpretation**

by Arlene Haack

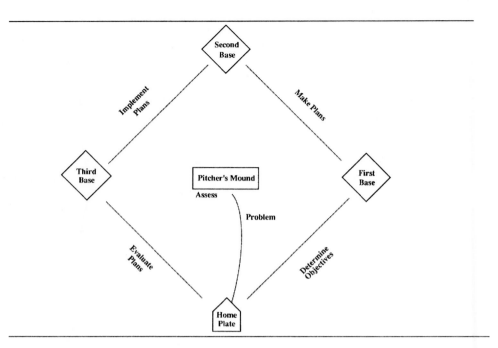

**FIGURE 3–4   Consulting Field: A Stephens/Systems Model**

by Patti Pfeifley

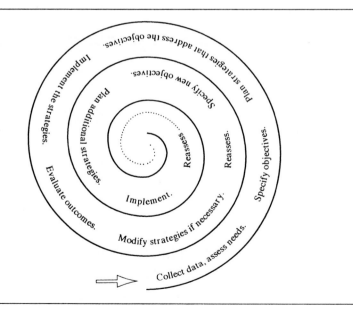

**FIGURE 3–5   Stephens/Systems Model**

by Sharon Arnold

2. How would you picture the Stephens/systems model? One person made the ball field form in Figure 3–4 which resembles the original circular graphic for this model. Another made the spiral form in Figure 3–5 which, if cut round and round, and lifted in the center, illustrates a three-dimensional, ongoing process. Consultation is effectively depicted through this round-and-round, ever upward more focused approach.

3. Try visualizing the Resource/Consulting Teacher Program model. What benefits can this interaction have for students with special needs? (See Figure 3–6 and its elaboration in Figure 3–7.)

4. An illustrator might select a more linear design for illustrating components of the School Consultation Committee model. One possible interpretation is a mobile design (see Figure 3–8), and another is a computer–type flow chart.

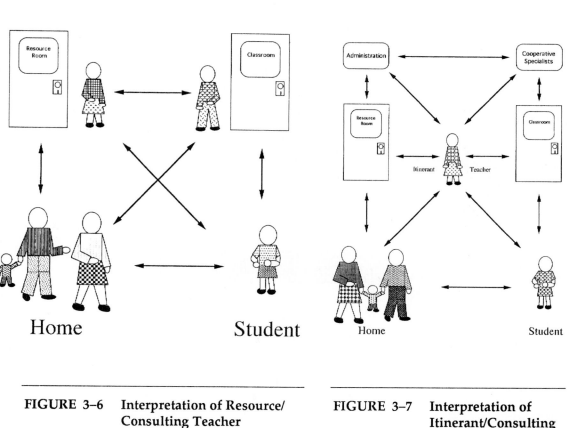

| **FIGURE 3–6** | **Interpretation of Resource/ Consulting Teacher Program Interaction** | **FIGURE 3–7** | **Interpretation of Itinerant/Consulting Teacher Interaction** |

by Candy Denk

by Eric Ross

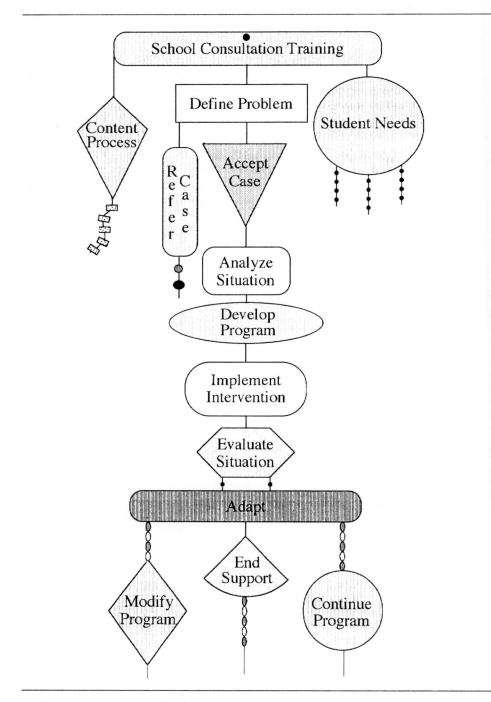

**FIGURE 3–8  A School Consultation Committee Model**

5. An interpretation of the Vermont Consulting Teacher Program model could include a backdrop or foundation that represents a state agency or university (see Figure 3–9).

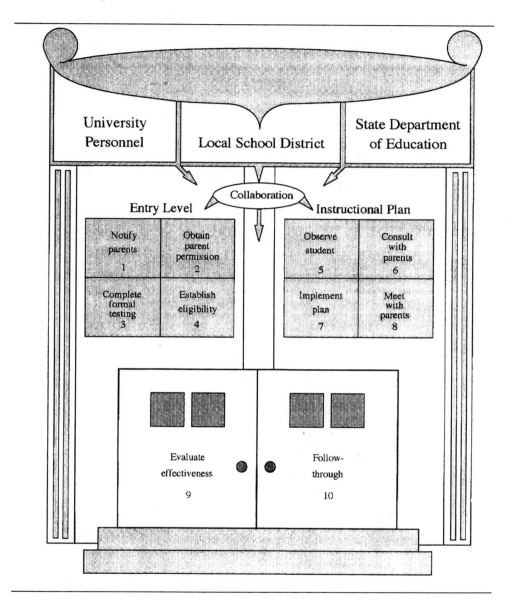

**FIGURE 3–9  Vermont Counsulting Teacher Model**

6. Note the development of triadic consultation interpretation (see Figure 3–10) into a more collaborative method for consultation (see Figure 3–11). Collaborative consultation also can be depicted effectively with an integrative, overlapping visual as shown in Figure 3–12. How would it look to you?

**FIGURE 3–10  Interpretation of a Triadic Foundation for Collaborative Consultation**

by Sharon Arnold

**FIGURE 3–11  Interpretation of Collaborative Consultation Based on Triadic Consultation**

by S. Arnold and P. Dettmer

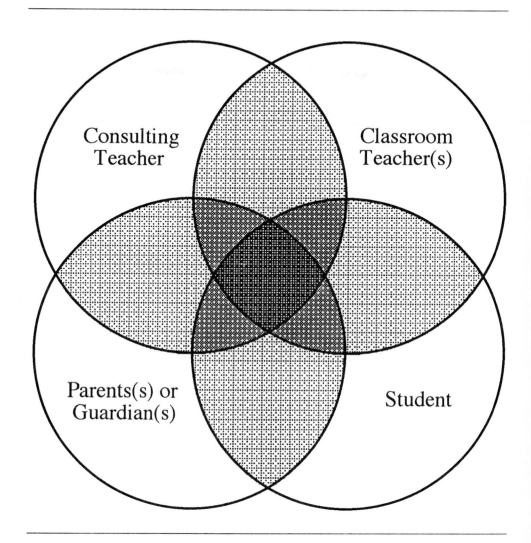

**FIGURE 3–12    Another Interpretation of Collaborative Consultation**

by Janet Stark

**Application 1—Explaining Models**
*Describing an Effective Model*

Now, after creating your mental models, try explaining their key steps with words, either in outline or paragraph form. Then reread the advantages/amber light suggestions for using each model (Table 3–1), and test your graphics to see if they point out the most important benefits and avoid the potential shortcomings of each one.

**Application 2—Selecting an Appropriate Method**
*What Consultants Can Choose for Specific Situations*

Seven potential situations for school consultation, collaboration, and/or teamwork are presented below. There are no right or wrong configurations for structuring methods to address the needs presented within these seven situations. Each should be approached by considering several points:

1. Is this a situation in which consultation and collaboration will be beneficial for the person(s) in need? (If the answer is yes, proceed to next points.)
2. Who best fits the consultant, consultee, and client roles in each?
3. How might interaction among roles be structured? What should happen first? Who will do what? When will the interaction conclude? (Do not dwell on the specific consultation process at this time. That will be addressed in Chapter 5.)
4. Consider the structural elements that will be included in the method you develop for addressing each of the situations:

   4.1 In what *system* (school, home, medical) will the consultation be conducted?
   4.2 Will the most helpful *perspective* be a purchase, a doctor-patient, or a process relationship?
   4.3 Should the *approach* be formal or informal?
   4.4 Is the most descriptive *prototype* the mental health, behavioral, or advocacy pattern?
   4.5 Will the consultation be provided in a direct or an indirect service delivery *mode*?
   4.6 Which *model* seems to fit the need and the other five consultation components best?

   One person doing this exercise may decide the best way to address the identified problem is with the triadic model, using indirect service from the consultant to the client, in an informal behavioral interaction within the school system. Another person's problem may have been served most appropriately within a Vermont Consulting Teacher Program model, using direct service to administrators in an advocacy-type interaction, and a formal approach calling for the doctor-patient perspective in a community-wide system. To carry out this task, recall that *methods* of consultation should be designed by using facets of the six structural elements that will best meet each student's special needs.

5. What may be major obstacles in carrying out the consultation and collaboration process? Major benefits? (Remember the all-important multiplier effects—those positive ripple effects that allow educators to reach a wider area of need than the immediate client.)

## Situations for Application 2

*Situation 1:* A fourth-grade boy has been in the educable mentally handicapped (EMH) program since first grade. He was first diagnosed as learning disabled, but later staffed into the EMH program. The mother presented a birth history that supported the decision and seems to have accepted it. However, two older brothers living away from home insist that there is nothing wrong with their little brother. Each time the mother visits with them she becomes confused, intimidated, and frustrated. The child is becoming more resistant an passive, and is gaining weight rapidly. How should the EMH teacher address the problem?

*Situation 2:* The speech pathologist has been asked by the gifted program facilitator to consult with her regarding a highly gifted child who has minor speech problems but is being pressured by the parents and kindergarten teacher to "stop the baby talk." The child is becoming very nervous and at times withdraws from conversation and play. How can the speech pathologist structure consultation and collaboration?

*Situation 3:* A school psychologist is conferring with a teacher about a high school student she has just evaluated. The student is often a behavior problem, and the psychologist is discussing methods for setting up behavior limits with appropriate contingencies and rewards. The teacher makes numerous references to the principal as a person who likes teachers to be self-sufficient and not "make waves." How should the school psychologist handle this?

*Situation 4:* A fifth-grade student with learning disabilities (LD) is not having success in social studies. The student has a serious reading problem but is a good listener and stays on task. The LD resource teacher suspects that the classroom teacher is not willing to modify materials and expectations for the child. The teacher has not discussed this situation with the LD teacher, but the student has. Parent-teacher conferences are next week. What should happen here, and who will make it happen?

*Situation 5:* In a third-grade class a student is an average learner but is often seen in the halls walking near the wall with one hand touching the wall. He appears sad, lonely, and unsure of himself. The special education teacher of a self-contained classroom for students with behavioral disorders has heard of this child getting into fights on the bus and the playground. Today the third-grade teacher stops the special education teacher during the lunch break and says the student was crying at recess and resisting communication. He is not doing any work, but just sitting and eyeing his classmates with a look of frustration and anger. What should the special education teacher do?

*Situation 6:* A high school learning–disabilities consultant is visiting with a principal at the principal's request. The principal expresses concern about the quality of teaching of two faculty members and asks the consultant to observe them and then provide feedback. How should the consultant handle this situation?

*Situation 7:* A local pediatrician contacts the director of special education and asks her to meet with local doctors to discuss characteristics and needs of at-risk and handicapped children. How should this opportunity be structured for maximum benefit to all?

## Tips for Collaborating and Consulting

1. Locate articles focusing on consultation, collaboration, and teamwork, summarize highlights, and prepare a "fact sheet" for other school staff, including administrators.
2. Have articles shared in Tip 1 available for any who might ask to read the entire work.
3. Make a bulletin board for the teacher workroom depicting models you created with the material in this chapter.
4. Prepare a brief description of a consultation and collaboration method and add it to the model display in Tip 3.
5. Be on the alert for new methods or revisions of existing methods, through which consultation and collaboration can occur in your school context.

## Chapter Review

1. School consultation evolved from practices in the mental health and medical services fields. The earliest uses of school consultation were in areas of speech and language therapy, and services for visually-impaired and hearing-impaired students.
2. There are differing points of view concerning the existence of a theoretical base of school consultation. Some researchers consider school consultation theory-based if the relationship between consultant and consultee can be identified across more than one literature source.
3. Research in school consultation and collaboration has been conducted to assess situational variables, outcome variables, and organizational change. There is a need for more reliable and valid instrumentation, more specific definition of variables, and more careful control of variables during research.
4. Structural elements to develop effective methods of school consultation can be categorized as: systems (institutions and contexts); perspectives (purchase, doctor-patient, process); approaches (formal, informal); prototypes (mental health, behavioral, advocacy); modes (direct, indirect); and models (triadic, Stephens/systems, Resource/Consulting Teacher Program, School Consultation Committee, Vermont Consulting Teacher Program, and the collaborative consultation model).
5. Major models currently used in school consultation have unique features that make them useful in particular situations and for special needs of consultees and clients. Each of the models also has some areas that may make the model more difficult to implement or less effective within particular contexts and for certain student needs.
6. The most effective strategy for school consultation and collaboration will be a synthesis of appropriate features from the six elements, which are blended to create a situation-specific method for serving a student's special learning needs within that student's school context.

## Activities

**1.** Pinpoint several changes that have occurred in special education during the past twenty years, and suggest implications for school consultation methods.

**2.** Using other references and sources, make a time line of key educational policies and reform that helped initiate interest in school consultation, collaboration, and teamwork. (An old window shade is a good material on which to make and display this kind of project.)

**3.** Make sketches or three-dimensional representations of the models you visualized in the applications exercise above. Does your graphic capture the intent of the model? Does it permit analysis of the model to determine its advantages and cautions in a variety of school settings?

**4.** Visit schools where consultation and collaboration play an integral role in serving students' special needs. Using the information in Figure 3–1, analyze the consultation systems, perspectives, approaches, prototypes, modes, and models that seem to be in use in those schools. Then summarize the results into brief, innovative descriptions of the methods that seem to have evolved from the synthesis of these components.

## For Further Reading

(Note: The reader is advised to focus on the key points of these recommended readings without getting tangled in the maze of philosophies and terms which, as explained in this chapter, often are not consistent across authors and consultation structures.)

Brown, D., Pryzwansky, W. B., and Schulte, A. C. (1991). *Psychological Consultation: Introduction to Theory and Practice.* Needham Heights, MA: Allyn and Bacon. Chapters 1, 2, and 3 in particular.

Conoley, J. C., and Conoley, C. W. (1982). School consultation: *A Guide to Practice and Training.* New York: Pergamon Press.

*Journal of Educational and Psychological Consultation.* All issues.

Morsink, C. V., Thomas, C. C., and Correa, V. I. (1991). *Interactive Teaming: Consultation and Collaboration in Special Programs.* New York: Merrill. Chapter 2 in particular.

*Remedial and Special Education Journal.* Issues focusing on school consultation and collaboration.

## References

Babcock, N. L., and Pryzwansky, W. B. (1983). Models of consultation: Preferences of educational professionals at five stages of service. *Journal of School Psychology, 21*: 359–66.

Bergan, J. R. (1977). *Behavioral Consultation.* Columbus, OH: Merrill.

Bergan, J. R., and Tombari, M. L. (1976). Consultant skill and efficiency and the implementation and outcome of consultation. *Journal of School Psychology, 14*(1): 3–14.

Brown. D., Pryzwansky, W. B., and Schulte, A. C. (1991). *Psychological Consultation: Intro-

*duction to Theory and Practice.* Needham Heights, MA: Allyn and Bacon.

Brown, D., and Schulte, A. C. (1987). A social learning model of consultation. *Professional Psychology: Research and Practice, 18:* 283–87.

Brown, D., Wyne, M. D., Blackburn, J. E., and Powell, W. C. (1979). *Consultation: Strategy For Improving Education.* Boston: Allyn and Bacon.

Bush, G. (1991). *America 2000: An education strategy.* Washington, D.C.: U.S. Department of Education.

Caplan, G. (1970). *The Theory and Practice of Mental Health Consultation.* New York: Basic Books.

Chandler, L. A. (1980). Consultative services in the schools: A model. *Journal of School Psychology, 18*(4): 399–401.

Coleman, P. G., Eggleston, K. K., Collins, J. F., Holloway, G. D., and Reider, S. K. (1975). A severely hearing impaired child in the mainstream. *Teaching Exceptional Children: 8,* 6–9.

Conoley, J. C., and Conoley, C. W. (1982). *School Consultation: A Guide To Practice and Training.* New York: Pergamon Press.

Conoley, J. C., and Conoley, C. W. (1988). Useful theories in school–based consultation. *Remedial and Special Education, 9*(6): 14–20.

Curtis, M. J., and Zins, J. E. (1981). *The Theory and Practice of School Consultation.* Springfield, IL: Charles C. Thomas.

Dettmer, P. (1989). The consulting teacher in programs for gifted and talented students. *Arkansas Gifted Education Magazine, 3*(2): 4–7.

Dettmer, P., and Lane, J. (1989). An integrative model for educating very able students in rural school districts. *Educational Considerations, 17*(1): 36–39.

Dyck, N., and Dettmer, P. (1989). Collaborative consultation: A promising tool for serving gifted learning–disabled students. *Journal of Reading, Writing, and Learning Disabilities, 5*(3): 253–64.

Evans, S. (1980). The consultant role of the resource teacher. *Exceptional Children, 4 6*(5): 402–4.

Friend, M. (1984). Consultation skills for resource teachers. *Learning Disability Quarterly, 7:* 246–50.

Friend, M. (1988). Putting consultation into context: Historical and contemporary perspectives. *Remedial and Special Education, 9*(6): 7–13.

Friend, M., and Bauwens, J. (1988). Managing resistance: An essential consulting skill for learning disabilities teachers. *Journal of Learning Disabilities, 21,* 556–561.

Gallessich, J. (1973). Organizational factors influencing consultation in schools. *Journal of School Psychology, 11*(1): 57–65.

Gallessich, J. (1974). Training the school psychologist for consultation. *Journal of School Psychology, 12:* 138–49.

Gersten, R., Darch, C., Davis, G., and George, N. (1991). Apprenticeship and intensive training of consulting teachers: A naturalistic study. *Exceptional Children, 57*(3): 226–37.

Graubard, P. S., Rosenberg, H., and Miller, M. B. (1971). Student applications of behavior modification to teachers and environments or ecological approaches to deviancy. In E. A. Ramp and B. L. Hopkins (eds.), *A New Direction for Education: Behavior Analysis,* pp. 80–101. Lawrence, KS: University of Kansas.

Gresham, F. M., and Kendell, G. K. (1987). School consultation research: Methodological critique and future research directions. *School Psychology Review, 16*(3): 306–16.

Gutkin, T. B. (1986). Consultees' perceptions of variables relating to the outcomes of school-based consultation interactions. *School Psychology Review, 15*(3), 375–82.

Gutkin, T. B., and Curtis, M. L. (1982). School-based consultation theory and techniques. In C. R. Reynolds and T. B. Gutkin (eds.), *The Handbook of School Psychology,* pp. 796–828. New York: Wiley.

Gutkin, T. B., Singer, J., and Brown, R. (1980). Teacher reactions to school–based consultation services: A multivariate analysis. *Journal of School Psychology, 18:* 126–34.

Haight, S. L. (1984). Special education teacher consultant: Idealism versus realism. *Exceptional Children, 50*(6): 507–15.

Hall, G. E., and Hord, S. M. (1987). *Change in Schools: Facilitating the Process.* Albany: State University of New York Press.

Hansen, J. C., Himes, B. S., and Meier, S. (1990). *Consultation: Concepts and Practices.* Englewood Cliffs, NJ: Prentice Hall.

Happe, D. (1982). Behavioral Intervention: It doesn't do any good in your briefcase. In J. Grimes (ed.), *Psychological Approaches to Problems of Children and Adolescents,* pp. 15–41. Des Moines, IA: Iowa Department of Public Instruction.

Heron, T.E., and Harris, K.C. (1982). *The Educational Consultant: Helping Professionals, Parents. and Mainstreamed Students.* Boston: Allyn and Bacon.

Heron, T. E., and Harris, K. C. (1987). *The Educational Consultant: Helping Professionals, Parents, and Mainstreamed Students.* Austin, TX: PRO–ED.

Heron, T. E., and Kimball, W. H. (1988). Gaining perspective with the educational consultation research base: Ecological considerations and further recommendations. *Remedial and Special Education, 9*(6): 21–28, 47.

Idol, L., Paolucci–Whitcomb, P., and Nevin, A. (1986). *Collaborative Consultation.* Austin, TX: PRO–ED.

Idol, L., and West, J. F. (1987). Consultation in special education (Part II): Training and practices. *Journal of Learning Disabilities, 20*: 474–97.

Idol–Maestas, L. (1981). A teacher training model: The resource/consulting teacher. *Behavioral Disorders, 6* (2): 108–21.

Idol–Maestas, L. (1983). *Special Educator's Consultation Handbook.* Rockville, MD: Aspen.

Idol–Maestas, L., and Celentano, R. (1986). Teacher consultant services for advanced students. *Roeper Review, 9*(1): 34–36.

Jackson, R. M., Cleveland, J. C., and Merenda, P. F. (1975). The longitudinal effects of early identification and counseling of underachievers. *Journal of School Psychology, 13*: 119–28.

Johnson, D., and Johnson, R. (1980). The key to effective inservice: Building teacher–teacher collaborations. *Developer*, pp. 223–36.

Knight, M. T., Meyers, H. W., Paolucci–Whitcomb, P., Hasazi, S. E., and Nevin, A. (1981). A four–year evaluation of consulting teacher service. *Behavioral Disorders, 6*: 92–100.

Lilly, M., and Givens–Ogle, L. (1981). Teacher consultation: Present, past, and future. *Behavioral Disorders, 6*: 73–77.

McDonald, J. P. (1989). When outsiders try to change schools from the inside. *Phi Delta Kappan, 71*(3): 206–12.

McGlothlin, J. E. (1981). The school consultation committee: An approach to implementing a teacher consultation model. *Behavioral Disorders, 6*(2): 101–7.

Mc Loughlin, J.A., and Kass, C. (1978). Resorce teachers: Their role. *Learning Disability Quarterly, 1* (1), 56–62.

McKenzie, H. S., Egner, A. N., Knight, M. F., Perelman, P. F., Schneider, B. M., and Garvin, J. S. (1970). Training consulting teachers to assist elementary teachers in the management and education of handicapped children. *Exceptional Children, 37* (2), 137–43.

Medway, F. J., and Forman, S. G. (1980). Psychologists' and teachers' reactions to mental health and behavioral school consultation. *Journal of School Psychology, 18*: 338–48.

Miller, T.L., and Sabatino, D. (1978). An evaluation of the teacher consultant model as an approach to mainstreaming. *Exceptional Children, 45*: 86–91.

Morsink, C. V., Thomas, C. C., and Correa, V. I. (1991). *Interactive Teaming: Consultation and Collaboration in Special Programs.* New York: Macmillan.

Nazzaro, J. N. (1977). *Exceptional Timetables: Historic Events Affecting the Handicapped and Gifted.* Reston, VA: The Council for Exceptional Children.

Neel, R. S. (1981). How to put the consultant to work in consulting teaching. *Behavioral Disorders, 6*(2): 78–81.

Nelson, C. M., and Stevens, K. B. (1981). An accountable consultation model for mainstreaming behaviorally disordered children. *Behavioral Disorders, 6*(2): 82–90.

Pedron, N. A., and Evans, S. B. (1990). Modifying classroom teachers' acceptance of the consulting teacher model. *Journal of Educational and Psychological Consultation, 1*(2): 189–200.

Pryzwansky, W. B. (1974). A reconsideration of the consultation model for delivery of school–based psychological services. *American Journal of Orthopsychiatry, 44*: 579–83.

Pryzwansky, W. B. (1986). Indirect service delivery: Considerations for future research in consultation. *School Psychology Review, 15*(4): 479–88.

Pryzwansky, W. B. (1989). School consultation: Some considerations from a psychology perspective. *Professional School Psychology, 4*: 1–14.

Raymond, G. I., McIntosh, D. K., and Moore, Y. R. (1986). *Teacher Consultation Skills.* Report no. ED 182–912. Washington, D.C.: U.S. Department of Education. (ERIC Document Reproduction Service no. ED 170–915.)

Reynolds, M. C. (1962). A framework for considering some issues in special education. *Exceptional Children, 28*: 367–70.

Reynolds, M. C., and Birch, J. W. (1988). *Adaptive Mainstreaming: A Primer for Teachers and Principals.* White Plains, NY: Longman.

Salend, S. J., and Salend, S. (1984). Consulting with the regular teacher: Guidelines for special educators. *Pointer, 25:* 25–28.

Schein, E. H. (1969). *Process Consultation: Its Role in Organizational Development.* Reading, MA: Addison–Wesley.

Schein, E. H. (February, 1978). The role of the consultant: Context expert or process facilitator? *Personnel and Guidance Journal.*

Sondel, B. (1958). *The Humanity of Words.* Cleveland, OH: World Publishing.

Stephens, T. M. (1977). *Teaching Skills To Children with Learning and Behavioral Disorders.* Columbus, OH: Merrill.

Tharp, R. G. (1975). The triadic model of consultation: Current considerations. In C. A. Parker (ed.), *Psychological Consultation: Helping Teachers Meet Special Needs* pp. 135–51. Reston, VA: The Council for Exceptional Children.

Tharp, R. G., and Wetzel, R. J. (1969). *Behavior Modification in the Natural Environment.* New York: Academic Press.

Vasa, S. T. (1982). *The Special Education Resource Teacher as a Consultant: Fact or Fantasy?* Paper presented at the Sixth Annual Meeting of the Council for Exceptional Children, Houston. (ERIC Document Reproduction Service no. ED 218–918.)

Voltz, D. L., and Elliott, R. N., Jr., (1990). Resource room teacher roles in promoting interaction with regular educators. *Teacher Education and Special Education, 13*(3–4): 160–66.

West, J. F. (1985). *Regular and Special Educators' Preference for School–Based Consultation Models: A Statewide Study.* Report no. 101. Austin, TX: The University of Texas at Austin, Research and Training Project on School Consultation.

West, J. F., and Brown, P. A. (1987). State departments of education policies on consultation in special education: The state of the states. *Remedial and Special Education, 8*(3): 45–51.

West, J. F., and Cannon, G. S. (1988). Essential collaborative consultation competencies for regular and special educators. *Journal of Learning Disabilities, 21:* 56–63.

West, J. F., and Idol, L. (1987). School consultation (Part I): An interdisciplinary perspective on theory, models, and research. *Journal of Learning Disabilities, 20*(7): 385–408.

West, J. F., Idol, L., and Cannon, G. S. (1987). A curriculum for preservice and inservice preparation of classroom and special education teachers in collaborative consultation. Austin, TX: The University of Texas at Austin, Research and Training Project on School Consultation.

Witt, J. C., and Elliott, S. N. (1985). Acceptability of classroom intervention strategies. In T. R. Kratochwill (ed.), *Advances in School Psychology,* 4, 251–88. Hillsdale, NJ: Lawrence Erlbaum.

Witt, J. C., Moe, G., Gutkin, T., and Andrews, L. (1984). The effect of saying the same thing in different ways: The problem of language and jargon in school–based consultation. *Journal of School Psychology, 22:* 361–67.

# 4

# EFFECTS OF DIVERSITY ON SCHOOL CONSULTATION, COLLABORATION, AND TEAMWORK

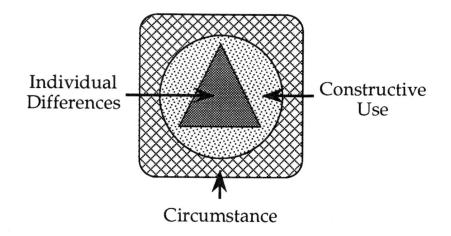

Individual Differences → ← Constructive Use

↑ Circumstance

## To Think About

Awareness of individual differences and the constructive use of those differences are extremely important teacher attributes. While many educators may "talk a good game" about individual differences of students, they rarely focus on individual differences among the *adults* who provide learning experiences for students. Even when teachers are well attuned to individual interests and preferred learning styles of their students, they may overlook the impact of differing values, styles, and interests on professional interactions among teaching colleagues.

Today's students are the future leaders of a shrinking global community. It is vital that educators prepare them to function successfully in diverse, multicultural societies. Teachers can model cooperation and collaboration skills they will need to survive in this increasingly complex, intertwined world. But to demonstrate these skills convincingly, educators must show their ability to work collaboratively as team members in school settings. As they interact with others, educators must demonstrate that they value diversity, respect differing philosophies, and accommodate individuality in teaching and learning styles. The consultant role is a natural and appropriate vehicle for promoting constructive use of adult individual differences within the school context.

## Focusing Questions

1. How do individual differences among adults affect interactions in the school context?
2. What are examples of adult differences that occur during consultation, collaboration, and teamwork?
3. How can educators benefit from study of their own preferred functions and styles?
4. How can adult differences be used constructively within the school context?
5. How does cultural diversity affect school consultation and collaboration practices?
6. How can consultation create needed links among various agencies that provide services for students with special needs?

## Key Terms

cultural diversity                  nonverbal behaviors
ethnic group                        paralanguage
kinesics                            proxemics
learning styles                     psychopest
macroculture                        rural
microculture                        temperament
Myers-Briggs Type Indicator (MBTI)  type preferences

---

**Scenario**

In an elementary school a sixth-grade boy enters the learning disabilities resource room visibly upset. He has come from his regular classroom for a two-hour block of reading remediation with the consulting teacher. He flings a stack of papers onto the table.

---

*LD TEACHER*: Things not going well today, Manuel?

*MANUEL*: It doesn't matter what I do! I can't please her.

*LD TEACHER*: Want to tell me about it?

*MANUEL*: I got an 80 on my English test.

*LD TEACHER*: 'Way to go!

*MANUEL*: And it would have been an 85 if I hadn't put two answers in the wrong place. Besides that, I passed the weekly spelling test and made up most of my homework from last week. But my teacher says I still have to do more.

*LD TEACHER*: What do you need to do?

*MANUEL*: I don't know. I asked, but she said we'll talk about it after school. She says she doesn't have time to go over it with me before then. And when she says "go over it" she means *really go over it*. She's going to call my mom to tell her I'll be late. Mama's supervisor doesn't like it when she gets called off the line to answer the phone. I don't see why my teacher doesn't just give me the list of page numbers and be done with it. She beats around the bush—talk, talk, talk—on and on, like she's trying to pry into things and make me over.

*LD TEACHER*: I see. Well, here's an idea. How about taking a few minutes to think about how to explain to your teacher what you need and why? Then together we can come up with a plan that will be better for everyone—you with your work at school, your mom at her work, and your teachers, both of us—who care about you a lot.

*MANUEL*: I guess so—O.K., if you think it will help. But I'll be glad when this year is over. This teacher is nice and all that, but we just never do see things the same. Next year I'll be going to different classes every hour. I may have someone like her again, but at least I won't be stuck with the same one all day!

## Valuing Individual Differences within the School Context

Patchwork fabric has appeal because it contains so many varieties of color, texture, and design. If each piece of fabric in the patchwork were identical, the fabric would be dull and lifeless. The most interesting patchworks are those in which each piece contributes uniqueness to the overall collage of colors and textures. Even if some of the colors or textures would clash elsewhere, when aggregated into a patchwork design they create a vibrant, colorful fabric that enlivens its setting (Meyer, 1977).

In much the same way, schools are a patchwork of attitudes, personalities, values, and interests. Each individual in the school setting is different, contributing uniqueness to enliven the whole. Sometimes individual characteristics may clash, but if the individuality of students *or* adults is repressed, the school climate becomes drab and lifeless.

Educators are challenged to treat each student as a unique learner. Individualization for student needs is an important aspect of teacher planning. However, for many educators, the individual traits of adult colleagues, which cause them to think and feel in unique ways, are too often overlooked. Tolerance for diverse perspectives toward problems and issues is one of an educator's most important assets when consulting, collaborating, and working in teams to facilitate student learning. Unfortunately, a study of adult differences is, for the most part, ignored in teacher preparation programs. But it is vital preparation for engaging in the professional interactions that help identify and serve student needs.

Much of the seemingly random variation in human behavior is actually quite orderly and consistent, because it is based on the way people prefer to use their perception and judgment (Lawrence, 1982; Keirsey and Bates, 1978). If one person views the world and reacts to it in ways unlike another, it is because that person processes information differently. Different viewpoints contribute diverse insights that help to broaden understanding of problems and generate promising alternatives for solving problems.

In order to serve students best, educators do not need to think alike—they just need to think together. Thinking together divergently can be very productive. Understanding and valuing adult uniqueness in information processing and orientation toward the world are key factors in the success of collegial relationships.

## Recognizing Adult Differences within the School Context

It is easy and convenient, but myopic, to endorse only one way of doing something—one's own—while wondering why everyone else is not clever enough, and agreeable enough, to concur. A situation perceived one way by one educator might be looked quite differently by another who has completely different values and attitudes.

"Why don't the rest of the people on the faculty support this method? It's working so well for some of us."

"Why are some faculty so negative toward new ideas before they even try them or give them a chance?"

"We never see eye-to-eye on anything in our department."

"I just can't figure out where that parent is coming from."

Conscientious educators who respect the individualism and independence of their students need to respect and protect these rights for colleagues and parents of students as well. Educator Madeline Hunter urges other educators to "come out of armed camps. . . w here we're not collaborating, so that 'I understand why you think it's right for your students to line up while I think it's better for them to come in casually'" (Hunter, 1985, p. 3). She stresses that, when educators show respect for other points of view, they model the cooperation that is so necessary for the future of communities, cities, nations, and the world.

As educators take the time to reflect on thoughts and feelings that drive their actions, they should realize that each person in the work team, classroom, family, or organization has sets of thoughts and feelings that govern individual behavior as well. The critical factor in teacher preparation is not more knowledge of subject matter and teaching techniques, but the ability to relate constructively to others, including colleagues, by responding to them and to their preferences and needs with emotional maturity (Jersild, 1955).

## *Assessing Adult Differences*

A number of theories and instruments are available for studying individual preferences in order to understand human behavior and improve human relationships. During the 1970s and 1980s, a plethora of concepts and assessments emerged to be used in such diverse social service areas as education, counseling (for marriage and family, personal, and career needs), religion, business and industry, and other social institutions. Personality theory, cognitive style theory, and aptitude-treatment interaction (ATI) were precursors to a mushrooming interest in learning styles paradigms (Keefe and Ferrell, 1990).

*Learning Styles*  Learning styles became an everyday word in the educational vocabulary of the 1970s and 1980s. In a synthesis of learning style research, Lawrence (1984) suggests that while the term *learning styles* is loosely defined, it does include:

- Cognitive style, in the sense of preferred or habitual patterns of mental functioning, information processing, and formation of ideas and judgment.
- Patterns of attitudes and interests that influence what a person attends to in potential learning situations.
- Disposition to seek out learning environments that are compatible with one's cognitive style, attitude, and interest, and to avoid those that are not.
- Disposition to use certain learning tools and avoid others.

Persons interested in learning styles assessment can choose among a wide range of well-known and widely-used tools and techniques, including Gregorc's concepts of learning style (Gregorc and Ward, 1977), aptitude-treatment interaction theories relating individual differences to instructional method, Kolb cognitive style concepts (Kolb, 1976), the McCarthy (1990) 4MAT system, and the Dunn and Dunn learning styles assessment (Dunn and Dunn, 1978), to name only a few of the more prominent examples. Each of these systems can contribute to increased understanding of human preferences that influence behavior. The Myers-Briggs Type Indicator (Myers, 1962) will be used here to focus on adult individual differences that affect consultation and collaboration.

***The Myers-Briggs Type Indicator***   The Myers-Briggs Type Indicator (MBTI) is one of the individual preference instruments that contributes richly to examination of individual differences. It is a useful choice for consultants and collaborators to study because it focuses on the *constructive use of individual differences* when people work in groups. The MBTI is a product of much reflection and research, with a substantial body of empirical data available on its use. It was developed during the late 1950s and early 1960s by Isabel Briggs Myers as a way of measuring personality variables identified by Jungian personality typology.

Carl Jung, noted Swiss psychologist, asserted that people are different in fundamental ways, even though all have the same instincts driving them from within (Jung, 1923). Jung believed that schools, as a part of the total world, contain in miniature most of the factors people face in their lives. Each person within the school is an experiment in life—an attempt at a new solution and adaptation (Jung, 1954). Any one of a person's instincts is not more important than that of another person. What *is* important is the person's own preferences for personal functioning. These individual preferences provide the "patchwork quilt" of human interaction that can be so constructive and facilitative for teamwork and group problem solving.

The MBTI examines either/or preferences toward patterns of natural interests, learning style, patterns of commitment, and work habits (Lawrence, 1984). For example, a person who indicates a preference for action and variety, shares experiences readily, prefers to work with others, and tends to get impatient with slow, tedious jobs, would have preferences quite different from one who prefers working alone, laboring long and hard on one thing, and seeking abundant quiet time for reflection. An individual who is interested in facts, works steadily and patiently, and enjoys being realistic and practical would contrast during group activity with one who prefers to generate multiple possibilities, attends to the whole aspect of a situation, and anticipates what will be said or done.

A person who wants logical reasons, holds firmly to convictions, and contributes intellectually while trying to be fair and impartial has a type of preferences different from one who relates well to most people, likes to agree with others, and cultivates enthusiasm among others. An individual who likes to have things decided and settled, functions purposefully, and seeks to make conditions as they "should be," does not have the same group work style as one who has a more live-and-let-live attitude, leaving things open and flexible while demonstrating adaptability and tolerance.

Any of the types characterized by the MBTI is derived from a collection of what a person *likes*, not what he or she lacks, and certainly not from what someone else thinks that person *should* like. An individual indicates which type of preferences are personally most satisfying. Every person has and can use all attributes when needed, but *prefers* to focus intensively upon one or the other at a time. Murphy (1987b) explains this point by using the example of color. Just as red cannot be blue, one type cannot be both polarities simultaneously. If a person prefers to apply experiences to problems, that person cannot also prefer to apply imagination to those problems. But he or she can use imagination if need be, and may benefit from practicing such skills in order to use that approach more productively. Jung believed that each individual has everything needed to function completely, with even the least preferred functions contributing to productivity and self-satisfaction. Less preferred functions provide balance and completeness. They are also the wellsprings of enthusiasm and energy. As an individual's most childlike and primitive functions, they can be quite useful by creating a certain awkwardness and unrest that cultivate innovation. The preferred functions are generally called on when ease and efficiency are desired.

## Self-Study of Preferred Styles and Functions

The individual personality is a result of inner forces acting and being acted on by outer forces (Hall and Lindzey, 1978). Until individuals engage in self-study, they are likely to see others through the biases and distortion of their own unrecognized needs, fears, desires, anxieties, and sometimes, hostile impulses (Jersild, 1955). School consultants would do well to analyze their own philosophy, values, and inclinations before attempting to work intensively with others and *their* preferences and values (Brown et al., 1979).

As educators reflect on their own characteristics and preferences, they often make comments such as these:

"I have lots of skills , but I don't seem to get them put together to do what I want."

"I am fed up with these reports that have to be done on such short notice. If data are turned in hastily and carelessly, what is their value?"

"I worked really hard on that project, and then everybody else seemed to forget that the ideas were mine when it came time to give out recognition."

"Should I state my views, or wait and see what everyone else thinks and then fall in line?"

"It seems like all I do with this faculty is put out fires."

"If I didn't show up tomorrow, I'm not sure any of my colleagues would notice or care, so long as there is a substitute teacher here to corral the kids."

Self-study can be undertaken through a variety of methods and settings, including group work, role playing, reading, conferences, and workshops. Tools such as the MBTI and others named earlier in this chapter can be studied and discussed in in-service and staff development sessions, department meetings, small-group activity, or conferences, in order to highlight the rich variety inherent in human nature. Of course, no single journal article, book, conference, or training package will be sufficient to fully understand the sophistication and complexity of individual differences. Nevertheless, teachers *can* deal more effectively with all students and their colleagues if they understand the basic principles of personality types and the effects on learning styles and teaching styles (Dettmer, 1981).

The importance of self-understanding is substantiated by these comments from an educator during coursework to prepare her for the consulting teacher role in special education:

> *Having now taken the Myers-Briggs Type Indicator two times, I have a better understanding of myself. More important, however, is that I have an increased understanding of type theory. Being a bit wary of typecasting, I was surprised to find that my type profile did not change from one administration of the of MBTI to the next. Of course, caution must be exercised in using the instrument. With little or no understanding of type theory, one easily could dismiss the instrument or misinterpret it. Even more detrimental would be using results to stereotype or place blame or make excuses.*
>
> *Without further study, I doubt I could determine anyone else's type. Yet being aware of different preferences is enough to foster my long-held beliefthat a teacher must approach the curriculum in a myriad of ways. By being sure there is 'something for everyone,' a teacher can make the best attempt at reaching all the students.*

Self-study helps educators become more aware of their own attributes and weave their own best qualities into new combinations for helping students with diverse interests and learning needs (Dettmer, 1981). Too few teacher preparation programs provide opportunities for this important self-exploration.

## Constructive Use of Adult Differences For School Consultation

Understanding differing preferences and types is particularly helpful when one person communicates with another, or lives with another, or makes decisions that affect another's life (Myers, 1980a). Problems in human relationships are minimized when the basis of the misunderstanding is realized. Data from a variety of occupational and academic groups have been used to study vocational preferences, aesthetic preferences, aptitudes, work habits, family and marriage relationships, creativity, and values. Isabel Briggs Myers (1975) liked to help married couples reconcile their different points of view by pointing out three alternatives:

> *You can consider that it is wrong of your partner to be different from you, and you can be indignant. That diminishes your partner and gets you nowhere. Or you can consider that it is wrong of you to be different from your partner and be depressed. That diminishes you and gets you nowhere. The proper solution is to consider that*

*the two of you are justifiably and interestingly different, and be amused. (Myers, keynote address, October 16, 1975)*

Differences among people in interaction techniques, preferred outcomes, work habits, and communication styles are important for school consultants to acknowledge when they are facilitating consultations and collaborations. Teachers often differ dramatically in their preferences. A consultant may work with one teacher who pays close attention to detail, examining every test score and asking questions about particular assignments, and another who scarcely looks at the test scores, preferring instead to solicit verbal, generalized assessment of the student's capabilities from other professionals.

A study by Lawrence and DeNovellis (1974) revealed that teachers with different preferences tend to behave differently in the classroom. Carlyn (1977) studied the relationship between personality characteristics and teaching preferences of prospective teachers. Some are more interested in administrative functions and others have a strong need for independence and creativity. Some prefer planning school programs, while others enjoy working with small groups of students. Some people like action and variety more than quiet and reflection. Some like to work in groups, whereas others prefer to work alone or with one person. Some people get impatient with slow jobs and complicated procedures. Others can work on one thing for a long time, and they resent interruptions. Carlyn concluded in her study that teachers of different personality-type preferences also preferred different kinds of teaching situations. These kinds of preferences and values help explain why some teachers will experiment with the modifications and materials a consultant suggests, while others resist or just never seem to get around to using them.

When a group of educators with different type preferences collaborate, they have the opportunity to contribute a variety of strengths. Those who like to bring up new possibilities and suggest ingenious ways of approaching problems will benefit from having other people supply pertinent facts and keep track of essential details. When some are finding flaws and holding to an existing policy, others contribute by selling the idea, conciliating, and arousing enthusiasm (Myers, 1980b).

Opposite types may or may not attract, but they definitely need to be present for greatest team productivity. Such differences can be useful, but managing them elegantly is a tremendous challenge for a consultant or consulting teacher. As stated earlier, the primary goal in consulting, collaborating, and working as a team is not to think alike, but to think together. Each person's individual preferences and values are important to the effectiveness of interaction. In the scenario, Manuel's teacher wants to discuss Manuel's assignments at length and in depth. Manuel prefers concrete assignments and minimal discussion about details. These differences are not just disagreement between adult and child or teacher and student. They reflect differing orientation to the world, learning styles, values, and work habits, and they can be constructive for serving the student's needs if managed wisely.

## Using Adult Differences to Facilitate Productive Interaction

Good teamwork calls for the recognition and use of certain valuable differences among all members of the team (Myers, 1974; Kummerow and McAllister, 1988). The most effective teams do not agree all the time, but they use individual differences within the group constructively (Kummerow and McAllister, 1988; Truesdell, 1983). Team success comes from division of labor, efforts toward mutual respect among members, openness to the contributions of others, and facilitative communication. Educators can learn a great deal from talking with colleagues with whom they differ both theoretically and methodologically (Gallessich, 1973).

Individuals have far more potential than they use at any one time, and the power of this potential in team settings is exponential. With a common vocabulary and a framework of respect for individuality, teamwork can be much more productive than individual effort.

### *Influence of Adult Differences on Communication*

Many communication problems among team members are due to individual differences. A statement that seems clear and reasonable to one person may sound meaningless or preposterous to another (Myers, 1974). One may want an explicit statement of the problem before considering possible solutions. Another member of the team might want at least the prospect of an interesting possibility before buckling down to facts. One may demand a beginning, a logically arranged sequence of points, and an end (*especially* an end, Myers cautions). Another will really listen only if the discussion starts with a concern for people and the direct effects of the issue on people.

Myers stresses, "It is human nature not to listen attentively if one has the impression that what is being said is going to be irrelevant or unimportant" (Myers, 1974, p. 4). Communication is such a critical part of successful consultation and collaboration that it will be the focus of concern in Chapter 6.

---

Application of Adult Preferences

*The Constructive Use of Individual Differences*

Pick a favorite lesson or subject area and imagine that you and a consultee will be team teaching this material. How would you go about this? Although it would be important to know something about your co-teacher's style and preferences, are there things you should study about *yourself* first, before embarking on this collaborative endeavor? How can you share that information with your colleague and learn comparable information about that person, in order to team more effectively?

---

## *Influence of Adult Differences on Problem Solving*

Personality type plays a significant role in the accuracy and efficiency of problem solving (Campbell and Kain, 1990). Some individuals are more accurate in problem identification, while others need less time to come up with possible solutions. One person may focus more on the problem and the facts, while another focuses on process and the meaning behind the facts. If an individual needs to solve a problem alone, he or she must manage multiple perspectives, but problem solving by a well-mixed team of individuals enables most perspectives to be represented.

No specific type preference is predictive of success in communication or problem solving within the group (Blaylock, 1983). Teams with a complete representation of types outperform virtually any single-type or similar-type team. The likelihood of having a versatile team is better than might be expected, for a single group of several individuals will contain many, if not most, of the type preferences.

## Using Knowledge of Adult Differences Appropriately

The phrase, "A little knowledge is a dangerous thing," should be heeded when addressing the issue of knowledge about individual differences. Just as teachers have learned to be discriminating in applying learning styles methodology to the classroom, so should consultants apply principles of type theory judiciously.

The following points summarize cautions along with possibilities for using knowledge about adult differences constructively:

**1.** Consultants can work from a knowledge of type theory, personality assessment, or learning styles concepts without knowing the type distribution of that group; in fact, they probably *should* do so. This premise will be more fully developed by the next several points.

**2.** It is not always possible, necessary, or even desirable to ascertain people's type preferences with a standardized instrument. The most important need is to develop the attitude that human differences are not behaviors intended to irritate and alienate each other. Rather, they are systematic, orderly, consistent, often unavoidable differences in the way people prefer to use their perception and judgment.

**3.** Each type is valuable, and at times indispensable, in every field.

**4.** Well-researched type theory does not promulgate labeling of individuals. Learning styles theory and right-left brain function research have fallen victim on occasion to unwarranted use of labels—"He's so right brained, that he can't . . ." and "She's a concrete sequential, so she won't . . . ." The world probably does not need any more labels for individuals, and this is particularly cogent in the field of special education. Such labels often contain hierarchical connotations (IQ tests, entrance exams); negative connotations ("stuck up" or "flaky"); derogatory overtones ("operates in the fast lane"); and trendy associations ("horoscope reader") (*Type Reporter, 37*, pp. 1–2). Consultants must take care to avoid such connotations, as well as phrases containing absolutes ("always . . . never . . .") and stereotyping through humor, anecdotes, excuses, and job division based on type (Lawrence, 1988).

**5.** Problems in human relationship caused by the conflict between opposite types can be lessened when the basis of the conflict is understood.

**6.** As the saying goes, "The map is not the territory." Type preferences never tell all there is to know about the rich and abundant variety of individuals that make up the human population of the world.

**7.** Any individual can reserve the right to change, experiment, or surprise another by being "out of character." Some of the most adamant resistance to type theory has come from those who regard type descriptions as stereotyping. Most people do not want to be regarded as completely predictable and unoriginal (*Type Reporter, 37*, p. 2.) People resent a "psychopest" (Luft, 1984) who professes to know everything about them.

**8.** Even among people with the same type preference, no two will function the same. It is like a garment of apparel—no two people look the same in it (*Type Reporter, 37*). It is inappropriate and unjust to assume too much from analysis of individual differences. No generalization should be applied to a single case, for any case could be an anomaly. As an example, Hammer (1985) stresses that a book (*Moby Dick,* for example) can be read in different ways by different people. One reader may have an eye toward the narrative as a thrilling sea adventure, while another may appreciate the symbolism of the whale's whiteness. The danger is in *assuming* what pleases others and how it pleases, to the point of denying opportunities for other experiences. Teachers who assume "her type does not like to read," may stop offering her books. If a teacher believes that a student will not enjoy a particular kind of learning experience, he or she may be denying the student necessary opportunities to develop (Hammer, 1985). These lessons were learned "the hard way" in uses and misuses of learning styles theory and should not have to be relearned.

**9.** Preferences should not be used to make decisions during hiring, voting, or similar selection processes. Their appropriate use is to explain a job or a role requirement to an applicant in terms of what it entails, allowing the applicant to determine whether or not he or she perceives a goodness-of-fit (*Type Reporter, 37*).

**10.** All good teaching methods have value for some students at certain times and in particular places. By the same token, each method will be received differently by each student (Murphy, 1987*a*). (Recall the analogy of the garment mentioned above.)

**11.** Valuing individual differences will require more than merely tolerating them. It means accepting the fact that people *are* different and the world is the better for the diversity (Murphy, 1987*a*).

**12.** Teacher preparation programs must be more enterprising and effective in preparing graduates to have a superlative ability to understand individual differences among educator colleagues as well as students.

**13.** Much more research is needed on the constructive use of individual differences, especially in the area of school consultation, collaboration, and working in professional teams.

## Effects of Cultural Diversity on School Consultation and Collaboration

After generations of being hailed as a cultural melting pot, the United States now is more appropriately referred to as a "salad bowl." Each component of the salad bowl has its own flavor and piquancy, but contributes significantly to the integrity and value of the whole. In a similar vein, each cultural, racial, ethnic, and religious group contributes to the value of the whole. The melting pot and salad bowl metaphors underscore ideas that form the crux of multicultural sensitivity at this point in history. As Hallahan and Kauffman propose (1991):

- Cultural diversity is to be valued.
- Common cultural values hold our society together.

Culture is composed of six major elements (Banks, 1988; Hallahan and Kauffman, 1991):

1. values and behavioral styles;
2. languages and dialects;
3. nonverbal communication;
4. awareness of one's cultural distinctiveness;
5. frames of reference, or normative world views and perspectives; and
6. identification, or feeling a part of the cultural group.

These six elements comprise a nation's culture (the macroculture), while smaller cultures (the microcultures) contain unique variations of them (Hallahan and Kauffman, 1991). Educators need to understand the microculture of exceptionality and its relationship to other microcultures within the macroculture.

Different regions of the country are becoming more unlike in important ways, so a policy or practice which benefits one region may be questionable or objectionable in another (Hodgkinson, 1985). Demographers project that by the year 2000, America will be a nation in which one of every three persons is nonwhite. Minorities will cover a broader socio-economic range than ever before, making simplistic treatment of their needs even less useful (Hodgkinson, 1985.) More and more, the educational system will be called on during the next several decades to serve new pluralities. Old concepts about cultural affiliations will no longer suffice. As just one example, the term *Asian-American* does not differentiate between Japanese and Korean, nor does *Hispanic* differentiate between Puerto Rican and Chicano.

## Assessing Multicultural Awareness among Educators

Hallahan and Kauffman (1991) stress that teachers must become comfortable with their own microcultural identification. Only after they have assessed their own attitudes and values toward cultural diversity will they be able to promote understanding and appreciation of diverse cultural groups. Educators must examine their spoken and unspoken attitudes about cultures different from their own, taking care to ferret out narrow viewpoints and shallow thinking. As an example of a teacher's narrow perspective, a student of native American heritage brought home from school a program with an illustration of "The Pilgrims' First Thanksgiving." The child's father was indignant on reading the caption under the illustration: "They served pumpkins and turkeys and corn and squash. The Indians had never seen such a feast!" (Dorris, 1979).

Sample items for assessing one's multicultural awareness are provided in Figure 4–1. The items can be used for personal reflection and self-study. Discussion of the items and expansion of the list would comprise a powerful staff development activity.

Efforts in the last several years to raise cultural awareness and improve the skills of educators for working with minority students and families have not caught up with the large cultural gap in many schools and communities (Preston et al., 1984). Problems in assuring truly multicultural education are compounded by the lack of minority group personnel in special education.

## Avoiding Confusion between Ethnicity and Exceptionality

Hallahan and Kauffman (1991) state the need to distinguish between ethnicity and exceptionality in serving students with special needs. In focusing on this need, they draw on Banks's definition of an ethnic group as one that shares a common ancestry, culture, history, tradition, and sense of peoplehood in becoming a political and economic interest group (Banks, 1988). Multicultural education relating to students with special needs must ensure that ethnicity is not mistaken for exceptionality (Hallahan and Kauffman, 1991). The word *disadvantaged* should not be paired with *cultural*. The more appropriate term is *cultural diversity*, and *not* cultural disadvantage. Ethnic standards for particular groups should not be held up as measuring sticks for standards of other groups. Doing so might cause individuals to be labeled as exceptional by virtue of their deviance and misfit in other groups.

*A = Always; U = Usually; S = Sometimes; R = rarely; N = Never*

*Personal Effort*

_____ 1. I realize that any individual in a group may not have the same values as others in the group.

_____ 2. I avoid words, statements, expressions, and actions members of other culture groups could find offensive.

_____ 3. I read books and articles to increase my understanding and sensitivity about the hopes, strengths, and concerns of people from other cultures.

_____ 4. I counteract prejudicial, stereotypical thinking and talking whenever and wherever I can.

*School Context*

_____ 5. I include contributions of minority populations as an integral part of the school curriculum.

_____ 6. I strive to nurture skills and develop values in students and colleagues that will help members of minority groups thrive in the dominant culture.

_____ 7. I know where to obtain bias-free, multicultural materials for use in my school.

_____ 8. I have evaluated the school resource materials to determine whether or not they contain fair and appropriate presentation of minority groups.

*Parent/Community Relations*

_____ 9. I invite parents and community from various cultural backgrounds to be classroom resources, speakers, visiting experts, or assistants.

_____ 10. I value having a school staff composed of people from different cultural backgrounds.

_____ 11. I exhibit displays showing culturally diverse people working and socializing together.

_____ 12. I advocate for schools in which all classes, including special education classes, reflect and respect diversity.

**FIGURE 4–1  Examples of Multicultural Assessment Items**

Cross-cultural variations have important effects on collaborative problem solving. Examples of ethnically based values and behaviors that affect group interaction are preferences regarding (Sue and Sue, 1990):

- Proxemics (personal space), such as physical distance between communicants and arrangement of furniture for seating.
- Kinesics (or body movement), such as posture, facial expression, and eye contact.
- Time orientation.
- Paralanguage (vocal cues beyond words), such as loudness, hesitations, inflections, and speed; and both verbal and nonverbal messages.

The consultant can model respect for diversity and assist other school personnel in cultivating the ethnic identity of students through classroom activities that range from traditional through atraditional styles. This reduces stereotyping and accommodates diversity, much to the advantage of multicultural students with special needs (Heron and Harris, 1987).

Consultants will want to encourage parents of students from culturally diverse groups to become involved in their child's education to the greatest extent possible. However, Heron and Harris (1987) caution that parent training programs must demonstrate respect for parents' language, culture, knowledge, and environmental constraints, when these exist. Barriers to active parent participation include work responsibilities, time conflicts, transportation problems, and child care needs. These findings (Lynch and Stein, 1990) have been supported across all ethnic and income groups. One study determined that Hispanic families were satisfied with their children's special education programs but less knowledgeable about them and less involved than parents of Anglos and blacks receiving special services (Lynch and Stein, 1990). See Chapter 11 for further discussion on parent involvement.

### Language Needs of Students from Culturally Diverse Groups

Linguistics will play a major role in the ways parents and school personnel communicate about students (Lynch and Stein, 1990). Non-English speaking students in the schools present major new challenges in education. Consultants should consider language and culture as means to appropriate programs and not as ends (Baca and Cervantes, 1984; Heron and Harris, 1987). The cultural background of many minorities dictates different patterns of communication (Sue and Sue, 1990). School personnel will need to articulate student needs carefully so that suitable programs are designed for special needs students who are from culturally diverse populations.

There has been much emphasis in recent years on programs for bilingual education and English as a second language. Bilingual education is a controversial area, with educators not in agreement about the most effective processes. However, it does seem that bilingual programs using both English and non-English languages for instruction are more beneficial than those emphasizing only one language (Heron and Harris, 1987). English as a Second Language (ESL) is a program that can be offered independently or incorporated into bilingual programs.

### Needs of Rural and Isolated Populations

What is rural? Perhaps more than anything else, it is a state of mind—an "I can do it" attitude growing out of the necessity of functioning independently without the built-in support system that is more available in urban settings (Teagarden, 1989). Rural schools in remote areas are characterized by geographic isolation, cultural isolation, too few students for some kinds of grouping, too few staff members covering too many curricular and special program areas, resistance of students to being singled out, limited resources, and most of all, distance that necessitates great amounts of personnel time spent in travel. Some special education resource personnel spend up to half of their workday on the road (Meyen and Skrtic, 1988). The consulting teacher has become a mainstay of school districts in which miles and more miles separate students who have special learning and behavior needs.

Communication is more likely to be person-to-person in rural areas, whereas it may be written or phoned in urban settings. In the rural setting, teachers are highly visible, therefore more vulnerable to community pressure and criticism. Rural educators are left much to themselves to solve problems and acquire skills for their roles (Thurston and Kimsey, 1989). These qualities of rural school life create advantages for consulting teacher approaches, yet certain disadvantages for the indirect service delivery. Few rural schools are fully prepared and able to meet the needs of special needs students without consulting and indirect services. Therefore, it is necessary for consultants and consulting teachers to become intensively involved in providing learning options and alternatives for students. The consulting teacher can coordinate collaborative effort among teachers, administrators, parents, and other community members so that few resources seem like more.

In a comparative study of consultant roles and responsibilities in rural and urban areas, Thurston and Kimsey (1989) found that rural and urban teachers conduct similar consulting activities, but rural teachers have less formal recognition of their consulting roles. They seem less confident in their consulting skills than their urban counterparts. Major obstacles include too many other responsibilities, no time, lack of administrative support, travel hardships, and too much paperwork. In contrast, obstacles for urban-area consulting teachers include too many other responsibilities, too much paperwork, and disinterested parents.

In no other setting is the positive ripple effect, or multiplier effect, more useful than in rural areas with limited access and resources. These multiplier benefits can be maximized by playing on the strengths of the rural community, including smaller class sizes, more frequent interaction between students and staff, greater involvement of parents in the school and its activities, and active students who participate in most phases of school life. Rural-area students tend to be resourceful, open to a wide range of experiences, somewhat independent, and capable of self-direction. These pluses can be used to advantage by consultants in designing collaborative arrangements for special needs. Students in rural areas often dislike being singled out; therefore, it is important to involve them in planning learning programs in which they are comfortable and interested.

## Needs of Military-Dependent Students

Military-dependent children and youth, and others who move frequently, are largely overlooked as a population having special needs who can benefit significantly from consultation services. When families move from site to site, they frequently become frustrated with the tangled web of records, referrals, screenings, and conferences. They need accurate, clear records to ease their transition from school to school. Consultants can be a lifeline for military and other students who move frequently by assisting busy classroom teachers with coordination and synchronization of student records and coordination of orientation activities and conferences.

Consultants also can facilitate the integration of students into activities with their new peers. Much more could be done in the way of making military-dependent and transitory students feel welcome in new environments. Curricular units and learning centers that highlight their travels and former experiences would be constructive for other students even as they make the military dependent child feel more welcome. Their strengths can be used to remediate gaps they may have incurred from dissimilar educational programs and frequent adjustments to new situations. Furthermore, students who have traveled widely can be valuable resources for their classmates and teachers.

## Practices for Promoting Multicultural Education

Educators will want to design activities that not only reduce prejudice and stereotyping, but promote the contributions from culturally diverse groups representing minority populations. Multicultural education is not an activity for the last thirty minutes of school on Friday. The principles of multicultural awareness and acceptance should be infused throughout the entire school program. Consultant roles can be particularly facilitative and supportive in this endeavor. The consultant can assist in assessing the instructional environment and designing effective instruction for culturally diverse groups.

The hidden curriculum is a critical area for multicultural awareness and acceptance. Informal discussions, bulletin board displays, selections read to the class, speakers brought into the classroom—all are helpful if planned carefully. Selected teaching activities can promote an acceptance of and even a fascination for differences, as well as an allowance for different opinions and points of view, and an increased understanding of how people sometimes are limited by their cultural assumptions. Consultants must work to ensure the hidden curriculum builds, and does not destroy, positive attitudes and understanding.

Consultants also are in a position to encourage fuller use of the resources within the entire community. They might bring in successful citizens who represent culturally diverse groups to tell about their heritage, their interests, and their roles in society. They might pair these resource people with students having special needs, particularly if these people have the same cultural background as the student. Since studies show that ethnically diverse parents tend to be less knowledgeable about and involved in their children's education than other parents (Ramirez, 1990; Lynch and Stein, 1990), consultants will be challenged to find ways of collaborating with them to inform and involve them. Awareness, appreciation and sensitivity toward individual differences and cultural diversity are vital attributes for consultants as they communicate, cooperate, and coordinate with a wide range of resource and support personnel, teachers, parents, and the students themselves.

## Consultants as Links among Social Agents

A vast array of social service agencies exists for serving students with special needs; however, their services often overlap and many are large, unwieldy bureaucracies with a maze of bewildering requirements (Guthrie and Guthrie, 1991; Hodgkinson, 1989). The situation calls for extensive collaboration among agencies for productive integration of services.

Educators may be the most feasible linkage in developing cooperation and coordination among organizations and agencies which serve children with special needs. Special educators, from experience and professional training, recognize the strengths and the needs of children and the families who nurture them. As budget constraints restrict the continuation or growth of many educational and social programs, special education consultants can play pivotal roles in the future for serving children with special needs. They are in good positions to become effective, cost-efficient links between education and other social agencies.

It will be a challenge for educators to form new paradigms that decompartmentalize services for students with special needs. Guthrie and Guthrie (1991) state that service providers must step outside the boundaries of their job descriptions on occasion to do what needs to be done for students. They suggest going to community centers, schools, and homes, devoting more time than usual to families and outside resources. These functions are compatible with the processes and content familiar to those in school consultation roles. Guthrie and Guthrie warn against the "all-talk, no action" posture, excessive jargon, and failure to follow up. These points are readily recognizable to school consultants, who have developed skill in avoiding such pitfalls.

Collaboration and team effort can begin in any agency. These strategies become powerful forces for education when they create positive ripple effects for students in schools, social services, business partnerships, and most of all, neighborhoods and homes.

## Tips for Consulting and Collaborating

1.   Listen to the other person's point of view. Seek to understand the content of the person's ideas and the meaning it has for that person.

2.   Encourage each member of a collaborative group to share knowledge and perceptions about an issue, in order to establish a solid framework in which to discuss the issue.

3.   Take the time to assess preferences of consultees before deciding upon a consultation method.

**4.** Encourage input from as many sources as possible when deliberating upon a difficult problem, in order to take advantage of many styles, preferences, and cultural perspectives.

**5.** Appreciate perceptions and preferences different from one's own by engaging in a dialectical conversation. Do not feel that it is necessary to change your position, or to convert the other person to your position.

**6.** When students with special needs are mainstreamed, share with their receiving teachers any helpful information about the students' learning styles and preferences; however, take care not to stereotype students or alter teacher expectations inappropriately.

**7.** Everyone is not an expert at everything. Find ways to acknowledge and use suggestions from others.

**8.** Respect the rights of others to hold different beliefs. While one may not agree with others, one must assume they are acting in ways they believe appropriate.

**9.** Really care about another person's feelings and ideas, and show it through actions.

**10.** There is always a reason that people do or say the things they do, so try to discover it.

## Chapter Review

**1.** Most educators are attuned to the need for responding to individual differences of their students; however, little attention has been given to individual differences among school personnel and ways in which those differences affect the school context and professional interactions.

**2.** Adult differences affect professional interactions in communicating, identifying problems, generating solutions to problems, and evaluating performance.

**3.** Before educators attempt to understand the uniqueness and individuality of their colleagues, they should analyze their own preferences and individuality.

**4.** Problems caused by disharmony between opposite types can be lessened when the basis of the disagreement is understood. Adult differences can be used to advantage in teamwork and problem solving. When all preferences are available through contribution of varying preferences among team members, all facets of a problem can be studied and a wide range of options generated.

**5.** School consultants are ideal for infusing multicultural education into the school context. They can facilitate greater parent involvement from culturally diverse populations, coordinate bilingual and English-as-a-second-language programs, and develop awareness and sensitivity toward needs of culturally diverse groups. Their services are particularly valuable in rural areas, as well as with military dependent children and others who move frequently.

**6.** School consultants recognize the strengths as well as the needs of children and youth; therefore, they can serve an important role in promoting integrated programming among all agencies that are involved with a child's development. They are in excellent positions to link the personnel and the services of school, social agencies, business partnerships, homes, and other community organizations into collaborative efforts that will help students who have special needs.

## Activities

**1.** Discuss ways that provocative issues related to individual preferences and styles might be explored without endangering professional collegiality and school morale.

**2.** Design a bulletin board that celebrates individual differences among adults.

**3.** Interview teachers from schools having multicultural populations, asking them to suggest ways in which consultation and collaboration might help meet students' special needs. What steps should be taken to carry out these ideas?

## For Further Reading

Jersild, A. T. (1955). *When Teachers Face Themselves*. New York: Teachers College Press, Columbia University.

*Journal of Psychological Type* (formerly named Research in Psychological Type). All issues.

Jung, C. G. (1923). *Psychological Types*. New York: Harcourt Brace.

Keirsey, D., and Bates, M. (1978). *Please Understand Me*. Del Mar, CA: Prometheus Nemesis.

Kummerow, J. M., and McAllister, L. W. (1988). Team-building with the Myers-Briggs type indicator: Case studies. *Journal of Psychological Type, 15*: 26–32.

Lawrence, G. (1982). *People Types and Tiger Stripes: A Practical Guide to Learning Styles* (2d ed.). Gainesville, FL: Center for Applications of Psychological Type, Inc.

Morsink, C. V., Thomas, C. C., and Correa, V. I. (1991). *Interactive Teaming: Consultation and Collaboration in Special Programs*. New York: Macmillan. Chapter 6, on considering cultural diversity in the interactive process, and Chapter 10, on implementation with culturally diverse students.

Myers, I. B. (1980). *Gifts Differing*. Palo Alto, CA: Consulting Psychologists Press.

Sue, D. W., and Sue, D. (1990). *Counseling the Culturally Different: Theory and Practice* (2d ed.). New York: Wiley.

## References

Baca, L. M., and Cervantes, H. T. (1984). *The Bilingual Special Education Interface*. Columbus, OH: Merrill.

Banks, J. A. (1988). Multiethnic education and practice (2nd ed.). Boston: Allyn & Bacon.

Banks, J. A., and McGee Banks, C. A. (1989). *Multicultural education: Issues and Perspectives*. Needham Heights, MA: Allyn and Bacon.

Blaylock, B. K. (1983). Teamwork in a simulated production environment. *Research in Psychological Type, 6:* 58–67.

Brown, D., Wyne, M. D., Blackburn, J. E., and Powell, W. C. (1979). *Consultation: Strategy for Improving Education.* Boston: Allyn and Bacon.

Campbell, D. E., and Kain, J. M. (1990). Personality type and mode of information presentation: Preference, accuracy, and efficiency in problem-solving. *Journal for Psychological Type, 20:* 47–51.

Carlyn, M. (1977). An assessment of the Myers-Briggs type indicator. *Journal of Personality Assessment, 41*(5): 461–473.

Clancy, S. G. (1985). Psychological type as context for understanding group effectiveness. *MBTI News, 7* (2), 3-4.

Dettmer, P. (1981). The effects of teacher personality type on classroom values and perceptions of gifted students. *Research in Psychological Type, 3:* 48–54.

Dorris, M. (1979). Why I'm not thankful for Thanksgiving. *Midwest Race Desegregation Assistance Center Horizons, 1*(5): 1.

Dunn, R., and Dunn, K. (1978). *Teaching Students through Their Individual Learning Styles* Reston, VA: Reston Publishing.

Gallessich, J. (1973). Organizational factors influencing consultation in schools. *Journal of School Psychology, 11*(1): 57–65.

Gregorc, A. F., and Ward, H. B. (1977). A new definition for individual: Implications for learning and teaching. *NASSP Bulletin, 61:* 20–26.

Guthrie, G. P., and Guthrie, L. F. (1991). Streamlining interagency collaboration for youth at risk. *Educational Leadership, 49*(1): 17–22.

Hall, C. S., and Lindzey, G. (1978). *Theories of Personality* (3d ed.). New York: Wiley.

Hallahan, D. P., and Kauffman, J. M. (1991). *Exceptional Children: Introduction to Special Education.* Englewood Cliffs, NJ: Prentice Hall.

Hammer, A. L. (1985). Typing or stereotyping: Unconscious bias in applications of psychological type theory. *Journal of Psychological Type, 10:* 14–18.

Heron, T. E., and Harris, K. C. (1987). *The Educational Consultant: Helping Professionals, Parents, and Mainstreamed Students* (2d ed.). Austin: TX: PRO-ED.

Hodgkinson, H. L. (1985). *All One System: Demographics of Education, Kindergarten through Graduate School.* Washington, D.C.: American Council on Education.

Hodgkinson, H. L. (1989). *The Same Client: The Demographics of Education and Service Delivery Systems.* Washington, D.C.: Institute for Educational Leadership, Center for Demographic Policy.

Hoffman, J. L. (1986). Educational administrators: Psychological types. *Journal of Psychological Type, 11:* 64–67.

Hunter, M. (1985). Promising theories die young. *ASCD Update,* May 1985, 1, 3.

Jersild, A. T. (1955). *When Teachers Face Themselves.* New York: Teachers College Press, Columbia University.

Jung, C. G. (1923). *Psychological Types.* New York: Harcourt Brace.

Jung, C. G. (1954). *The Development of Personality* (R.F. C. Hull, trans.). New York: Pantheon.

Keefe, J. W., and Ferrell, B. G. (1990). Developing a defensible learning style paradigm. *Educational Leadership, 48*(2): 57–61.

Keirsey, D. and Bates, M. (1978). *Please Understand Me: Character and Temperament Types.* Del Mar, CA: Prometheus Nemesis.

Kolb, D. A. (1976). *Learning-Style inventory: Technical Manual.* Boston: McBer and Co.

Kummerow, J. M. and McAllister, L. W. (1988). Teambuilding with the Myers-Briggs Type Indicator: Case studies. *Journal of Psychological Type, 15:* 26–32.

Lawrence, G. (1982). *People Types and Tiger Stripes.* Gainesville, FL: Center for Applications of Psychological Type.

Lawrence, G. (1984). A synthesis of learning style research involving the MBTI. *Journal of Psychological Type, 8:* 2–15.

Lawrence, G. (September, 1988). *Type and Stereotype: Sorting out the Differences.* Speech presented at the 1988 conference of Association for Psychological Type—Southwest, Albuquerque, NM.

Lawrence, G., and DeNovellis, R. (1974). Correlation of teacher personality variables (Myers-Briggs) and classroom observation data. Paper presented at American Educational Research Association conference.

Luft, J. (1984). (3rd ed.) *Group Processes: An Introduction to Group Dynamics.* Palo Alto, CA: Mayfield Publishing.

Lynch, E. W., and Stein, R. C. (1990). Parent participation by ethnicity: Comparison of Hispanic, Black, and Anglo families. *Educating*

*Exceptional Children* (5th ed.). Guilford, CT: Dushkin.

McCarthy, B. (1990). Using the 4MAT system to bring learning styles to schools. *Educational Leadership, 48*(2): 31–37.

Meyen, E. L., and Skrtic, T. N. (eds.). (1988). *Exceptional Children and Youth: An Introduction,* (3rd ed.). Denver: Love.

Meyer, S. (May, 1977). Personal correspondence.

Morsink, C. V., Thomas, C. C., and Correa, V. I. (1991). *Interactive teaming: Consultation and collaboration in special programs.* New York: Macmillan.

Murphy, E. (1987a). *I Am a Good Teacher.* Gainesville, FL: Center for Applications of Psychological Type.

Murphy, E. (1987b). *Questions children may have about type differences.* Gainesville, Fl: Center for Applications of Psychological Type.

Myers, I. B. (1962). *The Myers-Briggs Type Indicator Manual.* Palo Alto, CA: Consulting Psychologists Press.

Myers, I. B. (1974). *Type and Teamwork.* Gainesville, FL: Center for Applications of Psychological Type.

Myers, I. B. (October 16, 1975). Making the most of individual gifts. Keynote address at the first national conference on the uses of the Myers-Briggs Type Indicator. Gainesville, FL: University of Florida.

Myers, I. B. (1980a). *Gifts Differing.* Palo Alto, CA: Consulting Psychologists Press.

Myers, I. B. (1980b). *Introduction to Type.* Palo Alto, CA: Consulting Psychologists Press.

Myers, I. B., and McCaulley, M. H. (1985). *Manual: A Guide to the Development and Use of the Myers-Briggs Type Indicator.* Palo Alto, CA: Consulting Psychologists Press.

Preston, D., Greenwood, C. R., Hughes, V., Yuen, P., Thibadeau, S., Critchlow, W., and Harris J. (1984). Minority issues in special education: A principal-mediated inservice program for teachers. *Exceptional Children, 51*: 112–121.

Ramirez, B. A. (1990). Culturally and linguistically diverse children. *Educating Exceptional Children* (5th ed.). Guilford, CT: Dushkin.

Staff. "I don't think it's right to type people." *Type Reporter 37*: 1–4.

Sue, D. W., and Sue, D. (1990). *Counseling the Culturally Different: Theory and Practice* (2d ed.). New York: Wiley.

Teagarden, J. (Spring, 1989). Acres Wrap-up from a Teacher's Perspective. *Take Heart*, p. 4. Manhattan, KS: Kansas State University.

Thurston, L. P., and Kimsey, I. (1989). Rural special education teachers as consultants: Roles and responsibilities. *Educational Considerations, 17*(1): 40–43.

Truesdell, C. B. (1983). The MBTI: A win-win strategy for work teams. *MBTI News 5*: 8–9.

# 5

# PROBLEM-SOLVING STRATEGIES FOR CONSULTATION, COLLABORATION AND TEAMWORK

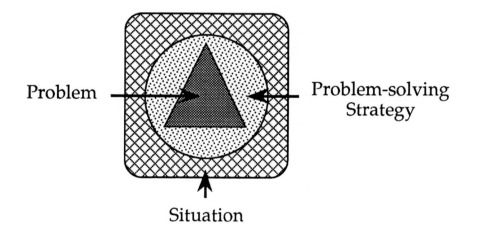

Problem — Problem-solving Strategy

Situation

## *To Think About*

The development of a structured format for consultation is integral to promotion of collaboration and teamwork among educators. Using a consulting process within a structured format is like preparing food according to a recipe. After the fundamental processes have been mastered, proficient cooks can adapt their procedures to just about any setting, individual need, preference, or creative impulse. In similar fashion, a basic "recipe" for consultation, once mastered, can be adapted to any school context, grade level, content area, or special learning need.

Consultation and collaboration increase the flexibility and expand the teachers' repertoire for identifying both student and personnel needs, and for developing plans to address the needs resourcefully. When consulting teachers, classroom teachers, support personnel, and parents complement and reinforce each other by using effective problem-solving methods and strategies, schools will become better places for learning.

## *Focusing Questions*

1. What are the fundamental components in a problem-solving process?
2. In what ways are communication, cooperation, and coordination needed in the consultation process?
3. Why is problem identification so important in consultation and collaboration?
4. What basic steps should be included in the consultation process?
5. What kinds of things should consultants and consultees say and do during their professional interaction?
6. What group problem-solving tools and techniques are particularly helpful for consultants and collaborators?

## *Key Terms*

| | |
|---|---|
| brainstorming | POCS (problem, options, consequences, |
| concept mapping | solution) |
| follow-up | problem identification |
| idea checklist | problem-solving process |
| interfering themes | process for consultation |
| lateral thinking | |

---

**Scenario**

The setting is the office area of an elementary school, where a special-education staff member has just checked into the building and meets a fourth-grade teacher.

*CLASSROOM TEACHER*: I understand you are going to be a consulting teacher in our building to work with learning and behavioral disorders.

*CONSULTING TEACHER*: That's right. I hope to meet with all staff very soon to determine your needs and work together on plans for addressing those needs.

CLASSROOM TEACHER: Well I, for one, am glad you're here. I have a student who is driving me and my other twenty-four students up the wall.

CONSULTING TEACHER: In what way?

CLASSROOM TEACHER: Since she moved here a few weeks ago, she has managed to upset completely the classroom system that I've used successfully for years.

CONSULTING TEACHER: Is your new student having trouble with the material you teach?

CLASSROOM TEACHER: No, she is a bright child who finishes everything in good time, and usually correctly, I might add. But she is extremely active, almost frenetic as she busy-bodies around the room making a nuisance of herself.

CONSULTING TEACHER: What specific behaviors concern you?

CLASSROOM TEACHER: Well, for one thing, she tries to help everyone else when they should be doing their own work. I've worked a lot on developing independent learning skills in my students, and they've made good progress. They don't need to have her tell them what to do.

CONSULTING TEACHER: So her behavior keeps her classmates from being the self-directed learners they can be?

CLASSROOM TEACHER: Right. I have to monitor her activities constantly, so my attention is diverted time after time from students I'm working with. She bosses her classmates in the learning centers and even when they play organized games outside. At this rate she will have serious difficulties with peer relationships.

CONSULTING TEACHER: Which of those behaviors would you like to see changed first?

CLASSROOM TEACHER: Well, I need to get her settled into some additional activities by herself rather than bothering other students.

CONSULTING TEACHER: What have you tried until now to keep her involved with her own work?

CLASSROOM TEACHER: We use assertive discipline in this school, so when she disrupts, I put her name on the board. By the way, the parents don't like this at all.

CONSULTING TEACHER: We could make a list of specific changes in behavior you would like to see and work out a program to accomplish them. . . There's the bell. Shall we meet tomorrow to do that?

CLASSROOM TEACHER: Sounds good. I'd like to get her on track so the class is more settled. The other children will like her better and she will be able to learn other things, too. *And* the parents will be happier as well. I'll see you here tomorrow. This consulting process may be just what we need!

# The Problem-Solving Process

Educators today must focus on a multitude of student needs and educational goals. This requires astute judgment, in order to select the most effective and efficient means of maximizing gains for all students' educational goals (Lanier, 1982). It also necessitates information from a variety of sources, in order to be knowledgeable about methods and materials that will serve diverse needs of students in a wide range of school contexts. Educators must focus on identifying learning and behavior problems and making appropriate decisions about educational programs. In order to do so, they need excellent problem-solving skills. Problem-solving ability comes more naturally and easily to some than to others. It is not likely that most problem-solving activity is carried out by any specific formula or "recipe." But skills for solving problems efficiently and effectively, particularly in groups, can be improved with training and practice. For this kind of professional development, it is helpful to begin with a fundamental problem-solving process.

Gordon (1977) outlines six steps for solving problems effectively:

1. identification and definition of the problem,
2. generation of alternative solutions,
3. evaluation of alternative solutions,
4. decision-making,
5. implementing the decisions, and
6. following up to evaluate the solution.

These components include the basic elements of the problem-solving processes that are most frequently employed in a wide variety of business and professional areas. It can be helpful to use the thought experiment concept introduced in an earlier chapter to picture the problem-solving process. A graphic illustration of the problem-solving process could be pictured by someone as a stepwise procedure (see Figure 5–1). A colleague might have fun depicting the problem-solving process as a fishing trip to come up with solutions to the problem (see Figure 5–2). Another might portray the process as a mechanic would approach problem solving (see Figure 5–3). Graphic representations are useful when discussing collaboration and teamwork with consultees and with the administrators who assist with consultation structures.

## *Communication, Cooperation, and Coordination in Problem Solving*

Communication, cooperation, and coordination are basic ingredients of good consultation. A problem-solving process that reflects high levels of each of these will allow educators to share expertise bearing on the problem. Learning and behavior problems are not always outcomes of student deficits. Many students are simply "curriculum disabled" (Conoley, 1985), needing a modified or expanded approach to existing curriculum so they can function successfully in school (Pugach and Johnson, 1990). In order to modify the learning environment both in school and at home, consultation must identify those aspects of students' educational programs that are interfering with their development.

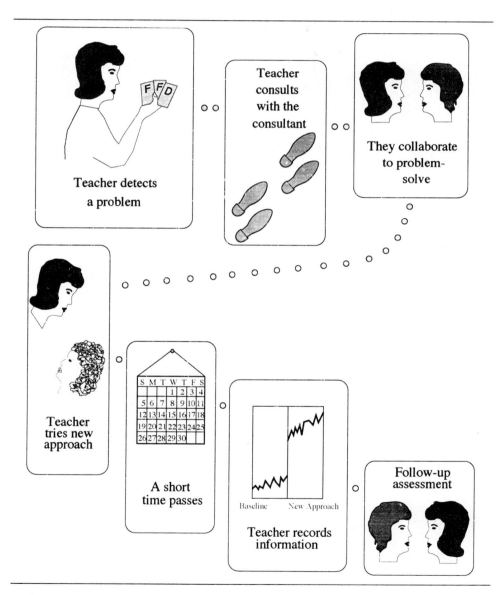

**FIGURE 5–1   Step by Step Problem Solving**

by Jane More Loeb

**FIGURE 5–2 Catching the Solution**

by Eileen Vega

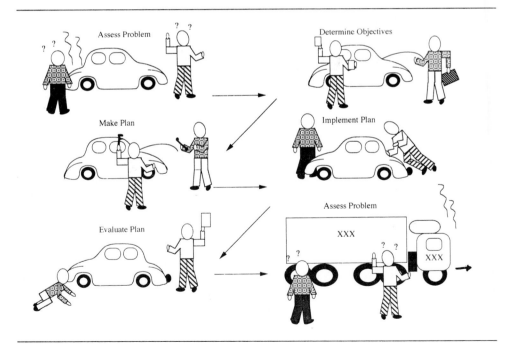

**FIGURE 5–3 "Tuning Up" for Success**

by Robin Corbin

*Interfering Themes* Consultation provides an arena in which to address four interfering themes which can restrict an educator's ability to facilitate student development. These interfering themes, identified by Caplan (1970), include:

lack of knowledge about students' needs;
lack of skills in dealing with the needs;
lack of confidence in using appropriate strategies; and
lack of objectivity in assessing the situation.

During collaboration, consultants should use every opportunity to reinforce the efforts and successes of classroom teachers and also convey a desire to learn from them and their experiences. Too often, classroom teachers, who occupy the lowest position in a hierarchy of specialists (Pugach, 1988), and parents, who can be somewhat detached from the school setting, are overlooked as possibilities for solutions when learning and behavior problems are explored.

When communicating and cooperating with consultees to identify the learning or behavior need, it is important that consultants avoid sending messages intimating that classroom teachers and parents are deficient in skills only special education teachers can provide (Friend and Cook, 1990; Huefner, 1988; Idol, Paolucci-Whitcomb, and Nevin, 1986). Nurturance of communication skills and cooperative attitudes will encourage feelings of parity and voluntariness among all school personnel and parents during the problem-solving process. Students who are assigned to resource settings in other schools for part of the week or school day may have teachers in each setting who never communicate about those students and their programs. This is a serious drawback of some cluster group arrangements in which students travel from one school to another, and no planned interaction among school personnel takes place.

Coordination of collaborative effort is a necessity. Special education teachers who cannot identify basal reading curriculum used in various levels, and classroom teachers who cannot identify the nature of instruction taking place in the resource room, make problem identification more difficult (Idol, West, and Lloyd, 1988). They may even intensify the problem. All parties must think about their own roles in the problem situation and endeavor to learn from each other by interacting, deferring judgment, and coordinating their services.

A team approach can be a most productive way to assess the context, conditions, interfering themes, and circumstances surrounding the student's needs and the school programs designed to meet those needs. A noted politician who had been endeavoring to get his colleagues to cooperate and collaborate reminded them that astronomers from all parts of the world collaborate because there is no one place from which every part of the sky can be observed. This message is cogent to educators as well, who need to observe each student and consider all needs in the cognitive, affective, emotional, physical, and social domains while problem solving for student programs. The perceptions and perspectives of each educator, including parents, are invaluable in identifying learning or behavior problems of students and developing goals to remediate the problems.

## The POCS Method of Problem Solving

The value of communication, cooperation, and coordination in collaborative problem solving can be stressed through use of the POCS method of problem solving (Thurston, 1987):

> *problem* identification (P),
> generating *options* (O),
> determining the *consequences* (C), and
> planning the *solution* (S).

A worksheet of POCS (problem, options, consequences, and solution) for taking notes on ideas generated is helpful for consultants as a problem-solving guide (see Figure 5–4).

**The Problem.**   The first and most critical step in the POCS method of problem solving is to identify the problem (Schein, 1969; Bolton, 1986). The most sophisticated teaching methods and the most expensive instructional materials are worthless if the student need is misidentified or overlooked. It can even be argued that inaccurate definition of the problem situation has potential for iatrogenic results. These hurt more than help, just as identifying an illness incorrectly can delay help or cause inappropriate medication that might be seriously counterproductive.

Problem identification requires special emphasis, if the consultation process is to produce results. In problem identification, consultation variables such as interview skills, flexibility, and efficiency have greatest impact on problem solving (Bergan and Tombari, 1976). Consultants who are skilled in problem analysis are most able to identify appropriate target behaviors and develop workable interventions (Bergan and Tombari, 1976). Information on the student's behaviors, discrepancies between current and desired performance, and baseline data are needed to determine the level of potential target behaviors (Polsgrove and McNeil, 1989).

When information about student needs is multisourced, it can give a more accurate perspective on learning and behavior problems, the settings in which they are demonstrated, severity and frequency of the problems, and persons who are affected by those behaviors (Polsgrove and McNeil, 1989). The need for multiple sources of information to help solve problems will be discussed later, in the section on the ten-step consultation process.

Obtaining information from multiple sources requires effective communication skills by all who can contribute information. Communication is such an important aspect of successful school consultation that it is addressed

Problem: _____

_____

Expected Outcome: _____

_____

| *Options* | *Consequences* |
|---|---|
| 1. _____ | _____ |
| 2. _____ | _____ |
| 3. _____ | _____ |
| 4. _____ | _____ |
| 5. _____ | _____ |
| 6. _____ | _____ |

Chosen Solution: _____

_____

Responsibilities and Commitments: _____

_____

Follow-up Date and Time: _____

**FIGURE 5–4  The POCS Method of Problem-Solving**

separately in Chapter 6. Expressing thoughts and feelings with clarity and accuracy entails effective listening and appropriate assertiveness. The problem will never be solved if all parties think they are working on different issues. Problems are like artichokes—they come in layers. Only after the outside layers are stripped away can problem solvers get to the heart of the matter. Good listening facilitates movement to the heart of the problem.

**Options.**   Problem solving also involves generating options to solve the problem. Brainstorming, or thinking of many solutions without judging or criticizing, is important in order not to get stuck in routines and answers. Some consultants find it helpful to encourage the person who "owns" the problem to make the most suggestions. For example, if the problem is making a decision about post-secondary education for a student with learning disabilities, the student and the parents should be encouraged to generate the most options. This is important for several reasons. When people participate in decision making, they feel more ownership toward the resultant activities than when the decision is forced on them (Wood, 1981). Also, as explained by Johnson and Johnson (1987), people are more apt to support decisions they helped create than those imposed on them, regardless of the merit of the ideas.

An important second reason for prompting the owner of the problem to give initial suggestions is that a consultant should avoid giving advice and being presented or perceived as the expert. Several researchers have shown that the nonexpert model of educational consulting is more successful in special education (Margolis and McGettigan, 1988; Idol-Maestes, Lloyd, and Lilly, 1981). The suggestions and opinions of others need to be listened to with respect and fully understood before additional suggestions are offered.

Finally, teachers and others are more likely to be resistant if the problem-solving process is perceived as advice giving by the consultant. Problems that come up in school consultation often reveal the need for changed classroom practices. This can engender resistance that will not yield to an "I'm the expert and you're not" model. Advice giving and hierarchical structure may be unintentionally communicated if consultants promote the options generated as being their ideas.

If a consultant is regarded as *the* expert, there is pressure on that consultant, and false expectations are created. It is hard to win in this kind of situation. The best practice for the consultant is to communicate equality, flexibility, and a sharing attitude. Three questions assess the equality that is or is not present in a professional consulting relationship:

- Does the consultant recognize the consultee's expertise and opinion?
- Does the consultant encourage the consultee to generate ideas and make decisions?
- Do consultees feel free to *not* do as the consultant might recommend?

Eager, competent consultants who are ready to solve problems and produce quick results, instant cures, and dramatic increases, too often jump in and try to solve problems alone. Consultees may react with resistance, negativism, or hostility by hiding their feelings, withdrawing, or blaming others if things do not work out.

It is difficult for consultants to avoid the "quick fix." But the quick fix is inappropriate (DeBoer, 1986). It is demeaning to the one who has been struggling with the problem. Others need to feel that the consultant fully understands their unique situation and the source of their frustrations before they are ready to participate in problem solving and listen to the suggestions of colleagues. Consultants must listen before they can expect to be listened to, treated with parity, or approached again voluntarily by consultees.

All learning situations and all students are unique. In response to a question about classroom management, a high school teacher replied, "I don't know all the answers, because I haven't seen all the kids." While students and situations may appear similar in some ways, the combinations of student, teacher, parents, and school and home contexts are unique for each problem.

Furthermore, in many cases, people with problems already have their answers. They just need help to clarify issues or an empathic ear to face the emotional aspects of the concern. If people keep talking, they often can solve their own problems. Joint problem identification and idea generating assure that professional relationships are preserved, professional communication is enhanced, and professionals maintain a greater feeling of control and self-esteem.

Good consultants do not solve problems—they see that problems get solved. So they facilitate problem solving, and "nix the quick fix." As Gordon (1977) asks, whose problem is it? Who really owns the problem? Busy consultants do not need to take on the problems of others, and such action would inhibit consultees from learning and practicing problem-solving skills. Everyone who owns a part of the problem should participate in solving it. That may involve collaboration among several people—teachers, administrators, vocational counselors, students, parents, and others. When problem ownership is a question, consultants and consultees should focus on the problem rather than on establishing ownership for the problem. All individuals will need to attend carefully to minimizing roadblocks and maximizing assertion and listening skills.

**Consequences.**  Effective consultants facilitate problem solving in such a way that all members of the group feel their needs are being satisfied and an "equitable" social and professional relationship is being maintained (Gordon, 1977). Members of the problem-solving team work together to evaluate all the suggestions made, with each discussing the disadvantages and merits of the suggestion from his or her own perspective. Agreement is not necessary at this point, because the barriers and merits important to each person are taken into account. Honest and open communication, good listening skills, and the appropriate level of assertiveness, are vital at this step.

**Solution.**  The group selects a workable solution all are willing to adopt, at least on a trial or experimental basis. The consultant promotes mutual participation in the decision. Group members more readily accept new ideas and new work methods when they are given opportunity to participate in decision making (Gordon, 1977). Many times a complex problem can be solved as each person in the group discovers what the others really want or, perhaps, fear. Then solutions can be formulated to meet the goals and protect the concerns of all involved.

In collaborative problem solving, whether using the POCS method or another effective method, the role of the consultant is to facilitate interaction and teamwork. This involves good listening, assertive responses, and successful resolution of conflicts, which will be discussed in greater detail in Chapter 6. Consultation encourages collective thinking for creative and imaginative alternatives and allows all involved to have their feelings and ideas heard and their goals met. The ultimate goal for effective problem solving is to provide the best education possible for children with special needs.

## The Ten-Step Process for Consultation

Now that problem identification, options, consequences, and solution finding have been discussed, it is appropriate to coordinate these activities into a structured consultation process. The ten-step process outlined in Figure 5–5 can help consultants and consultees communicate, cooperate, and coordinate their efforts in identifying educational problems and planning for student needs.

### Step 1: Planning prior to the Consultation

As consultants plan for consultation and collaboration, they focus on the major areas of concern. They prepare helpful materials and organize them in order to use collaborative time efficiently. It is useful to distribute information beforehand so that valuable interaction time is not consumed reading new material. But consultants must take care to present the material as tentative and open to discussion. Of course, it is not always expedient to plan in depth prior to consultations. Sometimes they happen informally and without notice—between classes, during lunch periods, or on playgrounds. While consultants will want to accommodate these occasions for interacting with colleagues, they also need to look beyond them for opportunities to engage in more in-depth sessions.

Consultants will want to provide convenient and comfortable settings for the interaction, arranging seating so there is a collegial atmosphere with no phone or drop-by interruptions. Serving coffee or tea can help set congenial climates for meetings.

### Step 2: Initiating the Consultation

Consultants need to exert much effort in this phase. When resistance to consulting is high, or the teaching staff has been particularly reluctant to collaborate, it will be difficult to establish first contacts. This is the time to begin with the most receptive staff members in order to build in success for the consulting program. Rapport is cultivated by addressing every consultee as special and expressing interest in what each one is doing and feeling. Teachers should be encouraged to talk about their successes. The consultant needs to display sensitivity to teachers' needs and make each one feel important. The key is to *listen*.

1. Plan prior to the consultation.

   1.1 Focus upon major topic or area of concern.
   1.2 Prepare and organize materials.
   1.3 Prepare several possible actions or strategies.
   1.4 Arrange for a comfortable, convenient meeting place.

2. Initiate the consultation.

   2.1 Establish rapport.
   2.2 Identify the agenda.
   2.3 Focus on the tentatively defined concern.
   2.4 Express interest in the needs of all.

3. Collect information.

   3.1 Make notes of data, soliciting it from all.
   3.2 Combine and summarize the data.
   3.3 Assess data to focus on areas needing more information.
   3.4 Summarize the information.

4. Identify the problem.

   4.1 Encourage all to listen to each concern.
   4.2 Identify issues, avoiding jargon.
   4.3 Encourage ventilation of frustrations and concerns.
   4.4 Keep focusing on the pertinent issues and needs.
   4.5 Check for agreement.

5. Generate options and alternatives.

   5.1 Engage in collaborative problem solving.
   5.2 Generate several possible options.
   5.3 Suggest examples of appropriate classroom modifications.
   5.4 Review options, discussing consequences of each.
   5.5 Select the most reasonable alternatives.

6. Formulate a plan.

   6.1 Designate those who will be involved, and how.
   6.2 Set goals.
   6.3 Establish responsibilities.
   6.4 Generate evaluation criteria and methods.
   6.5 Agree on a date for reviewing progress.

7. Evaluate progress and process.

   7.1 Conduct a review session at a specified time.
   7.2 Review data and analyze the results.
   7.3 Keep products as evidence of progress.
   7.4 Make positive, supportive comments.
   7.5 Assess contribution of the collaboration.

*(Continued)*

**FIGURE 5–5 The Ten-Step Process for Consultation**

8. Follow up on the situation.

8.1 Reassess periodically to assure maintenance.
8.2 Provide positive reinforcement.
8.3 Plan further action or continue the plan.
8.4 Adjust the plan if there are problems.
8.5 Initiate further consultation if needed.
8.6 Bring closure if goals have been met.

9. Interact informally with the consultee when possible.

9.1 Support effort and reinforce results.
9.2 Share information where it is wanted.
9.3 Enjoy the communication.

10. Repeat consultation as appropriate.

**FIGURE 5–5** *(Continued)*

The consultant will want to identify the agenda and keep focusing on the concern. It is helpful to have participants write down their concerns before the meeting and bring them along. Then the consultant can check quickly for congruence and major disagreements.

## Step 3: Collecting Information

The data should be relevant to the issue of focus. However, data which seem irrelevant to one person may be the very information needed to identify the real problem. So the consultant must be astute in selecting appropriate data that include many possibilities but do not waste time or resources. This becomes easier with experience, but for new consultants, having too much information is probably better than having too little.

Since problem identification seems to be the most significant factor in planning for special needs, it is wise to gather sufficient data from multiple sources. A case-study method of determining data sources and soliciting information is particularly effective in planning for students who have special learning and behavior needs. See Figure 5–6 for a case-study framework that includes up to sixteen data sources to provide information for problem solving. When a number of these sixteen are tapped, the central problem becomes much more clear and easily addressed.

## Step 4: Identifying the Problem

As discussed earlier, the most critical aspect of problem solving is identifying and defining the problem at hand. Bolton (1986) emphasizes that consultants and consultees must define the problem by focusing on the need, not the solution. Without problem identification, problem solving cannot occur (Bergan and

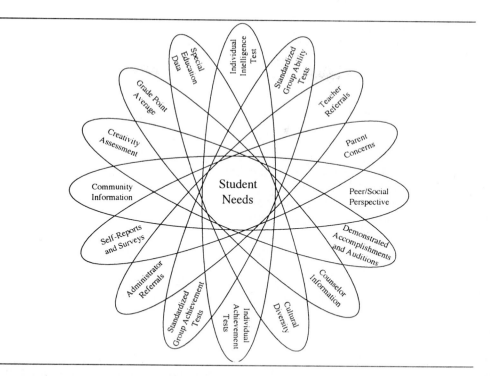

**FIGURE 5-6  Case Study Information**

Tombari, 1976). All concerns and viewpoints relevant to the problem should be aired and shared. A different viewpoint is not better or worse, just different. An effective consultant keeps participants focusing on the student need by listening and encouraging everyone to respond. However, a certain amount of venting and frustration is to be expected and accepted. Teachers and parents will demonstrate less resistance when they know they are free to express their feelings without retaliation or judgment. Consultants should remain nonjudgmental and assure confidentiality, always talking and listening in the consultees' language.

As information is shared, the consultant will want to make notes. It is good to have everyone look over the recorded information from time to time during the consultation as a demonstration of trust and equality, as well as a check on accuracy. (A log format for recording information and documenting the consultation is provided in Chapter 7.)

## Step 5: Generating Options and Alternatives

Now is the time for creative problem solving. If ideas do not come freely, or if participants are blocking productive thinking, the consultant might suggest trying one or more of the techniques described later in the chapter. A problem-solving technique not only unleashes ideas, it sends a message about the kind of behavior that is needed to solve the problem.

### Step 6: Formulating a Plan

Participants should be kept on task and reinforced positively for their contributions. Consultants will want to have suggestions available for sharing, but defer presenting them so long as others are suggesting and volunteering. They must avoid offering solutions prematurely or addressing too many issues at one time. Other unhelpful behaviors are assuming a supervisor/expert role, introducing your own biases, and making suggestions that conflict with existing values in the school context.

As the plan develops, the consultant must make clear just who will do what, and when, and where. Evaluation criteria and methods that are congruent with the goals and plan should be developed at this time, and arrangements made for assessment and collection of data on student progress.

### Step 7: Evaluating Progress and Process

This step and the final three steps are frequently overlooked. Consultation and collaboration experiences should be followed by assessment of student progress resulting from the collaborative plan, and also by evaluation of the consultation process itself. Figure 2–2 in Chapter 2 and additional information in Chapter 8, are useful for this purpose.

The consultant will want to make positive, supportive comments while drawing the interaction to a close, and at that time can informally evaluate the consultation with consultee help or formally evaluate by asking for brief written responses. This is a good time also to plan for future collaboration.

### Step 8: Following Up the Consultation

Of all ten steps, this may be the most neglected. Ineffective consultation often results from lack of follow-up service (Neel, 1981). It is in the best interest of the client, consultee, consultant, and future possibilities for consultation to reassess the situation periodically. Participants will want to adjust the student's program if necessary, and initiate further consultation if the situation seems to require it. Consultants should follow through immediately on all promises of materials, information, action, or further consultation, and reinforce things that are going well. They also need to make a point of noting improved student behaviors and performance, especially those that relate to the classroom teacher's efforts.

## Step 9: Interacting with the Consultee

Informal conversations with consultees subsequent to the consultation are reinforcing. During follow-up, consultants can help consultees feel good about themselves. Also, they may volunteer to help if things are not going as smoothly as anticipated, or if consultees have further needs. As stressed in an earlier chapter, the sweetest words a consultee can hear are, "What can I do to help you?" However, this question *must* be framed in the spirit of:

- "What can I do to help you *that you do not have the time and resources to do?*"

and *not* as

- "What can I do for you that you do not have the skill and expertise to accomplish?"

## Step 10: Repeating the Consultation If Needed

Further consultation and collaboration may be needed if the plan is not working, or if one or more parties believes the problem was not identified appropriately. On the other hand, consultation also may be repeated and extended when things are going well. The obvious rationale here is that if one interaction helped, more will help further. This is reinforcing for processes of consultation, collaboration, and teamwork. It encourages others to participate in the consultation and collaboration activity.

## What to Say During the Consultation

The ten-step consultation procedure, committed to memory or stapled into a plan book, is a good organizational tool and a reassuring resource for the consultant, particularly for those engaging in their first consultations. Of course, the consultant does not want to parrot points from an outline as though reading a manual for programming the VCR! But by practicing verbal responses that are helpful at each step, you will more naturally and automatically use facilitative phrases when the need arises. For example:

- *When planning the consultation.* (The comments in this step are made to yourself.)

  (What styles of communication and interaction can I expect with these consultees?)

  (Have I had previous consultations with them and if so, how did they go?)

  (Do I have any perceptions at this point about client needs? If so, can I keep them under wraps while soliciting responses from others?)

  (What kinds of information might help with this situation?)

- *When initiating the consultation.* (In this step and the rest of the steps, say to the consultee—)

   You're saying that . . .

   The need seems to be . . .

   May we work together along these lines . . . ?

   So the situation is . . .

   I am aware that . . .

   What can we do in regard to your request/situation . . . ?

- *When collecting information.*

   Tell me about that . . .

   Uh-huh . . .

   What do you see as the effects of . . . ?

   So your views/perceptions about this are . . .

   The major factors we have brought out seem to be . . .

   Tell me more about the background of . . .

   Sounds tough . . .

   To summarize our basic information then, . . .

- *When identifying the problem.*

   You say the major concern is . . .

   But I also hear your concern about . . .

   You'd like this situation changed so that . . .

   How does this affect your day/load/responsibility?

   You are concerned about other students in your room . . .

   You're feeling . . . because of . . .

   This problem seems formidable. Perhaps we can isolate part of it . . .

   Perhaps we can't be sure about that . . .

   If you could change one thing, what would you change first?

- *When generating possibilities.*

   How does this affect the students/schedule/parents?

   Do we have a good handle on the nature of this situation?

   We need to define what we want to happen . . .

   How would you like things to be?

   What has been tried so far?

   What happened then?

How could we do this more easily?

Could we try something new such as . . . ?

What limitations fall upon things we might suggest?

Let's try to develop some ideas to meet the need . . .

Your idea of . . . also makes me think of . . .

- *When formulating a plan.*

    Let's list the goals and ideas we have come up with . . .

    So, in trying . . . you'll be changing your approach of . . .

    To implement these ideas, we would have to . . .

    The actions in this situation would be different, because . . .

    We need to break down the plan into steps.

    What should come first? Second . . .

    When is the best time to start with the first step?

- *When evaluating progress.*

    Have we got a solid plan?

    One way to measure progress toward the goals would be . . .

    Some positive things have been happening . . .

    How can we build on these gains?

    Now we can decide where to go from here . . .

    In what ways did our getting together help?

    I can see the student progress every day . . .

    You're accomplishing so much with . . .

    How could I serve you and your students better?

- *When following up.*

    How do you feel about the way things are going?

    We had set a time to get back together. Is that time still O.K., or should we make it sooner?

    I'm interested in the progress you have observed.

    I'm following up on that material/action I promised.

- *When interacting with the consultee.*

    I just stopped by . . .

    Since we bumped into each other . . .

    I wondered how things have been going for you . . .

How are things in your corner of the world these days?

I'm glad you've hung in there with this problem.

You've accomplished a lot, which is hard to recognize when you're with it every day . . .

You know, progress like this makes teachers look very good!

- *When repeating the consultation.*

    Should we have another go at discussing . . . ?

    Perhaps we overlooked some information that would help . . .

    We got so much accomplished last time.

    How about getting together again to . . . ?

    That's a fine progress report.

    Would another plan session produce even more fantastic results?

---

**Application of the Ten-Step Consulting Process**

1. Select one or more of the following situations and simulate a school consultation experience, using the ten-step process and any of the application verbalizations that are appropriate:

*Situation A*: A ninth-grade student is considered lazy by former teachers, has failed several courses, and cannot grasp math concepts. He has difficulty locating information but can read and understand most material at his grade level. He is never prepared for class, seldom has pencil and paper, and loses his assignments. Yet he is pleasant, seemingly eager to please, and will try things in a one-to-one situation. His classroom teachers say he will not pass, and you have all decided to meet about this. How will you, the learning disabilities consulting teacher, address the situation?

*Situation B*: You are attending a confrence on behalf of a third-grade student who is emotionally disturbed and classified as borderline–educable mentally handicapped. You believe she should be served in a general classroom with supportive counseling service and reevaluated in a year. The other staff participants feel she should be in special education placement with mainstreaming into music, art, and physical education. The mother is confused about the lack of agreement among school personnel. How will you address the concerns of all in this situation, particularly the mother?

*Situation C*: A sixth-grade student's mother is known as a perfectionist. Her son did not receive all As on the last report card, and she has requested a conference with you, the classroom teacher, the principal, and the school psychologist. As gifted program facilitator, how will you address this situation?

*Situation D:* A first-year kindergarten teacher has learned that one of her students is a child with cerebral palsy. Although the child's history to date has included continuous evaluation, home teaching, group socialization experiences, special examinations, and therapy sessions as well as family counseling for three years, the teacher is nervous about her responsibilities with this child. As the speech pathologist, how will you build her confidence in caring for the kindergartner's language needs and her skill in helping the little girl to develop her potential?

2. As a team effort with colleagues who share your grade level and subject area, construct a scenario to demonstrate the ten-step collaborative school consultation process at your teaching level and in your content area(s). . . Role-play it for others, stopping at key points—for example, after problem identification and after formulation of the plan, to ask others what they might do at that point. . . If several promising alternatives are suggested, try each one and follow it to its conclusion. What techniques worked best? How did individual differences influence the consultation? Were these individual differences used constructively, and if not, what could have been done instead?

## What to Consider if Group Problem Solving Is Not Successful

There is no universal agreement on what makes consultation effective, and little empirical support exists to guide consultants as to what should be said and done in consultation (Gresham and Kendell, 1987; Heron and Kimball, 1988), However, the ten steps outlined in this chapter have worked well for many consultants and consulting teachers, with few resultant problems. If this method of ten steps does not work, consultants should ask several questions:

- Were feelings addressed?
- Was the problem defined accurately?
- Were the nitty-gritty details worked out?
- Was the consultation process evaluated?
- Was there follow-up to the consultation?
- Were any hidden agendas brought to light and handled?
- Could any other problem-solving tools facilitate the process?

## Tools to Facilitate Group Problem Solving

The collaborative format of working together and drawing on collective expertise is widely practiced in the business and professional world. In their efforts to use the best ideas of bright, innovative minds, astute business managers employ a number of group problem-solving techniques. These techniques allow individuals to extend their own productive thinking powers and enhance those of their colleagues by participating in structured group problem-solving activities. Such techniques, often utilized in business and industry, are yet to be promoted to any great extent in educational settings, where autonomy and self-sufficiency have traditionally been valued more than collaboration and teamwork.

Several easy and convenient problem-solving techniques suitable for group participation are: brainstorming, lateral thinking, concept mapping, idea checklists, and attribute listing. Ironically, many teachers incorporate these kinds of group problem-solving activities into curriculum planning for their students but overlook the potential that the techniques can contribute to carrying out their own responsibilities more effectively and pleasurably.

*Brainstorming* Brainstorming is a mainstay of creative problem-solving methodology. It facilitates generating many unique ideas. When a group is brainstorming, participants should be relaxed and having fun. There are no right or wrong responses during the process, because problems seldom have only one right approach. No one may critique an idea during the brainstorming process. All ideas are accepted as plausible and regarded as potentially valuable. Each idea is shared and recorded. In large group sessions, it is most efficient to have a leader for managing the oral responses and a recorder for getting them down on a board or chart visible to all.

Rules for brainstorming are:

1. Do not criticize any ideas at this time.
2. The more wild and zany the ideas, the better.
3. Think up as many ideas as possible.
4. Try to combine two or more ideas into new ones.
5. Hitchhike (piggyback) on another's idea. A person with a hitchhike idea should be called on before those who have unrelated ideas (Osborn, 1963.)

This technique is useful when the group wishes to explore as many alternatives as possible and defer evaluation of the ideas until the options have been exhausted. People who cannot resist the urge to critique ideas during brainstorming must be reminded that evaluation comes later. Leaders should call on volunteers quickly.

---

**Application of Brainstorming**

*Example of Using the Brainstorming Technique*

A brainstorming session might be held for the following situation:

A first-grade student has read just about every book in the small, rurally situated school. The first-grade teacher and gifted program facilitator brainstorm possibilities for enhancing this student's reading options and benefiting the school resources as well.

---

---

**Application of Lateral Thinking**

*Example of Using the Lateral Thinking Technique*

Lateral thinking might be used in this situation:

A high school student with learning disabilities has a serious reading problem, but teachers in several classes are not willing to make adjustments. The teachers have not discussed any problems with you recently, but the student has. How might you as consultant, and student as consultee, think of ways to approach the situation and modify classroom practices to help this student succeed? To think laterally, the consultant might regard the teachers as clients and consult with the student about ways of reinforcing teachers when they *do* make things easier. The student would be modifying the behavior of teachers, rather than the vertical thinking approach of asking teachers to modify student behavior.

---

When the flow of ideas slows, it is a good idea to persevere a while longer. Often the second wave of thoughts contains the most innovative suggestions. Each participant should be encouraged to contribute.

*Lateral Thinking*   The conventional method of thinking is vertical thinking, in which one moves forward mentally by sequential and justifiable steps. Vertical thinking is logical and single purposed, digging down more deeply into the same mental hole. Lateral thinking, on the other hand, digs a "thinking hole" in a different place. It moves out at an angle, so to speak, from vertical thinking to change direction, attitude, or approach so that the problem can be examined in a different way (deBono, 1973).

Lateral thinking should not replace vertical thinking, but complement it. While many educators emphasize vertical thinking at the expense of more divergent production, both are necessary to arrive at creative solutions for complex problems. The ability to use a lateral thinking mode by suspending judgments and generating alternatives should be cultivated by school personnel.

*Concept Mapping*   Concept mapping (referred to by some as mind mapping, semantic mapping, or webbing) is a tool for identifying concepts, showing relationships between them, and reflecting on the degree of generality and inclusiveness that envelops them (Wesley and Wesley, 1990). The technique allows users to display ideas, link them together, elaborate on them, add new information as it surfaces, and review the formulation of the ideas. The process begins with one word, or issue, written on paper or the chalkboard and enclosed in a circle. Then other circles of subtopics, ideas, words, and concepts are added to that central theme by lines or spokes that connect and interconnect where the concepts relate and interrelate. More and more possibilities and new areas open up as the webbing grows. Relationships and interrelationships that can help verbalize problems and interventions are recorded for all participants to see. If

**Application of Concept Mapping**

*Example of Using the Concept-Mapping Technique*

A classroom teacher has agreed to work with a student new to the district and identified as behavior disordered. The student has acceptable social skills in some instances and is friendly and cooperative. But he also requires individual instruction, is working about two years below grade level, and makes threats impulsively to other students. On one occasion he brought a weapon to school. During previous visits with the teacher, she indicated that things were going well. Now, in the middle of November, she asks to see you, the consultant for behavioral disorders, immediately. She is upset, saying things such as "It just isn't working," and "I've tried so hard," but she has not described the problem. How might concept mapping or webbing help in this situation?

the concept map is not erased or discarded, the process can go on and on as more ideas are generated and added.

Concept mapping is being taught to students at all grade levels for reading comprehension. Buzan (1983) offers strategies for mind mapping in which learning techniques such as note taking can be structured to show interrelationships easily. Many students in gifted programs have been introduced to the concept of webbing to focus on a problem of interest and plan an independent study. Sometimes college students are encouraged to try mind mapping by combining lecture notes and text reading to study for exams. Concept mapping is a powerful tool. It is useful not only for enhancing individual learning, but for leading to more meaningful and productive staff development (Bocchino, 1991).

*Idea Checklist*  Checklists that suggest solutions for problems can be created from sources such as college texts, teaching manuals, and instructional media manuals. More unusual checklists include the Yellow Pages of directories, referral agency listings, gift catalogs, and instructional resource center guides. Asking a question such as "How can we help Shawn improve in math proficiency?"

**Application of Idea Checklists**

*Example of Using the Idea Checklist*

A high school sophomore, seventeen years old and in the educable mentally handicapped program, is ready for a vocational training program. As EMH resource teacher, you believe the Vocational Rehabilitation Unit's four-month job-training program would be the most appropriate program for the student. However, the parents feel very protective of their son and are concerned that the environment will be noncaring. They resist suggestions that he leave their home. How might an idea-checklist process help during this consultation?

and scanning a Yellow Pages section or an off-level teaching manual may generate new ideas. Several chapters of this book contain checklists.

## Tips for Consulting and Collaborating

1.  Have materials and thoughts organized before consultations. Develop a list of questions that will help ferret out the real problem. Be prepared for the meeting with a checklist of information typically needed. Do not be afraid to say that you do not have the answer. If it is something you should know, find out, when you can, and get back to the person who asked.

2.  Have strategies and materials in mind that may be helpful to the situation, but do not try to have all the answers. This discourages involvement by others. Do not offer solutions too readily, and try not to address too many topics at once. Avoid jargon and shun suggestions that conflict with policies or favored teacher practices.

3.  Make it a habit to look for something *positive* about the teacher, the room, and the student, and comment on those things. Use feedback as a vehicle that can provide *positive* information, not just negative comments.

4.  Don't try to fix it if it is not broken.

5.  Don't wait for the consultee to make the first move. But do not expect that teachers will be enthused or flattered to have questions asked about their classrooms and teaching methods.

6.  When a teacher asks for advice about a student, first ask what the teacher has already observed. This gets the teacher involved in the problem and encourages ownership in serving the student's special need. Whenever possible, use the terms *we* and *us*, not *I*.

7.  Know how to interpret test results and how to discuss those results with educators, parents, and students.

8.  When possible, provide parents with samples of the child's schoolwork to discuss during the conference. Have a list of resources ready to share with parents for help with homework, reinforcements, and study tips. When providing materials, explain or demonstrate their use, and then keep in touch so that no problems develop.

9.  Maintain contact with teachers during the year. You may find that the teacher has detected an improvement that is directly related to your work, and this reinforcement will be valuable for you and your own morale.

10.  Remember that minds, like parachutes, work best when they are open.

## Chapter Review

1.  While many variants of a problem-solving process exist, basic steps are similar for all. They include identifying the problem, generating options,

analyzing consequences, and developing plans for solutions. When these steps have been taken, implementation of the plan and follow-up activity can occur.

2. Communication, cooperation, and coordination are vital components of effective group problem solving.

3. Problem identification is the most critical phase of problem solving. Information from multiple sources and collaborative input by a team of educators will help identify the real problem and facilitate its solution.

4. Ten steps important in a problem-solving consultation are: planning; initiating the consultation; collecting information; identifying the problem; generating options and alternatives; formulating a plan; evaluating progress; following up; interacting informally; and repeating the consultation as appropriate.

5. Consultants will benefit from practicing key phrases to use during each phase of the consultation.

6. Divergent production of ideas during problem solving can be enhanced by the use of techniques and tools such as brainstorming, lateral thinking, concept mapping, and idea checklists. Teachers often use these techniques with students, but overlook their possibilities for contributing to professional activity.

## Activities

1. When consultants introduce themselves to consultees, what are four or five things they can mention about themselves in order to develop rapport?

2. Discuss at least five things a consultant does *not* want to happen while consulting and collaborating, along with the conditions that might cause these unwanted events, and how the conditions might be avoided or overcome.

3. For a challenging assignment, select a school issue or student problem and create a method for engaging in consultation by designating a system, perspective, approach, prototype, mode, and model, as discussed in Chapter 3. Carry out the consultation as a role play or simulation, using the ten steps and verbal responses suggested in this chapter. In a "debriefing" session with your colleagues, discuss which parts of the method development and consultation process were most difficult, possible reasons, and what could be done to improve the method for more successful consultation.

## For Further Reading

Buzan, T. (1983). *Use Both Sides of Your Brain.* New York: E. P. Dutton.

Davis, G. A., and Rimm, S. B. (1989). *Education of the Gifted and Talented.* Englewood Cliffs, NJ: Prentice Hall. Chapters 10, 11, and 12, on creativity and thinking skills.

deBono, E. (1973). *Lateral Thinking: Creativity Step by Step.* New York: Harper and Row.

Osborn, A. F. (1963). *Applied Imagination: Principles and Procedures of Creative Problem-Solving.* New York: Scribner's.

# References

Bergan, J. R., and Tombari, M. L. (1976). Consultant skill and efficiency and the implementation and outcome of consultation. *Journal of School Psychology, 14,*(1): 3–14.

Bocchino, R. (March, 1991). Using mind mapping as a note–taking tool. *Developer,* pp. 1, 4.

Bolton, R. (1986). *People Skills: How to Assert Yourself, Listen to Others, and Resolve Conflicts.* New York: Simon and Schuster.

Buzan, T. (1983). *Use both sides of your brain.* New York: E. P. Dutton.

Caplan, G. (1970). *The Theory and Practice of Mental Health Consultation.* New York: Basic Books.

Conoley, J. (1985). Personal correspondence.

Davis, G. A., and Rimm, S. B. (1989). *Education of the Gifted and Talented.* Englewood Cliffs, NJ: Prentice– Hall.

DeBoer, A. L. (1986). *The Art of Consulting.* Chicago: Arcturus.

deBono, E. (1973). *Lateral Thinking: Creativity Step by Step.* New York: Harper and Row.

Friend, M., and Cook, L. (1990). Collaboration as a predictor for success in school reform. *Journal of Educational and Psychological Consultation,* 1(1): 69–86.

Gordon, T. (1977). *Leader effectiveness Training. L.E.T.: The no-lose way to release the production potential in people.* Toronto: Bantam.

Gresham, F. M., and Kendall, G. K. (1987). School consultation research: Methodological critique and future research directions. *School Psychology Review,* 16(3): 306–316.

Heron, T, ., and Kimball, W. H. (1988). Gaining perspective with the educational coonsultation research base: Ecological considerations and further recomendations. *Remedial and Special Education,* 9(6): 22–28, 47.

Huefner, D. S. (1988). The consulting teacher model: Risks and opportunities. *Exceptional Children,* 54(5): 403–414.

Idol, L., Paolucci–Whitcomb, P., and Nevin, A. (1986). *Collaborative Consultation.* Austin, TX: PRO–ED.

Idol, L., West, J. F., and Lloyd, S. R. (1988). Organizing and implementing specialized reading programs: A collaborative approach involving classroom, remedial, and special education teachers. *Remedial and Special Education,* 9(2): 54–61.

Johnson, D. W., and Johnson, F. P. (1987). *Joining Together: Group Theory and Group Skills* (3rd ed.). Englewood CLiffs, NJ: Prentice-Hall.

Lanier, J. E. (1982). Teacher education: Needed research and practice for the preparation of teaching professionals. In D. C. Corrigin, D. J. Palmer, and P. A. Alexander (eds.), *The Future of Teacher Education.* College Station, TX: Dean's Grant Project, College of Education, Texas A and M University.

Margolis, H., and McGettigan, J. (1988). Managing resistance to instructional modifications in mainstream settings. Remedial and Special Education, 9: 15–21.

Neel, R. S. (1981). How to put the consultant to work in consulting teaching. *Behavioral Disorders,* 6(2): 78–81.

Osborn, A. F. (1963). *Applied Imagination: Principles and Procedures of Creative Problem–Solving.* New York: Scribner's.

Polsgrove, L., and McNeil, M. (1989). The consultation process: Research and practice. *Remedial and Special Education,* 10(1): 6–13, 20.

Pugach, M. C. (1988). The consulting teacher in the context of educational reform. *Exceptional Children,* 55(3): 273–275.

Pugach, M. C., and Johnson, L. J. (1989. Prereferral interventions: Progress, problems, and challenges. *Exceptional Children,* 56, 117–126.

Schein, E. H. (1969). *Process consultation: Its role in organizational development.* Reading, MA: Addison-Wesley.

Thurston, L. P. (1987). *Survival Skills for Women: Facilitator Manual.* Manhattan, KS: Survival Skills and Development.

Wesley, W. G., and Wesley, B. A. (1990). Concept–mapping: A brief introduction. *Teaching Professor,* 4(8): 3–4.

# 6

# COMMUNICATION PROCESSES FOR CONSULTANTS AND COLLABORATORS

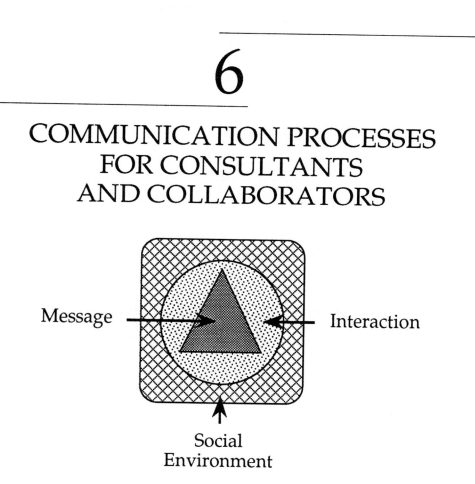

Message — Interaction

Social Environment

## To Think About

Communication is one of the greatest achievements of humankind. A vital component of human relationships in general, it is also the foundation of cooperation and collaboration among educators.

Communication involves talking, listening, managing interpersonal conflict, and addressing concerns together. Components for successful communication are understanding, trust, autonomy, and flexibility. People who can communicate effectively do so by withholding judgmental behavior and minimizing efforts to control others (Lippitt, 1983).

While problems and conflicts are unavoidable elements of life, good communication skills facilitate problem solving and resolution of conflicts. On the other hand, ineffective communication creates a void that breeds misunderstanding and distrust. Elements of trust, commitment, and effective interaction are critical for conflict-free relationships (Lippitt, 1983). Effective communication becomes a foundation for cooperation and collaboration among school personnel and parents.

## Focusing Questions

1. What is a primary reason people fail at work?
2. What are key components of the communication process?
3. How does one establish rapport in order to facilitate effective communication?
4. What are major verbal and nonverbal skills for communicating effectively?
5. What are the primary roadblocks to communication?
6. How can a school consultant be appropriately assertive and cope with resistance when the need arises?
7. What techniques and skills are useful for conflict management?

## Key Terms

| | |
|---|---|
| assertiveness | nonverbal communication |
| body language | rapport |
| communication | resistance |
| conflict management | Responsive Listening Checklist |
| empathy, empathic | roadblocks to communication |
| high-context communication | verbal communication |
| low-context communication | |

---

### Scenario

The setting is the hallway of a junior high school in midafternoon, where the general math instructor, a first-year teacher, is venting to a colleague.

*MATH TEACHER:* What a day! On top of the fire drill this morning and those forms that we got in our boxes to be filled out by Friday, I had a disastrous encounter with a parent.

*COLLEAGUE:* Oh, one of those, huh?

*MATH TEACHER:* Jay's mother walked into my room right before fourth-hour, and accused me of not doing my job. It was awful!

*COLLEAGUE:* (frowns, shakes head)

*MATH TEACHER:* Thank goodness there weren't any kids around. But the music teacher was there to see me about next week's program. This parent really let me have it. I was stunned, not only by the accusation, but by the way she delivered it. My whole body went on "red alert." My heart was pounding, and that chili dog I had for lunch got caught in my digestive system. Then my palms got sweaty. I could hardly squeak out a sound because my mouth was so dry. I wanted to yell back at her, but I couldn't!

*COLLEAGUE:* Probably just as well. Quick emotional reactions don't seem to work very well in those situations. I found out the hard way that it doesn't help to respond at all during that first barrage of words. Sounds like you did the right thing.

*MATH TEACHER:* Well, it really was hard. So you've had things like this happen to you?

*COLLEAGUE:* Um-humm. I see we don't have time for me to tell you about it, because here come our troops for their next hour of knowledge. But I can tell you all about it later if you want. Come to my room after school and we'll compare notes—maybe even plan some strategies for the future just in case. And, by the way, welcome to the club!

## Communication for Effective Relationships

People typically communicate in one form or another for about 70 percent of their waking moments. They spend about 10 percent of that time writing, 20 to 40 percent speaking, and 45 to 65 percent listening (Bolton, 1986). Unfortunately, as many as eight out of ten people who fail in their work roles do so for one reason—they do not relate well with others (Bolton, 1986).

Communication skills clearly are keys to success in any field, and they are indispensable in consulting with other professionals. A supportive, communicative relationship among special education teachers, general classroom teachers, and parents is critical to the success of mainstreamed children with special learning needs. Trends in education emphasize the necessity for greatly strengthened communication among all who are involved with the student's educational program. Special educators must model and promote exemplary communication and interaction skills if they are to serve as consultants and team members for helping mainstreamed students succeed (Dickens and Jones, 1990).

Consulting is not a one-person exercise. A consultant will pay a high price for a "Rambo" style of interaction ("My idea can beat up your idea," or "I'm right and that's just the way it is"). Communication that minimizes conflict and enables teachers to maintain self-esteem may be the most important and most "delicate" process in consulting (Gersten et al., 1991.) Unfortunately, development of communication skills is not usually included in the formal preparation of educators. Because the development and use of "people skills" is the most difficult aspect of collaboration for many educators, more and more educators are stressing the need for specific training in consulting and communication skills to serve special needs students.

# Components of Communication

Communication requires three elements:

- a message;
- a sender of the message, and
- a receiver of the message.

Semantics play a fundamental role in both sending and receiving messages. A person who says, "Oh, it's no big deal—just an issue of semantics" is missing a major point. The semantics frequently *are* the issue and should never be taken for granted. The vital role of semantics in consultation, collaboration, and teamwork was introduced in Chapter 1, revisited in Chapter 3, and will be important in this chapter, with its focus on communication skills.

## *Barriers to Communication*

In their program for building relationships through negotiation, Fisher and Brown (1988) identify three major barriers to communication:

- assuming there is no need to talk;
- communicating in one direction ("telling" people); and
- sending mixed messages.

In order to communicate effectively, the message sender must convey the purpose of the message in a facilitative style with clarity to the receiver. Miscommunication breeds misunderstanding (Ozturk, 1992). A gap in meaning between what the message sender gives and what the message receiver gets can be described as distortion at best, or as communication trash in severe cases. A person may send the message, "You look nice today," and have it understood by the receiver as, "Gee, I never do look very good." A classroom teacher wanting to reinforce the learning disabilities teacher might say "Gerry certainly gets better grades on tests in the resource room, "but the resource teacher may hear, "You're helping too much and Gerry can't cope outside your protection."

In addition to vague semantics and distorted messages, many filters disrupt the message as it passes (or doesn't pass) between the sender and the receiver. Examples of filters are differing values, ambiguous language, stereotypes and assumptions, levels of self-esteem, and personal experiences. Static from pre-conceived ideas works constantly to prevent people from hearing what others are saying and provide only what people want to hear (Buscaglia, 1986). This can be demonstrated with the well-known game of "Gossip." Players stand in a long line or a circle, while one of them silently reads or quietly receives a message. Then that person whispers the message to the next one, and that message continues to be delivered to each one in turn. After passing through the filters of many people and stated aloud by the very last one, the message in most cases is drastically different from the original message. The game results are usually humorous. Real-life results are not so funny.

In order to be effective communicators, senders and receivers of messages need skills that include rapport building, responsive listening, assertiveness, tools for dealing with resistance, and conflict management techniques. After effective communication skills have been cultivated, consultants and consultees are able to engage more effectively in collaborative problem solving.

## Rapport-Building to Enhance Communication

Collaboration with other professionals that is in the best interest of students with special needs often means simply sitting down and making some joint decisions. At other times, however, it must be preceded by considerable rapport building. Successful consultation necessitates good rapport between the participants in the consulting relationship. Johnson and Johnson (1987) contend that it is more difficult to reject ideas offered by persons who are liked and respected than by those who are disliked. It is important to keep in mind that both the consultant and the consultee should provide ideas toward solving the problem. Respect must be a two-way condition for generating and accepting ideas. Rapport building becomes a vital need for building an appropriate consultation climate.

What behaviors are central to the process of building a trusting, supportive relationship? When asked this question, many teachers mention trust, respect, feeling that it is O.K. not to have all the answers, feeling free to ask questions, and feeling all right about disagreeing with the other person. People want to feel that the other person is *really* listening.

Respecting differences in others is an important aspect of building and maintaining rapport. Although teachers and other school personnel are generally adept at recognizing and respecting individual differences in children, they may find this more difficult to accomplish with adults. Accepting differences in adults may be particularly difficult when the adults have different values, skills, and attitudes. Effective consultants accept people as they really are rather than wishing they were different. Rapport building is not such a formidable process when the consultant respects individual differences and expects others either to have this respect or to develop it (Margolis and McGettigan, 1988).

## Skills For Communicating

Four major sets of skills are integral to successful communication:

- responsive listening;
- assertion skills;
- conflict management skills; and
- collaborative problem-solving skills.

Responsive listening skills enable a person to understand what another is saying and to convey that the problems and feelings have been understood. When listening methods are used appropriately by a consultant, the consultee plays an active role in problem solving without becoming dependent on the consultant.

Assertion skills include verbal and nonverbal behaviors that enable collaborators to maintain respect, satisfy their professional needs, and defend their rights without dominating, manipulating, or controlling others. Conflict management skills help individuals deal with the emotional turbulence that typically accompanies conflict. Conflict management skills also have a multiplier effect of fostering closer relationships when a conflict is resolved. Collaborative problem-solving skills help resolve the conflicting needs so that all parties are satisfied. Problems then "stay solved," and relationships are developed and preserved.

### *Responsive Listening Skills*

Plutarch said, "Know how to listen and you will profit even from those who talk badly." Shakespeare referred to the "disease" of *not* listening. Listening is the foundation of communication. A person listens to establish rapport with another person. People listen when others are upset or angry, or when they do not know what to say or fear speaking out will result in trouble. People listen so others will listen to them. Listening is a process of perpetual motion that focuses on the other person as speaker and responds to that other person's ideas, rather than concentrating on one's own thoughts and feelings. Thus, effective listening is *responsive listening* because it is responding, both verbally and nonverbally, to the words and actions of the speaker.

Listening responsively and empathetically is associated with the development of trust and understanding (Margolis and Brannigan, 1986; Nichols and Stevens, 1957) and with effective consulting practices (Gutkin and Curtis, 1982). It improves relationships, promotes exploration of prospective solutions (Egan, 1982), minimizes resistance (Murphy, 1987), and fosters collaboration (Idol-Maestas, Lloyd, and Lilly, 1981). Although most people are convinced of the importance of listening in building collegial relationships and preventing and solving problems, few are as adept at this skill they would like or need, to be. There are several reasons for this. First, most people have not been taught to listen effectively. They have been taught to talk—especially if they are teachers, administrators, or psychologists. Educators are good at talking and regard it as an essential part of their roles. But effective talkers must be careful not to let the lines of communication get tangled up in their need to talk too much or too often.

***Reasons for Listening***   Listening helps keep the "locus of responsibility" with the one who owns the problem (Gordon, 1977). Therefore, if one's role as a consultant is to promote problem solving without fostering dependence on the part of the consultee, listening will keep the focus of the problem solving where it belongs. Listening also is important in showing empathy and acceptance, two vital ingredients in a relationship that fosters growth and psychological health (Gordon, 1977).

Listening can prevent or minimize misunderstandings that occur in schools when educational roles are overloaded with responsibilities. It is very difficult for one person to understand the variety and complexity of another's problems. The receiver of a communication cannot know the sender's experiences or the nuances of the message. Katz and Lawyer (1983) define communication as the exchange of meaning that allows each to influence the other's experience. Listening helps one person "experience" the other's attitudes, background, and problems.

If listening is so important, why is it so hard? First, as discussed earlier, people often are not taught to listen and do not develop the skills needed to be effective listeners. Also, people may be hesitant to listen because they think listening implies agreeing. However, listening is much more than just hearing. A speaker can utter perhaps 125 words a minute, but a listener can process from 400 to 600 words a minute. What happens in the "listener's gap?" Too often listeners think about what they will say next, what they are going to recommend about the problem, or what they are going to do over the weekend.

Listening is also difficult because it is hard to keep an open mind about the speaker. Openness certainly is important in effective communication. Consultants must demonstrate tolerance toward differences and appreciation of richly diverse ideas and values while they are engaged in consulting relationships. A consultant's own values about child rearing, education, or the treatment of children with special needs become personal filters that make it difficult to really listen to those whose values are very different. For example, it may be hard to listen to a consultee parent who thinks it is appropriate for a very gifted daughter to drop out of school at the age of sixteen to help on the family farm because "She'll be getting married before too long and farm work will prepare her to be a wife better than schoolwork ever can." It takes discipline to listen to comments such as this when your mind is reacting negatively and wants to put together some very pointed comments to argue against this kind of thinking. A good rule of thumb to remember in such cases is that "when we add our two cents' worth in the middle of listening, that's just about what the communication is worth!" (Murphy, 1987.)

Feelings of the listener also act as filters to impede listening. Listening is very hard work. If the listener is tired or anxious or bursting with excitement and energy, it is particularly hard to listen carefully. While listening is demanding and difficult, it is vital for the collaborative relationships that are an integral part of the school consultation process. Improving listening skills can help establish collaborative relationships with colleagues, even those with whom it is a challenge to communicate. When consultants and consultees improve their listening skills, they have a head start on solving problems, side-stepping resistance, and preventing conflicts.

There are three major components of responsive listening:

- nonverbal listening;
- encouraging the sending of messages (talking); and
- showing understanding of the message.

*Nonverbal Listening Skills* Responsive listeners use minimal and appropriate body language to send out the message that they are listening effectively. Some body language cues reflect ethnic background (Schein, 1969). Hall (1981) discusses a wide range of nonverbal cues that must be understood in order to interpret messages correctly. The high-context communication identified by Hall (1981) relies heavily on nonverbals and group understanding (Sue and Sue, 1990). An example is the communication that develops between twins. Another example is the shortened communication by people who know each other well and can omit much verbal communication without loss of meaning. Low-context communication puts greater reliance on the verbal part of the message.

Studies in kinesics, or communication through body language, show that the impact of a message is about 7 percent verbal, 38 percent vocal, and 55 percent facial. The eyebrows are particularly important in conveying messages. Nonverbal listening behavior of a good listener is described by Tony Hillerman in his 1990 best-seller *Coyote Waits:* "Jacobs was silent for awhile, thinking about it, her face full of sympathy. She was a talented listener. When you talked to this woman, she attended. She had all her antennae out. The world was shut out. Nothing mattered but the words she was hearing" (Hillerman, 1990, pp. 148–149).

Nonverbal listening may be particularly difficult for those amazing people who can do several things at once, such as watch a television show and write a letter, or talk to a parent and grade papers, or prepare supper while listening to a child's synopsis of the day. This is because nonverbal components of listening should demonstrate to the speaker that the message receiver is respecting the speaker enough to concentrate on the message and is following the speaker's thoughts to find the *real* message. Careful listening conveys attitudes of flexibility, empathy, and caring, even if the speaker is using words and expressions that cloud the message.

A person who is attentive leans forward slightly, engages in a comfortable level of eye contact, nods, and gives low-key responses such as "oh," and "uh-huh," and "umm-humm." The responsive listener's facial expression matches the message. If that message is serious, the expression reflects seriousness. If the message is delivered with a smile, the listener shows empathy by smiling.

The hardest part of nonverbal listening is keeping it nonverbal. It helps the listener to think about a tennis game and remember that during the listening part of the "game," the ball is in the speaker's court. The speaker has the privilege of saying anything, no matter how silly or irrelevant. The listener just keeps sending the ball back by nodding, or saying "I see" or other basically nonverbal behaviors, until he or she "hears" the sender's message. This entails using nonverbal behaviors and "listening" to the nonverbal as well as the verbal message of the sender. The listener recognizes and minimizes personal filters, perceives and interprets the filters of the sender, and encourages continued communication until capable of understanding the message from the sender's perspective. Responsive listeners avoid anticipating what the speaker will say and *never* complete a speaker's sentence.

After listeners have listened until they really hear the message, understand the speaker's position, and recognize the feelings behind the message, it is their turn to speak. But they must be judicious about what they do say. Several well-known, humorous "recipes" apply to this need.

- Recipe for speaking—stand up, speak up, then shut up.
- Recipe for giving a good speech—add shortening.
- It takes six letters of the alphabet to spell the word *listen*. Rearrange the letters to spell another word that is a necessary part of responsive listening.
- In the middle of listening, the *t* doesn't make a sound.

*Verbal Listening Skills*  Although the first rule of the good listener is to keep your mouth shut, there are several types of verbal responses that show that the listener is following the thoughts and feelings expressed by the speaker. Verbal responses are added to nonverbal listening responses to communicate that the listener understands what the other is saying from that speakers specific point of view. Specific verbal aspects of listening also keep the speaker talking. There are several reasons for this that are specific to the consulting process:

The consultant will be less inclined to assume ownership of the problem.

Speakers will clarify their own thoughts as they keep talking.

More information will become available to help understand the speaker's point of view.

Speakers begin to solve their own problems as they talk them through.

The consultant continues to refine responsive listening skills.

Three verbal listening skills that promote talking by the speaker are inviting, encouraging, and cautious questioning. Inviting means providing an opportunity for others to talk, by signaling to them that you are interested in listening if they are interested in speaking. Examples are "You seem to have something on your mind," or "I'd like to hear about your problem," or "What's going on for you now?"

Verbal responses of encouragement are added to nodding and mirroring of facial responses. "I see," "Uh-hum," and "Oh" are examples of verbal behaviors that encourage continued talking. These listener responses suggest: "Continue. I understand. I'm listening."(Gordon, 1977)

Cautious questioning is the final mechanism for promoting continued talking. Most educators are competent questioners, so the caution here is to use minimal questioning. During the listening part of communication, the message is controlled by the speaker. It is always the speaker's serve. Intensive and frequent questioning gives control of the communication to the listener. This is antithetical to the consulting process, which should be about collaboration rather than power and control. Questions should be used to clarify what the speaker has said, so the message can be understood by listener—for example "Is this what you mean?" or "Please explain what you mean by 'attitude problem.'"

*Paraphrasing Skill* Responsive listening means demonstrating that the listener understands the essence of the message. After listening by using nonverbal and minimal verbal responses, a consultant who is really listening probably will begin to understand the message of the speaker. To show that the message was heard, or to assess whether or not what was "heard" was the same message the sender intended and not altered by distortion, the listener should paraphrase the message. This has been called active listening (Gordon, 1977) and reflective listening (Bolton, 1986). Paraphrasing is an even more intricate skill than skills discussed earlier. It requires the listener to think carefully about the message and reflect it back to the speaker without changing the content or intent of the message.

There is no simple formula for reflecting or paraphrasing, but two good strategies are to be as accurate as possible and as brief as possible. A paraphrase may begin in one of several ways: "It sounds as if . . . ," or "Is what you mean . . . ?" or "So, it seems to me you want (think) (feel) . . . ," or "Let me see if I understand. You're saying . . . " Paraphrasing allows listeners to check their understanding of the message. It is easy to mishear or misinterpret the message, especially if the words are ambiguous. Correct interpretation of the message will result in a nod from the speaker, who may feel that at last someone has really listened. Or the speaker may correct the message by saying, "No, that's not what I meant. It's this way . . . " The listener may paraphrase the content of the message. For example, "It seems to me that you're saying . . . " would reflect the content of the message back to the speaker. "You appear to be very frustrated about . . . " reflects the emotional part of the message. It is important to use the speaker's words as much as possible in the paraphrase words and to remain concise in responses. By paraphrasing appropriately, a listener demonstrates comprehension of the message or receipt of new information. This aspect of hearing and listening is essential in communication, and in assertion, problem solving, and conflict management as well.

Just by recognizing a consultee's anger, sadness, or frustration, a consultant can begin to build a trusting relationship with a consultee. The listener doesn't necessarily have to agree with the content or emotion that is heard. It may appear absurd or illogical. Nevertheless, the consultant's responsibility is not to change another's momentary tendency; rather, it is to develop a supportive working relationship via effective communication, paving the way to successful cooperation and problem solving while avoiding conflict and resistance.

Parents often comment that they have approached a teacher with a problem, realizing they didn't want a specific answer, but just a kindly ear—a sounding board, or a friendly shoulder. Responsive listening is important in establishing collaborative relationships and maintaining them. It is also a necessary precursor to problem solving in which both parties strive to listen and get a mutual understanding of the problem before it is addressed.

So when is responsive listening to be used? The answer is—*all* the time. Use it when establishing a relationship, when starting to problem solve, when emotions are high, when one conversation doesn't seem to be getting anywhere, and when the speaker seems confused, uncertain, or doesn't know what else to do.

This complex process may not be necessary if two people have already developed a good working relationship and only a word or two is needed for mutual understanding. It also may not be appropriate if one of the two is not willing to talk. Sometimes "communication postponement" is best when you are too tired or too emotionally upset to be a responsive listener. When a consultant cannot listen because of any of these reasons, it is not wise to pretend to be listening, while actually thinking about something else or nothing at all. Instead, a reluctant listener should explain that he or she does not have the energy to talk about the problem now, but wishes to at a later time, for example: "I need a chance to think about this. May I talk to you later?" or "Look, I'm too upset to work on this very productively right now. Let's talk about it first thing tomorrow." Figure 6–1 summarizes responsive listening skills that help avoid blocked communication.

## Roadblocks to Communication

Roadblocks (Gordon, 1977) are red flags to interaction, halting the development of effective collaborative relationships. They may be verbal behaviors or nonverbal behaviors that send out messages such as, "I'm not listening," or "It doesn't matter what you think," or "Your ideas and feelings are silly and unimportant." Roadblocks discourage the speaker and erode feelings of being able to handle problems, complete tasks, or live up to standards (Gordon, 1977).

|  | Yes | No |
|---|---|---|
| **A.** *Appropriate Nonverbals* | | |
| 1. Good eye contact | _____ | _____ |
| 2. Mirrored facial expression | _____ | _____ |
| 3. Body orientation toward other person | _____ | _____ |
| **B.** *Appropriate Verbals* | | |
| 1. Door openers | _____ | _____ |
| 2. Good level of encouraging phrases | _____ | _____ |
| 3. Cautious questions | _____ | _____ |
| **C.** *Appropriate Responding Behaviors* | | |
| 1. Reflected content (paraphrasing) | _____ | _____ |
| 2. Reflected feelings | _____ | _____ |
| 3. Brief clarifying questions | _____ | _____ |
| 4. Summarized | _____ | _____ |
| **D.** *Avoidance of Roadblocks* | | |
| 1. No advice-giving | _____ | _____ |
| 2. No inappropriate questions | _____ | _____ |
| 3. Minimal | _____ | _____ |
| 4. No judging | _____ | _____ |

**FIGURE 6–1  Responsive Listening Checklist**

Thurston, 1989

Responsible school consultants most assuredly do not intend to send blocking messages. But by being busy, not concentrating, using poor listening skills, or allowing themselves to be directed by filters such as emotions and judgment, well-meaning consultants inadvertently send blocking messages.

*Nonverbal Roadblocks*  Nonverbal roadblocks include facing away when the speaker talks, displaying inappropriate facial expressions such as smiling when the sender is saying something serious, distracting with body movements such as repetitively tapping a pencil, and grading papers or writing reports while "listening." Interrupting a speaker to attend to something or someone else—the phone, a sound outside the window, or a knock at the door—also halts communication and contributes in a subtle way toward undermining the spirit of collaboration.

*Verbal Roadblocks*  Gordon (1977) lists twelve verbal barriers to communication. These have been called the "Dirty Dozen," and they can be grouped into three types of verbal roadblocks that prevent meaningful interaction (Bolton, 1986):

- judging;
- sending solutions; and
- avoiding others' concerns.

The first category, judging, includes criticizing, name-calling, and diagnosing or analyzing why a person is behaving a particular way. False or nonspecific praise, and evaluative words or phrases, send a message of judgment toward the speaker. "You're not thinking clearly," "You'll do a wonderful job of using curriculum-based assessment!" and "You don't really believe that—you're just tired today," are examples of judging. (Notice that each of these statements begins with the word "you.") Nonjudgmental communication expresses interpersonal equity (Gibb, 1974), which is a vital component of a collaborative relationship.

Educators are particularly adept with the next category of verbal roadblocks—sending solutions. These include directing or ordering, warning, moralizing or preaching, advising, and using logical arguments or lecturing. A few of these can become a careless consultant's entire verbal repertoire. "Not knowing the question," Bolton (1986, p. 37) says, "it was easy for him to give the answer." "Stop complaining," and "Don't talk like that," and "If you don't send Jim to the resource room on time . . . " are examples of directing or warning. Moralizing sends a message of "I'm a better educator than you are." Such communication usually starts with "You should . . . " or "You ought to.. . . ". When consultees have problems, the last thing they need is to be told what they *should* do.

Avoiding others' concerns is a third category of verbal roadblocks. This category implies "no big deal" to the message receiver. Avoidance messages include reassuring or sympathizing, such as "You'll feel better tomorrow" or "Everyone goes through this stage," or interrogating to get excessive information and thus delay problem solving. Other avoidance messages include intensive questioning in the manner of the Grand Inquisition, and humoring or distracting, "Let's get off this and talk about something else." Avoiding the concerns others express sends the message that their concerns are not important.

Advising, lecturing, and logical argument are all too often part of the educator's tools of the trade. Teachers tend to use roadblock types of communication techniques frequently with students. The habits they develop cause them to overlook the reality that use of such tactics with adults can drive a wedge into an already precarious relationship. Consultants must avoid tactics such as assuming the posture of the "sage-on-the-stage," imparting wisdom in the manner of a learned professor to undergraduate students, lecturing, moralizing, and advising. Unfortunately, these methods imply superiority, which is detrimental to the collaborative process.

Strong emotions and logic are like air and water—they cannot be in the same space at the same time. Being rational with someone who is emotional leads to frustration. (More will be said about the advising roadblock in another section.) These tools have no place in the consultant's work box. They create irritation and resistance even if the consultant is "right," and they reinforce the false hierarchy of expert/dumb person. When consultants use roadblocks, they are making themselves, their feelings, and their opinions the focus of the interaction, rather than allowing the focus to be the issues, concerns, or problems of the consultee. When they set up roadblocks, listeners do not listen responsively or encourage others to communicate clearly, openly, and effectively. Because it is so easy to inadvertently use a communication block through speaking, it is wise to remember the old adage, "We are blessed with two ears and one mouth, a constant reminder that we should listen twice as much as we talk." Indeed, the more one talks, the more likely a person is to make errors, and the less opportunity that person will have to learn something.

## Assertiveness

By the time the consultant has listened effectively and the collaborative relationship has been developed or enhanced, many consultants are more than ready to start talking. Once the sender's message is understood and emotional levels are reduced, it is the listener's turn to be the sender. Now the consultant gets to talk. However, it is not always easy to communicate your thoughts, feelings, and opinions without infringing on the rights, feelings, or opinions of others. This is the time for assertiveness.

Being assertive involves achieving your goals without damaging the relationship or another's self-esteem (Katz and Lawyer, 1983). The basic aspects of assertive communication (Sundel and Sundel, 1980; Alberti and Emmons, 1974; Thurston, 1987) are:

Use an "I" message instead of a "you" message.
Say "and" instead of "but."
State behavior objectively.
Name your own feelings.
Say what you want to happen.
Express concern for others.
Use assertive body language.

Open and honest consultants say what they want to happen and what their feelings are. That does not mean they always get what they want. Saying what you want and how you feel will clarify the picture and assure that the other(s) won't have to guess what you want or think. Even if others disagree with the ideas and opinions, they can never disagree with the feelings and wishes. Those are very personal and are expressed in a personal manner by starting the interaction with "I," rather than presenting feelings and opinions as truth or expert answer.

*Concern for Others during the Interaction* Expressing concern for others can take many forms. This skill demonstrates that although people have thoughts and feelings which different from those of others, they can still respect the feelings and ideas of others. "I realize it is a tremendous challenge to manage thirty-five children in the same classroom." This statement shows the consultant understands the management problems of the teacher. As the consultant goes on to state preferences in working with the teacher, the teacher is more likely to listen and work cooperatively. The consultee will see that the consultant is aware of the problems that must be dealt with daily. "It seems to me that . . . " and "I understand . . . " and "I realize . . . " and "It looks like . . . " are phrases consultants can use to express concern for the other person in the collaborative relationship. If the consultant cannot complete these sentences with the appropriate information, the next step is to go back to the listening part of the communication.

*How to Be Concerned but Assertive* Assertive people own their personal feelings and opinions. Being aware of this helps them state their wants and feelings. "You" sentences sound accusing, even when that is not intended, which can lead to defensiveness in others. For example, saying to a parent, "You should provide a place and quiet time for Hannah to do her homework," is more accusatory than saying, "I am frustrated when Hannah isn't getting her homework done, and I would like to work with you to think of some ways to help her get it done." Using "and" rather than "but" is very important in expressing thoughts without diminishing a relationship. This is a particularly difficult assertion skill. To the listener the word "but" tends to erase any preceding phrase and prevents the real message from coming through.

It is important to state behavior specifically. By describing behavior objectively, a consultant or consultee sounds less judgmental. It is easy to let blaming and judgmental words creep into language. Without meaning to, the speaker throws up a barrier that blocks the communication and the relationship.

---

**Application for Communicating Positively**

Compare the first statement with the second one:

1. "I would like to have a schedule of rehearsals for the holiday pageant. It is frustrating when I drive out to work with Maxine and Juanita and they are practicing for the musical and can't come to the resource room."

2. "When you don't let me know ahead of time that the girls won't be allowed to come and work with me, I have to waste my time driving and can't get anything accomplished."

In reflecting on these statements, which one is less judgmental and accusatory? Can these two contrasting statements create differing listener attitudes toward the speakers? For many listeners the judgmental words and phrases in the second sentence ("you don't let me," "won't be allowed," "waste my time") sound blaming. They introduce a whole array of red flags.

---

Assertive communication includes demonstrating supportive body language. A firm voice, straight posture, eye contact, and body orientation toward the receiver of the message will have a desirable effect. Assertive body language affirms that the sender owns his or her own feelings and opinions but also respects the other person's feelings and opinions. This a difficult balance to achieve. Body language and verbal language must match or the messages will be confusing. Skills for being assertive are listed in Figure 6–2.

When consultants and consultees communicate in ways that accurately reflect their feelings, focus on objective descriptions of behavior and situations, and think in a concrete manner about what they want to happen, assertive communication will build strong, respectful relationships. Assertive communication is the basis for solving problems and resolving conflicts.

## Managing Resistance, Anger, and Conflict

Sometimes, regardless of how skillful and diplomatic people are in dealing with the emotions of others, they run into barriers of resistance in their attempts to

|  | Usually | Sometimes | Never |
|---|---|---|---|
| 1. Conveys "I" instead of "you" message | | | |
| 2. Says "and" rather than "but" | | | |
| 3. States behavior objectively | | | |
| 4. Says what he/she wants to have happen | | | |
| 5. States feelings | | | |
| 6. Expresses concern | | | |
| 7. Speaks firmly, clearly | | | |
| 8. Has assertive posture | | | |
| 9. Avoids aggressive language | | | |

**FIGURE 6–2  Assertiveness Checklist**

communicate with others. It is estimated that as much as 80 percent of problem solving with others is getting through the resistance. The theme of teacher resistance and how to deal with it is a prominent one in recent school consultation literature (Pugach and Johnson, 1990).

Resistance is a trait of human nature that surfaces when people are asked to change. A wise person once suggested, "How can we ask others to change when it is so hard to change ourselves?" Resistance often has nothing to do with an individual personally or even with a new idea. The resistance is simply a reaction to change of any kind. It requires new ways of thinking and behaving (Margolis and McGettigan, 1988). Change implies imperfection in the way things are being done, and this makes people defensive.

## Why Educators Resist

As discussed in Chapter 1, teachers value their autonomy (Parish and Arends, 1983). They tend to interpret instructional modifications for exceptional learners as limits on their freedom to make instructional decisions (Truesdell, 1988). When people experience such threats to their freedoms, they often demonstrate resistance (Hughs and Falk, 1981).

Ample evidence exists that many general education teachers resist mainstreaming and the movements to curtail student classification and placement in special education. Idol-Maestas and Ritter (1985) note that consulting teachers regard the negative attitude of classroom teachers toward mainstreaming disabled students as a major obstacle in school consultation. Twenty-two percent of graduates from the early resource/consulting teacher preparation programs reported resistance later from their teaching colleagues toward consultation. It is unrealistic to expect all classroom teachers to adopt instructional modifications comfortably and willingly. A gifted program facilitator explained to a new gifted education staff member, "Before I enter any classroom to confer with a teacher or collect a group of students for the resource room, or make suggestions in special education staffings, I ask myself, 'How would I feel if I were on the other side of this door and a colleague asked me to modify the way I am teaching these students?' This helps me to convey concern and helpfulness rather than judgment and superior expertise."

It is human nature to be uncomfortable when another person disagrees. It is also human nature to get upset when someone resists efforts to make changes, implement plans, or modify systems to be more responsive to children with special needs. The need for change can generate powerful emotions. Most people are uncomfortable when experiencing the strong emotions of others. When someone yells or argues, the first impulse is to become defensive, argue the other point of view, and defend your own ideas. Although a school consultant may intend to remain cool, calm, and collected in the interactions that involve exceptional children, occasionally another individual says something that pushes a "hot button" and the consultant becomes upset, angry, or defensive.

Special education consulting teachers have been asked to describe examples of resistance toward their roles. Their responses include these examples:

Consultees (classroom teachers) won't share how they feel.

They act excited about an idea, but never get around to doing it.

They won't discuss it with you, but they do so liberally with others behind your back.

They may try, but give up too soon.

They take out their frustrations on the students.

They are too quick to say that a strategy won't work in their situation.

They dredge up a past example where something similar didn't work.

They keep asking for more and more details or information before trying an idea.

They change the subject, or suddenly have to be somewhere else.

They state that there is not enough time to implement the strategy.

They intellectualize with a myriad of reasons it won't work.

They are simply silent.

When resistance spawns counter-resistance and anger, an upward spiral of emotion is created that can make consulting unpleasant and painful. Bolton (1986) describes resistance as a push, push-back phenomenon. When a person meets resistance with more resistance, defensiveness, logical argument, or any other potential roadblock, resistance increases and dialogue can develop into open warfare. Then the dialogue may become personal or hurtful. Nobody listens at that point, and a potentially healthy relationship is damaged and very difficult to salvage.

## How to Deal with Resistance and Anger

An important strategy for dealing with resistance and defensiveness is to handle your own defensiveness, stop pushing so that the other person will not be able to push back, delay reactions, keep quiet, and *listen*. This takes practice, patience, tolerance, and commitment. It is important to deal with emotions such as resistance, defensiveness, or anger before proceeding to problem solving. People are not inclined to listen until they have been listened to. They will not be convinced of another's sincerity and openness, or be capable of thinking logically, when the filter of emotions is clouding their thinking.

Consultants must "hear their way to success" in managing resistance. This may take five minutes, or months of careful relationship building. Colleagues cannot always avoid disagreements that are serious enough to create anger and resistance. A comment or question delivered in the wrong manner at the wrong time may be the "hot button" that triggers the antagonism. Consider remarks such as these:

"If you want students to use good note-taking skills, shouldn't you teach them how to take notes?"

"Not allowing learning disabled students to use calculators is cruel."

"Why don't you teach in a way that accommodates different learning styles?"

"You penalize gifted students when you keep the class in lockstep with basal readers."

Such remarks can make harried, overworked classroom teachers defensive and resentful. If an occasion arises in which a teacher or parent becomes angry or resistant, responding in the right way will prevent major breakdowns in the communication that is needed.

Kroth (1985) suggests several do's and don'ts for dealing with anger:

Do:
  Listen.
  Write down what the other person says.
  Ask what else is troubling, when the other slows down, .
  Exhaust the person's list of complaints.
  Ask for clarification of any complaints that are too general.
  Show the list to the person and ask if it is complete.
  Ask for suggestions for solving the problems.
  Write down the suggestions.
  In so much as possible, mirror the other's body posture during the process.
  Speak more softly, as that person speaks loudly, .

Don't:
  Argue.
  Defend or become defensive.
  Promise things you can't produce.
  Take ownership of problems that belong to another.
  Raise your voice.
  Belittle or minimize the problem.

Lipshitz, Friedman, and Owen (1989) contend that the power approach to problem solving almost always breeds resistance. They suggest two strategies:

1. *Assume a one-down position.*

   This avoids the power game. An example of assuming the one-down position in a collaborative situation is saying, "Please bear with me if I offer inappropriate suggestions. I don't pretend to understand the organization of your classroom. I know about classwide management procedures that have been successful with mainstreamed students."

2. *Preempt.*

   This means anticipating a difficulty or emotional block by explaining that while a block may occur, it is normal and temporary, and need not become a serious barrier to problem solving. Just mentioning the possibility of resistance before it occurs can be helpful in managing resistance.

Robinson and Brosh (1980) offer other suggestions for dealing with resistance.

Inquire into resistance. Treat an objection as a learning experience and use questions rather than arguments. Rebutting creates conflict rather than solves problems.

Use the bottom line. Respond to questions with bottom-line answers and be as direct as possible. Never exaggerate and do not "lead up" to potential problems or benefits. Begin with them.

Stop and establish. Stop the talking and take a step back to establish your goal and intention. Seek the goal and intention of others in the situation. For example, you might say, "Let's stop arguing about the merits of this pre-assessment procedure. My goal is to find a workable solution to John's difficulties in the classroom. What is your goal?" Another example is asking the question, "Can anyone help us understand why we are having trouble finding an acceptable solution? What is impeding our progress?"

Look for understanding. Examine the situation and discover where you agree and disagree. Then start with the agreements (Schindler and Lapid, 1989).

## Conflict Management

Conflicts are a part of life. They occur when there are unreconciled differences among people in terms of needs, values, goals, and personalities. If conflicting parties cannot give and take by integrating their views and utilizing their differences constructively, interpersonal conflicts will escalate.

School consultants and collaborators are not exempt from the dysfunction that often accompanies conflict. So it is important to for them to develop tools for transforming vague and ambiguous sources of conflict into identified problems that can be solved collaboratively. Lippitt (1983) suggests that conflict, as a predictable social phenomenon, should not be repressed, because there are many positive aspects to be valued. Conflict can help clarify issues, increase involvement, and promote growth, as well as strengthen relationships and organizational systems when the issues are resolved.

Gordon (1977) contends it is undesirable to avoid conflict when there is genuine disagreement, because resentments build up, feelings get displaced, and unpleasantries such as backbiting, gossiping, and general discontent may result.

*Reasons for Conflict among Educators*    Teachers, administrators, and parents face many possible occasions for conflict when they are involved with educating children who have special needs. Some conflicts occur because there is too little information or because misunderstandings have been created from incorrect information. These instances are not difficult to resolve because they require only the communication of facts. Other areas of conflict arise from disagreement over teaching methods, assessment methods, goals, and values. Parent goals and teacher goals for the exceptional student may differ significantly, and support personnel may add even more dimensions to the conflict. For example, if a child is instructed by the reading specialist to read more slowly, urged by the learning disabilities teacher to read more rapidly, required by the classroom teacher to read a greater amount of material, and ordered by the parent to get better grades or *else*, communication is tenuous or nonexistent, and conflict is inevitable.

Perhaps the most difficult area of conflict relates to values. When people have differing values about children, education, or educator roles within the learning context, effective communication is a challenging goal. As discussed earlier in this chapter, rapport building, listening, and paraphrasing are significant in building relationships among those whose values conflict. The most important step is to listen courteously until a clear message about the value comes through, demonstrating respect for the value even if it conflicts with yours. Then it is time to assert your own values and, along with the other person, try to reach a common goal or seek a practical issue on which to begin problem solving.

*How to Resolve Conflicts in the School Context*    Some conflicts, particularly those involving values, are difficult to prevent and may seem at the time to be unresolvable. However, if all can agree to common goals or common ground for discussion, conflicts can be resolved.

Gordon (1977) and many others suggest that conflict resolution can follow one of three paths:

> I win, you lose.
> You win, I lose.
> I win, you win.

The first two paths are frequently taken because people fear conflict and wish to avoid it. The third path, with the win/win outcome, is hard because those involved must confront their emotions and the emotions of others, and work diligently to turn conflict into cooperation. This method focuses on needs rather than solutions. It is based on two-way communication with lots of listening. During conflict situations, the immediate purpose of interaction is improving communication, not changing points of view.

The first step in resolving conflicts within an "everybody wins" philosophy is to use those listening skills described earlier in the chapter to find common ground. In dealing with emotions of the speaker, the listener must concentrate with an open mind and attend to the speaker's feelings as well as the facts or ideas that are part of the message. The listener must strive to hear the whole story without interrupting, even if there are strong feelings of disagreement. Conflict usually means that intense emotions are involved. Only by concentrating on the message with an open mind can all parties begin to deal with the conflict. Emotional filters often function as blinders. If the emotions cannot be overcome, the best tactic is to postpone the communication, using assertive responses to do so.

Listening establishes a common intent and develops a starting attitude. Listening to one who is upset helps that person focus on a problem rather than an emotion. Listening lets people cool down. Bolton (1986) calls this the spiral of resistance, suggesting that if one listens with empathy and does not interrupt, the speaker's anger or high emotion will dissipate. Without saying a word, the listener makes the speaker feel accepted and respected.

It is hard to argue with someone who does not argue back. It is hard to stay mad or upset with someone who seems to understand and empathize. Each time a person listens, a small victory for the advancement of human dignity has been achieved (Schindler and Lapid, 1989). Only after emotions are brought into the open and recognized can all parties involved move on to seek a common goal.

The initial intent for resolving a conflict should be to learn. This enables all factions to increase mutual understanding and think creatively together. Most people could agree to such a start because it does not address goals or values. It does not even require agreement that a problem exists. It simply establishes the intent to learn by working together. Establishing intent for dialogue should follow the reduction of emotional responses. Of course, as discussed earlier, it is important to avoid roadblocks at all stages of the process.

Consultants and consulting teachers must put aside preconceived notions about their own expertise and learn from those who often know the student best—parents and classroom teachers. These consultees respond positively to open-ended questions that let them know they are respected and needed. When consultants open their own minds, they unlock the potential of others.

After listening constructively, consultants need to help establish ground rules for resolving the conflict. The ground rules should express support, mutual respect, and a commitment to the process. Again, this requires talking and listening, dialoguing, and keeping an open mind. It is important not to dominate the dialogue at this time and, by the same token, not to let the other person dominate the conversation. This part of the communication might be called "agreeing to disagree," with the intent of "agreeing to find a point of agreement." It is important to share the allotted interaction time equitably and in a way that facilitates understanding. Consultants must use precise language without exaggerating points, or, as discussed earlier, flaunting "educationese" and taking inappropriate shortcuts with jargon and "alphabet soup" acronyms.

Dealing with conflict productively also requires asserting your ideas, feelings, or opinions. While listening enables the consultant to understand the speaker's perspectives, wants, and goals, assertion skills allow consultants to present their perspective. This often follows a pattern of listen—assert—listen—assert—listen, and so on, until both parties have spoken and have been heard.

Although there may be resistance after each assertion, it will gradually dissipate so that *real* communication and collaboration can begin to take place. Only after this process has happened can collaborative goal setting and problem solving occur. Figure 6–3 summarizes useful steps for managing resistance and conflict.

There is a well-known story of a man who had three sons. He stipulated in his will that the oldest son should inherit half his camels, the middle son should get one-third of the camels, and the youngest should be the new owner of one-ninth of his camels. When the old man died, he owned seventeen camels. But the sons could not agree on how to divide the camels in accordance with their father's will. Months and months of bitter conflict went by. Finally the three young men sought the advice of a wise woman in the village. She heard their complaints and observed their bitterness and felt sorry that brothers were fighting and putting the family into turmoil. So she gave the brothers one of her camels. The estate then was divided easily according to the father's wishes. The eldest took home nine camels, the second put six camels beside his tent, and the youngest took home two camels. The men were happy, the father's last wishes were honored, and the wise woman took her own camel back and led it home.

Conflict management is the process of becoming aware of a conflict, diagnosing its nature, and employing an appropriate problem-solving method in such a way that it simultaneously achieves the goals of all involved and enhances relationships among them. If the consulting relationship is treated as a collaborative one in which each person's needs are met (the win/win model), then feelings of self-confidence, competence, self-worth, and power increase, enhancing the overall capacity of the system for responding to conflict in the future (Katz and Lawyer, 1983). The win/win relationship is based on honesty, trust, and mutual respect—qualities stressed earlier as vital to a successful consulting relationship. Win/win allows all involved parties to experience positive outcomes. The model works best when all parties use effective communication skills (Fisher and Ury, 1981).

A. *Responsive Listening*

1. Had assertive posture _____

2. Used appropriate nonverbal listening _____

3. Did not become defensive _____

4. Used minimal verbals in listening _____

5. Reflected content _____

6. Reflected feelings _____

7. Let other do most of the talking _____

8. Used only brief, clarifying questions _____

B. *Assertiveness*

9. Did not use roadblocks such as giving advice _____

10. Used "I" messages _____

11. Stated wants and feelings _____

C. *Recycled the Interaction*

12. Used positive postponement _____

13. Did not problem solve before emotions were controlled _____

14. Summarized _____

15. Set time to meet again, if applicable _____

**FIGURE 6–3 Checklist for Managing Resistance and Conflict**

The opposite of successful conflict management is avoiding conflict, ignoring feelings, and bypassing the goals of others. The relationship becomes adversarial, if it is not already so, because for someone to win, another must lose. When conflicts are approached with responsive listening and dealt with honestly and openly, the underlying problem or need can be resolved.

When engineers stress collaboration, they often use the bumblebee analogy. According to the laws of aerodynamics, bumblebees cannot fly. But as everyone knows, they do. By the same token, some might say that groups cannot function productively because of the conflicts, personal agenda, and individual preferences that exist among the members. But they do. Groups of people play symphonies, set up businesses, write laws, and develop IEPs for student needs. An understanding of adult individual differences, styles, and preferences, as discussed in Chapter 4, will encourage participants in consultation and collaboration to listen more respectfully and value differences among colleagues. This knowledge, when combined with responsive listening, avoidance of roadblocks, and assertiveness, will enable consultants to deal with resistance and conflict productively. Conflict management puts these skills to practical use in educational settings of school and home.

## Tips for Consulting and Collaborating

1. Avoid communication roadblocks.

2. Listen. This helps dissipate negative emotional responses and often helps the other person articulate the problem, perhaps finding a solution then and there.

3. Use assertion. Say what you feel and what your goals are.

4. Be aware of your "hot buttons." Knowing your own responses to certain "trigger" behaviors and words will help you control natural tendencies to argue, get defensive, or simply turn red and sputter.

5. Attend to nonverbal language (kinesics, or body language) as well as to verbal language when communicating.

6. Don't "dump your bucket" of frustrations onto the other person. Jog, shout, practice karate, but avoid pouring out anger and frustration on others. Instead, fill the buckets of others with "warm fuzzies" of empathy and caring.

7. Develop a protocol within the school context for dealing with difficult issues and for settling grievances.

8. Deal with the present. Keep to the issue of the current problem rather than past problems, failures, or personality conflicts.

9. Use understanding of individual differences among adults to bridge communication gaps and manage conflicts in educational settings.

10. Advocate for training that focuses on communication, problem solving, and conflict management.

## Chapter Review

1. The primary reason people fail at work is because of communication problems. It is too often assumed that communication skill develops with no special attention to the complexities of social interaction.

2. The sender, the message, and the receiver are three key components of the communication process. Each component is vital. When a message is missent or misheard, many distortions occur that prevent open, honest communication. This happens because of differences in values, language, attitudes, perceptions, and background of sender and receiver.

**3.** Listening is the most important skill educational professionals can use to establish rapport with partners in addressing educational goals for children. Responsive listening means using nonverbal and verbal responses to the content of the message and the emotions of the speaker. Verbal responses include brief messages and messages that show understanding. Listening responsively is a challenge because of the temptation to talk about your own thoughts and ideas.

**4.** Major skills in effective communication are responsive listening, asserting, managing conflict, and collaborative problem solving. Both verbal and nonverbal components are included in these skills. The skills form the basis of a respectful, egalitarian relationship and a successful team on behalf of the student with special needs. They pave the way to effective problem solving and mutual collaboration.

**5.** Communication can be hampered by verbal and nonverbal roadblocks. Verbal roadblocks include responses that are judgmental, responses that send solutions, and responses that avoid the concerns of others. Nonverbal roadblocks include body language that conveys lack of empathy and concern.

**6.** Assertive communication allows speakers to state their own views, feelings, and opinions, without impeding the ongoing consulting process. Assertiveness means stating your wants or feelings by starting sentences with "I," using "and" rather than "but," and showing concern for the other person. Resistance sometimes occurs when a speaker is assertive. This resistance is a natural reaction to the request for change. It can be managed by using a combination of assertiveness and responsive listening.

**7.** Conflict arises when members of educational teams have different feelings, values, needs, and goals. Conflict resolution should follow a win/win model if collaborative efforts are to be maintained. Listening instead of arguing, establishing ground rules, and seeking a common goal help bring teams to the problem-solving stage without any "losers."

## Activities

**1.** Discuss the following:
What roadblock does each of these comments set up?

> What you need is more activity. Why don't you develop a hobby?
>
> You are such a good friend. I can count on you.
>
> Let's talk about something more positive.
>
> I know just how you feel.
>
> Why did you let her talk to you that way?
>
> Which of these lines create resistance and defensiveness?
>
> What you should do is . . .

Do you want to comment on this?

Everyone has problems like that.

That's a good thought.

You mean you'd actually do that?

Let's change the subject.

What should I do?

What assertive statements could be made for each situation?

A colleague talks to you about his personal problems and you can't get your work done.

The paraprofessional comes in late frequently.

During a committee meeting one member keeps changing the subject and getting the group off task.

A colleague wants to borrow some material but has failed to return things in the past.

During a phone conversation with a wordy parent, you need to get some information quickly and hang up soon.

The class next door is so rowdy that your class can't work.

2.  Discuss these basic assumptions about communication for consultation and add more to the list.

The reactions of others depend on your actions, word choices, body language, and listening skills.

People generally want to do a good job.

People have a powerful need to "save face."

No one can force another person to change.

Learning to communicate, be assertive, and facilitate conflict resolution is awkward at first.

3.  During initial attempts at paraphrasing, the process often feels and sounds awkward and phony. What might be done about that?

4.  Practice the following situations:

expressing anger in constructive ways;

requesting the return of an item borrowed from you;

stating a contrasting view to a supervisor-type;

recommending a better way of doing something;

asking again, and again, for materials you loaned some time ago and you need now.

**5.** Restate the following message so the language is assertive but nonthreatening to the receiver.

"You penalize gifted students when you keep the class lockstepped in the basal texts and the workbooks."

"If you want students to use good note-taking skills, you should teach them how to take notes."

"Not allowing students to use calculators is poor teaching practice and terribly outmoded."

"It is not fair to insist that learning disabled students take tests they cannot read."

## For Further Reading

Bolton, R. (1986). *People Skills: How to Assert Yourself, Listen to Others, and Resolve Conflicts.* New York: Simon and Schuster.

DeBoer, A. L. (1986). *The Art of Consulting.* Chicago: Arcturus.

Fisher, R., and Brown, S. (1988). *Getting Together: Building Relationships as We Negotiate.* New York: Penguin Books.

Fisher, R. and Ury, W. (1981). *Getting to yes: Negotiating agreement without giving in.* New York: Penguin.

Gordon, T. (1977). *Leader Effectiveness Training. L. E. T.: The No-Lose Way to Release the Productive Potential in People.* Toronto: Bantam.

Hall, E. T. (1959). *The Silent Language.* New York: Doubleday.

## Reference

Alberti, R. E., and Emmons, M. L. (1974). *Your Perfect Right: A Guide to Assertive Behavior* (2d ed.). San Luis Obispo, CA: Impact.

Bolton, R. (1986). *People Skills: How to Assert Yourself, Listen to Others, and Resolve Conflicts.* New York: Simon and Schuster.

Buscaglia, L. (1986). *Loving Each Other: The Challenges of Human Relationships.* Westminister, MD: Fawcett.

DeBoer, A. L. (1986). *The Art of Consulting.* Chicago: Arcturus.

Dickens, V. J., and Jones, C. J. (1990). Regular special education consultation: A teacher's education strategy for implementation. *Teacher Education and Special Education, 13:* 221–24.

Egan, G. (1982). *The Skilled Helper: A Model for Systematic Helping and Interpersonal Relating* (2d ed.). Monterey, CA: Brookes/Cole.

Fisher, R., and Brown, S. )1988). *Getting Together: Building Relationhips As We Negotiate.* New York: Penguin Books.

Fisher, R., and Ury, W. (1981). *Getting to Yes.* New York: Penguin

Gersten, R., Darch, C., Davis, G., and George, N. (1991). Apprenticeship and intensive training of consulting teachers: A naturalistic study. *Exceptional Children, 57:* 226–36.

Gibb, J. R. (1974). Defensive communication. In R. S. Cathcart and L. A. Samovar (eds.): *Small Group Communication: A Reader* (2d ed.): pp. 327–33. Dubuque, IA: Brown.

Gordon, T. (1977). *Leader Effectiveness Training, L.E.T.: The No-Lose Way to Release the Productive Potential in People.* Toronto: Bantam.

Gutkin, T., and Curtis, M. J. (1982). School–Based Consultation: Theory and Techniques. In C. R. Reynolds and T. B. Gutkin (eds.): *The Handbook of School Psychology,* pp. 796–828. New York: Wiley.

Hall, E. T. (1959). *The Silent Language.* New York: Doubleday.

Hillerman, T. (1990). *Coyote Waits.* New York: Harper and Row.

Hughs, J., and Falk, R. (1981). Resistance, reactance, and consultation. *Journal for School Psychology, 19(2):* 139–42.

Idol–Maestas, L., Lloyd, S., and Lilly, M. S. (1981). Non-categorical approach to direct service and teachers education. *Exceptional Children, 48*: 213– 20.

Idol–Maestas, L., and Ritter, S. (1985). A follow-up study of resource/consulting teachers: Factors that facilitate and inhibit teacher consultation. *Teacher Education and Special Education, 8*: 121–31.

Johnson, D. W., and Johnson, F. P. (1987). *Joining Together: Group Theory and Group Skills* (3rd ed.). Englewood Cliffs, NJ: Prentice Hall.

Katz, N. H., and Lawyer, J. W. (1983). Communication and conflict management skills: Strategies for individual and systems changes. *Nonviolence and Change National Forum, 63*: 31.

Kroth, R. L. (1978). *Communication with Parents of Exceptional Children: Improving Parent–Teacher relationships.* Denver: Love.

Lippitt, G. L. (March, 1983). Can conflict resolution be win–win? *School Administrator*, pp. 20–22.

Lipshitz, R., Friedman, V., and Owen, H. (1989). Overcoming resistance to training and a nonconfrontive approach. *Training and Development Journal*, pp. 46–50.

Margolis, H., and Brannigan, G. G. (1986). Building trust with parents. *Academic Therapy, 22*: 71–74.

Margolis, H., and McGettigan, J. (1988). Managing resistance to instructional modifications in mainstream settings. *Remedial and Special Education, 9*: 15–21.

Murphy, K. D. (1987). *Effective Listening: Hearing What People Say and Making it Work for You.* New York: Bantam.

Nichols, R. G., and Stevens, L. A. (1957). *Are You Listening?* New York: McGraw–Hill.

Ozturk, M. (1992). Education for cross-cultural communication. *Educational Leadership, 49*(4): 79-81.

Parish, R., and Arends, R. (1983). Why innovation programs are discontinued. *Educational Leadership, 40*: 62–65.

Pugach, M. C., and Johnson, L. J. (1990). Fostering the continued democratization of consultation through action research. *Teacher Education and Special Education, 13*: 240–45.

Robinson, E. H. III, and Brosh, M. C. (1980). Communication skills training for resource teachers. *Journal of Learning Disabilities, 13*: 55–58.

Schein, E. H. (1969). *Process Consultation: Its Role in Organization Development.* Reading, MA: Addison–Wesley.

Schindler, C., and Lapid, G. (1989). *The Great Turning: Personal Peace, Global Victory.* Santa Fe: Bear.

Sue, D. W., and Sue, D. (1990). *Counseling the Culturally Different: Theory and Practice* (2d ed.). New York: John Wiley.

Sundel, S. S., and Sundel, M. (1980). *Be Assertive: A Practical Guide for Human Service Workers.* Beverly Hills: Sage.

Thurston, L. P. (1987). *Survival Skills for Women: Facilitator Manual.* Manhattan, KS: Survival Skills Education and Development.

Thurston, L. P. (1989). Rural special education teachers as consultants: Strategies, practices, and training. Presented at American Council for Rural Special Education national conference, Ft. Lauderdale, FL.

Truesdell, L. A. (1988). Mainstreaming in an urban middle school: Effects of school organization and climate. *Urban Review, 20*(1): 42-58.

# 7

# MANAGING RESPONSIBILITIES OF CONSULTATION AND COLLABORATION

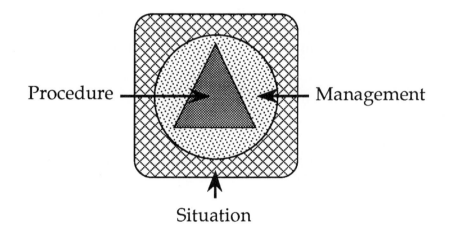

Procedure → Management

↑
Situation

## To Think About

Schools are bustling arenas of activities that often seem to have little to do with books and studies. Not only do school personnel teach students in academic settings, they also feed them, transport them, keep records, counsel and advise, dispense materials and resources, address social and health problems, and much, much more. If other school-related roles as diverse as librarian, speech pathologist, school psychologist, social worker, and nurse were included, the list would increase exponentially.

The complexity of contemporary school life is immense. In this daily hubbub the demands on school personnel for efficiency, expertise, and accountability can be overwhelming. Stress and fatigue take a toll, with burnout and attrition from the field all too frequent results. But role-related stress can be minimized and controlled by managing time and resources wisely and by organizing procedures for carrying out responsibilities of the role efficiently.

## *Focusing Questions*

1.  Why are school consultants particularly vulnerable to stress, burnout, and attrition?
2.  What organizational techniques will help consultants perform their roles effectively?
3.  What procedures for conducting meetings, interviews, and observations contribute to consultation and collaboration success?
4.  How can school consultants manage records and resources efficiently?
5.  How do support personnel contribute to collaboration for helping students with special needs succeed in school?
6.  What ethical considerations guide the practice of school consultation?

## *Key Terms*

| | |
|---|---|
| attrition | observation |
| burnout | related services personnel |
| consultation log or journal | stress management |
| ethics of consultation | support personnel |
| interview | time management |

---

**Scenario**

The setting is the kitchen of a home where a middle school student and mother are sitting at the kitchen table.

*MOTHER*: I see a note here from your teacher saying that you need to make up an important math test you missed yesterday . . .

*CHILD*: Uh-huh, I missed it because yesterday was Tuesday.

*MOTHER*: What does that have to do with the math test?

*CHILD*: Well, on Tuesdays I'm supposed to see Mrs. Evans, but she wasn't there. So I went to Mr. Bowman instead.

*MOTHER*: Who is Mrs. Evans?

*CHILD*: She's the reading teacher. I see her Tuesdays and Thursdays, from 1:30 to 2:30, but she was sick yesterday.

*MOTHER*: So you saw Mr. Bowman. Who is he?

*CHILD*: The special education teacher I see for more help with reading, but mostly with spelling and my workbooks. He got called to another school for a meeting, so he sent me to Jeanette.

*MOTHER*: Now wait a minute—who is Jeanette?

*CHILD*: Gee, mom, I thought you told the principal you and dad would keep up with my school program.

*MOTHER*: *I'm trying!*

*CHILD*: Anyway, Jeanette is the high school girl who tutors me in reading.

*MOTHER*: Oh?

*CHILD*: It's O.K. She's nice. She wants to be a teacher someday. Mrs. Bagley helped me work it out.

*MOTHER*: And *who* is Mrs. Bagley?

*CHILD*: The counselor. She says working with Jeanette is good for me, and for her, too.

*MOTHER*: And just what does Miss Anderson think about all of this?

*CHILD*: Uh, who's she?

*MOTHER*: Your *classroom teacher!*

*CHILD*: Oh, yeah, I forgot all about her.

(This child's schedule underscores the complexity of role responsibilities among educators, accentuating the need for communication, cooperation, and coordination in schools and homes.)

adapted from Michelle Berg.

## Stress, Burnout, and Attrition of School Consultants

Each year a significant number of teachers experience symptoms of burnout, with feelings of physical and emotional fatigue, loss of enthusiasm for their jobs, and sometimes depression or guilt. Burnout disproportionately affects those in human service professions (Maslach, 1982). High levels of emotional exhaustion and depersonalization, when accompanied by low feelings of personal accomplishment, signal burnout for teachers, social workers, nurses, and others who serve people's needs. They feel used up and exhausted physically, emotionally, and attitudinally. Truch (1980) describes the condition as "chronically miserable" and prone to "rust out." Up to fifty percent of educators have indicated they may leave the profession because of burnout (Raschke, Dedrick, and DeVries, 1988).

Overwhelming responsibilities and pressures involved in working with special needs students make teachers particularly vulnerable to stress and burnout. In a study of more than six hundred special educators, Zabel and Zabel (1982) found those who function as consulting teachers rank higher in emotional exhaustion and depersonalization than those in other service deliveries. The researchers propose that this occurs because consulting teachers serve large geographic areas, many students, and a wide range of expectations of others. As advocates for children with special learning and behavior needs, special education teachers may set unreasonably high expectations for themselves and others. Lack of role clarity and discrepancy between their own role perceptions and expectations of others contribute to this syndrome (Bensky et al., 1980). Dettmer (1982) identifies lack of recognition and reinforcement for their work, as well as heavy responsibilities without much decision-making authority, as additional stressors.

Undue levels of stress reduce productivity, motivation, and, eventually, compassion for others (Shaw, Bensky, and Dixon, 1981). Maslach and Pines (1977) have determined that, at the extreme stage of burnout, human service workers are likely to view clients as somehow deserving of their problems.

There may be a cyclical or reciprocal relationship between teacher stress and student behavior (Shaw, Bensky, and Dixon, 1981). For example, short-term results of teacher stress such as irritability, inability to concentrate, disorganization, and poor management of work flow can affect the behavior and performance of students. Teacher stress also affects interactions with other professionals. One unfortunate outcome of burnout is attrition from the field, resulting in fewer professionals available to serve children with special needs.

Stress and burnout at such debilitating levels can be prevented. While enough has been written about this subject in recent years to cause some to say they are *burned out* with the term burnout, stress levels for educators continue to rise. If even one teacher can be rescued from burnout by focusing on the subject, many children will benefit. For students with special needs it is crucial that their general classroom and special education teachers do not "fizzle out," "coast out," or "rust out" in their profession. Teachers who do so risk slipping further and further into cynicism and disillusionment. Students with learning and behavior disorders are particularly vulnerable to such attitudes by their teachers.

Organizational procedures and strategies can be adopted to make responsibilities and work loads less overwhelming. Consultants and consultees must learn to "work smarter, not harder" to accomplish goals for students who are at risk of failure in school. This chapter will focus on suggestions for working smarter—and not necessarily harder—to become more comfortable and productive in consultive and collaborative roles.

---

**Application for Thinking Positively**

Start with a stack of three by five cards, preferably bright colored. On five of them write a positive feature about yourself: an ability you are proud of, an accomplishment you have made, or something about yourself that indicates what a wonderful person you are. Then select an activity you enjoy doing every day, such as reading the paper, getting into the car to go home from school, or having that first cup of coffee. Each day before doing this activity, read over your cards. Do this daily and particularly at any time you feel your flame starting to burn out. Add to your cards each week. Thinking positively and noting your accomplishments can help prevent burnout.

---

## Developing a Positive Attitude

A positive attitude helps reduce stress. Zabel and Zabel (1982) suggest keeping a diary, or developing positive self-talk such as "I can't change it, so I won't worry about it," or "What difference will this one thing make ten years from now?" Truch (1980, p. 95) advises, "Take it easy, take it as it comes. If it doesn't come, go out and get it. If it is still not there, create it. Do what you need to do. It is never too late."

Another effective strategy is working to change negative thoughts to more positive ones. Instead of thinking, "She shouldn't have reacted that way," it helps to think, "I wish she hadn't reacted that way." Instead of thinking, "It ruins my day when that happens," a better thought is, "It is inconvenient that happened."

## Maintaining Good Health

A nourishing diet keeps the body fit and more resistant to stress. Avoiding liquor, caffeine, and foods with artificial additives will help. Reducing intake of saturated fat, processed sugar and salt, and increasing consumption of fiber are healthful. So is cutting out, or down on, smoking.

Exercise is extremely important. A creative way to exercise and problem solve simultaneously has been developed by Caro and Robbins (1991). They encourage colleagues to "TalkWalk," which is talking while walking together in an unrestricted outdoor environment. It is a way to exercise physically and mentally while reflecting, discussing professional issues, and problem solving together. TalkWalking provides a change of venue that can lead to open, trusting, productive communication.

## Building Networks of Support

Developing mutually supportive networks will minimize, if not eliminate, feelings of isolation and helplessness in the demanding role of school consultant. It helps to talk things out with others as one tackles the complex responsibilities inherent in meeting special needs. Consultants will want to develop comfortable relationships with supervisors and others at work and in the community. A support system is an effective outlet for frustration and also provides a backup in times of crisis.

One special education staff made a commitment to meet each Friday at a local restaurant for lunch and lively conversation. Ground rules stipulated no talking about students, schools, or personnel in this public place, of course. But the camaraderie and conviviality of the weekly event, which was looked on favorably by district administrators, was an effective system of support for teachers whose roles entail stress and frustration.

## Setting Realistic Goals

School consultants will benefit from developing realistic goals and making sure their daily activity focuses on those goals. The goals should be stated positively. Say, "I will use my plan time today to prepare a science test," not, "I will try not to waste my plan period today"; "I will evaluate these compositions before I leave school," not, "I won't let these compositions go until tomorrow." Positive language promotes action.

Consultants must understand their role before committing to it (as discussed in Chapter 2) and avoid trying to be a "superperson." They should update their goals periodically, reviewing progress often and revising where necessary. Goal setting will be discussed more fully in the time management section.

## Taking Time to Relax

Relaxing does not mean sitting down to eat a meal or to watch television. Deep relaxation requires that you do nothing else, relaxing mentally as well

---

### Application for Setting Goals

To check for potential stress factors, use a grid that determines whether or not your behavior matches your goals (see Figure 7–1). On the left-hand column list your personal goals. Include family, school, personal, community, and organizational goals as appropriate. Across the top write your most frequent behaviors, such as reading, going to meetings, grading papers, gardening. Then check the behaviors that are helping you meet your goals. If you have behaviors that are not helping meet any of your goals, reflect on the value of those behaviors at this point in your life. If you have goals you are not accomplishing, examine the behaviors list to see what might be added for helping you accomplish these goals. If you still find gaps, take care, for your flame of enthusiasm and feeling of accomplishment may begin to sputter. Some changes may be in order.

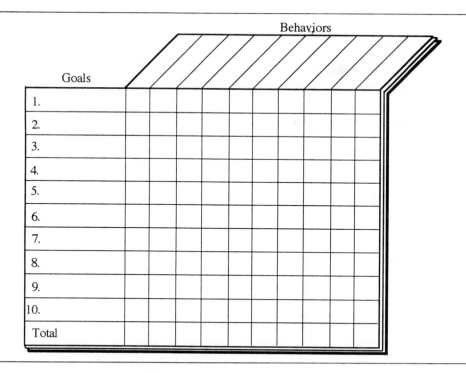

**Figure 7-1  Stress Management Grid**

as physically. Imagery, biofeedback, yoga, and meditation are examples of deep relaxation techniques. Several helpful relaxation activities are deep breathing, counting backward, imagining a favorite place, and relaxing the entire body, part by part. It is good to reserve time for relaxation by putting it on your daily "To Do" list. Then it will not be so easy to neglect.

## Making Environmental Changes

Consulting teachers can improve the learning environment by altering it in a variety of ways and at various times during the school year. The classroom or resource area can be set up so the environmental systems control student behavior (DeShong, 1981). It is helpful to take a critical look at the room arrangement, looking for ways to change the traffic flow and manage trouble spots of congestion efficiently. This may involve moving the pencil sharpener or having two trash cans instead of one and locating them more strategically. Teachers need to sit in each area and every desk in the room, asking, "Am I comfortable here? Can I see and hear well? Is there a glare? Are there distractions? Is this a pleasant place?" Comfortable students are happier, more productive students. Learning and teaching are more effective when the environment is pleasant and comfortable.

Consultants will want to structure their consultation areas to increase opportunities for talking with colleagues. Privacy for confidential conversations, room arrangements for collegial interaction, and often-overlooked amenities such as fresh air, comfortable chairs, and attractive displays will encourage collaboration.

## Taking Control of Your Own Life

Educators can take control of their lives by being prepared and efficient. An initial step is to examine the frustrating facets of your life and work to remove them (Goldfein, 1977). Potentially frustrating aspects of daily living and suggestions from Goldfein and others for managing them, include the following:

*Keys.* Have four sets made.

*Greeting Cards.* Prepare cards for your full list. Note date in upper right hand of card, where stamp goes. Keep them handy so you don't forget them.

*Family Control Center.* Display a cork bulletin board with a large calendar for writing on, push tacks, pad and pencil. Write clear, concise directions to family members. For example, keep track of who has ball practice and won't be home for dinner.

*Planning and Appointment Book.* Into this put all current addresses. Carry it with you, placing messages, numbers, dates, and appointments in it, and throw away all your tiny scraps of paper.

*Surprise Drawer.* Buy ahead for special occasion gifts. Buy at leisure (and on sale!), and place wrapped, tagged gifts in your surprise drawer. Have extra child's birthday gifts and baby shower gifts available.

*Emergency Phone List.* On a mailing label write names, addresses, and phone numbers you use often, and put the list beside your phone. If you live in a rural area, write out specific directions to your home in case of an emergency.

*Information Book.* In this three-ring binder put laminated or plastic-sleeved sheets of step-by-step guidelines for procedures in case you must be away suddenly. Include car license plate number and what to do if the electricity goes off. Have one set of the guidelines for home and one for school.

The list can be expanded to include individual preferences and life-styles. By controlling these daily life details, busy educators have more time and energy for being productive in their demanding roles as well as having time for fun and relaxation as well.

**Controlling Your Life and Role**

What if burnout has struck already? What if you feel low self-esteem, emotional and physical exhaustion now? Then these intervention techniques may be helpful.

1. Talk to someone. Say hello, give a positive comment to someone, share ideas.

2. Pretend you are O.K. Remember that problems in life are inevitable and demonstrate we are alive and still functioning. Smile. Stand up straight and walk with a bouncy step. Wear bright, happy clothes—a funny tie or long, dangling earrings shaped like dinosaurs or pea pods.

3. Sit in the warm, fresh air. Natural light helps your body function better.

4. Laugh out loud. Each person should have his or her "laugh ration" every day for mental and physical health. Listen to a comedy tape. Read a joke book. Watch children play.

5. Move. Oxygenate. Mild exercise gets the blood flowing and transports more oxygen throughout the body, helping you feel alert and alive.

6. Play energetic, happy music. Classical music is effective. Rock music is tiring and drains energy from many people.

7. Break that routine. Take a different route to work. Rearrange your schedule or your furniture. Take a vacation if you possibly can. When you do, leave worries and cares behind. Give yourself over to relaxation and rejuvenation.

8. Schedule appointments with yourself. Keep a jar of little treats on your desk, such as encouraging statements or envelopes with a five-dollar bill inside, to be good to yourself every now and then.

9. Use reminders to help remember these and other prevention and intervention strategies. They could be colored ribbons, stick-on happy faces, ads from magazines, letters to yourself. Put the reminders on your tote bag or briefcase, on your watch, calendar, or rearview mirror.

10. Remind yourself often that prevention and remediation of stress and burnout are the concern of the individual, not family or friends or colleagues. Each must become aware of the factors and variables in his or her own personal formula of strategies for keeping the flame of motivation alive.

## Management of Time and Energy

When school consultants are asked about the biggest obstacle to their role, the majority responds, "Time, time, time!" As time goes by, seemingly more and more swiftly each year, busy people compensate by trying to do more things and to do them faster. Time is a critical factor in the plans and purposes of educators, particularly for school consultants in their complex, multifarious roles. Wouldn't it be wonderful if each educator could have time for these activities?

- preparation of the learning environment;
- teamwork and interaction with colleagues;
- work periods with varying groups of students;
- development and revision of learning materials; and
- office hours, just as many other professionals have to use for consulting, reading, filing, grading, planning, phoning, evaluating, and reflecting.

Educators are probably decades away from enjoying this ideal schedule. But school consultation and collaboration can become catalysts for arranging more professional work schedules.

When a group of consultants were tracked over a two-year period (Nelson and Stevens, 1981), researchers found their time was distributed among consultations, meetings, preparation and planning, administrative assistance, supplementary services, and direct services to general and special education. The majority of their time was spent in indirect service, with only 25 to 30 percent in actual consultation. Other indirect services demanding time were preparation and planning, administration, observations, and meetings. A more recent study by Tindal and Taylor-Pendergast (1989) revealed consultants spent 35 percent of their professional time with students, 14 percent with teachers, 10 percent with other staff, and about 41 percent alone. Their activities included:

- 15 percent for problem identification and program evaluation,
- 32 percent for interactive testing,
- 22 percent for interpersonal communication,
- 22 percent for noninteractive observation, and
- 9 percent for review of records and preparation of materials.

Managing time and schedules to conduct consultation and collaborate effectively is one of the biggest challenges for school consultants. Caseload is a critical factor in managing time and arranging schedules. One consultant devoted 76.8 hours over 13 weeks to just 1 case. The experience of Idol (1988) and others suggests that special education consultants should serve a maximum of 35 students. Those having both direct and indirect service roles should have their ratios classified for each category, and students receiving consultation services as well as direct services should be counted twice.

Problems concerning time management contribute to teacher stress and burnout and possibly, to attrition from the field. Since time is not replaceable or expandable, it must be allocated judiciously to provide the most service for the greatest number of people.

Time management practices encourage efficient use of abilities and strengths. The purpose of time management is not to get *everything* done, but to accomplish professional and personal goals (Maker, 1985). Being busy is not the same as being productive. Time management is a skill that can be learned and improved. Personality differences and cultural diversity affect the value and use of time and will need to addressed accordingly.

A basic four-step plan is useful for achieving productive time management practices:

1. Establish goals and make plans.
2. Identify and eliminate time wasters.
3. Use positive time management strategies.
4. Take care of yourself.

When these steps are followed, educators are more able to achieve satisfaction with their work, progress toward their goals, and enjoy feelings of self-worth and accomplishment. They also have more time for fun and leisure activities.

## Goal Setting and Planning

"Where do I want to go?" and "What are my goals for going there?" are vital questions for consultants to ask themselves. Reflecting on such questions activates the planning process. Careful planning prevents waste of time, energy, and resources. It keeps individuals on target toward their personal and professional goals, enabling them to do what needs to be done purposefully rather than spontaneously.

A busy school consultant might think about a perfect day five years into the future—and what that day would contain. Further education? Another home? A different job? A new car? A stimulating school day with happy, successful students and colleagues who work together enthusiastically? After reflecting on this perfect day and thinking of words that describe it, the consultant can formulate long-term goals for attaining such a day and many more. These goals may be personal or professional, related to educational degrees, home, family, job setting, or job description.

Once goals are established, they become a yardstick by which to plan the use of time. When people know where they are going, they can plan the actions to get there. By putting the actions on the "To Do" list, they are working constructively toward where they want to be.

## Identifying and Eliminating Time Wasters

According to Alan Lakein (1973), an authority in time management, there are four kinds of time:

1. Pay-off time, resulting in an immediate reward. This might be preparing your tax forms, grading papers, or meeting with an angry parent.
2. Investment time, for long-term development. This could be attending classes, going to a conference, reading professional journals, establishing professional networks.
3. Organization time, to maintain the system. This includes reports, procedures, and routines required within the system.
4. Wasted time, which is gone forever.

Time wasters make things take longer than they should, or have no use. Examples of teacher time wasters are phone interruptions, overscheduling due to an inability to say no, ineffective communication, excessive socializing, indecision, procrastination, confusion about responsibilities, and fretting about unfinished tasks. The consultant role is particularly vulnerable to all of these factors.

The strategies in this chapter are just a few of many educators can use to manage their time and lives. It takes self-discipline to identify and avoid situations that lead to inappropriate use of time. Use of time is a very personal decision. There are no universal *shoulds*. Managing time carefully enhances both productivity and personal well-being and is an important professional goal.

---

**Application for Using Time Wisely**

Physicists define time as nature's way to keep everything from happening at once. By planning time and managing time-wasters, educators can be more productive and less stressed. These strategies are helpful:

1. Make a "To Do" list. Some make monthly, weekly, and daily lists. Others divide their lists into professional and personal categories. Still others designate categories such as meetings, direct service, or observation. Each time you make your list, do it at the same time of day and on the same kind of paper. Write down all that needs to be done and plan all activities, even those such as talking with friends or playing with the family.

Then prioritize the list. Lakein (1973) suggests "ABCing" the list, with A as top priority. It is not good to let C, or lesser priorities of others priorities become your A priorities. Designate as A priorities only those that must be done, regard B priorities as nice if done, and treat C jobs as those that may be done later. You might even end up with a D or Z pile, which you could regard as your "So What?" list. Some jobs turn into "so whats" if left untended long enough, and then they can be discarded.

2. Learn to say no. Avoid saying "Well . . . ," or "I'll think about it." Perhaps the very worst response is,"I will if you can't find anyone else." There will be little doubt as to who will end up doing the job. Say no, give a brief reason, and offer an alternative if one comes to mind easily. If it does not, try

these responses, "Yes, if you will do something for me," or "This is so important that it needs more attention than I can give it now," or "Please take a number and be seated, because I'm inundated right now." Saying no is a difficult social skill that should be practiced until it feels comfortable and guilt-free.

3. Rearrange your personal schedule. If you are most alert at 6:00 A.M., get up earlier than usual and do the most difficult tasks at your peak efficiency time. If you are least efficient at 8:00 P.M., then write letters, talk with friends, iron, fix a broken towel rack, or anything that does not take your best effort. Trying to do difficult tasks at low-efficiency times is frustrating and often requires doing the task over.

4. Plan for bits of time. Keep "can do" lists for periods of five minutes, fifteen minutes, and thirty minutes. When waiting for a meeting to start or classes to begin, do something on your list. This is a good chance to get some C priority things done. It is reasonable at times to sit and think, read a mystery, or listen to music. Time spent relaxing is not wasted time.

5. Delegate. This is the perfect solution for C priorities, if a helper is available. Teachers are habituated into functioning autonomously, but at times others may be just waiting for a chance to contribute and develop their own skills. Performing delegated tasks can be good learning experiences for students.

6. Break mountains of work into molehills. Do a task analysis or break down the job into smaller steps that you can complete with satisfaction. This is a reinforcing process, and after enough small steps have been taken, the job is done. To practice this process, think about a task that has needed doing for awhile—cleaning out files, organizing a parent volunteer program, painting the living room. Then conduct a task analysis of the job. Carve that job into small, manageable steps. Put deadlines on the steps. Finally, put the first step on your "To Do" list for tomorrow. Then you have a firm start toward accomplishing it.

7. Set deadlines and time limits. Plan a treat for accomplishing a task by deadline. Time limits help get things done efficiently, help overcome procrastination, and prevent simple tasks from becoming major projects. They prevent letting the intention to clean out one drawer become major cleaning of the whole desk, file cabinet, and bookshelves.

8. Organize your desk and office area. MacKenzie (1975) describes the "stacked desk syndrome," in which the desk is so cluttered with things not to forget that you cannot find things, concentrate, or work efficiently.

9. Handle the C tasks. If they can't be delegated or ignored, try putting them on the "Can Do" list. If that is not an option, consider bartering, pooling resources, and consolidating activities.

10. Overcome procrastination. Entire books have been written about this phenomenon, but most of us put off reading them! Several previously
*(Continued)*

---

**Using Time Wisely** *(Continued)*

mentioned suggestions will help break the procrastination habit. The hardest part is simply getting started on a task. Do a more pleasant step first or have a friend do the first step with you. Think hard about the cost of putting things off.

**11.** Take less time to do routine things. For example, make a list of tasks that require attention once a month, twice a month, weekly, and daily. Look at the list. What would happen if the daily list became a weekly list, the weekly list moved to semimonthly, and the twice-monthly to once a month? Probably nothing drastic. It may not be necessary to vacuum weekly, or wash twice a week, or grade every worksheet, or communicate with parents weekly.

**12.** Get a "Do Not Disturb" sign, and use it adamantly, without guilt. Some teachers have had great success making and using work-status cubes for their desk *and* even encouraging their students to do the same. Faces on the cube can convey messages such as "Do Not Disturb," "I need help," "This is not a good day, so be patient, please," or "May I help someone?"

**13.** Plan time for yourself. Busy educators often devote much time and energy to taking care of others at the expense of themselves. Take time to relax, visit with others in the building, talk to a child, read a book, go for a walk, sketch a picture.

**14.** Plan treats to reinforce your own efficiency and measurable progress toward goals. Many teachers are quite goal directed but fail to build self-rewards into their planning schedules (Davis, 1983).

---

One additional benefit educators can obtain from managing time effectively is the ripple effect it has for students. Not only do students profit from a more organized and productive teacher, they benefit from modeled techniques they can apply in their own lives.

## Techniques for Meetings, Interviews, and Observations

Who has not winced at the thought of yet another meeting? Meetings, interviews, and classroom observations command precious time as well as physical and mental energy. Tremendous amounts of collective time and energy are wasted when many people are trapped in unproductive meetings. Educators aiming to "work harder, not smarter," should strive for group interactions that are efficient and productive for all.

### Conducting Efficient Meetings

School consultants are busy, but classroom teachers may be the most overextended of all. Furthermore, many classroom teachers such as Miss Anderson in this chapter's scenario find the total time for having all their students together for a class period is appallingly short. Consultation and collaboration will be accepted more readily when consultees know that consultants respect their time and their students' time. So they suggest a meeting only if it promises to contribute significantly in serving client needs.

The first rule of thumb in planning an efficient meeting is to ask, "Do we really need to have this meeting?" If the answer is not a resounding "Yes," then the business probably can be handled a more efficient way, perhaps by memo, phone, or brief face-to-face conversations with individuals. Good reasons for having a meeting are:

> meeting legal obligations (such as an IEP conference);
> problem solving with several people in a variety of roles involved;
> brainstorming so that many ideas are put forth;
> reconciling conflicting views; or
> building a team to implement educational decisions.

Unnecessary meetings waste school time. They also erode participants' confidence in the value of future meetings that may be called. Sigband (1987) recommends that meetings be held only when there is verifiable need, basing each one on an overall purpose and series of objectives. Only people who can make a definite contribution need to be there. An agenda should be prepared, and the meeting room and any needed equipment should be ready. Most important, the meeting must begin on time and end on time, or early if possible.

*Preparing for the Meeting* Leaders or chairs of meetings will be more prepared and organized if they follow a planning checklist (see Figure 7–2 for an example). The planning sheet should include general planning points such as date, time, participants, and goals. Checklists designed to stipulate preparations for the room and to note participant needs also will be useful.

*Participants* After determining a need for a meeting, leaders and chairs will want to request attendance from only those who can contribute. They should keep the group as small as possible, adhering to the rule of thumb that the more people involved, the shorter the meeting should be. Experts on group interaction recommend that the maximum to have for problem solving is five, for problem identification about ten; for hearing a review or presentation, as many as thirty; and for motivation and inspiration as many as possible. If a group includes more than six people, it is likely someone will not have an opportunity to speak.

*Agenda* Meeting chairs should develop an agenda that reflects the needs of all participants. If the agenda is distributed beforehand, participants will be more productive and less apprehensive. (See Figure 7–3 for an example of a premeeting communication to prepare participants.) Sometimes leaders of large group meetings draw on a teaching technique of placing a short, high-interest activity, related to the topic but needing little explanation, on the chalkboard or overhead screen. Participants focus on the task as they arrive, becoming focused on the meeting topic.

It is important to allocate time for each item on the agenda. Estimating the time needed will allow the chair to monitor progress during the meeting. It is counterproductive to persevere on early items and fail to get to the last ones. If more important items are placed far down the agenda, it might even appear, if time becomes limited, that they have been put there by the convener to avoid action or decision making. Consultants seeking to build collaborative interactions among their colleagues will not want that to happen.

Date: _____  Place: _____

Time: _____  Topic: _____

Participants: _____

_____

Goals for Meeting: _____

_____

_____

Preparation for Room

_____ Overhead projector

_____ Screen, bulbs, cord

_____ Chalkboard, chalk

_____ Charts, pens, tape

_____ Tape recorder, tapes

_____ Podium, lectern

_____ Tables, chairs

_____ Breakout arrangements

_____ Other?

Room Arrangement: _____

_____

_____

_____

_____

Preparation for Participants

_____ Name tags

_____ Pads and pens

_____ Handouts

_____ Agenda

_____ Icebreakers activity

_____ Map of location

_____ Refreshments

_____ Follow-up activity

_____ Other?

(Sketch of Room)

FIGURE 7–2  Checklist to Prepare for Meetings

*Seating Arrangements* Comfortable chairs and seating arrangements that facilitate interaction are important factors in the success of a meeting. Full size chairs (not kindergarten furniture) with a little padding, but not too much, should be provided. For best interaction, there should be an arrangement where all can face each other. A circle for six to ten people, a U shape with peripheral seating if there is to be a visual presentation, and a semicircle of one or more rows for large groups work well (Lawren, 1989).

*Participant Responsibilities* Along with the responsibility of each participant to interact and help problem solve, brainstorm, or decide, three other responsibilities are important—chair, recorder, and timekeeper. In many cases the consultant will take care of all three roles, particularly if the meeting includes only two or three people. However, if the meeting is long, or or the issues are complex and there is much discussion and brainstorming, it is efficient for the chair to call on another to record the plans and decisions.

---

Date: _____     Place:_____

Time Start: _____ Time End _____ Topic:_____

Participants: _____

_____

_____

Goals for Meeting: _____

_____

_____

_____

_____     Minutes of Prior Meeting Attached _____

_____     Advance Preparation Needed _____

---

At the Meeting

| Action | Person(s) Responsible | Target Date | Done |
|--------|----------------------|-------------|------|
|        |                      |             |      |
|        |                      |             |      |
|        |                      |             |      |

---

FIGURE 7–3  **Checklist to Prepare Participants**

*During the Meeting* Whether the meeting involves two persons or twenty, all participants should feel they have important contributions to make. All should listen attentively to each other, think creatively and flexibly, and avoid disruptive communication such as jokes, puns, sarcasm, or side comments (Gordon, 1974). Talking and whispering in subgroups can be particularly distracting. Ironically, some teachers who will not tolerate such behavior by their students in the classroom are the biggest offenders. Astute group leaders have various ways of handling this disagreeable occurrence. They might go over to the offenders and stand alongside or between them, direct questions to them, or request information from them. In the right circumstance, a touch on the arm or shoulder can bring a talker back into focus toward the business of the group. Each participant in a meeting should be thinking at all times, "What will help move us ahead and solve the problem?" and "What does the group need and how can I help?" (Gordon, 1974).

*Minutes of the Meeting* Sometimes a committee is accused of keeping minutes to waste hours! Minutes should reflect the group's decisions about what is to be done, by whom, and by what date, but not each point of the discussion. Minutes are a record for naming those who will have a responsibility, for describing plans and decisions, and for listing projected dates for completion of tasks. This is an important aspect of the consultation that should not be slighted.

*Assessment of the Meeting* Some time should be reserved at the end of the meeting to discuss progress made and to evaluate the effectiveness of the meeting. If a meeting agenda becomes sidetracked, leaders should redirect the group's attention by making a point to refocus the discussion (Raschke, Dedrick, and DeVries, 1988).

Compromise for consensus is not always the best solution. It may signify a weak decision, a watered-down plan, or a failure by some participants to express their concerns as firmly as they should. During the meeting leaders should encourage opposing views to be aired, so that these do not surface later when the matter has been closed. If any participant wishes to dissent, the time to do so is in the meeting, not in hallways after the matter has been decided.

Of course, many consultations and collaborations involve only two individuals—consultant and consultee. But these procedures recommended for groups of several or more are often pertinent to interactions between only two individuals as well.

## Conducting Effective Interviews

School consultants often need to interview school personnel, community resources, and family members to plan programs for helping students with special needs. Interviewees can provide information for case studies and formulation of learning goals. They help generate options and alternatives for special needs and provide data for program evaluation.

Successful interviews require effective communication skills (see Chapter 6), and postures of onedownsmanship, parity, and cooperativeness. Queries such as "Tell me more," and "Could you expand on that?" and "Let me see if I understand what you are saying . . . " are examples of the responsive listening and paraphrasing that help to elicit the most useful information.

The interviewer should take notes, allowing interviewees to look them over at the conclusion of the interview. If a tape recording is desired, the interviewer must ask permission beforehand to make one. Some feel it is best to avoid taping, because respondents are often less candid if their comments are being recorded.

Interviews must be conducted ethically, collegially, and for a purpose not attainable by less intrusive, time-consuming methods. Keys to a successful interview by the school consultant are asking the right questions and valuing the expertise of the interviewee. A follow-up interaction soon after the interview session is affirming and reassuring, thus facilitating further collaboration.

## Making Prudent Observations

Consultants often need to observe a student, groups of students, or an entire program in operation. This is not an easy professional task. Consultants who go into classrooms to observe can expect some discomfort and anxiety on the teacher's part. There may be latent resentment because the consultant is free to visit in other classrooms, something many teachers would like but are rarely given the opportunity to do.

Consultants can facilitate the process of observation and ease the minds of those being observed in several ways. First, they should provide a positive comment on entering the room and then sit unobtrusively where the teacher has designated. They should avoid getting involved in classroom activities or helping students. Effective observers can blend into the classroom setting so they are hardly noticed. Regular visits minimize the likelihood of having students know who is being observed and for what reason. It is a sad thing to hear a student say, "Oh, here's that learning disabilities teacher to check up on Jimmy again." Records of behaviors must be done in code so that writing, watching, and body language of the consultant do not reveal the intent of the observation. Each consultant should develop a personal coding system for recording information. (Chapters 8 and 9 provide more information on documenting observations.) Sometimes observers watch the targeted student for one minute, and then divert their attention to another student for one minute continuing the process with other peers. In this way the student's behavior can be compared with that of classmates. The consultant may teach a lesson and have the classroom teacher observe. This can be helpful for both consultant and consultee.

An observer should exit the room with a smile and a supporting glance at the teacher. Then very soon after the observation, the observer will want to get back to the classroom teacher with positive, specific comments about the classroom, feedback on the observation, and suggestions for entering into problem solving. Although consultants do not observe in classrooms for the purpose of assessing teacher behaviors and teaching styles, it would be myopic to assume they do not notice teaching practices that inhibit student success in the classroom. In a nonthreatening, nonexpert way, the consultant might ask the consultee if the student achieved the goals of the lesson. If not, is there something the teacher would like to change so this could occur? Then what might the consultant do to help?

To avoid gathering inaccurate information, consultants will want to make repeated observations. In doing so, they can also obtain additional information on antecedents to the problem (Cipani, 1985).

Achieving rapport with a consultee while targeting a teaching strategy for possible modification requires utmost finesse by consultants. This underscores the need for providing feedback and continuation of the problem solving process as soon as possible after a classroom observation.

## Management of Consultation Records and Resources

A prominent scientist for space research commented that physicists can lick anything, even gravity, but the paperwork is overwhelming. Special education teachers can relate to that. They cite excessive paperwork and record keeping, along with insufficient time in which to do them, as major causes of stress and burnout. Writing and monitoring IEPs, individual pupil record keeping, and completion of records and forms rank high as major usurpers of their personal and professional time (Davis, 1983). When asked to estimate the amount of time they spend performing their responsibilities, resource teachers often overestimate the time spent on direct pupil instruction and staffings and underestimate their time preparing for instruction and performing clerical duties such as record-keeping.

Nevertheless, if teaching is to be an important service profession, careful record keeping is essential. Record keeping must be written into the consultant's role description as a significant responsibility, with time allowed for its accurate completion. Who would want to be treated by a doctor who did not write down vital information after each visit, or served by a lawyer who failed to record and file important documents? The key for educators is to manage their paperwork so it does not manage them. Developing efficient systems and standardized forms for record keeping will help educators, and consultants in particular, work smarter and not harder.

## Using a Consultation Log

One of the most important formats for consultants to develop is a consultation log or journal. Consultants can record the date, participants, and topic of each consultation on separate pages, along with a brief account of the interaction and the results agreed on. Space should be provided for follow-up reports and assessment of the consultation (see Figure 7–4 for a sample format). Records should be kept noting the time spent in consultation and any positive results accomplished, if consultation is to gain credibility as an essential educational activity. While consultants cannot control the type of

---

Client (coded): _____ Consultee (initials): _____

Initiator of Consultation: _____

General Topic of Concern: _____

_____

Purpose of Consultation: _____

_____

_____

_____

Brief Summary of Consultation _____

_____

_____

_____

Steps Agreed On—By Whom, by When: _____

_____

_____

_____

Follow-up: _____

_____

Most Successful Part of Consultation: _____

_____

Consultation Areas Needing Improvement: _____

_____

---

**FIGURE 7–4  Consultation Log Format**

records required, they can determine processes and procedures for collecting and using information (Davis, 1983).

One caution must be noted about consultation logs. Important points of the discussion about student needs and progress might be entered in the log. However, no diagnostic classification or plan requiring parent permission should be recorded (Conoley and Conoley, 1982), and confidentiality of the information must be preserved. Consultants will want to develop procedures for coding that will ensure confidentiality yet identify pertinent information efficiently.

### Creating a Logo for Consultant Memos

A consultation memo is a communication tool and also a record of that communication. Consultants will find it helpful to include a personalized logo on the memo forms they use to communicate with consultees. This logo, at a glance, identifies the memo as from the consultant. A busy recipient immediately recognizes its source and can make a quick decision about the need to respond now or at a later time. It personalizes professional interaction by providing a bit of information about the consultant, a humorous touch, or the creative element that educators enjoy and appreciate. A carefully designed logo can put consultation, collaboration, and team effort in a positive light. (See Figure 7–5 for an example of a personalized memo pad design.)

Another item that improves consultant efficiency is the professional card. Business cards have been a mainstay for communicating basic information in many professions, and it is surprising that they are so seldom used in education. Administrators can increase the visibility of their staff and enhance morale as well by providing them with attractive, well-designed professional cards. Educators find these cards helpful when they interact with colleagues at other sites, or when they attend conferences and conventions. The cards are convenient for quickly jotting down requests for information, for building communication networks among colleagues with similar interests, and even for promoting your own school district and educational area.

### Organizing a Consultation Notebook

Consultants often use a loose-leaf notebook divided into sections with index tabs. The sections can be categorized by buildings, students, or teachers served. Each consultant will want to develop the style that works best in his or her school context and role. Figure 7–6 is a list of suggestions for notebook sections. Consultants may not want or need all of these sections and may come up with others of their own. Here again, personalization for your role and school context determines the notebook's usefulness.

A primary responsibility of the consultant is to ensure confidentiality of information for both student and staff. This can be accomplished in at least

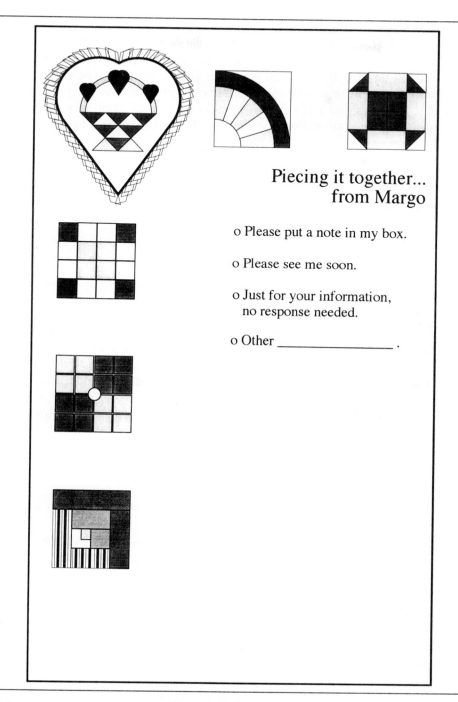

**FIGURE 7–5 Consultation Logo Designs**

By Margo Hosie

two ways—coding the names with numbers or symbols while keeping the code list in a separate place, and marking person-specific files as confidential. A "Confidential" rubber stamp prepared for this purpose can be used to alert readers that the information is not for public viewing. These practices, along with the usual protection of information and data, and the practice of seeing that the recorded information is as positive and verifiable as possible, are common-sense rules that should be sufficient for handling all but the most unusual cases.

| | |
|---|---|
| *Appointments:* | One for week, one for year. |
| *To-Do Lists:* | By day, week, month, or year as fits needs. List commitments. |
| *Lesson Plans:* | If delivering direct service, outline of activities for week. |
| *Consultation Logs:* | Chart to record consultation input and outcomes (Figure 7-4). |
| *Phone Call Log:* | Consultation time by phone. |
| *Observation Sheets:* | Coded for confidentiality. |
| *Contact List:* | Phone numbers, school address, times available. |
| *Faculty Notes:* | Interests, social and family events and dates, teaching preferences of staff. |
| *Student List:* | Coded for confidentiality, birthdates, IEP dates, other helpful data. |
| *Student Information:* | Anecdotal records, sample products, events, awards, interests, birthdays, talents. |
| *Medication Records:* | If part of responsibilities. |
| *Materials Available:* | Title, brief description with grade levels, location. |
| *Services Available:* | School and community services for resources. |
| *State Policies:* | Guidelines, procedures, names and phone of agencies/personnel. |
| *School Policies:* | Brief description of school policies, regulations, handbook. |
| *Procedural Materials:* | Forms, procedures, for standard activities. |
| *Evaluation Data:* | Space and forms to record data for formative and summative evaluation (see Chapter 8, and coded if confidential). |
| *Idea File:* | To note ideas for self and for sharing with staff and parents. |
| *Joke And Humor File:* | To perk up the day, and for sharing with others. |
| *Three-Year Calendar:* | For continuity in preparing, checking, and updating IEPs. |
| *Pockets:* | For carrying personalized memos, letterhead, stamps, hall passes, paper, letterhead. |

**FIGURE 7–6  Consultation Notebook Format**

An itinerant consulting teacher who serves several schools may want to prepare a simple form stating the date, teacher's name and child's code, along with the topic to be considered, for each school. The list can be scanned before entering the building, so no time is lost in providing the consultative or teaching service. Some consulting teachers block off and color-code regular meeting times and teacher responsibilities. This practice permits a clearer picture of available consultation times.

Another helpful strategy is development of a comprehensive manual that includes standard procedures and forms used in the school district and required by the state. An example of a frequently used message form that was made into a pad by the consultant is shown in Figure 7–7.

*Consultation Schedules* The consultation schedule is a vital tool. It not only allows the consultant to organize time productively, but demonstrates to administrators and other school personnel that the school consultant is goal directed, productive, and facilitative. Schedules should be left with

---

(tear-off messages)

HIGH SCHOOL PASS

STUDENT'S NAME: _____    HOUR: _____

TEACHER'S NAME: _____    DATE: _____

*Test Directions:*

_____ 1. Student will work independently on test.

_____ 2. Teacher will read test to student.

_____ 3. Student will answer orally. Teacher records answer.

_____ 4. Can use textbook on test.

_____ 5. Can use notes on test.

_____ 6. Can use review sheets on test.

_____ 7. Give test with these modifications: _____

_____ Yes _____ No    Should student return before period ends?

_____ Time dismissed from class to come to resource room.

_____ Time dismissed from resource room.

---

**FIGURE 7–7  Message Pad Format**

By Wendy Dover (adapted from Farmers Branch ISD, Texas)

secretaries of all buildings assigned to the consultant and posted in teacher workrooms, so colleagues have easy access to the information.

Consultations and collaborative experiences can be keyed on the consultant's schedule with code letters, for efficiency. One consulting teacher uses this code in her notebook:

- ID  — informal discussion, spontaneous meeting;
- PM  — planned, formal meeting;
- PC  — phone conversation;
- MM — major meeting of more than two people;
- FT  — follow-through activity; and
- SO  — scheduled observation.

Standardized forms are helpful for collecting and using basic information. The forms that produce multiple copies may be more expensive in the short run but can save valuable time and energy in the long run. A story is told of a miser who took overly long strides in his $80 shoes in order to save his shoe leather, but in doing so ripped the cloth of his $100 slacks. In similar fashion, the time spent on developing systems and standardizing conventional forms will be well spent. It frees up more time and energy for individualizing and personalizing the instruction for special needs of the students.

Commercial resources are available that provide sample letters and forms adaptable to a variety of educational purposes, from writing a letter of congratulations to answering concerns and criticisms (Tomlinson, 1984). Although educators will not want to use these patterns verbatim, they can get a "jump start" in preparing some of the more difficult communications.

Coordination and organization of student files, consultation logs, school procedures, and schedules will necessitate more time for paperwork at the outset, but once the procedures are set up, they will be time efficient and cost effective in the long run.

## Organizing and Distributing Materials

Many school districts now have extensive instructional resource centers where school personnel can check out a variety of material for classroom use. Even with the busiest resource center in full operation, consultants usually have their own field-related materials and information about special areas that teachers want and need. With little or no clerical help, and oftentimes little storage space available beyond the seats, floor, and trunk of their own vehicles, traveling school consultants would be wise to develop a simple, orderly checkout system for loaned materials. Without such a system, consultants will soon have little left to use and share.

Materials belonging to the schools should be marked with a school stamp, and personal materials should be labeled with a personal label. Library pockets and checkout cards facilitate checkout and return. The consultant should keep an up-to-date inventory of available personal and school library materials that are loanable and specific to student needs teachers must address. Before traveling to a school, the consultant can scan the checkout file for materials that are due, and stop by classrooms or put memos into message boxes asking for their return. Efficient consultants leave request cards so school staff can let them know of their needs. They also periodically assess the usefulness of their materials by querying teachers and students who used them. These kinds of interactions build positive attitudes toward collaboration and teamwork, promote the effectiveness of school consultation, and extend the ripple effect of special services.

## Related Services and Support Personnel as Partners in School Consultation

An ancient proverb reminds us a child's life is like a piece of paper on which every passerby leaves a mark. Several years ago Bronfenbrenner (1973) stressed that all members of society have the responsibility to teach society's children. A typical community has three kinds of social agencies for educating children—informal, nonformal, and formal (Seay, 1974). Families and neighborhoods are informal agencies for education. Churches, media, and cultural centers are nonformal educator agencies, and schools and universities represent formal agencies. A multitude of educator roles exists among the informal, nonformal and formal agencies, ranging from Scout leaders, to 4-H leaders, to private music and art instructors, to church school teachers. Doctors and dentists teach within their professional roles. Some request information from schools and seek interaction with teachers. One frequently overlooked educational role that more and more schools are learning to value and use is senior citizens, including grandparents of students.

Schools and universities house a variety of support personnel who can assist with student needs. These people also are catalysts for the increasingly popular use of community resources to accentuate learning among students (Dettmer, 1980). Related services and support personnel for students include those serving in areas such as transportation, speech pathology, audiology, psychological services, physical and occupational therapy, recreation, counseling, medical and school health, social work, parent counseling and training, cultural agencies, and mentors or internship supervisors. Each school also has a number of ancillary personnel without whom school life would be uncomfortable, disorganized, and ineffective. These include people in roles such as food-service staff, secretaries, librarians and media specialists, transportation staff, paraprofessionals, custodians, and volunteer aides.

Related services and support personnel offer services and guidance in academic, emotional, social, physical, career, and transition areas. Support also is provided by coordinators, supervisors, evaluators, and building administrators. Special resource services include media, speakers, mentors, tutors, judges of events and products, and community partners. Extender services can be provided by libraries, parks, colleges, industries, businesses, and professions. Special activities, managed through clubs, workshops, interest or travel groups, and the like, are an important part of special services for special needs.

Most students with special needs are assigned to general classrooms, even though they may attend resource rooms or work with consulting teachers for a portion of the school day. In order to serve their special learning and behavioral needs, support services and classroom extender services should be integrated into their educational programs.

Just as the roles of consultant, consultee, and client are interrelated and interchangeable according to the focus of the consultation, the roles and responsibilities of related, support, and ancillary services personnel interrelate and interchange according to the part each plays in the student's education. For example, transportation personnel are integral to the programs of special education students. They are a key link between home and school. They sometimes play an active role in a referral process for special education, and they can help determine the effects of interventions. They may be involved as partners in reward and reinforcement systems for students, or to extend learning activities beyond the classroom.

The teacher for an educable mentally handicapped student might be a consultee for a bus driver in a consultant role. A librarian might be a consultant to help a gifted program teacher, as consultee, select and locate resources. The school psychologist can contribute valuable information about the purposes, interpretation, and uses of tests. The training of counselors in both individual and group guidance techniques makes them helpful resources in staff development activities and problem-solving sessions. An understanding custodian has always been regarded as a teacher's best friend and helpmate in the school setting. This is especially relevant to the special education teacher's responsibilities. Consultants can encourage custodians to be involved in planning and monitoring special programs for students with special needs.

School nurses and social workers contribute valuable data in consultations and staffings. They are often able to target seemingly insignificant data toward important aspects of problem identification. Transportation staff provide support when they collaborate on scheduling, reinforcement plans, and other special arrangements. One driver of the special education bus displays schoolwork in the bus. She also has a chart for the "star" bus student of the week. She explains that because it is the special education bus, she wants to make their bus ride special. She makes an effort to collaborate with teachers, adapting to special schedules so students are not late or left stranded at a building.

Paraprofessionals and teacher aides interact frequently with other staff members and often are able to view students in different ways. They can share their concerns and contribute information that helps teachers and consultants provide appropriate learning experiences for their students.

Building principles have roles and responsibilities that are just short of overwhelming. So many school issues compete for their time and energy that, when the consultants ask for their participation in consultation and collaboration, special efforts must be made to accommodate administrator schedules. Administrators can assist immeasurably by freeing up teacher time, staggering schedules, and arranging for substitute staff, so that consultation and collaboration among school personnel can take place. Administrators can work with consultants to clarify roles and ensure consultants obtain parity among the school staff. One of their most significant contributions is to encourage interaction and staff development among school personnel. When in-service and staff development are arranged, promoted, and *attended* by building principals, the multiplier ripple effects are profound. It is vital that all related services and support personnel are included in in-service and staff development sessions, so they are aware of special needs and the programs being implemented to serve those needs.

Labels and categories for school personnel are relatively unimportant within a collaborative climate. The service provided for a child's need determines the role. Thousand et al. (1986) emphasize that schools have many natural, untapped pools of skills and interests across a wide range of unassigned areas. When teachers can form teams and move among roles, positive ripple effects occur. Examples are an increased adult-to-pupil ratio in a learning program and the ability of the school to provide more personalized instruction (Nevin, Thousand, and Paolucci-Whitcomb, 1990).

In order to facilitate appropriate support services for students, consultants can do several things:

Become knowledgeable about the roles and responsibilities of support personnel.

Strive for IEPs and informal learning plans that include all facets of the student's learning and involve all roles that will help the student succeed.

Within the bounds of necessary confidentiality and ethical school practices, ask support personnel for their viewpoints and opinions about helping students with special needs.

Inform suport personnel about the consultation role, schedule, and responsibilities.

Monitor the student's performance across all kinds of school, home, and community learning in a variety of situations.

Include support services personnel in staff development activities, encouraging their involvement and collaboration.

Have specific in-services for them, to provide awareness and encourage collaboration.

## Referral Agencies

Every community, large or small, urban or rural, accessible or isolated, wealthy or poor, has agencies and potential resources for contributing to learning programs that serve special needs of children and adolescents. The consulting teacher will find it helpful to develop a directory of referral agencies, with addresses and phone numbers, to have available for consultations and staffings. As one example, a consultant in a mid-size town in the Midwest prepared a referral directory containing more than one hundred sources of assistance. Some were national sources that could be called with a hot line or an 800 number, such as the Missing Children's Network. Others were state-level agencies, including the Resource Center for the Handicapped. Still others were county agencies, such as the County Family Planning Clinic. But within this average town, many sources were available "just down the street," including a crisis center and a community theater. Resourceful consultants will regularly involve personnel from a variety of agencies to collaborate in planning and implementing student programs that provide support to students' special needs.

## Ethics of Consulting and Collaborating

Consultation and collaboration in the school setting require particular emphasis on ethical interaction for several reasons:

Special needs of students are involved.

Confidential data must be shared among several individuals.

Consultants are out and about much more than classroom teachers, interfacing with many people in several buildings.

Parent permission may not be required, but many of the issues approximate the sensitivity of special education issues that do require parental consent.

Consultants have complex roles with many demands on them, but often receive little or no training in how to adapt to those roles.

Consultation implies power and expertise until the collaborative spirit can be cultivated.

Consultants may be asked, on occasion, to act inappropriately as a middle person, or to form alliances or carry information, and they must respond ethically.

Adults often have difficulty adapting to individual differences in teaching styles and preferences of colleagues, and many of them demonstrate resistance.

The persuasive aspects of consultation require a close, careful look at ethical practice (Ross, 1986). Ethical consultation is demonstrated by adhering to principles of confidentiality in acquisition and use of information about students, families, and individual school settings. It also includes a high regard for individual differences among colleagues and the constructive use of those differences—concern and empathy for all, onedownsmanship in the consultative role, and mutual ownership of problems and rewards in the school environment (as discussed in Chapter 4) to serve students' special needs.

Consultants and collaborators should review legal requirements relating to confidentiality, such as the Family Educational Rights and Privacy Act of 1974 (Buckley Amendment), and truth-in-testing laws within states that legislate them. Requirements such as these stipulate the need for confidentiality of student data and regulate parental access to information about their children.

Hansen, Himes, and Meier (1990) present several suggestions for school consultants to follow in order to exercise ethical behavior in their roles:

1. Promote professional attitudes and behaviors among staff about confidentiality and informed consent.
2. Take care with the quality of information you enter in written records.
3. Take care in discussing problems of children and their families.
4. Focus on strengths of clients and share information only with those who need it to serve the student's needs.

School consultants will be more successful in their roles and more widely accepted by their professional colleagues if they base consultation, collaboration, and teamwork on a code of consultation ethics that includes the following recommendations:

Avoid any activity that might embarrass colleagues.

Do not violate confidences or carry tales.

Limit the consultative activities to things for which you are trained.

Take care not to distort or misrepresent information.

Openly share helpful data, but only in ways that protect the rights of students and families.

Make as few remarks about specific teaching practices as possible.

Know when to stay in the consultation and when it would be best to get out and seek another approach.

Be open to new ideas and knowledge.

Give colleagues the benefit of wanting to help.

Leave therapy to therapists who are trained for it.

Maintain good records that provide confidentiality.

Keep consultative channels and doors open.

Refrain from taking issues personally.

Above all, advocate for the child, letting student needs guide your actions and decisions.

Several well-known maxims apply to the implementation of planful, efficient, collegial, and ethical practices for consultation:

- "What breaks in a moment may take years to mend."
- "Keep your words sweet, for you may have to eat them."
- "Better to bend than to break."
- "Only a fool would peel a grape with an ax."

## Tips for Consulting and Collaborating

**1.** At the end of the year, write thank-you notes to school personnel you have worked with, including principals, secretaries, and custodians. When writing notes to colleagues, sign your name in a distinctive color on pads of an individualized design. Send a note on a "reminder" memo and staple a bag of nuts, or a valentine cookie, or a doughnut, to it. Remember those who collaborate with you in special ways by delivering a treat to their room and a brief note of appreciation.

**2.** Color code folders for schools if you serve several. Use a file box with a card for each day to list reminders, and a schedule book. Keep an idea file of filler activities.

**3.** Use tubs for storage of materials. Plan ahead and put materials in the tub for one week, one month, a season, or a thematic unit.

**4.** Have a retrieval box in a certain place for receiving borrowed items that are returned. Keep a checkout catalog so you will know where your materials are. When materials are due, remove due cards for the buildings where you will be that week and collect the materials while there.

**5.** Listen to conversations in the workroom, lunchroom, and faculty meetings. When a topic surfaces for which you have materials, offer to share. Prepare a list of instructional material that is for loaning and distribute copies of it. Make sure grade level and sample objectives of the material are given.

**6.** Don't schedule yourself so tightly that you have no time for informal interactions and impromptu consultation. These can open the door for more intensive and productive collaboration. Also, be more protective of colleagues' time than you are of your own, and make good use of it.

7. Furnish treats often. For diet-conscious schools, make the treats vegetables or fruit.

8. Develop rapport with librarians. Give advance notice of upcoming topics and try not to make too many spur-of-the-moment requests. Make friends with custodians and refrain from making excessive demands on their time and energy.

9. Keep public remarks about colleagues on a positive, professional level. If you must vent, try using a journal at home. Reviewing it now and then may show you the way to improve the situation.

10. Remember special things about the faculty in each school, and start a card file with comments that will be useful in personalizing the interactions. If you find a news article pertaining in a positive way to a colleague or a student, clip it out and send it along with a congratulatory note.

11. Send a note weekly to classroom teachers of mainstreamed students.

12. Make efficient checklists for procedural activities, such as general items to tell parents at conferences or items to tell new students and their parents.

13. If doing a demonstration lesson, give the classroom teacher a paper stating the name and type of activity, and learning objectives. State your name at the bottom and specify that it comes from "Consultant _____'s Lesson Plan," thereby establishing your identity.

14. Go to classroom teachers and ask *them* for help in their area of expertise. Ask for a copy of something you have seen that would be a good addition to your file, but be sure a teacher means for you to use it or share it before you do so.

15. Generate alternatives to having more and more meetings, try them out, and get input from colleagues on their value. When a meeting *is* needed, and it promises to be a difficult one, on the night before the meeting, try visualizing a successful one in which everything goes very well.

## Chapter Review

1. Stress that is encountered in many human service roles can lead to burnout and subsequent attrition from the field. Positive attitudes, health maintenance, supportive networks, realistic goals, relaxation, environmental changes, and taking control of your life will minimize stress and help prevent burnout, fizzle out, rust out, and coast out among consultants and teachers.

2. Careful management of time and energy decreases stress and increases productivity for those in consultative roles. School personnel will want to establish goals to manage their resources, identify and remediate time wasters, use positive time management strategies, and take good care of themselves.

**3.** Meetings, interviews, and observations must be kept as efficient and positive as possible. With careful planning, each of these activities can be more productive for consultants and collaborators. It is important to provide a comfortable meeting environment, prepare an agenda, keep minutes of decisions and plans, and assess the success of the meeting. When consultants observe in classrooms, they should demonstrate caring attitudes and provide positive support for those being observed.

**4.** Record-keeping systems and resource management systems are necessary for busy consultants who serve many schools. Consultants must keep records and materials in order, maintain confidentiality, and be on the lookout for helpful material with which to consult and collaborate. Consulting journals and notebooks are tools that facilitate management of complex responsibilities. Personalized touches for memos and messages help develop rapport with consultees.

**5.** Support personnel are key components in constructing a complete plan for serving students who have special needs. They can be involved as consultants, consultees, and clients in identifying problems, setting goals, planning and implementing programs, reinforcing success, and evaluating outcomes. Consultants should have updated lists of referral agencies available for their use and for sharing with consultees and parents.

**6.** Ethical and conscientious considerations must guide consultants in every consultative and collaborative effort. The primary aim of any school interaction is the welfare of the student.

## Activities

**1.** Discuss some record-keeping and managerial tasks that most people really don't like to do, such as preparing income tax returns, and consider ways the activities could be made less unpleasant and more manageable. Then consider how these techniques could be used creatively by school consultants.

**2.** Describe "The Perfect Meeting." What would need to be done in order for this meeting to transpire?

**3.** How many support services, related services, and ancillary personnel categories can you list, and how many ways can you find for individuals in these categories to become educational partners with teachers, students, and parents?

**4.** Create ideas for the following management tools, and if your present situation warrants, construct them and try them out:

a logo for personalized note pads or memo sheets that will identify you and will feature school consultation in a positive, collaborative spirit;

an observation checklist that would work in your school situation;

a consultation log or journal format to record the consultation and follow-through, as well as a brief assessment of the consultation;

a table of contents for a notebook in which to organize information, data, and material needed to carry out the school consultation role;

a system for cataloguing materials to be shared with consultees, and for checking the material in and out.

5.   Select a time management strategy and try it for a predetermined length of time.

6.   Find out more about several related services roles that you are not familiar with—for example, the occupational therapist, the audiologist, the social worker, or the school psychologist. What are their responsibilities? What preparation did their roles require? What does a typical day entail for each of them? Interview them and ask their views about consultation and collaboration.

7.   Develop a plan for ways in which at least three related services and support personnel could be involved in consultation and collaboration to provide a team effort toward serving students with special needs.

8.   Compile a reference list of referral agencies, support groups, and community resources in your area that could be helpful in meeting special needs of students. Preface the list with a brief description of the community where the school is located. Then compare your list with a colleague's list that represents a different type of geographic area.

9.   Think ahead to your own professional growth and future. Where do you see yourself five years from now? What will it take to get there? Develop some steps that can help you attain your vision.

## For Further Reading

Collins, C. (1987). *Time Management for Teachers: Practical Techniques and Skills That Give You More Time to Teach.* West Nyak, NY: Parker.

Conoley, J. C., and Conoley, C. W. (1982). *School Consultation: A Guide to Pactice and Training.* New York: Pergamon Press. Chapter 9, on ethical considerations in consultative practice.

Davis, W. E. (1983). *The Special Educator: Strategies for Succeeding in Today's Schools.* Austin, TX: PRO-ED. Chapter 2, on burnout, Chapter 5 on meetings, Chapter 6, on paperwork, record keeping, and time management, and Chapter 8, on ethical, legal, and professional dilemmas.

Douglass, M. E., and Douglass, D. N. (1980). *Manage Your Tme, Manage Your Work, Manage Yourself.* New York: AMACOM.

Lippitt, G., and Lippitt, R. (1978). *The Consulting Process in Action.* San Diego: University Associates. Chapter 5, on ethical dilemmas and guidelines for consultants.

Maker, C. A. (1985). *Professional Self-Management: Techniques for Speical Service Providers.* Baltimore: Brookes.

Sugai, G. (Winter, 1986). Recording classroom events: Maintaining a critical incidents log. *Teaching Exceptional Children,* pp. 98–102.

# References

Bensky, J. M., Shaw, S. F., Gouse, A. S., Bates, H., Dixon, B., & Beane, W. E. (1980). Public Law 94–142 and Stress: A problem for educators. *Exceptional Children, 47* (1), 24–29.

Bronfenbrenner, U. (October, 1973). Tear down the walls. *Scholastic Teacher*, pp. 78–79.

Collins, C. (1987). *Time Management for Teachers: Practical Techniques and Skills That Give You More Time to Teach.* West Nyak, NY: Parker.

Caro, D. J., and Robbins, P. (1991). TalkWalking—Thinking on Your Feet. *Developer*, November 1991, 3–4.

Cipani, E. (1985). The three phrases of behavioral consultation: Objectives, intervention, and quality assurance. *Teacher Education and Special Education, 8,* 144–152.

Conoley, J. C., and Conoley, C. W. (1982). *School consultation: A Guide to Practice and Training.* New York: Pergamon Press.

Davis, W. E. (1983). *The Special Educator: Strategies for Succeeding in Today's World.* Austin: PRO–ED.

DeShong, B. R. (1981). The special educator: Stress and survival. Rockville, MD: Aspen.

Dettmer, P. (1980). The extended classroom: A gold mine for gifted students. *Journal for the Education of the Gifted, 3*(3): 133–42.

Dettmer. P. (1982). Preventing burnout in teachers of the gifted. *G/C/T,* 21: 37–41.

Douglass, M. E., and Douglass, D. N. (1980). *Manage Your Tme, Manage Your Work, Manage Yourself.* New York: AMACOM.

Goldfein, D. (1977). *Everywoman's Guide to Time Management.* Millbrae, CA: Les Femmes.

Gordon, T. (1974). *T.E.T.: Teacher Effectiveness Training.* New York: Wyden.

Hansen, J. C., Himes, B. S., and Meier, S. (1990). *Consultation: Concepts and Practices.* Englewood Cliffs, NJ: Prentice Hall.

Idol, L. (1988). A rationale and guidelines for establishing special education consultation programs. *Remedial and Special Education, 9*(6): 48–58.

Lakein, A. (1973). *How to Get Control of Your Time and Your Life.* New York: McKay.

Lawren, B. (September, 1989). Seating for success. *Psychology Today, 16:* 18–19.

Lippitt, G., and Lippitt, R. (1978). *The Consulting Process in Action.* San Diego: University Associates. Chapter 5, on ethical dilemmas and guidelines for consultants.

MacKenzie, R. A. (1975). *The Time Trap.* New York: McGraw Hill.

Maker, C. A. (Ed.). (1985). *Professional Self–Management: Techniques for Special Service Providers.* Baltimore: Brookes.

Maslach. C. (1982). *Burnout: The Cost of Caring.* Englewood Cliffs, NJ: Prentice Hall.

Maslach. C., and Pines, A. (1977). The burnout syndrome in the daycare setting. *Child Care Quarterly, 6,* 100–113.

Nelson, C. M., and Stevens, K. B. (1981). An accountable consultation model for mainstreaming behavioral disordered children. *Behavioral Disorders, 6:* (2), 82–91.

Nevin, A., Thousand, J., and Paolucci–Whitcomb, P. (1990). Collaborative consultation: Empowering public school personnel to provide heterogeneous schooling for all—or, who rang that bell? *Journal of Educational and Psychological Consultation, 1*(1): 41–67.

Raschke, D., Dedrick, C., and DeVries, A. (1988). Coping with stress: The special educator's perspective. *Teaching Exceptional Children, 21*(1): 10–14.

Ross, R. G. (1986). *Communication Consulting as Persuasion: Issues and Implications.* Report no. CS 506–027. Washington, D.C.: U.S. Department of Education. (ERIC Document Reproduction Service no. ED 291–115.)

Seay, M. (1974). *Community Education: A Developing Concept.* Midland, MI: Pendell.

Shaw, S. F., Bensky, J. M., and Dixon, B. (1981). *Stress and burnout: A primer for special education and special services personnel.* Reston, VA: Council for Exceptional Children.

Sigband, N. B. (February, 1987). The uses of meetings. *Nation's Business*, p. 28R.

Sugai, G. (Winter, 1986). Recording classroom events: Maintaining a critical incidents log. *Teaching Exceptional Children*, pp. 98–102.

Thousand, J., Fox, T., Reid, R., Godek, J., Williams, W., and Fox, W. (1986). *The Homecoming Model: Educating Students Who*

*Present Intensive Educational Challenges Within Regular Education Environments.* Monograph no. 7–1. Burlington, VT: University of Vermont, Center for Developmental Disabilities.

Thurston, L. P. (1987). *Survival Skills for Women: Facilitator manual.* Manhattan, KS: Survival Skills Education and Development.

Tindal, G. A., and Taylor–Pendergast, S. T. (1989). A taxonomy for objectively analyzing the consultation process. *Remedial and Special Education, 10*: (2), 6–16.

Tomlinson, G. (ed.). (1984). *School Administrator's Complete Letter Book.* Englewood Cliffs, NJ: Prentice Hall.

Truch, S. (1980). *Teacher Burnout and What to Do About It.* Novato, CA: Academic Therapy.

Zabel, R. H. and Zabel, M. K. (1982). Factors in burnout among teachers of exceptional children. *Exceptional Children, 49*(3): 261–63.

# 8

# ASSESSMENT AND EVALUATION OF SCHOOL CONSULTATION AND COLLABORATION

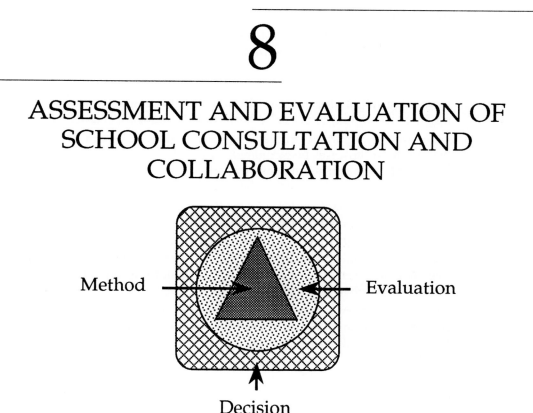

Method ← → Evaluation

Decision

## To Think About

Setting goals and evaluating the achievement of those goals are integral parts of education. This was most vividly illustrated in the requirements of Public Law 94-142 stipulating the development of individual education programs (IEPs). The basic philosophy that supports IEP development and evaluation is also the backbone of all good program development. A critical part of any educational program is the evaluation plan. Without such a plan, it is impossible to determine whether or not the goals have been achieved.

A consultation program requires evaluation, just as any other educational program does. Indeed, evaluation is particularly important in programs that strive for abstract skills and intangible outcomes.

## *Focusing Questions*

1. How are evaluation data helpful in developing and improving consultation programs? Who will want to see data from the consultation program for accountability purposes?

2. When should evaluation plans for school consultation and collaboration be developed? When should evaluation procedures for consultation be implemented?

3. Why do school consultants need to evaluate aspects of classroom environments that might affect student behavior? What classroom environments might affect student behavior? What variables might affect assessment?

4. What are the important processes in consultation? How can the effectiveness of these processes be evaluated? How might objective information be obtained to help consultants improve specific process skills? Are there parallels to the way teachers gather data about student skills?

5. What is the important content of consultation? What types of data might be collected to document the effectiveness of using this content?

6. What data might a consulting teacher collect about student (or client) progress that could be included as part of an evaluation plan? How might that type of information indicate whether or not the consulting teacher is doing a good job in the consultation?

7. How can a consultation program be justified, considering all possible sources of information available in the school and other information that might be gathered for this purpose?

## *Key Terms*

accountability
assessment
behavioral observation
Curriculum-Based Assessment
Curriculum-Based Measurement
evaluation
evaluation plan
formative evaluation

ongoing systematic assessment
outcomes-based education
portfolio assessment
rating forms
self-assessment
self-monitoring of behavior
summative evaluation

---

### Scenario

The setting is the conference room of a special education program office where the principal, the director of special education, the special education consulting teacher, and a parent are seated.

*PRINCIPAL*: Mrs. James, I have asked Mrs. Garcia, our director of special education, and Mr. Penner, our special education consulting teacher, to meet with us today to help address your questions. I've explained to them that you're concerned about the new program for your daughter. As I understand your concerns, you feel she is not learning as much as she did last year when she went to the resource room for special help. Is there anything you would like to add?

*PARENT*: Well, I don't like to complain, but I just don't understand this new way of doing things for her. I was glad when she qualified for special education, because I thought she would finally get some help. Now she isn't getting it any more. Besides that, I wonder how this consulting program affects the other children. As you know, I am president of the local Parent Teachers Association, and questions about the special education program have come up at several of our meetings. I told parents I would try to get more information from you.

*CONSULTING TEACHER*: I've been working closely with your daughter's classroom teacher this year, and we've worked out some special learning activities in the classroom such as cooperative learning. She loves that, and when she needs a little extra help, we have arranged for a sixth-grade girl to tutor her. Besides that, she goes to the resource room for math.

*SPECIAL EDUCATION DIRECTOR*: I understand that the placement team agreed to all these special experiences at the IEP meeting last spring.

*PARENT*: Yes, I know we agreed to try them, but I don't think they are working. I would like more evidence that this is a good way to educate children that have special learning needs.

*PRINCIPAL*: Mr. Penner, do you have data that we can show Mrs. James?

*CONSULTING TEACHER*: Well, I could get some test scores from teachers, I guess.

*SPECIAL EDUCATION DIRECTOR*: Our consultation program is rather new. I believe it is already producing some positive outcomes, but it is evident that we must provide more documentation of the results. We will need a more structured evaluation plan to get the appropriate data for assessing our results.

*PRINCIPAL*: I agree. Thank you, Mrs. James, for being involved with your daughter's program and helping us to think through what we need to do. After we do some further work on this topic, may we call on you to collaborate with us on developing a plan?

## Assessing and Evaluating the Consultation

Assessment and evaluation—the words produce apprehension and uneasiness over the use of tests, observations, and rating scales. Who has not dreaded the prospect of having their work and progress evaluated? Yet in these days of accountability, evaluation is an essential part of professional responsibilities. Consultants cannot know if the consultation activities are effective unless they conduct some type of evaluation. Administrators and policymakers cannot support their programs unless meaningful data are available.

Conoley and Conoley (1982) articulate the critical importance of evaluation to consultants with the following statement:

> *It will make little difference to a consultee organization if the consultant does everything with textbook perfection. The decision-makers are interested in positive outcomes in terms of cost, increased services, or staff feedback. Consultants must be prepared not only to provide assistance to others who are planning, implementing, and evaluating programs (i.e., program consultation) but must also* give priority *[emphasis added] to such activities in their own service delivery systems. (p. 82)*

Engaging in an ongoing systematic assessment process is the best way to make sure appropriate decisions are made.

## Components of Consultation Evaluation

A model of consultation evaluation is shown in Figure 8–1. The model features the accumulation of information for two primary purposes—formative evaluation and summative evaluation. Formative evaluation is used when making decisions to modify, change, or refine a program during its implementation. Summative evaluation documents the attainment of program goals and is used most often by administrators in determining whether or not programs should be started, dropped, maintained, or chosen from among several alternatives (Scriven, 1967; Popham, 1988; Posavac and Carey, 1989).

Data gathered during formative evaluations are often included as part of summative evaluations (Tuckman, 1985). The key in selecting evaluation procedures is to consider the purposes of assessment—the questions that need to be answered. Formative evaluations provide information for making changes and improvements. The focus is on individual concerns and the local school context. Summative evaluations are used to make decisions about program goals; therefore, they require collection of data from larger groups. Formative and summative evaluations also differ in the audiences to whom the results will be targeted and the way in which those results will be communicated (Popham, 1988). The authors of this book propose that a good consultation evaluation will include context, processes, and content of consultation. These three elements are used for both formative and summative purposes. Examples of questions that might be answered in each situation are presented in Figure 8–2.

*Evaluation of Consultation Context*   Formative evaluation of the context yields information about all elements that are expected to have an impact on the effectiveness of the consultation, such as students, teachers, parents, or home and classroom environments. This information helps in selecting and modifying consultation processes and content and is particularly useful during the initial stages of a consultation episode. Summative evaluation of context provides

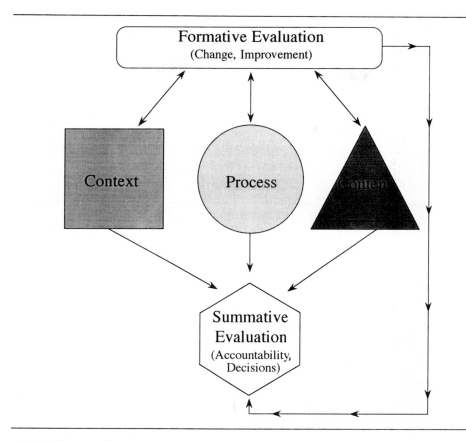

**FIGURE 8–1 Evaluation of School Consultation**

information to help decide whether or not the program should be continued in a particular school.

*Evaluation of Consultation Processes* Formative evaluation of consultation processes provides information about skills and procedures the consultant should develop or improve during the consultation process. Summative evaluation of processes gives information that demonstrates whether or not the skills and procedures used by the consultant were appropriate and effective.

*Evaluation of Consultation Content* Formative evaluation of the content of consultation provides information about effectiveness of the interventions planned by the consultant and consultee and, when the interventions are not effective, provides data to guide school personnel in making program changes. Summative evaluation of content indicates whether or not the student is receiving the appropriate level or type of service. For example, a student might need more in-depth psychotherapy than the school counselor can provide.

| Focus On: | FORMATIVE<br>Change/Improvement | SUMMATIVE<br>Accountability |
|---|---|---|
| **Program**<br>**Success** | **Development/Change**<br>What program aspects<br>should be changed to fit<br>this school and community? | **Status Decisions**<br>Should the consulting<br>program continue<br>next year? |
| **Consultation**<br>**Skills** | **Growth/Development**<br>What interpersonal<br>management skills need<br>to be changed? | **Self-Analysis**<br>Do I have the skills<br>to be an effective<br>consultant? |
| **Student/**<br>**Client**<br>**Progress** | **Growth/Progress**<br>Are achievement and<br>behavior improving? | **Placement Decisions**<br>Does the student need<br>more or less restrictive<br>service? |

(left vertical labels: Process Context / Content)

**FIGURE 8-2  Purposes of Assessment and Evaluation**

## Developing an Evaluation Plan

Consultants should clearly identify data collection methods in the initial stages of program development and at the beginning of each school year thereafter. A consultant who does not determine how to evaluate the program until the end of the school year will be working "harder, not smarter." Summative evaluation procedures should be extensive enough to document achievement of each annual goal. This language probably sounds familiar; the requirements are exactly the same when an IEP is developed. The similarity is not coincidental. Principles guiding IEP development must guide all good program development.

Once goals are determined, consultants can begin to list the types of data needed and determine ways of obtaining the data. Much of the data will exist within classrooms, in student files, or in school computer data banks. The challenge is to know what is needed and plan a strategy for collecting and summarizing the data in a meaningful, time-efficient way.

## *Example of an Evaluation Plan*

Anita, a certified learning disabilities teacher, was excited about the prospects for the coming school year. Her school had set goals to address the educational needs of students at risk and to decrease the number of students labeled as disabled. Since many of these formerly labeled students were placed in LD programs, she volunteered to change her program delivery model to consultation and collaboration, with only limited resource room services. It was a challenge for which she hardly knew where to begin.

Anita had studied literature on consultation and collaboration, and she knew that the first step was to think through the program goals. She also knew it would be important to gather appropriate data so she and her administrators could decide whether or not their goals were met by this program change. She carefully considered the types of data she would gather throughout the school year in order to make a good decision about the effectiveness of the program. As she thought about her evaluation plan, Anita also wanted to make sure she continued to improve her consultation skills during the year. So she included several goals that addressed that need.

Her plan is shown in Figure 8–3.

## *Components of a Good Plan*

The evaluation plan should contain at least one measure to document achievement of each program goal and a projected time line for gathering the information. Many different sources of information should be used, including but not limited to: direct observations of behavior; portfolios of student work; long-term projects; logs and journals of consultation activities; interviews; videotaped conferences; anecdotal records; and student grades.

Assessment methods and procedures should be as objective and unbiased as possible. Sometimes unbiased opinions and objectivity are not easily attained. For example, a consultant might ask consultees to complete checklists such as the ones presented in this chapter, but respondents may not be willing or able to offer objective opinions. As noted in earlier chapters, lack of objectivity was cited by Caplan (1970) as theme interference in working with the special needs of students. Consultees sometimes give high ratings indiscriminately. This failure to discriminate may be due to fear of the consequences of being truthful (such as losing a colleague's friendship) or not knowing enough about the questioned behavior to offer a constructive opinion. High ratings are of little benefit for evaluation, and if inaccurate, they may be another example of an iatrogenic effect, compounding problems rather than creating solutions. For

| Program Goals | Evaluation Procedures | Dates |
|---|---|---|
| Student progress in general classroom, with grades no less than D | Curriculum-Based Measurement Grade reports Student portfolios | Daily 9-wks on-going |
| Increase in skills of teachers for teaching special needs students | Inservice evaluation | each session |
| Student use of study skills in the classroom | Classroom observation Teacher reports | 9-wks 9-wks |
| Positive interaction with peers and teachers in classroom settings | Classroom observation Behavior rating scale | on-going 9-wks |
| Parent satisfaction with child's school experiences | Questionnaire | Dec.– May |
| Teacher satisfaction with consultation services | Self-assessment checklists and rating forms | 9-wks |
| Teacher use of suggested materials and methods in teaching | Classroom Environment Checklist | Sep., Jan., May |
| Consultant use of effective communication and problem-solving | Video-tapes, behavior rating form, consultation verbal analysis system | 9-wks |
| More student service with less labeling | Consultation activity report Consultation log | Daily By need |

**FIGURE 8-3 Consultation Evaluation Plan**

these reasons, consultants need information from multiple sources, in different circumstances within the context, and at varying times throughout the school year.

The following points list key elements in developing an effective evaluation plan:

1. It should be an ongoing process.
2. Multiple sources of information should be used.
3. Valid and reliable methods of gathering information should be used.
4. It should be limited to gathering data that will answer pertinent questions and document attainment of consultation goals.
5. It should be realistic, diplomatic, and sensitive to multicultural considerations.
6. Legal and ethical procedures, including protection of rights of privacy, should be followed.
7. Anonymity of respondents should be maintained whenever possible.
8. It should be cost-effective in time and money. For example, whenever possible, existing data should be used.

## Evaluating the Context of Consultation

Contextual evaluation is a relatively new conceptual framework through which consultants can examine their efforts. This approach to evaluation grew in importance as part of the educational reform of the 1980s. It is based on the premise that educational events occur in a context and the elements of the context play important parts in determining whether or not educational processes result in the desired outcomes (Field and Hill, 1988).

Contextual evaluation acknowledges the interdependence of all aspects of the school experience, including teachers, parents, students, administrators, classroom environment, school facilities, policies, procedures, and legal requirements. Contextual evaluation should consider the impact of students on teachers as well as that of teachers on students. It must assess the effect of teachers on consultants as well as the effect of consultants on teachers. It also should provide information on the professional interactions among individuals involved within the consultation environment(s).

Contextual evaluation is discussed here as it might be applied by individual consultants or collaborators. Administrators interested in a more extensive discussion of contextual appraisal for special education evaluation will find the work of Field and Hill (1988) a helpful reference.

Part I of this book discussed many contextual elements that play a role in school consultation, including societal values, legal requirements, community climate, home environment, school reform movements, teacher attitudes, and student characteristics. That information can provide background for appraising all elements when evaluating a consultation program. Evaluators will want to give careful attention to environmental factors that are related to student outcomes (Ysseldyke and Christenson, 1987). These factors include:

*school district conditions* such as teacher-pupil ratio, extent of emphasis on basic skills, amount of homework, emphasis on test taking, or grading policies;

*within-school conditions* such as class size, school ambience, leadership from the principal, cooperative environment, collaborative staff relations, degree of structure, or classroom rules and procedures; and

*general family characteristics* such as socio-economic status, educational level, use of out-of-school time, and peer groups outside the school.

Assessment of student characteristics and general classroom conditions is needed in order for a consultant to determine whether or not any mismatch between student characteristics and classroom situation is a factor in the problem. If the classroom environment is a problem, analysis of the information can be used to formulate appropriate solutions. Information about student progress will be discussed in the section on content of consultation, because student academic and behavior change is the most valid measure of the effectiveness of content.

## Assessment of Classroom Environments

The major contextual element to be assessed is the classroom learning environment in which the student is expected to function. Bender (1988) suggests that educational placement teams conduct extensive evaluations of every classroom in the building at least every five years, keeping the information available for the use of preassessment team members, consultants, and other school staff. He articulates the importance of this type of assessment information for consultants:

> . . . *some of the most useful services presently performed by special education consultants depend on knowledge about the standard functioning of general classrooms. When a consultant visits a class to observe the student and to consult, prior knowledge of what general types of strategies are commonly used in that class is likely to greatly enhance the consultant's ability to make meaningful strategy suggestions. (Bender, 1988, p. 19)*

Other reasons for including this type of assessment in the evaluation plan are: (1) it is recognized that planning for instruction based on student learning styles and characteristics alone has been unsuccessful (Bender, 1988; Bursuck and Lessen, 1987; Ysseldyke and Christenson, 1987); (2) research on effective instruction now provides useful information for determining which elements of the classroom environment should be evaluated (Bursuck and Lessen, 1987; Ysseldyke and Christenson, 1987); and (3) the assessment has the potential to help classroom teachers better understand their own needs in facilitating learning for students with special needs (Bender, 1988).

Classroom elements (Bender, 1988) that should be assessed appear in Figure 8–4. This list of elements will be helpful for consultants who wish to prepare

---

*Teaching Strategies and Approaches*

Analysis in this category determines types of effective teaching practices used by the teacher, such as:

1. Precision teaching
2. Cooperative learning
3. Self-monitoring
4. Peer tutoring
5. Use of learning strategies
6. Use of alternative or supplementary reading materials, alternative testing and grading strategies

*Typical Modifications Made in the Classroom*

Analysis in this category includes strategies for effective teaching behaviors, such as:

1. Pacing
2. Monitoring
3. Providing feedback and follow-through
4. Using alternative presentation modes, including visual and auditory presentations
5. Alternative classroom organizations
6. Use of cognitive organizers for reading
7. Use of individualized instruction

*Unusual Aspects of the Local Curriculum*

Elements assessed in this area include:

1. Average achievement levels of the school
2. Type of curriculum presented to students in prior years
3. Reading level of classroom texts

---

**FIGURE 8-4  Classroom Elements to be Assessed**

their own checklists or rating forms. The forms should be completed by classroom teachers and discussed in consultations with the teacher. Other sources of rating forms and checklists that can be used for this purpose are cited in the section for further reading.

## Evaluating the Process of Consultation

One of the most important reasons for conducting process evaluation is to glean information for professional development. According to some authorities, self-assessment and self-direction are preferred methods of professional development for teachers (Bailey, 1981). The rationale for self-assessment applies even more to school consultants than to teachers, because in most school contexts there will be few, if any, opportunities for consultants to receive any assistance from administrators or supervisors. Without some type of self-assessment, a consultant may perpetuate ineffective processes and the quality of the consultation may decline over time. The value of engaging in self-assessment of consultation is illustrated by this journal entry by a graduate student in consultation:

> *Before involvement in the consulting project at this university, I had never seriously examined my communication skills. The video-taping has been the hardest for me; however, I have come to realize the importance of it and I have gained a better insight into areas that can be improved.*
>
> *The first video-tape recording was a real eye-opener, revealing lack of skill in handling resistance. The second recording surprised the consultee, as she realized that during the consultation she had thought of a solution to the problem for herself. The third video-tape revealed more areas in need of work: Conflict resolution, assertiveness, and controlling facial responses. I feel I did a good job of using the problem-solving technique, and the best part was to hear two consultees say they were going to use it themselves in problem situations. They feel it helped them focus on the problem and think of real solutions. It gave them a base from which to work.*
>
> *Setting time limitations is something I'm not comfortable doing. I would rather allow the consultee enough time to work through feelings and identify the issues. However, looking back over my consultation log, I see that six of the consultations took more than 45 minutes and might well have concluded earlier if I had set time limits.*
>
> *Now that I have identified this baseline of strengths and weaknesses, I have set the following goals to achieve by the end of the school year:*
>
> 1. *Reduce resistance from consultees to no more than 95% of the time.*
> 2. *Resolve conflicts at least 80% of the time.*
> 3. *Use assertive behavior during consultation 100% of the time.*
> 4. *Eliminate inappropriate facial responses. I will video-tape consultation episodes every nine weeks and tabulate the target behaviors to see if I am making progress in reaching my goals. In addition, I will use a simplified version of the Consultant Behaviors Checklist to get feedback from my consultees every nine weeks. I will periodically interview consultees after consultation episodes to gather more immediate feedback about the target behaviors I am trying to improve.*
>
> *This project has made me aware of the importance of evaluation and how to use the information gathered. It does no good to gather the information if one does not make use of it. This was a valuable experience for me!*

## Consultant Self-Assessment Procedures

While many individuals engage in some self-appraisal or mental reflection, few do so systematically. Thus, the assessment or appraisal might not lead to meaningful improvement. Effective self-assessment should consist of a systematic, comprehensive program in which the consultant can gain information that leads to improvement or to a change of behavior.

The following suggestions for developing a self-assessment program are adapted from the work of Bailey (1981).

1. *Gain a philosophical overview of self-assessment.* Understand that self-assessment is not synonymous with the accountability required by administrators. Its purpose is personal change and improvement, and you should not share the results with supervisors unless you want to. The activities may not be easy to do, and some are rather time-consuming. They require selection of objective methods to gather data, in order to be most effective. Data should be collected in several consulting sessions with different types of consultees and various problem situations.

2. *Use media for self-assessment.* An objective way of gaining feedback about your behavior is to monitor it through use of audio- or videotaped material. Students in consulting preparation programs have been reluctant initially to use this type of feedback, but most are grateful later for its helpfulness. These tips for preparing and analyzing videotapes are helpful:

2.1 Set the consultee at ease by explaining the purpose of the videotape recording.

2.2 Do a few "trial runs" before involving a consultee, in order to become comfortable with the video camera and accustomed to seeing yourself on tape.

2.3 Don't focus on traits that have nothing to do with the quality of consultation. Taping distorts your voice and visual image, so don't worry about them.

2.4 Observe or listen to the tape several times, each time focusing observations on just one or two behaviors.

2.5 Tabulate behavior using a systematic observation method so the information can be interpreted meaningfully and progress followed objectively.

2.6 Be sensitive to the rights of privacy of the consultee. Arrange the seating during a videotape-recording session so that you face the camera and the consultee's back is to the camera.

2.7 Do not show the tape to an audience without receiving signed permission from the consultee.

3. *Identify the important consultation skills to be observed.* Merely watching and listening to yourself with the help of media will not provide enough information to guide personal development. Specific skills must be designated for recording the observation. Checklists and rating forms such as the Consultant Behaviors Checklist, Figure 8–5 can be used to identify behaviors to observe while viewing or listening to the taped consulting sessions. These checklists were developed from lists of important consulting behaviors described by researchers in the field.

**4.** *View or listen to taped consulting sessions and tabulate observation data.* Systematic behavioral observation techniques discussed later in this chapter are useful for observing consultant behavior, just as they are useful in observing student behavior in the classroom. Tabulate only one or two behaviors in each viewing, perhaps starting with a verbal behavior such as the number of times you said "O.K." or a nonverbal behavior such as looking away from the consultee. After tabulating the target behaviors, summarize strengths and behaviors that should be improved.

**5.** *Write down goals and objectives.* Prioritize the behaviors needing change and write behavioral objectives for them. Remember to state some type of criterion such as saying "O.K." no more than two times in a 20-minute consultation session. Include dates for achievement of each objective.

**6.** *Select strategies to help make the needed changes.* Formulate the strategies from material presented in other chapters of this text.

**7.** *Gather feedback and chart progress in achieving goals.* Periodic checks to determine whether or not you are making progress in the area you selected for change is essential. It is very easy to believe falsely that the change has taken place, if this step is bypassed. If goals focus on verbal skills, audio tapes probably will be sufficient for follow-up data, but if they include nonverbal skills, use of videotapes should continue. Perhaps it would be most efficient to reevaluate consultation skills at every marking period for students. The advantage of using consultee feedback is that consultee information can be contrasted with the consultant's own information. If there is much difference between the two sets of information, causes of the discrepancy need to be determined.

**8.** *When a criterion is met, a self-reward is due for a job well done!* The objective data can be shared with a supervisor. The consultant may wish to chart consultation growth, just as student progress growth is documented. Charts tell the story much more quickly than a list of numbers or a narrative description. Self-assessment should be an ongoing process propelled by realistic expectations.

## Records of Consultation Activities

Administrators are interested in more than how effectively consultants communicate or engage in problem solving. They want to know about practical issues such as how the consultant uses time, how many consultees have been helped, the types of problems addressed, and whether or not the consultation services were helpful to the consultees.

Consultants should keep records of consultation activities in order to answer these types of questions. The consultation log in Chapter 7 is a useful form for documenting these data. Those who want to develop their own forms would find the work of Tindal and Taylor-Pendergast (1989) a helpful reference. It may be productive also to check with your administrator to find out what specific information would be most desired. Busy consultants should not spend time collecting information that is not wanted or needed.

CONSULTANT_____ OBSERVER _____ DATE_____

|  | yes | needs work | does not apply |
|---|---|---|---|
| **1. Welcome** | | | |
| Sets comfortable climate | | | |
| Uses commonly understood terms | | | |
| Is nonjudgmental | | | |
| Provides brief informal talk | | | |
| Is pleasant | | | |
| **2. Communication Exchange** | | | |
| Shares information | | | |
| Is accepting | | | |
| Is empathic | | | |
| Identifies major issues | | | |
| Keeps on task | | | |
| Is perceptive, providing insight | | | |
| Avoids jargon | | | |
| Is encouraging | | | |
| Gives positive reinforcement | | | |
| Sets goals as agreed | | | |
| Develops working strategy | | | |
| Develops plan to implement strategy | | | |
| Is friendly | | | |
| **3. Interpretation of Communication** | | | |
| Seeks feedback | | | |
| Demonstrates flexibility | | | |
| Helps define problem | | | |
| Helps consultee assume responsibility for plans | | | |
| **4. Summarizing** | | | |
| Is concise | | | |
| Is positive | | | |
| Is clear | | | |
| Sets another meeting if needed | | | |
| Is affirming | | | |

**FIGURE 8-5  Consultant Behaviors Checklist**

## Evaluating the Content of Consultation

The content of consultation consists of the problem solutions, instructional techniques, or behavioral interventions selected through the consultation process. The content can be judged effective if the goals of the consultation are achieved. In school consultation the goals usually address improved achievement or behavior.

### Assessing Student Academic Performance

School consultants need training in the traditional approach of examining students through use of formal and informal testing procedures to identify their special learning needs. Skill in observing classroom performance, as differentiated from performance in a testing situation, is also necessary. The most functional approach to making these observations is Curriculum-Based Assessment (CBA).

*Curriculum-Based Assessment (CBA)*   It is important to identify accurately the student's current level of performance in the classroom and monitor progress in a systematic, ongoing manner. Standardized tests are not designed for this type of monitoring. Curriculum-Based Assessment is the most appropriate approach for the purpose (Bender, 1988; Bursuck and Lessen, 1987; Deno, 1987; Wang, 1987).

"There is nothing new about Curriculum-Based Assessment. In many respects it is like coming home to traditional classroom instruction" (Tucker, 1985, p. 199). What *is* new are more precise and practical ways of examining student progress in the classroom curriculum. The basic concept of CBA is use of the actual curriculum materials, or the course of study adopted by a school system, in making the assessment (Tucker, 1985). CBA differs from traditional testing, which uses material representing a composite of items taken from many different curricula. While standardized tests tell us how students perform in relation to a large reference group, CBA tells us how students perform in the classrooms where they are expected to function. Since most school consultants will be addressing problems that occur in general classrooms, they will need this type of information to formulate good solutions to problems and to document effectiveness of their efforts.

Consultants can choose among several ways to conduct CBA. The method chosen will depend on the circumstances within the school. Caution should be taken in adopting commercially prepared CBA measures because they probably will not be accurate measures of the curriculum in a particular school. Some criterion-referenced test batteries use the term *Curriculum-Based Assessment*, but are actually based on composites of many curricula. While criterion-referenced testing certainly is an appropriate way to conduct CBA, the measures should be based on the *local* curriculum. A commercial battery usually will not have that feature. However, criterion-referenced tests that accompany the textbooks adopted by school personnel would be very appropriate CBA measures for a consultant to use.

Some school districts and states require a type of criterion-referenced testing for all students. A term commonly used for this practice is *outcomes-based education*. For a school that utilizes the principles of outcomes-based education, the information generated from outcomes-based education data might be sufficient for evaluation needs. The consultant would need only to gain access to the information as it applies to the program being evaluated.

Other CBA measures are informal reading inventories (assuming the reading materials are taken from school texts), and mastery tests in content subject matter. "CBA is the ultimate in 'teaching the test,' because the materials used to assess progress are *always* drawn directly from the course of study" (Tucker, 1985, p. 200). The disadvantages of teacher-made Curriculum-Based Measurement are the time it takes teachers to develop them and the unknown reliability and validity of the measures (Fuchs, Fuchs, and Hamlett, 1990).

Many special educators are familiar with approaches to evaluation of student learning such as Precision Teaching (Lindsley, 1964) and Data-Based Instruction (Mercer and Mercer, 1989). These approaches require specification of observable and measurable objectives that can be recorded as the number of correct and incorrect movements or responses per minute. One-minute probes are given daily and the scores are plotted on charts. The charts are analyzed frequently to observe trends that indicate whether or not instructional program changes are needed. A variation of this approach was developed and refined at the University of Minnesota (Deno, 1987). This CBA system is called Curriculum-Based *Measurement* (CBM), emphasis added to differentiate it from other forms of CBA.

Deno (1987) specified two distinctive features of Curriculum-Based Measurement: (1) the procedures possess reliability and validity to a degree that equals or exceeds that of most achievement tests; and (2) growth in each curriculum area is measured on a single global task performed repeatedly across time. This approach differs significantly from criterion-referenced testing, which uses many different tasks, each measuring a different skill in a sequence. CBM has been widely researched in elementary schools using different types of curricula. It measures effectively the growth in academic areas of reading, writing, math, and spelling. The research has not singled out particular situations where it is most appropriate, but CBM is likely to be more useful than criterion-referenced tests for students in classrooms where whole language instruction is being used, because of its emphasis on global measures. It is very appropriate for use with students who have learning problems. It might also be an attractive approach to use with gifted students when basic skill development is of less interest to the evaluator than progress on more global measures.

A major disadvantage of CBM is the time needed to keep records and chart results. However, this process can be facilitated by use of software that automatically generates, administers, and scores tests; saves student scores and responses to the items on the tests; graphs scores; and automatically analyzes the student's rate of progress in comparison to the goal line (Fuchs, Hamlett, and Fuchs, 1990).

*Portfolio Assessment*   Other types of student performance, including sample worksheets, copies of projects, extra-credit reports, and samples of artwork, can be collected to help document the content of consultation. Evaluation of such products is an alternative that has much potential for assessing a wide range of student abilities and needs. A number of educational pioneers are leading the movement toward alternative assessment by promoting portfolios as a means for attesting to student progress over time (Maeroff, 1991).

Paulson, Paulson, and Meyer (1991) describe the portfolio as a purposeful collection of student work that exhibits efforts, progress, and achievements in one or more areas. They propose that students participate in selecting the contents to put into their portfolios and in developing the criteria for selection and for judging merit. Such processes are arenas for involving students in collaborative experiences to improve their learning and productivity.

A portfolio is larger and more elaborate than a report card, but smaller and more focused than a trunkful of artifacts (Valencia, 1990). A convenient storage device is the expandable file folder. This is to be a working folder; therefore, it should be easily accessible to the student owner and the teacher. Suitable products to be added to the portfolio, after self-assessment by the student and consultation with the teacher, might include: progress charts; completed learning packets, artwork; a student-made book; lists of mastered vocabulary or spelling words; notes on informal conversations; research reports; clever doodles; original songs; creative writing samples; descriptions of good deeds and helpful behavior; an autobiography; journal entries; tests; records of scores; teacher observation notes; audio- or video-tapes; solutions to problems; and much more. It is helpful to have a summary sheet, table of contents, or other organizing format. The construction of this format provides another valuable opportunity for the teacher and student to collaborate and discuss learning.

Portfolio assessment is a procedure that focuses on both the process and the product of learning. It is authentic in purpose and task, multidimensional, and contributes to an ongoing learning process. The material can be continuously evaluated, streamlined, and sent with the student from grade level to grade level as visible evidence of growth and improvement. It provides an effective vehicle for partnership in learning between teacher and student and contributes valuable support material for staffings and parent conferences.

Problems to be overcome in using this alternative form of assessment center around the additional work, storage space, patience, and time for teacher interaction with each student. A school consultant can ease the load of a teacher who wishes to use portfolio assessment by working as a team member to consult with students as they reflect on their work, and by collaborating with the teacher to develop ways of organizing and using the procedure.

Implementation of a portfolio assessment system in collaboration with students and colleagues includes the following steps:

1. Inform students and involve them.
2. Determine types of contents to be included (with flexibility for adding new types that may be determined later).
3. Prepare formats to organize portfolio contents, such as a table of contents or a summary sheet.
4. Determine criteria for evaluating the contents.
5. Determine the final destination of the portfolio and its contents.

**Maintaining Student Academic Records** If consultants have been using curriculum-based assessment and systematic behavioral observation procedures, a summary of the information can provide a summative record of consultation content. This information can report the number of goals met or not met, student grades or test scores, and interviews with teachers and parents.

As suggested earlier, one disadvantage of collecting and maintaining records generated by types of assessment such as student portfolios is the amount of space needed for filing them. Minner, Minner, and Lepich (1990) illustrate this point by stating, "If a teacher had a caseload of 15 students and each student worked in four academic content areas, the teacher would collect over 2,000 work samples in an academic year if he or she collected only one sample per week in each area" (pp. 32–33). The volume of papers would be even greater for a consultant who wished to monitor the progress of a caseload of thirty or more students. One solution to this dilemma is to require students to keep their own portfolios of their work (Wolf, 1989). This strategy seems especially valuable for use by consultants for gifted and talented students in content areas of art, music, design, written expression, computer programming, and other subjects which do not lend themselves easily to conventional forms of assessment.

Another method involves collaboration among classroom teacher, special education consultation, *and student* to develop criteria for assessing portfolio products, selecting the best or most representative ones, and removing others. Thus the portfolio volume is reduced while the student is gaining valuable self-assessment skills.

## Assessing Student Behaviors

Finding solutions to classroom behavior problems constitutes one of the major content areas of consultation. Consultants will need to gather objective information to document behavior changes. Systematic behavior observations, as well as subjective measures such as rating scales and checklists, should be used for this purpose.

**Behavior Observations** Many students with learning and behavior problems, as well as some gifted and talented students, demonstrate social difficulties, lack of motivation, poor work habits, or other behaviors that need to be monitored as part of the consultation evaluation program. Several researchers have studied general classroom settings and have identified the emotional, social, and work skills most important for success in those settings (Bursuck and Lessen, 1987; Fad, 1990; Wood and Meiderhoff, 1989). These data can be used to develop a checklist or rating scale most appropriate for your level of service. An alternative is to use one of several commercially developed rating scales and checklists that are available—for example, the Walker Problem Behavior Identification Checklist (Walker, 1970) or the Behavior Problem Checklist (Quay and Peterson, 1987). Caution should be exercised when selecting from existing rating scales, so that those chosen will be appropriate for the classroom situation in which they are to be used.

Several individuals, such as classroom teachers, parents, teacher aides, or peer tutors, can be asked to complete the rating scales. There are two advantages in asking the classroom teacher. First, the behaviors to observe can be more closely targeted. Second, teachers can be encouraged to focus attention on behaviors not previously considered. Bursuck and Lessen (1987) emphasize that a combination of behavioral observation by a consultant and completion of a behavior checklist by the teacher will be preferable to either one alone.

It is not sufficient to observe that the student does not pay attention or is noisy. The educator needs to know precisely the rate and frequency of the behaviors and under what conditions the student displays the behaviors. Systematic, direct observation of the student in the environments in which the problems occur is the best assessment procedure for gathering the information.

Data collected on specific behaviors can help collaborators set goals, plan programs, and evaluate interventions. In preassessment and problem solving, it is much easier to deal with "is at least fifteen minutes tardy 85 percent of the time," or "screams and kicks heels on the floor an average of six times per day," or "writes 90 percent of the 4s, 5s, and 7s backward," than it is to collaboratively work on problems described as "irresponsible," "aggressive," and "has problems writing her numbers."

Consultants may select from among several types of ongoing measurement of behavior when they wish to observe a student's behavior in the classroom, on the playground, or in the halls. There are many excellent resources about the methodology of behavior observation (Alberto and Troutman, 1990; Wolery, Bailey, and Sugai, 1988; Rusch, Rose, and Greenwood, 1988).

*Documenting Changes in Student Behavior*   Several methods of behavior measurement are useful for consultants:

- frequency recording,
- interval recording,
- time sampling, and
- duration.

Each method begins with identifying and defining a specific, concrete behavior or a set of behaviors to be observed.

Behavior should be defined so precisely that when measured by two different people, the numbers will be virtually the same, assuring reliability of the measurement. Two people measuring "aggression" or "irresponsibility" would not have very high interrater reliability of the measurement! Sometimes it will take several visits to the classroom to develop an observable and measurable definition of the behavior.

Frequency recording determines the number of times the event happens. It is used to measure discrete behaviors that can be discriminated, such as swearing in class or episodes of crying. Consultants will want to observe in the environment in which the behavior occurs for a number of times to get a representative sample of the behavior. It may be necessary to spend time in the classroom before observation, so that the student becomes accustomed to the observer's presence and is not "on best behavior." Then the measurement will be more realistic. Teachers and students themselves can record frequency of specific behaviors. Trial recording is a variation of frequency recording. This method adds the dimension of recording the opportunities a student has to perform a behavior. For example, if the observer uses frequency recording to measure "compliance with teacher instructions," it will be necessary to know how many teacher instructions were presented before a compliance rate or percent can be obtained. A tally mark could be made on the data sheet for every instruction, and those that are followed would then be circled. A sample data sheet for frequency recording is provided in Figure 8–6.

In interval recording and time sampling, the observation period is marked into intervals such as fifteen-second sections, two-minute sections, or ten-minute sections. Although the measure is more precise with smaller sections of time (intervals), it is not always possible to use these when the observer is teaching the class or leading a discussion. For interval recording, the observer would mark whether or not the behavior in question occurred during the interval. Did Jay spit at another student during that five-minute period (mark +), or refrain from doing so (mark -)? Did Tracy work on the workbook lesson during the interval (mark +), or did she get up and wander around, look out the window, or comb her hair (mark -)? After the observation period, the consultant or teacher should divide the number of intervals in which the behavior occurred by the total intervals observed to get a percent of intervals (or time) that the behavior in question happened.

Time sampling is similar to interval sampling and usually is easier because it does not require looking at the student for the entire observation period. After the observation time is divided into blocks of time (intervals), the observer only marks whether or not the behavior is occurring at the end of the interval. For example, at the end of fifteen seconds, the observer checks to see if Ryan is carving on the desk, the learning materials, or his flesh with a pencil, pen, or some other instrument. If so, the observer would mark +, and if not, the observer would mark -. Although some teachers might wish to stop Ryan's behavior rather than measure it, for the purposes of behavior observation, an observa-

Student _____   Observer _____
Dates _____   Time _____   Place _____

Definition _____

_____

_____

_____

_____

| Date | Time | | Behavioral Episodes Tally | Total |
| | Start | Stop | | |
|------|-------|------|---------------------------|-------|
| | | | | |
| | | | | |
| | | | | |
| | | | | |
| | | | | |
| | | | | |
| | | | | |
| | | | | |
| | | | | |
| | | | | |

**FIGURE 8–6   Sample Data Sheet for Frequency Recording**

tional posture rather than a disciplinary posture is needed. A percent of intervals is reported, in order to describe the behavior.

Duration recording requires using a watch or clock to measure how long a behavior occurs. This type of behavior measurement is often used with time on task, time in seat, or time required to complete an assignment or task. The observer starts the stopwatch or notes the time the behavior begins and ends. Using a stopwatch to measure time performing a specific behavior is an alternative to interval recording or time sampling.

Additional procedures for measuring and recording student behavior are included in the section on behavior management in Chapter 9. When these measures are used to assess a behavior, and used again after an intervention to reassess the same behavior, observed changes can be very obvious and dramatic. Then the results of collaboration are precise. It is a real boost to a collaborative partnership when a student's homework completion rate soars from 10 percent to 85 percent, or when the number of times a student puts on her coat independently changes from zero percent of opportunities to 100 percent after some work at home by parents.

*Self-Monitoring of Behavior*   Teaching students to monitor their behavior is a powerful instructional technique (Lovitt, 1984) that can provide useful information for evaluation purposes. It helps consultants because ongoing data can be collected without asking classroom teachers to provide constant monitoring of behavior. The records made by the students can be summarized and used by consultants for accountability purposes.

---

**Examples for Self-Monitoring of attention:**

1. Teacher instructs student about behaviors and actions that represent attention, and discusses ways student can help self.
2. Teacher prepares audiotape that plays tones every ten to ninety seconds, or an average of forty-five seconds, and provides record sheets to mark yes or no during monitoring.
3. Teacher models use of audiotape as follows:

   "Each time a tone sounds, I ask, 'Was I paying attention?'"

   "If I was paying attention, I mark *yes* on my record sheet. If I was not paying attention, I mark *no* on my record sheet."

   "Now I return to my work."

4. After one or two training sessions, student is expected to use the procedure without teacher assistance.
5. If desired, teacher can do spot checks to see if student is being honest about marking, but generally it is not necessary. Improvement in attention seems to occur due to the process of thinking about it periodically through this technique.
6. When student has improved in giving attention to the task, use of the audiotape can be omitted. Student is instructed to ask, "Was I paying attention?" each time the thought occurs, and mark the record sheet accordingly. If desired, self-recording can be eliminated at this time.
7. It is not always necessary to use tangible reinforcers for the procedure, but if they are used, they should be withdrawn as soon as possible.

*Audio or Video Tape Records* Another possibility for accumulating records of student behavior, particularly social behavior in the classroom, is the use of audio- or video-taped sessions (Minner et al., 1990). "Teachers have told us that tapes are especially useful when showing parents how their son or daughter has progressed" (p. 33). This approach to data collection, while very effective, is often difficult to arrange. The suggestions discussed for using video-tapes in self-assessment are applicable for this situation. Consultants should be very cautious about protecting the confidentiality of the observed student as well as other students in the classroom.

## Tips for Consulting and Collaborating

**1.** Evaluate consultations, in order to improve on effectiveness.

**2.** Suggest to teachers a variety of evaluation tools for monitoring student progress.

**3.** Acknowledge that less-than-desirable consultations occur occasionally, and build on the experience.

**4.** Share results of evaluation with key groups as appropriate—consultees, administrators, decision makers, parents—maintaining confidentiality and rights of privacy for those involved.

**5.** Celebrate even small gains in consultation success.

**6.** Promote instances of high-quality consultation and collaboration, not just the frequency and time spent in the activities.

## Chapter Review

**1.** An evaluation program is essential for documenting the effectiveness of any educational program. Evaluation is necessary to make program improvements and to defend the quality of the program to administrators and other decision makers.

**2.** During the initial stages of program development, consultants should create a plan for ongoing evaluation. Formative and summative information of the context, processes, and content of consultation must be gathered in the most efficient manner possible. Methods of gathering data should come from multiple sources and should be as objective and unbiased as possible.

**3.** Consultants should evaluate the context that has the most impact on student performance, with emphasis on student characteristics and their relationships to classroom environmental conditions. Context evaluation is used primarily for formative evaluation and should include careful appraisal of classroom setting demands.

**4.** Formative and summative evaluation should include evaluation of consultation processes. Consultants need to engage in systematic self-assessment, in order to gain information for improving their consultation skills, because it is not likely most will have the administrator feedback and monitoring needed for professional growth in this area. They should also keep careful records of their activities, to justify the program to decision makers.

5. No matter how good the processes of consultation may be, the program will not be effective unless students make progress in learning or behavior goals. The content of the consultation must work. It will be critical for consultants to keep records of student achievement and behavior change, in order to document the effectiveness of the program.

6. Data collected on learning achievement and specific behaviors can help collaborators set goals, plan programs, and evaluate the effectiveness of interventions. The desired student behavior should be defined precisely. Data collection methods from which to select include Curriculum-Based Assessment, student portfolio assessment, frequency recording, interval recording, time sampling, duration recording, and audiotape and videotape records.

7. Consultation effectiveness is three-dimensional. The consulting will be a great success if it results in:

- consultee satisfaction;
- problem resolution for the client's need(s); and
- a strengthened consultation system.

## Activities

1. Evaluation is an essential aspect of education. While classroom teachers assume responsibility for evaluating student learning, it is administrators who usually are responsible for evaluating the effectiveness of programs and educational methods such as school consultation. Discuss how the role of school consultants requires that they become actively involved in evaluating consultee satisfaction, problem resolution, and the strength of the consultation system.

2. Name several consumer and decision-making target groups within a school district who are likely to ask for data to support a consultation program. What would be the most effective formats for presenting the data to each target group for its purposes?

3. Study the evaluation model in Figure 8–1 and the example of one consultant's plan described in this chapter. Then develop an evaluation plan for consultation service during the coming school year in your school setting.

4. Work with a group of other consultants or teachers. Have each person make a copy of one of the checklists or rating scales of classroom environment cited in this chapter's section for further reading. Collaborate to compare the rating scales, and create a rating scale that would be useful in a typical school setting.

5. Conduct a self-assessment of consultation skills. Give careful attention to each step of the process as described in this book. Make an effort to videotape the consultation in a real or simulated experience at least every nine weeks

throughout an entire school year. Chart behavioral data to demonstrate progress on at least two specific objectives.

**6.** Use the consultation log in Chapter 7 for at least six weeks. Meet with other consultants to modify the form as needed, and then use the revised form for the remainder of the school term.

**7.** Read the references about Curriculum-Based Measurement cited in the section for further reading. Then work with other consultants and teachers to see if this type of assessment could be implemented in a way that would be beneficial to all involved.

**8.** Practice using the behavior observation techniques described in this chapter. Refine those that are most useful to you.

## For Further Reading

### Behavior Observation

Cautela, J. R., Cautela, J., and Esonis, S. (1982). *Forms for Behavior Analysis with Children*. Champaign, IL: Research Press.

Hall, R. V., and Houten, R. V. (1980). *The Measurement of Behavior*. Austin, TX: PRO-ED.

Maag, J. W. (1989). Assessment in social skills training: Methodological and conceptual issues for research and practice. *Remedial and Special Education, 10*(4): 6–17. Discusses criticisms of assessment of social skills training and suggests procedures to improve this type of assessment.

### Checklists and Rating Scales of Classroom Environments

Bender, W. N. (1988). The other side of placement decisions: Assessment of the mainstream learning environment. *Remedial and Special Education, 9*(5): 28–33.

Renzulli, J. S., and Reis, S. M. (1985). *The School-Wide Enrichment Model: A Comprehensive Plan for Educational Excellence*. Mansfield Center, CT: Creative Learning Press. Contains figures, charts, checklists, and text for assessing enrichment activities, process development, and independent study for gifted and talented students.

Salend, S. J., and Viglianti, D. (1982). Preparing secondary students for the mainstream. *Teaching Exceptional Children, 14*: 137–40.

Wood, J. W., and Miederhoff, J. W. (1989). Bridging the gap. *Teaching Exceptional Children, 21*(2): 66–68.

Ysseldyke, J. E., and Christenson, S. I. (1987). Evaluating students' instructional environ-ments. *Remedial and Special Education, 8* (3): 17–24.

### Comprehensive Classroom Assessment Programs

Bursuck, W. D., and Lessen, E. (1987). A classroom-based model for assessing students with learning disabilities. *Learning Disabilities Focus, 3*(1): 17–29. Describes the elements of curriculum-based assessment and instructional design, a well-designed, comprehensive system utilizing academic probes, work habit perception check, and environmental inventory.

Steele, J. (1982). *The Class Activities Questionnaire*. Mansfield Center, CT: Creative Learning Press. Evaluates those skills and factors related to the instructional climate that indicate the presence of enrichment opportunities for students. Obtains feedback from both teachers and students.

Ysseldyke, J. E., and Christenson, S. I. (1987). Evaluating students' instructional environments. *Remedial and Special Education, 8*(3): 17–24. Discusses the rationale for assessing a student's instructional environment and describes The Instructional Environment Scale (TIES), a set of assessment tools produced by PRO-ED.

### Contextual Appraisal of Special Education Programs

Field, S. L., and Hill, D. S. (1988). Contextual appraisal: A framework for meaningful evaluation of special education programs. *Remedial Education, 9*(4): 22–30. Explains the importance of contextual appraisal for special education programs. Of primary interest to administrators.

## Curriculum-Based Measurement

The first four references, a set of short papers, explain different aspects of CBM, such as how to develop and administer measurement devices, how to graph performance, and practical suggestions for teachers using the system.

Deno, S. L. (1987). Curriculum-based measurement. *Teaching Exceptional Children, 20*(1): 41–47.

Fuchs, L. S. (1987). Program development. *Teaching Exceptional Children, 20*(1): 42–44.

Tindal, G. (1987). Graphing performance. *Teaching Exceptional Children, 20*(1): 44–46.

Wesson, C. L. (1987). Increasing efficiency. *Teaching Exceptional Children, 20*(1): 46–47.

Fuchs, L. S., Fuchs, D., and Hamlett, C. L. (1990). Curriculum-Based Measurement: A standardized, long-term goal approach to monitoring student progress. *Academic Therapy,*

25(5): 615–32. Provides a reasonably detailed description of how CBM can be used to help teachers formulate effective instructional programs using the charted data to make relevant decisions.

## Evaluation of Consultation Processes

Conoley, J. C., and Conoley, C. W. (1982). *School Consultation: A Guide to Practice and Training.* New York: Pergamon Press. Contains more than a half-dozen forms to be used or adapted for gathering consultee feedback about the effectiveness of the consultation process.

## Work Habits and Social Skills

Fad, K. S. (1990). The fast track to success: Social behavioral skills. *Intervention in School and Clinic, 26*(1): 39–43. Reports the results of a survey of classroom teachers to identify the social and behavior skills considered essential for classroom survival. The author lists the ten most critical skills. A helpful resource for developing behavior checklists.

# References

Alberto, P. A., and Troutman, A. C. (1990). *Applied Behavior Analysis* (3d ed.). Columbus, Ohio: Merrill Publishing Co.

Bailey, G. D. (1981). Self–directed staff development. *Educational Considerations, 8*(1): 15–20.

Bender, W. N. (1988). The other side of placement decisions: Assessment of the mainstream learning environment. *Remedial and Special Education, 9*(5): 28–33.

Bursuck, W. D., and Lessen, E. (1987). A classroom–based model for assessing students with learning disabilities. *Learning Disabilities Focus, 3*(1): 17–29.

Cautela, J. R., Cautela, J., and Esonis, S. (1982). *Forms for Behavior Analysis with Children.* Champaign, IL: Research Press.

Conoley, J. C., and Conoley, C. W. (1982). *School Consultation: A Guide to Practice and Training.* New York: Pergamon Press.

Deno, S. L. (1987). Curriculum–based measurement. *Teaching Exceptional Children, 20*(1): 41–47.

Fad, K. S. (1990). The fast track to success: Social behavioral skills. *Intervention in School and Clinic, 26*(1): 39–43.

Field, S. L., and Hill, D. S. (1988). Contextual appraisal: A framework for meaningful evaluation of special education programs. *Remedial and Special Education, 9*(4): 22–30.

Fuchs, L. S. (1987). Program development. *Teaching Exceptional Children, 20*(1): 42–44.

Fuchs, L. S., Fuchs, D., and Hamlett, C. L. (1990). Curriculum–based measurement: A standardized, long–term goal approach to monitoring student progress. *Academic Therapy, 25*(5): 615–32.

Fuchs, L. S., Hamlett, C. L., and Fuchs, D. (1990). *Basic Math, Basic Reading, Basic Spelling* [Computer programs]. Austin, TX: PRO–ED.

Hall, R. V., and Houten, R. V. (1980). *The Measurement of Behavior.* Austin, TX: PRO–ED.

Lindsley, O. (1964). Direct measurement and prosthesis of retarded children. *Journal of Education, 147*: 62–81

Lovitt, T. C. (1984). *Tactics for Teaching.* Columbus, OH: Merrill.

Maag, J. W. (1989). Assessment in social skills training: Methodological and conceptual issues for research and practice. *Remedial and Special Education, 10*(4): 6–17.

Maeroff, G. I. (1991). Assessing alternative assessment. *Phi Delta Kappan, 73*(4): 273–81.

Mercer, C. D., and Mercer, A. R. (1989). *Teaching Students with Learning Problems* (3d ed,). Columbus, OH: Merrill.

Minner, S., Minner, J., and Lepich, J. (1990). Maintaining pupil performance data: A guide. *Intervention in School and Clinic, 26*(1): 32–37.

Paulson, F. L., Paulson, P. R., and Meyer, C. A. (1991). What makes a portfolio a portfolio? *Educational Leadership, 48*(5): 60–63.

Popham, W. J. (1988). *Educational Evaluation* (2d ed.). Englewood Cliffs, NJ: Prentice Hall.

Posavac, E. J., and Carey, R. G. (1989). *Program Evaluation: Methods and Case Studies* (3d ed.). Englewood Cliffs, NJ: Prentice Hall.

Quay, H. C., and Peterson, D. R. (1987). *Manual For The Revised Behavior Problem Checklist.* Coral Gable, FL.

Renzulli, J. S., and Reis, S. M. (1985). *The School-wide Enrichment Model: A Comprehensive Plan for Educational Excellence.* Mansfield Center, CT: Creative Learning Press.

Rusch, F. R., Rose, T., and Greenwood, C. R. (1988). *Introduction to Behavior Analysis in Special Education.* Englewood Cliffs, NJ: Prentice Hall.

Salend, S., and Viglianti, D. (1982). Preparing secondary students for the mainstream. *Teaching Exceptional Children, 14*: 137–40.

Scriven, M. (1967). The methodology of evaluation. In R. W. Tyler, R. M. Gagne, and M. Scriven (Eds.): *Perspectives of Curriculum Evaluation.* Chicago: Rand McNally.

Steele, J. (1982). *The Class Activities Questionnaire.* Mansfield Center, CT: Creative Learning Press.

Tindal, G. (1987). Graphing performance. *Teaching Exceptional Children, 20*(1): 44–46.

Tindal, G. A., and Taylor–Pendergast, S. J. (1989). A taxonomy for objectively analyzing the consultation process. *Remedial and Special Education, 10*(2): 6–16.

Tucker, J. A. (1985). Curriculum–based assessment: An introduction. *Exceptional Children, 52*(3): 199–204.

Tuckman, B. W. (1985). *Evaluating Instructional Programs* (2d ed.). Boston: Allyn and Bacon.

Valencia, S. (January, 1990). A portfolio approach to classroom reading assessment: The whys, whats, and hows. *Reading Teacher,* pp. 338–40.

Walker, H. M. (1970). *Walker problem behavior identification checklist manual.* Los Angeles: Western Psychological Services.

Wang, M. (1987). Toward achieving educational excellence for all students: Program design and student outcomes. *Remedial and Special Education, 8*(3): 25–34.

Wesson, C. L. (1987). Increasing efficiency. *Teaching Exceptional Children, 20*(1): 46–47.

Wolery, M., Bailey, D., and Sugai, G. (1988). *Effective Teaching: Principles and Procedures of Applied Behavior Analysis with Exceptional Students.* Boston: Allyn and Bacon.

Wolf, D. P. (1989). Portfolio assessment: Sampling student work. *Educational Leadership.* 46(7): 35–40.

Wood, J. W., and Meiderhoff, J. W. (1989). Bridging the gap. *Teaching Exceptional Children, 21*(2): 66–68.

Ysseldyke, J. E., and Christenson, S. I. (1987). Evaluating students' instructional environments. *Remedial and Special Education, 8*(3): 17–24.

# 9

# CONSULTATION, COLLABORATION, AND TEAMWORK FOR EFFECTIVE SCHOOLS

Adaptation —————→ ←————— Consultation

School Setting

## To Think About

Educators in the last decade of the twentieth century are witnessing an explosion of reports, proposals, and legislative mandates calling for educational reform. The school reform movement, along with conditions revolving around world concerns and demands for the future, has brought about organizational change, school restructuring, program revisions, and extensive staff development. Teachers, administrators, and support personnel face significant changes in the ways they function. Educational reformers propose comprehensive, schoolwide changes. One of the most significant changes to be made during the next decade and beyond will be collaboration to living about full inclusion of students with special learning and behavior needs into the total school environment. Education of students with special needs requires teaching a wide range of functional skills. Special education personnel are called on often to consult with teachers, parents, administrators, work-study supervisors, and others about social and learning behaviors that are disruptive in the educational setting and detrimental to the student's progress.

Cosmetic alterations will not be sufficient to address the plethora of issues, concerns, and demands on schools and their students in the next century. Many of the changes in the way schools function will necessitate strong efforts in consultation, collaboration, and teamwork among school personnel and parents.

## Focusing Questions

1. What characteristics distinguish effective schools?

2. How have some schools reorganized to incorporate the research on effective schools? What are similarities and differences in the intensity of teamwork, consultation, and collaboration among these programs?

3. What are the distinguishing characteristics of effective teachers, according to research? How can consultants use the research about effective teachers to help teachers structure and present effective lessons?

4. How can school consultants use principles of behavior management to improve student learning and behavior?

5. What are appropriate reinforcers for increasing desired behaviors, and punishers for decreasing undesired behaviors, of students with learning and behavioral disorders?

## Key Terms

Adaptive Learning Environments Model (ALEM)
antecedent
baseline
behavior
behavior management
Class-Within-a-Class (CWC)
consequence
effective lesson structure
effective presentation skills
effective schools
effective teachers
full inclusion

Mainstream Training Project (MTP)
negative reinforcement
positive reinforcement
preassessment
Premack Principle
punisher
reinforcer
school improvement
Schoolwide Enrichment Model
stimuli
stimulus control
Success-For-All (SFA)
team teaching

**Scenario**

The setting is a high school where the last scheduled period of the day is over and teachers are alone in their classrooms preparing for the next day. Several of them are reflecting silently on the special needs of their students that have been demonstrated in so many ways this day.

*BIOLOGY TEACHER* (thinking to herself about Diane): Diane knows the content for this class, but she can't pass the tests because they are above her reading level. How can I help her make a better grade on the next test?

*GOVERNMENT TEACHER* (pondering his lesson plan for tomorrow): I'd like to make some of these economics concepts more concrete for the kids who can't deal with abstractions, but I need to see some examples of how to do it.

*PHYSICAL SCIENCE TEACHER* (admonishing herself): Nothing I'm trying with J.D. is working. Even the behavior contract I set up is a flop. I wonder what other teachers have found to help them deal with his behavioral disorder.

*ENGLISH TEACHER* (worrying about tomorrow's schedule): No one prepared me for my first year of teaching and a whopping five preparations a day! As if that weren't enough to exhaust anyone, I feel that I also need to find low-vocabulary, high-interest reading for the ninth-grade English class.

*COMPUTER SCIENCE TEACHER* (shaking her head in frustration): I just don't understand why these learning-disabled students can't pay attention and take notes in class. They're going to need this stuff when they interview for jobs some day.

*HEALTH TEACHER* (organizing his desk to leave for home): Better get a good night's sleep—tomorrow's topic is a hard one. Birth defects. Just once I'd like to *really* get their attention and bring in some people who have serious disabilities, to show students what a person can do with positive attitudes and a few special resources. But I can't find the time to make all those arrangements.

*PSYCHOLOGY TEACHER* (looking at the clock and thinking): Hope I don't run into Ginger's mom at the grocery store again this evening. I can't handle one more tirade about how bored Ginger is in school, including my class. Ginger may know a lot about psychology already, but her social skills leave much to be desired.

## Characteristics of Effective Schools

Education is viewed by many as the key to a nation's success in global leadership and strength in the international marketplace. Schools are called on to prepare students for becoming informed citizens and productive workers, not just in their own communities and nation, but within an international perspective. These lofty goals can be attained only by competent educators and effective schools. Part of the school reform of the 1970s and 1980s included research to determine what made some schools more effective than others. The results of this research provide important background information for consultants to apply in making decisions that can significantly improve schools. The vast amount of data can be categorized into two groups:

- characteristics of effective schools, and
- characteristics of effective teachers.

Consultants will play important parts in encouraging these characteristics in the schools where they work. They can provide valuable leadership in helping the school to become more effective.

Characteristics that distinguish effective schools from other schools (Bickel and Bickel, 1986; Morsink et al., 1986) include:

1. Strong leadership by building principals who are actively committed to the goals of the school.
2. An orderly school climate that includes student awareness of the requirements for order.
3. High expectations that students will achieve academically.
4. A process of systematically monitoring student performance.
5. Holding basic skills achievement as a central outcome measure.
6. Students participating in engaged learning at a high frequency level.

In reviewing the effective schools literature and the research supporting programs for addressing needs of at-risk students, such as Chapter 1 programs, special education programs, and other remedial programs, Slavin and Madden (1989) determined that:

1. Retention is one of the most frequently used strategies for dealing with at-risk students, but is the least effective in long-term results.

2. The diagnostic/prescriptive pull-out program might keep at-risk students from falling further behind their peers, but that effect is limited to the early grades and occurs only in reading and math.

3. In-class models in which special education or remedial teachers work in the classroom are no more effective than pull-out programs.

4. Both pull-out programs and in-class models are  probably too limited in instructional strategy to make a significant difference.

5. Reducing class size produces few substantial gains in student achievement until class size approaches one student.

6. Preschool, kindergarten, and first-grade programs  focusing on prevention show strong positive effects immediately after the preschool experience. But the  effects diminish each subsequent year, until by grade two or three they are undetectable. "Preschool may be seen as a means of getting students off to a good start in school, not as a program that, used in isolation,

is likely to reduce substantially students' risk of school failure" (Slavin and Madden, 1989, pp. 7–8).

**7.** Programs with the most long-term positive effects on student achievement fall into one of two categories: *continuous progress models,* with students proceeding at their own pace through a sequence of well-defined instructional objectives, and certain forms of *cooperative learning,* in which students work in small learning teams to master material that is presented initially by the teacher.

**8.** Remedial diagnostic-prescriptive pull-out programs show convincing evidence of effectiveness when they involve one-to-one tutoring, often by peers and/or volunteers or by computer-assisted instruction.

Slavin and Madden (1989) concluded, "If we are to ensure that all students attain an adequate level of basic skills, then we must organize schools differently" (p. 11). Slavin and Madden recommend the following school changes:

State that it is the school's responsibility to see everyone succeeds.
Recognize that success for everyone will not be cheap.
Emphasize prevention of learning and behavior problems.
Emphasize classroom change.
Use remedial programs as a last resort.

These data cast a dismal shadow on traditional programs such as resource rooms and itinerant teaching models. Educators must determine ways in which they can reorganize and restructure learning environments in order to improve their effectiveness in meeting student needs. Consultation, collaboration, and teamwork are key components in reform efforts to make schools more effective.

## Effective School Programs

Since consultants will be key personnel in reorganization and restructuring, several examples of exemplary models are presented in this chapter. In each instance, consultation, collaboration, and teamwork structures replace traditional pull-out and push-in approaches to increase the possibilities for full inclusion of students with disabilities into the total school environment. These new structures encourage the development of integrated, comprehensive, multidimensional educational programs that are particularly relevant for students with special needs, who are at risk within current educational systems.

### Preassessment

One of the most widely used approaches for addressing the needs of students at risk of failing in general education settings is a team problem-solving approach known as preassessment. This approach sometimes is termed pre-referral, teacher support team, teacher assistance team, building team, or some other variation implying a team effort in a general education setting (Chalfant, Pysh, and Moultrie, 1979; Graden, Casey, and Christenson, 1985; Pugach and Johnson, 1989). One element these team approaches have in common is inclusion of a multidisciplinary team of school personnel who meet on a regular basis to provide assistance to classroom teachers *before* engaging in referral and evaluation for placement in special education. The goal typically is to *prevent* special education placement if at all possible. A typical preassessment takes place in this manner:

1. A multidisciplinary team is formed. This team usually includes the building principal as leader, two or three experienced classroom teachers, one or two special education teachers, and other support personnel as deemed necessary.

2. The team meets on a regular schedule (from every week to once per month) with classroom teachers who request assistance in dealing with the needs of students in their classrooms.

3. Team members engage in problem solving and make suggestions to the requesting teacher.

4. The requesting teacher selects strategies to try for a predetermined period of time.

5. The teacher collects data during the trial period to document whether or not the strategies are effective. Team members sometimes assist with the data collection.

6. The team and requesting teacher meet at the predetermined time to evaluate the data. If the interventions have been effective, the case is dismissed. If they have not been effective, the team can generate other interventions to try, or refer the case for comprehensive evaluation, if there is reasonable evidence that a student's needs are exceptional and require special education services.

Preassessment team interactions are meant to be informal. Team members must use effective consultation and collaboration skills if the program is to be successful. When all team members engage in effective problem-solving processes, the students who are at risk will benefit. When team members do not problem solve effectively, students are often needlessly referred for special education services (Cooley et al., 1988).

A review of preassessment programs in Kansas (Cooley et al., 1988) showed that much of the success of preassessment teams depends on the clarity of the classroom teacher in describing the problem. In most cases, teams will be generating alternatives based on information about the problem, whether or not the information is accurate. Formal checks should be made to determine the use of appropriate procedures by the teacher. Also, there must be monitoring to assess whether or not evaluation data have been collected in valid and reliable ways, in order to make further decisions (refer to Chapter 8 for suggested procedures).

The challenge for consultants serving on preassessment teams is to find ways of helping classroom teachers clearly identify learning and behavior problems. The techniques presented in Chapters 5 and 7 of this book can help the consultant accomplish this task. Another important aspect of preassessment is discussing alternatives that can be used in the classroom. Chapter 10 contains ideas for strategy- and content-related issues. Collecting accurate follow-up data is critical to the success of the preassessment process. (Refer to Chapter 8 for a discussion of curriculum-based assessment. Chapter 8 and a later section of this chapter present behavioral observation techniques.) An example of a form for monitoring preassessment is given in Figure 9-1.

## *Team Teaching*

Another example of collaboration frequently practiced in effective schools is team teaching. It involves groups of teachers who instruct and interact with large groups of up to one hundred or more students, or small groups of ten to twenty, or individual students. The approach evolved from a report by the Commission on the Experimental Study of the Utilization of the Staff in the Secondary School, as appointed by the National Association of Secondary School Principals in 1956. Recommendations of the commission for creating a better high school included (Trump, 1960):

> small groups of students;
> flexible groupings of students;
> independent study;
> paraprofessionals;
> team teaching; and
> professional services.

By the mid-1960s, there were indications that one-quarter of secondary schools in the United States were trying out some form of team teaching. However, many of the schools used the team approach for only part of the curricular program. It was often the case that only a few teachers were involved in team teaching and planning. Educators were not trained for team teaching. Few research studies that were conducted addressed the critical issue of student achievement within the approach. Support for team teaching was fueled more by validation-through-affirmation than validation-by–empirical evidence (Armstrong, 1977). Over a fifteen-year period during the 1960's and 1970's, large amounts of money, personnel, and time were invested in the idea of team teaching, without any systematic evaluation of the effect on student achievement (Heidbrink, 1990).

Name of Student: _____ _____

Classroom Teacher(s): _____ _____

| Intervention/Modification | Date | Results |
| --- | --- | --- |
| _____ | _____ | _____ |

Modified Physical Environment:

_____ _____ _____

Peer Assistance:

_____ _____ _____

_____ _____ _____

Increased Time on Task:

_____ _____ _____

_____ _____ _____

Adapted Materials/Assignments:

_____ _____ _____

_____ _____ _____

Adapted Instruction/Presentation:

_____ _____ _____

_____ _____ _____

Reinforcement Strategies:

_____ _____ _____

_____ _____ _____

Changes/Modification:

_____ _____ _____

_____ _____ _____

**FIGURE 9-1  Preassessment Monitoring Form**

During the 1980's and early 1990's, team teaching received renewed interest, due to public demands for differentiated instruction that is more closely matched to individual student interests and needs. Proponents argue that while teachers can educate in their areas of expertise, they can also share teaching responsibilities and learn from each other.

Teachers need training and practice in consulting and collaborating, in order to be productive team members. This kind of training must begin in preservice teacher preparation programs. Goodlad (1990) reports that student teachers spend most of their time working with a single teacher in one classroom, not with teams of teachers in the total school context. Much more work is needed toward this approach if it is to be effective in meeting all students' needs.

## *Adaptive Learning Environments Model*

The Adaptive Learning Environments Model (ALEM) (Wang and Birch, 1984) uses a new approach to team teaching. It is one of the earliest attempts to change general classroom environments to accommodate the needs of all children, including those with disabilities. According to its developers, the ALEM concept depicts schools as social systems that must respond effectively to individual differences. Schools are accountable for ensuring that students acquire basic academic skills, a positive self-perception of academic and social competence, practical competence in coping with the social and academic demands of schooling, and a sense of responsibility to the broader social community. All students are taught in the regular classroom, as adapted to include:

A multi-age and team-teaching organization that increases flexibility in the classroom, where individual differences are viewed as the norm rather than the exception;

Highly structured diagnostic-prescriptive academic instruction, with each student expected to make steady progress when provided with learning experiences based on individual needs;

Student planning and monitoring of own learning;

An open-ended, exploratory learning element promoting social and personal development and often involving cooperative learning methods;

Built-in support systems that include consultation and collaboration by school administrators, health professionals, and special education teachers;

A family involvement program that attempts to reinforce the integration of school and home experiences.

ALEM has been researched in a variety of settings, including rural, suburban, and middle-class areas, with a wide range of students, including disadvantaged, handicapped, and gifted. The developers maintain it is one of the most multifaceted and visible efforts to integrate exceptional children into general classrooms. Wang (1986) reports consistently positive trends on student achievement in basic skills and social behavior. Improved attitudes toward differences among students occur in classes where exceptional students are integrated. The research base also supports the thesis that a high degree of implementation of ALEM can be attained in classroom settings that differ in terms of aims, needs, and contextual characteristics. Major strengths of ALEM are the data-based approach to improving the degree of program implementation, and an individualized staff development program (Wang and Walberg, 1988).

Other researchers (Fuchs and Fuchs, 1988) question such positive results. They contend that the research on the effectiveness of ALEM is equivocal at best. Therefore, they call for more research before educators embark on a large-scale, full-time mainstreaming program such as ALEM.

## Class-Within-a-Class

The Class-Within-a-Class (CWC) program was developed to be an alternative service delivery model as part of the Park Hill Secondary Learning Disability Project, funded by the Missouri Department of Elementary and Secondary Education, Special Education Section (Reynaud et al., 1987). The underlying philosophy of the program is that all children have the innate potential to learn, and it is the role and responsibility of the public school system to provide opportunities for all learners to be successful. The total program includes collaborative curriculum planning between teams of learning disabilities (LD) teachers and content area teachers, and use of a learning strategies curriculum (Deshler and Schumaker, 1986). The LD teachers are in the content classrooms during instruction and provide a variety of support services in classrooms to students who have special needs.

These are the essential elements of the Class-Within-a-Class approach:

1. Teachers who are compatible and willing to work in a team effort are selected by the administrators.
2. The teaching team meets regularly to plan classroom activities.
3. Teacher roles are defined with the general classroom teacher responsible for maintaining the integrity of the class, and with the special education teacher collaborating to support the classroom teacher and serve as a resource to students.
4. High school age learning-disabled students with achievement below fourth grade, and elementary-age students more than two years below grade level, are excluded.

5. When possible, all students of a certain grade level are in the same classroom, so the LD teacher can "go with them" to class.

The CWC approach is rapidly gaining widespread acceptance (Hudson, 1992). Although extensive research documenting the effectiveness of CWC has not been published at this time, preliminary results indicate that the approach is very effective, if teachers are adequately prepared for collaboration and the guidelines are carefully followed (Hudson, 1992). Before embarking on the use of this model, however, schools should consider carefully the work of Slavin and Madden (1989), which suggests that in-class models are no more effective than pull-out programs.

## Success-For-All (SFA)

The Success for All program was developed and implemented in an inner-city elementary school in Baltimore, Maryland (Madden et al.1989). The developers wanted to see what would happen if they decided (1) to ensure that each child in every school would reach the third grade on time with adequate basic skills; (2) no child would be assigned to special education for a learning problem unless he or she were seriously handicapped; and (3) no child should need to be retained in a grade or relegated to long-term remedial services. The program includes these elements:

1. Certified teachers with experience in Chapter 1 programs, special education programs, or primary reading programs are employed to work one-on-one with students who are having difficulty keeping up with their reading groups in the classroom.
2. Students in grades 1 through 3 are in age-grouped classes of about twenty-five for most of the school day but are regrouped for a ninety-minute reading period into classes of about fifteen students at the same performance level.
3. Curriculum-based assessments are made every eight weeks to determine each student's progress. Information from the assessments is used to make program modifications for each student and identify students who need other types of assistance.
4. Half-day preschool for four-year olds and full-day kindergarten for five-year-olds are provided. The curriculum in these programs places heavy emphasis on development and use of language, and provides a balance of academic readiness and nonacademic activities.
5. Two social workers and one parent liaison work full-time at the school as a family support team.
6. A program facilitator, along with the building principal, takes responsibility to oversee operation of the program.

**7.** Teachers are given detailed manuals developed for the program, supplemented by two days of in-service at the beginning of the school year, and followed by several brief in-service sessions throughout the year.

**8.** When a student's learning problems cannot be dealt with in the regular classroom and with the help of tutors, special-education resource services are provided.

The Success-For-All program evaluation at the end of the first year indicated that the preschool and kindergarten children in the experimental school scored higher than the children in the control group on several measures of language development and reading word attack. Children from first grade through third grade in the experimental school outscored the control children on every reading measure.

In contrast, Semmel and Gerber (1990) point out that the Success-For-All program is the most expensive and most ambitious approach for responding to the "problems of learner heterogeneity."

## *Mainstream Training Project (MTP)*

Some school districts have responded to concerns about meeting the diverse needs of students with projects that combine consultation, collaboration, and inservice. The Mainstream Training Project (MTP) is an example at the secondary school level (Tindal et al., 1987; Waltz, 1990). Within this model, the special education cooperative provides a five-phase training program designed to assist classroom teachers in accommodating all types of learners. During the first phase, all school staff are given in-service, dealing with general information about handicapped learners, description of services provided through special education, and due process procedures. The second and third phases involve summer workshops for classroom and special-education resource teacher teams from each school district. The topics included in the workshops are listed in Figure 9–2.

---

1. Literature review of effective teaching practices
2. Classroom management strategies
3. Cooperative learning methods
4. Individual mastery learning techniques
5. Use of learning centers
6. Direct instruction teaching techniques
7. Reading in the content areas
8. Writing as a tool for learning
9. Teaching study skills and actively engaged learning
10. Evaluation, grading options, and test-writing

---

**FIGURE 9-2  Workshop Topics for the Mainstream Training
Project (MTP)**

1. The regular education teacher assumes daily management of the program, including completion of student observations, evaluative checklists, or tests, and implements any curricular modifications established at the outset.

2. The special education teacher assumes responsibility for helping the teacher collect data, for consulting with the teacher about programs, and for coordinating modification if the student's performance is below the performance levels that are expected.

3. The student follows the agreement and completes all tasks and activities required at the appropriate times. Students are directed to seek assistance if they are having difficulty completing the tasks/requirements (Tindal et al., p. 100-101).

**FIGURE 9-3  Roles of Consultants, Teachers, and Students in the Mainstream Training Project (MTP)**

After the teachers have begun to master this content, phase four begins, and consultation support is provided for applying the knowledge in the teachers' classroom practices. Typical responsibilities for the consultant, consultee, and students are described in Figure 9–3.

Once teachers demonstrate competent application of the knowledge in their classrooms, they move into phase five, which involves assisting in training other teachers in phases one through four.

The Mainstream Training Project explicitly utilizes consultation and collaboration as integral parts of the success of the program. Data collected initially to determine the effectiveness of the program lacked sufficient research design control to draw strong conclusions. However, it is noteworthy that students receiving the consultation services earned grade-point averages no different from students who did not have consultation agreements. Since the consultation group students were predicted most likely to fail, data tend to support the effectiveness of the program.

Cancelli and Lange (1990) caution that within the in-service approach, the consultant owns the problem. By contrast, in most consultation, the teacher owns the problem and the consultant assists in problem clarification. These concerns should be kept in mind when planning the goals of in-service and staff development and will be addressed further in Chapter 12.

## Schoolwide Enrichment Model

Gifted program personnel often serve as consultants or consulting teachers to plan and coordinate appropriate learning opportunities for gifted and talented students. Most students identified as gifted or very talented in one or more areas spend the major portion of the school day in the general classroom. In order to provide more productive learning time for gifted students and redeem them from years and years of curriculum redundancy, gifted program consultants should work closely with classroom teachers and resource people in the community to challenge students in their areas of special interests and strengths.

Meaningful school experiences for very able students usually differ in pace, breadth, and depth from experiences offered by the regular school program. Differentiated curriculum can be provided by methods such as flexible pacing of subject matter, group activities for interaction with mental peers, personalized learning options, and relevant enrichment of the course content.

One of the most widely used systems for differentiating the curriculum of gifted and talented students is the Schoolwide Enrichment Model, a comprehensive plan developed by Joseph S. Renzulli and associates (Renzulli and Reis, 1985). This model serves gifted and talented students in both general classrooms and special resource rooms. In the Schoolwide Enrichment Model, the gifted education facilitator's role is similar to that of a varsity coach who is responsible for the general physical fitness of all students in the school, but who also facilitates the development of gifted athletes. A Schoolwide Enrichment Team of faculty members, parents, and students gives teachers and administrators the direction they need to expand the scope of school-based experiences toward special interests and talents.

Staff development, parent involvement, extensive use of resource personnel, long-range planning, and intensive evaluation are integral components of the Schoolwide Enrichment Model. The coordinator of the enrichment program—who may or may not have other school responsibilities, depending on the size and scope of the program—consults and collaborates with classroom teachers, administrators, resource persons, and parents, as well as the students, to facilitate learning at the pace and level very capable students need in order to develop their potential. The coordinator also provides direct service to identified gifted students, co-teaches process skills in the general classroom, and manages special projects carried out by students in their interest areas. The coordinator assists classroom teachers to eliminate unnecessary assignments. This gives students the opportunity to progress through the regular curriculum in an efficient, often accelerated, manner (Reis and Renzulli, 1986; Renzulli and Reis, 1986).

The roles and responsibilities carried out by the Schoolwide Enrichment Model coordinator point out the value of collaboration and consultation activities for serving the special needs of a particular student population. In addition, they underscore the contribution of consultation services toward an atmosphere of excellence as these services affect the total school program in positive ways.

Many research studies have been conducted on various components of the Schoolwide Enrichment Model. Several of the studies examine long-term effects of participation in the model across a period of more than ten years. Studies from the first part of that period are summarized in a two-volume technical report (Renzulli, 1984). Since publication of the technical report, numerous research articles have appeared in professional journals, substantiating the success of the Schoolwide Enrichment Model for students identified as gifted, talented, and creative (Renzulli, 1986).

Other widely used gifted program models that encourage consultation and collaboration among teachers, support personnel, parents, and students, include the Autonomous Learner Model (Betts, 1986), Talents Unlimited (Schlichter, 1986), the Individualized Programming Planning Model (Treffinger, 1986), the Integrative Model (Clark, 1992); the Purdue Three State Enrichment Model for Elementary Level (Feldhusen and Kolloff, 1986), and the Purdue Secondary Model (Feldhusen and Robinson, 1986). Each of these models supports the philosophy that gifted students must receive differentiated services regularly for their special needs—not just a few minutes once or twice a week in brief, isolated programs having little or no continuity with general classroom curriculum.

## Characteristics of Effective Teachers

Research has shown that teachers who are most effective in fostering student achievement engage in a number of common practices, many of which are critical for handicapped and other low-achieving students (ERIC, 1987a; 1987b; Bickel and Bickel, 1986; Morsink et al., 1986). Effective teachers will:

Direct classroom learning by using structured materials and solicit high levels of academically focused, engaged learning time among students.

Use teaching activities centering on academic issues, with clear goals communicated to students.

Allocate sufficient time for instruction.

Provide extensive content coverage.

Monitor student performance continuously.

Provide many opportunities for correct responses to appropriate teacher questioning.

Provide immediate and academically oriented feedback to students.

### Effective Lesson Structure

Research demonstrates that one set of effective teacher practices relates to lesson structure and another set addresses presentation of the lesson. Steps for developing an effective lesson structure, briefly stated, are (ERIC, 1987b; 1987a):

1. Gain the learner's attention. Use verbal prompts such as "look here" and "listen." Maintain 90 percent task engagement during teacher-directed activities.
2. Review relevant past learning. Teacher review, or correcting of homework, is recommended.
3. Communicate the goal of the lesson. Tell what is being learned and why it is important. Keep the goal statement brief.
4. Model the skill to be learned. Proceed in small steps that are not too difficult and give explicit verbal directions. Exaggerate steps to call attention to the critical features.
5. Prompt for correct response. Let students practice with many correct responses. Continue until very high levels of proficiency are demonstrated. The teacher should do each step as the students are doing it, providing modeling and verbal prompts.
6. Check for skill mastery. Students perform the behavior under teacher supervision without prompting. The teacher provides feedback after every trial and watches for many successful repetitions.
7. Close the lesson. Review the skill, discuss what will be in the next lesson, or introduce independent work.

## Effective Presentation of the Lesson

The following presentation skills are summarized from ERIC documents which are in the public domain and can be obtained from Council for Exceptional Children (ERIC 1987a; ERIC 1987b): should be used:

1. Elicit frequent responses. Responses can be verbal or written and can be in unison or given individually. Nonvolunteers should be called on in most instances, to ensure active involvement of all students.
2. Maintain an appropriate pace. A suitable pace is facilitated when teachers are well prepared, elicit many responses, and move quickly to questions or teacher input.
3. Maintain student attention. Strategies that are helpful when attention wanes include soliciting more responses from students, moving closer to the student whose attention is lost, or gaining eye contact with students.
4. Monitor student responses and adjust instruction. Keep correct response rates from 80 to 90 percent. Immediately acknowledge correct answers and then move quickly to new input.
5. Ensure all students have an equal chance to learn. Make sure all students are called on, not just those who volunteer. Use good eye contact with all students, and allow time for them to formulate answers.

## Managing the Behavior of Mainstreamed
## Students with Special Needs

Managing the behavior of mainstreamed students is one of the most common problems consultants are asked to address (Thurston and Kimsey, 1990). However, it is difficult for a consultant to deal with a behavior problem "from a distance." The most efficacious approach for helping the consultee resolve this kind of classroom problem is the collaborative approach. Collaborative problem solving for behavior management often requires specific guidance from the consultant, because the teacher has "tried everything" already. Parents also may need assistance from the consultant, in order to deal with behavior problems at home. Behavior management plans to reduce particular behaviors should include procedures for increasing or developing appropriate behaviors.

Characteristics of the behavioral approach to behavior management are defined by Martin and Pear (1988) as:

emphasis on defining problems in terms of behavior that can be measured and using the measure as the best indicator of success;

procedures and techniques for changing behavior as ways of rearranging the environment;

precise description of methods and rationales; and

high value on accountability.

These characteristics of behavior modification are important to consultants because they provide parameters for collaborating about behavior problems. Also, they include both contextual and process considerations.

There is much misunderstanding about the use of behavioral procedures. Although the principles of behavior management are familiar to experienced educators, effective implementation of the principles in classroom or home settings is more problematic (Alberto and Troutman, 1990). Many behavior analysis professionals express concern about the misuse of behavior management techniques. It is virtually impossible to learn enough from a few pages in one book to implement sophisticated programs of behavior management ethically and effectively. Alberto and Troutman (1990) caution that teachers who want to use behavior management procedures ethically and responsibly must address teacher and staff competence, selection of appropriate goals and procedures, voluntary participation, and accountability. The recommended reading list at the end of the chapter is an appropriate place to begin a more intensive study of behavior management principles.

Management of severe behavioral disorders among mainstreamed students is a complex area that requires intensive consultation and collaboration with well-prepared special education personnel. Consultants with no background in behavioral issues should undertake training in more formal applied behavior analysis to assure competence in their use of behavioral methods. They should also interact frequently with those who are specially trained as teachers for students with behavioral disorders.

## The ABC Approach

The ABC approach provides a helpful view of behavioral theory. A is the antecedent, B the behavior, and C the consequence of the behavior. Most approaches to behavior management concern themselves with these three aspects of student behavior. Antecedents and consequences are part of the context of student behavior. They can be manipulated or modified to cause a change in behavior.

Collaborative teams will need to examine the antecedent (A), the behavior (B), and the consequence (C) in problem situations and work together to define and measure behavior. Consultation should include responsive listening, assertion, and problem solving, in addressing each aspect of behavior management. Consultants and consultees, must mutually define behavior(s), and carry out analysis and modification of context together. In addition, evaluation of the procedures that are utilized must be conducted collaboratively. In these ways collaborators can plan effective means of altering the antecedents and/or the consequences of the behavior in the student's environment.

## Defining Behaviors

Student behavior problems must be defined carefully, in order to plan an effective behavior management program. This means the targeted behaviors must be observable, thus measurable. Clarification of the problem behavior facilitates communication among educators and allows ongoing evaluation in order to monitor progress of the student toward specific goals.

In pinpointing the behaviors to be changed or specific goals for student behavior, programs should target behaviors that, when changed, will benefit the student. This might appear to be a simplistic recommendation for an obvious condition. However, programs for initiating behavior change are often designed simply to reduce student behaviors that disrupt the smooth functioning of the school setting, rather than to improve the individual student's situation (Winett and Winkler, 1972). Appropriate goal selection involves careful examination of the purposes of a behavior change plan and must be congruent with the student's individual education plan (IEP) and individual rights.

**Application for Defining Behavior**

Consider the types of behaviors that are common complaints of teachers and parents. They might be problems such as "lazy," "unmotivated," "has a bad attitude," or "disruptive." Each of these problems needs to be defined more explicitly, so that it can be observed and measured. Think again about each of the behaviors you considered and define them in specific, measurable terms. This may not be easy. Many educators tend to think of behavior in broad, general terms. Figure 9-4 lists samples of nonspecific and specific behaviors that often concern teachers and parents.

To test your thought-problem definition, give it the IBSO test (Morris, 1985): "*Is the Behavior Specific and Objective?*" To answer yes, you would need to respond affirmatively to these two questions:

1. Can you count the number of times the behavior occurs in a particular period, such as fifteen minutes, one hour, or one day? Or can you count the number of minutes it takes for the student to perform the behavior?
2. Would another person know exactly what to look for when you name the target behavior you are planning to change?

Examine the behaviors and decide if attempts to change them would infringe on a student's rights. Is the behavior detrimental to the student? Could you name a behavior that might be increased for each behavior that you listed as needing to be decreased?

| Non-Specific | Specific |
|---|---|
| pays attention | faces the speaker, keeps eyes on speaker or materials speaker is using |
| has poor self-esteem | utters negative comments about self, destroys own work on completion |
| acts out | hits peers, curses, throws objects, kicks peers or objects |
| shows initiative | asks questions, volunteers for additional work |
| understands rules | says and demonstrates class rules |
| knows colors | points to colors when asked to |
| is shy | responds to questions, starts conversation, joins group |

**FIGURE 9–4 Non-Specific and Specific Behavior**

## *Measuring Behaviors*

Measurement of behavior provides a yardstick for assessing the success of the behavior management program. Behavior change data can be used to demonstrate success in the consultation relationship, too.

A chart or graph is an effective way to communicate about behavior with parents, teacher, and students themselves. Figure 9-5 is one example of a chart to record observations concerning student tardiness to class. Chapter 8 describes several behavioral observation methods appropriate for gathering information about specific problem behaviors, and Chapter 7 has information for making observations.

When measuring a specific behavior or several behaviors is particularly difficult, the consultant will want to spend several sessions observing the student. It is often helpful to keep an ongoing narrative about the problem, including the situation in which the behavior occurs and attitudes of teachers and other students toward that behavior. From this narrative, specific target behaviors can be identified.

A graph should be developed on which the collected data are charted. The ordinate, or vertical axis of the graph, is marked into numbers that represent the quantity or level of the behavior. Examples are: minutes late to class, percent of intervals on task, or number of temper tantrums. The abscissa, or horizontal axis, represents time and can be marked into sessions,

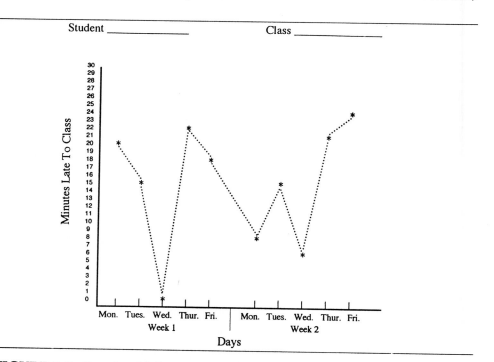

FIGURE 9-5 Graph of Minutes Late to Class

**Application for Measuring Behavior**

Choose one of the behaviors you considered previously in the application for defining behavior section. Look it over to be sure it passes the IBSO test. Then decide which behavioral observation method you could use to collect data on that behavior. (Refer to Chapter 8 for discussion of frequency recording, interval recording, time sampling, and duration recording.) Design a data collection sheet and create some mock data. Then draw a graph that labels the ordinate and the abscissa, and chart your data.

classes, hours, or days. The more specific the labeling of the axes, the more useful the graph will be as a communication tool.

Data should be collected for several days or sessions, until the chart shows a stable representation of the behavior. Observing a student for several days also allows the student to become accustomed to having the outside observer in the classroom. This helps ensure the behavior is a true representation of the student's usual behavior. Data collected before implementation of an intervention will form the baseline, or picture of the behavior. Additional data collected after intervention of the behavior management plan will be compared to the baseline data, in order to determine results of the intervention. Baseline data typically are collected for several days or across several sessions (refer again to Figure 9-5).

After a consultant has collected information about the target behavior during several sessions, it is time to implement the behavior change procedures that have been developed collaboratively by the team. During implementation it is important to continue observing the behavior and graphing the data.

## Manipulating Antecedents to Manage Behavior

An antecedent (A) is a cue or a stimulus that a student responds to, such as the presence of the principal in the hall, or instruction from the teacher, or teasing by another student. Each of these stimuli prompts student behavior. For example, seeing the principal in the hall may prompt the student to walk instead of run. An instruction from the teacher may prompt the student to follow the instruction. Teasing might prompt the student to hit the teaser or start an argument. When there is a high probability that a student behavior will occur in the presence of a particular antecedent or stimulus, we can say that there is stimulus control (Rusch, Rose, and Greenwood, 1988). Special educators use stimulus control to teach new behaviors and manage inappropriate behaviors. That is, they manipulate the antecedent stimuli in the student's environment so that appropriate behaviors will occur.

Any environmental stimulus may be an antecedent for a particular behavior. Physical arrangements, location of others in the environment, and behavior of others in that setting are the primary types of antecedents (Rusch Rose, and Greenwood, 1988). Therefore, teachers can set up or change physical arrangements, the location of others, and behavior of others to promote appropriate student behavior. Examples of changes made by teachers are: pointing, moving the desks of students, moving near a specific student, and providing rules, clues, hints, and reminders.

When arranging antecedents to prompt specific behaviors, it is important that the stimuli are clear and distinctive. Instructions and rules should be concise and appropriate to the age or developmental level of the students. If students respond unacceptably to stimuli that are inappropriate, such as teasing, or if students do not respond to cues for appropriate behavior such as instructions from the teacher, then they must be taught to respond to new or different antecedents. Learning to respond to specific antecedents requires that students learn to respond to certain stimuli and ignore others. Antecedent stimuli are important components in behavior management programs because the behaviors they precede will be followed by consequences that reinforce.

## Using Consequences to Manage Behavior

Explanation, modeling, practice, and reinforcement are all important for managing behavior. Of all these, reinforcement is the key. Reinforcement is a type of consequence. A consequence (C) is a stimulus event that follows a behavior. Consequences control either an increase or a decrease in student behavior.

*Punishment* Consequences that decrease undesirable behavior are punishers. Punishers may be something presented (presentation punishment)—for example, sitting on a bench during playtime, or writing a sentence ten times. Or punishers may be something withdrawn or removed (removal punishment)—for example, being grounded or having no snack. Whether the punisher presents something or removes something as a consequence, it is intended to *decrease undesirable behavior.*

*Reinforcement* Consequences that *increase* behaviors are reinforcers. Positive reinforcers provide pleasant stimuli, such as smiles, stickers, and money. For example, a student might receive a coin for a fast–food hamburger when he avoids a fight, or a parent might praise the child for a good report card.

Negative reinforcers remove an unpleasant stimulus. For example, a student might be excused from writing spelling words five times if she spells 90 percent of them correctly on the pretest, or a parent might excuse a child from doing dishes, for eating his vegetables. In order for negative reinforcement to be effective, the behavior that is reinforced must precede the reinforcement. Promises by the child to complete the behavior after enjoying the reinforcement are not acceptable.

Reinforcers can be the presentation of positive events for the student, or removal of unwanted events, but they are used to *increase desirable behavior*. In contrast to reinforcers, punishers are used to present or remove events, in order to *decrease undesirable behavior*. Examples of these four kinds of consequences—presentation punishment, removal punishment, positive reinforcement, and negative reinforcement—are provided in Figure 9–6.

*Determining Appropriate Consequences* Something that is reinforcing or punishing for one student is not necessarily reinforcing or punishing for another. Competency in determining appropriate consequences for students is one of the most important skills a teacher, parent, or consultant develops. If a student does not want to have recess and prefers to remain in the room with the teacher, having that student stay in the room would not be a punishment. If the student has a fear of success, profuse praise and tangible rewards may not be reinforcing. Children with special needs may react differently to some reinforcers and punishers than other children do. So educators must observe carefully children's reactions and know their preferences well, in order to select effective consequences.

(These are *examples* of reinforcers and punishers, *not recommendations* for use in any given situation.)

| *Positive Reinforcers* | *Negative Reinforcers* |
|---|---|
| Free time | No homework over weekend |
| Class party | No final exam required |
| Smile after hearing hello | Excused from chores |
| Watching a movie or t.v. | Removal of seating chart |
| Happy face marks, stickers | Can skip hard practice |
| Public recognition for work | A day off |
| More minutes on break | Probation |
| Attention, laughter | Buy one, no pay for second |

| *Presentation Punishers* | *Removal Punishers* |
|---|---|
| Go to principal's office | No free time |
| Stand by fence on playground | No recess |
| Write words 5 times | Not eligible for sports |
| Extra assignment | No talking to classmates |
| Scolding | No dessert |
| Sit on a chair, go to time-out | No snacks |
| Run laps | Kicked off team |
| Demerits | Cannot participate |

**FIGURE 9-6 Four Kinds of Consequences**

Natural contingencies such as a smile or peer approval are generally better than artificial consequences such as stickers and money. There is a higher probability that new behaviors will be generalized to other settings and to situations where teachers are not present. Ferster, Culbertson, and Boren (1975) caution that artificial consequences are sometimes used for the benefit of the instructor rather than the student. If teachers and parents provide artificial reinforcers such as stickers and edibles, they should pair them with natural reinforcers such as a smile and a compliment. Then the artificial reinforcers can be gradually reduced. (See Figure 9–7 for a list of possible reinforcers.)

Hall and Hall (1980) suggest a nine-step sequence for selecting potential reinforcers:

**1.** Consider the age, interests, and appetites of the person whose behaviors you wish to strengthen.

**2.** Consider the behavior you wish to strengthen through reinforcement.

**3.** List potential reinforcers, considering what you know about the person—age, interests, likes and dislikes, and the specific behavior you have defined.

**4.** Use preferred activities as reinforcers (Premack, 1959). However, the behavior must be performed before the reinforcer is given. Behaviors that occur frequently can be used as reinforcement for low probability behaviors.

| *Tangibles* | *Activities* |
|---|---|
| Stickers and decals | Helping in the cafeteria |
| Small school supplies | Stapling papers |
| Novelty buttons | Carrying messages to other rooms |
| Posters | Taking the class roll |
| Certificates of merit | Operating the film projector |
| Playing cards (1 at a time) | Sharpening pencils |
| Free-time certificate | Decorating a bulletin board |
| Magnets, rocks, shells | Assisting the custodian |
| Art supplies | Distributing materials |
| Balloons, whistles, tops, | Listening to music with earphones |
| unusual pencils | Recording behavior on a graph |
| A seat of honor | Going to the library |
| Food items | Giving an intercom message |
| Positive notes home | |

*Social*

That's great! I agree. This shows a lot of work. Best job I've seen today. Fine effort. Please show this good work to. . . . You're becoming expert at this! Good job.

**FIGURE 9-7 Examples of Reinforcers for Students with Special Needs**

For example, a child might be allowed to watch TV after working quietly for twenty minutes.

**5.** Try asking the student what he or she would like.

**6.** Make appropriate use of novel reinforcers.

**7.** Give preference to reinforcers that are natural.

**8.** Select the reinforcer(s) you will use.

**9.** Make a record of the behavior before and after reinforcement, to test the effectiveness of the reinforcer.

---

**Application for Determining Appropriate Consequences**

Imagine that you are consulting with a teacher or parent of the following students who have special needs. Identify the behavior to be changed and define it in measurable terms. Then list possible reinforcing and punishing consequences for each of these students.

1. Abby is a three-year-old child in a preschool program. She has very limited mobility in her limbs. When the teacher attempts to work with her on the exercises prescribed by the physical therapist, Abby screams and gets rigid. She loves music and watching the fish and gerbils in the classroom, and she loves to eat, but she is diabetic.

2. Jaimal has a math disability and is in the fourth grade. He is reading at the fifth-grade level and loves to read and draw pictures, often covering his number problem worksheets with drawings. He is a gregarious child and very popular with the students in his mainstreamed class. He has trouble sitting still and listening to the teacher. He would rather talk to his friends.

3. Alex is twelve years old and has several severe behavior problems. He is mainstreamed in physical education and language arts. In physical education he is usually chosen last for teams, primarily because he is very rude and unsportsmanlike. The teacher is concerned about his verbal aggressivenessduring gym class, in particular. Alex does not like much about school. However, he seems to like the gym teachers, individual sports, and fancy cars.

4. Juanita is twenty years old and in a group home with other developmentally delayed women. She works in a sheltered workshop and is very happy with her job and her roommates. Sometimes she wanders off from the group home or argues very loudly with supervisors on the job. She has poor social skills but enjoys doing things with people, such as making pizza with others in the group home.

When consulting with parents and other educators, a consultant should treat management of behavior as a collaborative effort. The more information that can be pooled about the student's behavior and environment, and the more appropriate the selection and arrangement of antecedents and consequences to improve the behavior, the more effective the behavior management program will be.

As stated earlier, reinforcers should be appropriate to age, developmental level, and gender. No matter how attractive a reinforcer is to a student, it will not be useful unless the student is developmentally, emotionally, and physically ready to perform a particular target behavior (Morris, 1985). Careful selection of a reinforcer is crucial to the success of a program to manage behavior. Chapter 10 provides examples of strategies that use specific individual and group reinforcement and punishment techniques for managing behavior.

Consequences must be contingent; that is, they must immediately follow the behavior. Consequences should be used frequently, especially at the beginning of a behavior change program, and they must be used consistently. When selecting punishers to decrease a behavior, include reinforcers to strengthen appropriate, acceptable behavior.

## Tips for Consulting and Collaborating

1. Team teach with a classroom teacher on a given topic, work with one child or a small group on a certain topic in the classroom, and arrange tutors or mentors for students with special needs.

2. Read about or observe in schools where models such as ALEM, CWC, and SFA have been implemented, and prepare a one-page fact sheet to share with interested staff.

3. Collaborate with teachers to provide support instruction in study skills and learning strategies that complements the content material being taught in the classroom.

4. Complete a college or university course on behavior management.

5. Tailor behavior modification techniques to the specific interests, needs, and situations of each individual student.

6. Monitor closely the effects on behavior that reinforcers and punishers produce. If desirable behavior does not increase, the reinforcer may be having the effect of a punisher. If undesirable behavior is not reduced, the punisher may be serving as a reinforcer.

## Chapter Review

1. The school reform research of the 1980's identified characteristics of effective schools and teachers. This knowledge base provides helpful background information for consultants to use when working with school staff.

2. A number of innovative delivery systems and models have been researched and developed during recent decades of school reform and restructuring. Several are particularly promising in serving the special needs of students who have learning and behavior problems.

Preassessment and team teaching incorporate team effort to help prevent school failure and minimize the need for diagnostic testing and possible placement in special education.

The Adaptive Learning Environments Model (ALEM) is one of the earliest attempts to integrate research about effective schools and teachers into school reorganization. The goal of ALEM is to eliminate the need for pull-out programs by providing classroom alternatives that will address the learning needs of all students. Extensive collaboration between parents, teachers, administrators, and other professionals is critical for the success of ALEM.

Class-Within-a-Class (CWC) is an innovative delivery model that strives to reduce pull-out programs by serving learning-disabled students full-time in general classes. Special education teachers go into the classrooms during instruction to collaborate and consult with the teacher and provide additional support to learning-disabled students in the class.

Success-For-All (SFA) is a comprehensive program aimed at preschool and primary levels. Its main purpose is to prevent failure by assuring reading success during the early school years. Individual tutoring, cross-age grouping, and extensive collaboration are important features of this program.

The Mainstream Training Project (MTP) uses in-service training for preparing secondary-level classroom teachers to serve students who have learning difficulties. When classroom teachers have been trained in using effective teaching methods for students with learning and behavior problems, special education consultants work closely with them to monitor student progress and assist in implementation of newly learned teaching techniques.

Gifted and talented students can have more challenging learning experiences in the classroom when their teachers are supported by consultation services within programs such as the Schoolwide Enrichment Model, Talents Unlimited, and the Integrative Model. Classroom teachers and gifted program consultants should collaborate in providing gifted and talented students with curriculum options and alternatives such as flexible pacing, enrichment, personalized instruction, and challenging group experiences.

3. Research has shown that effective teachers engage in a number of common practices that are critical for the success of low-achieving students in learning. Consultants need to be aware of these practices so they can help teachers incorporate them into their classroom activities. Effective practices include the way the teacher structures the lesson and the way the teacher presents the lesson.

4. Behavior problems have a variety of causes and exist in many forms, with varying degrees of severity and complexity. The consultant or another team member should be skilled and knowledgeable in the use of behavioral methods.

The targeted behavior should be important for the learning and behavior of the student, not primarily for the convenience of the teacher. The behavior should be defined so precisely that it can be measured by different observers with relatively the same outcome, and the student must be capable of performing the desired behavior.

**5.** It is difficult to determine appropriate reinforcers and punishers for some students. Teachers should collaborate with special education consultants and parents to ascertain the kinds of reinforcers and, if necessary, punishers for use as antecedents or consequences to enable students with special needs to be successful in school.

# Activities

**1.** Select an experimental program reviewed in this chapter that would serve the needs of the school where you teach or would like to teach. Modify the model in a way that would make it more appropriate for that setting.

**2.** Secure the ERIC documents summarized in this chapter. Plan how these documents could be used as a part of your consultation efforts.

**3.** Develop a two-column list of activities most students experience daily. Put on the left side those that:

- control students and require them to conform (line up, fold papers with names on outside, have only four people at the learning center. . . ).

Then put on the right side those that:

- allow students freedom and choice, encouraging creativity and individualism (have free time during the last ten minutes of class, decide whether or not you need to do a particular worksheet, get a drink without permission. . . ).

**4.** Think of ways the choice and self-management (right hand) side of your list in Activity 3 could be extended, while maintaining the learning and behavior goals that school and home contexts require. Also scan the conformity (left-hand) side to see if any of those requirements could or should be eliminated for the best interests of students.

# For Further Reading

Alberto, P. A., and Troutman, A. C. (1990). *Applied Behavior Analysis for Teachers: Influencing Student Performance*. Columbus, OH: Merrill.

Chalfant, J. C., Pysh, M. V. D., and Moultrie, R. (1979). Teacher assistance teams: A model for within–building problem solving. *Learning Disability Quarterly*, 2; 85–96.

Graden, J. L., Casey, A., and Christenson, S. L. (1985). Implementing a prereferral intervention system: Part I. The Model. *Exceptional Children*, 51; 377–84. This article and the one by Chalfant et al., above, provide clear explanations of the way preassessment (teacher assistance teams) can be organized and managed.

Lovitt, T. (1984). *Tactics for Teachers*. Columbus, OH: Merrill.

Madden, N. A., Slavin, R. E., Karweit, N. L., and Livermon, B. J. (1989). Restructuring the urban elementary school. *Educational Leadership, 46*(5); 14–18. This reference provides additional details about the Success–For–All program.

Morris, R. J. (1985). *Behavior Modification With Exceptional Children: Principles and Practices*. Glenview, IL: Scott, Foresman.

Morsink, C., Soar, S., Soar, R., and Thomas, R. (1986). Research on teaching: Opening the door to special education classrooms. *Exceptional Children, 53*(1);32–40. This article is helpful to consultants who want to read more about research on effective schools and effective teachers.

Renzulli, J. S. (ed.). (1986). *Systems and Models for Developing Programs for the Gifted and Talented*. Mansfield, CT: Creative Learning Press. This book provides comprehensive descriptions of fifteen widely used curricular systems and models for developing the potential of very able students.

Reynaud, G., Pfannenstiel, T., and Hudson, F. (1987). *Park Hill Secondary Learning Disability Project: An Alternative Service Delivery Model Implementation Manual*. Kansas City, MO: Park Hill School District. This manual provides extensive information about setting up Class–Within–a–Class.

Rusch, F. R., Rose, T., and Greenwood, C. R. (1988). *Introduction to Behavior Analysis in Special Education*. Englewood Cliffs, NJ: Prentice Hall.

Tindal, G., Shinn, M., Waltz, L., and Germann, G. (1987). Mainstream consultation in secondary settings: The Pine County model. *Journal of Special Education, 21*(3): 94–106. The Mainstream Training Project is described in this reference.

Wiedmeyer, D., and Lehman, J. (1991). The "House Plan" approach to collaborative teaching and consultation. *Teaching Exceptional Children, 23*(3): 6–10. Discusses partnerships between learning disabilities personnel and general classroom teachers, based on collaborative teaching and consultation. Has examples of specific activities and sample lessons, as well as evaluation strategies.

# References

Alberto, P. A., and Troutman, A. C. (1990). Applied behavior analysis (3rd ed.). Columbus, OH: Merrill.

Armstrong, D. G. (Winter, 1977). Team teaching achievement. *Review of Educational Research*, pp. 65–86.

Beckhoff, A. G., and Bender, W. N. (1989). Programming for mainstream kindergarten success in preschool: Teachers' perceptions of necessary prerequisite skills. *Journal of Early Intervention, 13*(3), 269–280.

Betts, G. T. (1986). The autonomous learner model for the gifted and talented. In J. S. Renzulli (ed.), *Systems and Models for Developing Programs for the Gifted and Talented*, pp. 27–56. Mansfield Center, CT: Creative Learning Press.

Bickel, W., and Bickel, D. (1986). Effective schools, classrooms and instruction: Implications for special education. *Exceptional Children, 20*(6):489–519.

Cancelli, A. A., and Lange, S. M. (1990). Considerations for future research in the institutionalization of school–based consultation. *Journal of Educational and Psychological Consultation, 1*(1):87–98.

Chalfant, J. C., Pysh, M. V. D., and Moultrie, R. (1979). Teacher assistance teams: A model for within–building problem solving. *Learning Disability Quarterly, 2*:85–96.

Clark, B. (1992). *Growing Up Gifted*. Columbus, OH: Merrill.

Cooley, S., McVey, D., and Barrett–Jones, K. (1988). Evaluation of identification and pre-assessment processes in Kansas. *ERIC Document Reproducation Service* no. ED 303928.

Deshler, C., and Schumaker, J. (1986). Learning strategies: An instructional alternative for low–achieving adolescents. *Exceptional Children, 52*(6):583–90.

*tion skills*. ERIC Digest #449. Reston, VA: Council for Exceptional Children.

ERIC Clearinghouse on Handicapped and Gifted Children. (1987b). *Lesson structure*. ERIC Digest #448. Reston, VA: Council for Exceptional Children.

Feldhusen, J. F., and Kolloff, P. B. (1986). The Purdue Three–stage Enrichment Model for gifted education at the elementary level. In J. S. Renzulli (ed.), *Systems and Models for Developing Programs for the Gifted and Talented*, pp. 126–52. Mansfield Center, CT: Creative Learning Press.

Feldhusen, J. F., and Robinson, A. (1986). The Purdue Secondary Model for Gifted and Talented Youth. in J. S. Renzulli (ed.), *Systems and Models for Developing Programs for the Gifted and Talented* pp. 153–79. Mansfield Center, CT: Creative Learning Press.

Ferster, C.B., Culbertson, S., and Boren, M.C. (1975). *Behavior Principles* (3rd. ed.). Englewood Cliff, N.J.: Prentice Hall.

Fuchs, D., and Fuchs, L. S. (1988). Evaluation of the Adaptive Learning Environments Model. *Exceptional Children*, 55: 115–27.

Goodlad, J. (1990). Better teachers for our nation's schools. *Phi Delta Kappan*, 72(3):185–94.

Graden, J. L., Casey, A., and Christenson, S. L. (1985). Implementing a prereferral intervention system: Part I. The Model. *Exceptional Children*, 51:377–84.

Hall, R.V., and Hall, M.C. (1980). *How to Use Systematic Attention and Approval (Social Reinforcement)*. Lawrence, KS: H and H Enterprises.

Heidbrink, C. (1990). *Team Teaching and Academic Achievement*. Unpublished manuscript, Kansas State University, College of Education, Manhattan, KS.

Hudson, F. (1992). *Teaming Through a Class-Within-a-Class Model*. Paper presented at Learning Disabilities Association international conference, Atlanta, GA.

Lovitt, T. (1984). Tactics for Teachers. Columbus, OH: Merrill.

Madden, N. A., Slavin, R. E., Karweit, N. L., and Livermon, B. J. (1989). Restructuring the urban elementary school. *Educational Leadership*, 46(5):14–18.

Martin G. and Pear, J. (1988). *Behavior Modification: What it is and How to Do It* (3rd ed.). Englewood Cliffs, N.J.: Prentice Hall.

Morris, R.J. (1985). *Behavior Modification with Exceptional Children: Principles and Practices*. Glenview, IL.: Scott Foresman.

Morsink, C., Soar, S., Soar, R., and Thomas, R. (1986). Research on teaching: Opening the door to special education classrooms. *Exceptional Children*, 53(1):32–40.

Premack, D. (1959). Toward empirical behavior laws: I. Positive reinforcement. *Psychological Review*, 66:219–233.

Pugach, M. C., and Johnson, L. J. (1989). Prereferral interventions: Progress, problems, and challenges. *Exceptional Children*, 56:117–26.

Reis, S.M., and Renzulli, J. S. (1986). The secondary triad model. In J. S. Renzulli (ed.), *Systems and Models for Developing Programs for the Gifted and Talented*, pp. 267–305. Mansfield Center, CT: Creative Learning Press.

Renzulli, J.S., and Reis, S.M. (1985). *The Schoolwide Enrichment Model: A Compprehensive Plan for Educational Excellence*. Mansfield Center, CT: Creative Learning Press.

Renzulli, J. S., and Reis, S. W. (1986). The Enrichment Triad/Revolving Door Model: A schoolwide plan for the development of creative productivity. In J. S. Renzulli (ed.), *Systems and Models for Developing Programs for the Gifted and Talented* pp. 216–66. Mansfield Center, CT: Creative Learning Press.

Renzulli, J. S. (ed.). (1984). *Technical Report of Research Studies Related to the Revolving Door Identification Model*. Bureau of Educational Research, University of Connecticut.

Renzulli, J. S. (ed.). (1986). *Systems and Models for Developing Programs for the Gifted and Talented*. Mansfield Center, CT: Creative Learning Press.

Reynaud, G., Pfannenstiel, T., and Hudson, F. (1987). *Park Hill Secondary Learning Disability Project: An Alternative Service Delivery Model Implementation Manual*. Kansas City, MO: Park Hill School District.

Rusch, F.R., Rose, T., and Greenwood, C.R. (1988). *Introduction to Behavior Analysis in Special Education*. Englewood Cliffs, N.J.: Prentice Hall.

Schlichter, C. (1986). Talents unlimited: Applying the multiple talent approach in mainstream and gifted programs. In J. S. Renzulli (ed.), *Systems and Models for Devel-*

*oping Programs for the Gifted and Talented*, pp. 352–90. Mansfield Center, CT: Creative Learning Press.

Semmel, M. I., and Gerber, M. M. (1990). If at first you don't succeed, bye, bye again: A response to general educators' views on the REI. *Remedial and Special Education*, 11(4):53–59.

Slavin, R.E., and Madden, N.A. (1989). What works for students at risk: A research synthesis. *Educational Leadership*, 47(4):52–54.

Thurston, L.P., and Kimsey, I. (1989). Rural special education teachers as consultants: Roles and responsibilities. *Educational Considerations*, 17(1):40–43.

Tindal, G., Shinn, M., Waltz, L., and Germann, G. (1987). Mainstream consultation in secondary settings: The Pine County model. *Journal of Special Education*, 21(3): 94–106.

Treffinger, D. J. (1986). Fostering effective, independent learning through individualized programming. In J. S. Renzulli (ed.), *Systems and Models for Developing Programs for the Gifted and Talented*, pp. 429–60.

Mansfield Center, CT: Creative Learning Press.

Trump, J. L. (April, 1960). Six suggestions for a better high school program. *Journal of the National Education Association*, pp. 41–43.

Waltz, L. (1990). Mainstream consultation and training. *The Consulting Edge*, 2(1):5–6.

Wang, M. C. (March, 1986). The Adaptive Learning Environments Model: Design and Effects. Paper presented at Association for Children with Learning Disabilities Conference, New York, NY.

Wang, M. C., and Birch, J. W. (1984). Effective special education in regular classes. *Exceptional Children*, 50 (4), 391–98.

Wang, M. C., and Walberg, H. J. (1988). Four fallacies of segregationism. *Exceptional Children*, 55:128–37.

Wiedmeyer, D., and Lehman, J. (1991). The "House Plan" approach to collaborative teaching and consultation. *Teaching Exceptional Children*, 23(3); 6–10.

Winett, R.A., and Winkler, R.C. (1972). Current behavior modification in the classroom: Be still, be quiet, be docile. *Journal of Applied Behvior Analysis*, 5:499–504.

# 10

# CONSULTATION, COLLABORATION, AND TEAMWORK FOR EFFECTIVE LEARNING

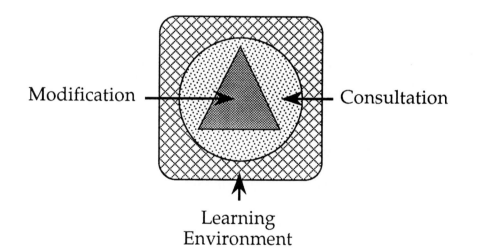

Modification — Consultation

Learning
Environment

## To Think About

One of the most common concerns to emerge during school consultation centers around the need for interventions to help students with learning and behavioral disorders succeed in school. Consulting teachers must not only be skilled in the processes of consulting, but comfortable with helping teachers generate and carry out appropriate interventions. After collaborative relationships have been developed, substantive content knowledge will enable consultants to facilitate successful problem-solving strategies. Without these strategies on which to build intervention plans, consultation and collaboration would result in nothing but talk. The interaction would facilitate process, but would be somewhat empty. As one national news magazine writer described consultations that are long on process but short in content, "The emperor has no clothes" (Britt, 1985, p. 30).

Many new ideas and innovations for use in the general classroom setting have been developed as part of the school reform movement. Guskey (1990) identifies seven major innovations:

> cooperative learning,
> the effective schools model,
> critical thinking,
> mastery learning and outcomes-based education (OBE),
> mastery teaching,
> Teacher Expectations and Student Achievement (TESA), and
> learning styles.

Most of these innovations, or variations of them, are discussed in this chapter. The focus is on educational content that can contribute practical substance to the consultation experience. These strategies and techniques can be discussed during consultation coursework, interviews, and practicum experiences as tools for helping students with special needs.

## Focusing Questions

1. What teaching methods increase opportunities for all students to learn in a mainstreamed, heterogeneous classroom?

2. What kinds of classroom arrangements encourage students to help one another learn?

3. What techniques can students use that allow them to monitor and direct their own learning?

4. What individual and group strategies are effective for managing student behavior?

5. How can the classroom setting be arranged and the learning tasks modified, so students with special learning needs have a better chance to succeed in learning tasks?

6. What factors need to be considered when consulting and collaborating with classroom teachers to plan interventions for those with special needs?

## Key Terms

Classroom Modification
Classwide Peer Tutoring
Cooperative Learning
Cross-Age Peer Tutoring
Curriculum Compacting
Enrichment
Flexible Pacing
Grading Policies
Improvement Points
Learning Strategies

Learning Styles
Mastery Learning
Modified Testing
Peer-Assisted Strategies
Readability
Same-Age Peer Tutoring
Test-Taking Skills
Textbook Adaptation
Tutee
Tutor

---

**Scenario**

The setting is an elementary school, where a learning disabilities resource teacher is consulting with a fourth-grade teacher.

*LD RESOURCE TEACHER*: I'm concerned about Jason when he's in the classroom. I've worked with his reading skills, but he is still far from being able to do fourth-grade work.

*CLASSROOM TEACHER*: I'm concerned about him, too. He's failing science and social studies in the classroom.

*LD RESOURCE TEACHER*: He has a wonderful background in science and social studies. I really think his problem is that he can't read and write the material used in the classroom.

*CLASSROOM TEACHER*: Would you have time to help teach him science and social studies? I hate to see him fail day after day.

*LD RESOURCE TEACHER*: Let's plan a time when we can talk about this and find ways to modify our techniques so Jason can learn more science and social studies. When would be convenient for you?

*CLASSROOM TEACHER*: How about Thursday during my break?

*LD RESOURCE TEACHER*: Good. In the meantime, it would help if you complete this observation checklist. And I'd like to come into your classroom during your social studies and science periods to make a few additional observations. It would also help for me to look at any worksheets, tests, or other products Jason has worked on in class. I'll look through my resource books for a few ideas to bring along when we meet. Will you do that, too?

*CLASSROOM TEACHER*: O.K. I hope the two of us can think of some way to help Jason.

## Effective Practices for Mainstreaming

Since the passage of Public Law 94-142 with its mandate for educating individuals with disabilities in the least restrictive setting, researchers have attempted to determine instructional approaches that would be most effective for mainstreamed students in general education classrooms. Early attempts to superimpose techniques from special education settings were not always successful, so researchers began exploring alternatives. Several of these are promising.

The most widely promoted approaches to addressing the learning needs of low-achieving students include effective teacher-directed instruction and mastery learning. These instructional approaches are used often in special education classrooms but might be less familiar to general classroom teachers. Many teachers express dismay about not having enough time to provide the necessary monitoring and corrective feedback that would help students who have special needs. One strategy that has been used successfully to provide more time and monitoring for special needs is peer assistance. Cooperative learning, class-wide peer tutoring, and cross-age/same-age peer tutoring are examples of peer assistance techniques consultants can help consultees implement in the classroom.

Teachers also face dilemmas over assigning grades to students who are struggling with learning and behavior problems. Consultants should be prepared to help teachers develop explicit plans for testing and grading students with special learning needs. Not all of the instructional interventions and techniques special education teachers use in special settings are appropriate for general classroom settings. The interventions must be feasible for each setting and for the individuals involved.

On occasion, consultants have been able to work with general classroom teachers, especially at the secondary level, to teach students learning strategies, study skills, and other behaviors needed for classroom success. Sometimes the strategies are taught to all students in the classroom. At other times they are taught to small groups of students in pull-out programs. In either case, the consultant's role becomes one of monitoring and reinforcing use of the strategies once they have been taught.

Special education teachers have training and experience in modifying tasks to match student strengths, weaknesses, and learning styles, as well as in evaluating progress and determining grades. They should draw liberally on their former experiences to make appropriate suggestions for classroom modifications. Even so, the key factor in the transfer of these ideas is the ability of the specialist to structure thinking into a collaborative consultation style.

Most of the strategies and interventions that will be discussed in this chapter could be implemented without teacher collaboration. However, there is strong evidence in research and practice that the outcomes will be more beneficial for mainstreamed students when special education teachers, support personnel, and classroom teachers collaborate to develop and implement them.

In addition to benefits for students, the outcomes generally provide reinforcement for school personnel who are deeply concerned about students with learning needs that cannot be met in the regular classroom environment without special assistance.

## Teacher-Directed Instruction and Mastery Learning

Effective teachers of low-achieving students use direct instruction methods. These strategies of effective teachers were addressed in Chapter 9. Mastery learning and outcomes-based education also have been identified as important elements of instructional programs to foster achievement of low-achieving and at-risk students (Bloom, 1984; Guskey, 1988; Reisberg and Wolf, 1988; Slavin and Madden, 1989; Wang; 1987). The terms refer to the process of setting explicit learning objectives for students and measuring progress toward attainment of the objectives by using frequent curriculum-based measurement. Students who have not achieved mastery of an objective are provided with reteaching and additional practice until mastery is met. This process is not new to special educators, who are required by law to use it in developing individualized education programs. However, the procedures are now being advocated for use in general classrooms (Guskey, 1990).

Most special education consultants will have no difficulty working with classroom teachers in the use of mastery learning techniques. When consultants are able to provide general education teachers with a set of procedures for mastery learning that is easily implemented using their existing curricula, teachers are more likely to overcome many of the negative attitudes toward low-achieving students (Reisberg and Wolf, 1988). (See Chapter 8 for further discussion of mastery learning techniques using curriculum-based assessment and Chapter 9 for material on effective teaching.)

## Peer-assisted Strategies

Classroom teachers who have mainstreamed students with disabilities often feel the most limiting aspect of their charge is not having enough time to give students the individual attention they need. The research about effective teaching identifies "academic engaged time" as highly related to achievement (Rosenshine and Berliner, 1978). Jenkins and Jenkins (1985) state it this way, "If teachers desire to increase academic engaged time through one-to-one instruction, they must expand their reserve of instructional personnel. They need not look far. Some of the best helpers are other students who can be recruited from inside their own school" (Jenkins and Jenkins, 1985, p. 2).

Researchers have studied several ways of using peers to help one another learn. When one or a combination of these peer-assisted approaches is used, the teacher or consultant manages and monitors the performance of peers as they engage in learning together. Cooperative learning and peer tutoring are two of the most common ways of using peers to help one another learn.

## Cooperative Learning

Cooperative learning methods are gaining widespread attention for use in many classrooms. When used appropriately, the methods result in improved student achievement and improved social relationships at the same time (Johnson and Johnson, 1987; Lloyd et al., 1988; Madden and Slavin, 1983). The term *cooperative learning* has become associated with a variety of structured approaches that arrange classrooms so students study in heterogeneous groups to meet academic goals (Johnson and Johnson, 1987; Slavin, 1986). In most of the models, all students in the classroom are assigned to heterogeneous groups and, under the guidance of the teacher, help one another master content previously presented by the teacher. Students are held individually accountable for the content, with individual performance scores pooled to determine group rewards. Thus, all students are rewarded for helping, sharing, and working together. School personnel should have sufficient information about cooperative learning in order to consult or collaborate in making modifications and adaptations with this strategy.

There are many ways to structure a cooperative learning lesson. Student Teams Achievement Divisions (Slavin, 1986) is one example of an effective way to set up cooperative learning. In Student Teams Achievement Division (STAD):

1.   Students are assigned to heterogeneous teams of four or five. The teacher makes sure each team has a proportional amount of diversity based on sex, ethnicity, personality, and ability—one high achiever, one low achiever, and two or three average achievers on each team. (Note Figure 10–1 which shows the desired diversity of team assignments.)

2.   Each time team membership changes (approximately every six to nine weeks), time and guidance are provided for a structured activity that allows team members to  become familiar with each other on a personal level. Each team selects a name that provides group identity in subsequent activities.

3.   Each cooperative learning lesson begins with teacher-directed instruction of important material (five minutes to two class periods, depending on the complexity of the material to be learned).

4.   Students work together in their teams to practice the skills, review the content, or expand its application. Worksheets usually are provided in order to structure the team study. One worksheet per two or three students is provided, to encourage cooperative study. Completing worksheets takes from fifteen minutes to two class periods, depending on the difficulty of the material being studied.

5.   Class rules for cooperative behavior are posted in the room. (An example appears in Figure 10–2.) Bonus points are awarded to teams, to reinforce students for following rules and using cooperative behaviors.

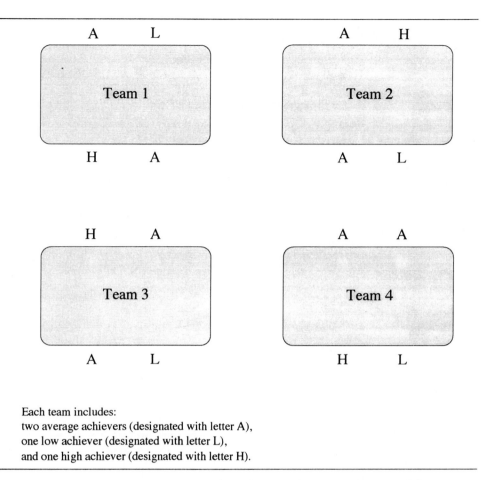

Each team includes:
two average achievers (designated with letter A),
one low achiever (designated with letter L),
and one high achiever (designated with letter H).

**FIGURE 10-1  Table Arrangements for Heterogeneous Groupings Of Students In Cooperative Learning Activities**

**6.** Each *individual* takes a quiz on the material. Individual quiz scores are compared to individual "base" scores, in order to determine improvement points, which then are pooled to formulate team scores. To use the improvement point system, the following steps are taken by the teacher:

6.1 Determine a base score for each student by computing an average percentage from previous work in the subject area.

6.2 Compare the actual quiz score to the base score. If the student exceeds the base score by 10 or more points, he or she contributes 30 *improvement points* to the team. If the score is at the base score or exceeds it by fewer than 10 points, the student contributes 20

*Speak to Each Other*

1. Speak softly.
2. Take turns talking.
3. Limit talking to the subject of study.
4. Look at the person speaking—be a good listener.
5. Ask teammates for help before asking the teacher.
6. Disagree agreeably.

*Help Each Other*

7. Tell your teammates how to find answers when they nee dhelp, instead of telling anwers.
8. Encourage everyone on the team to do his or her best work.
9. Make sure everyone on your team knows the material before you stop working together.
10. Don't get yourself or another person off task—pay attention to the assigned work.

**FIGURE 10-2   Class Rules For Cooperative Learning**

improvement points to the team. If the quiz score is no more than 10 points below the base score, he or she contributes 10 points to the team score. A perfect paper, regardless of the base score, contributes 30 improvement points to the team score.

7. Improvement point scores for each team are averaged and recorded (often on a chart in the classroom for recognition). Teams with an average of 15 points are recognized as Good Teams; those with an average of 20 points are Great Teams; and teams with averages of 25 points are Super Teams.

8. Quizzes are returned to individual students so each one is aware of his or her performance. Individual quiz scores can be used for grades. Slavin (1986) does not recommend using team scores for determining individual grades; however, they can be used for a portion of the grade to represent class participation.

There are many variations to this model of cooperative learning. Sometimes the students play a game with members from other teams to earn points for their teams. At other times the teacher assigns topics or jobs to individual team members. When students with special needs are involved, other modifications might be necessary. If a modification is made, teachers or consultants should make sure that these two elements are present (Slavin, 1990):

*Group goals or positive interdependence.*
The members within a group must work together in order to earn recognition, grades, rewards, and other indicators of group success.

*Individual accountability.*

All individuals within the group must demonstrate their learning in order for the group to experience success. This accountability could involve individual test scores that are averaged for group recognition or a report in which each person contributes a specific portion. It should not be a single product without differentiated tasks.

## Teaching Social Skills for Cooperation

Some authors (Dishon and O'Leary, 1990; Johnson and Johnson, 1987; Kagan, 1989) recommend direct instruction in the skills needed for cooperative behavior. This instruction probably will be necessary for many special education students and should be monitored closely by the teacher or consulting teacher. Supplemental instruction by the consulting teacher may be needed for children with serious emotional or social problems.

The social skills needed for cooperative learning range from basic skills, such as maintaining eye contact, to complex communication skills. Dishon and O'Leary (1989; 1990) identified the following essential social skills for cooperative learning:

Task skills for helping the group reach its goals
(checks for understanding, contributes ideas, stays on task), and

Maintenance skills to help build group feeling
(encourages and responds to ideas, and disagrees agreeably).

Suggestions for efficient teaching of social skills for cooperative learning are summarized from tips provided by Dishon and O'Leary (1989):

1. Discuss, describe, brainstorm one skill at a time.
2. Have students identify words and behaviors that might be seen or heard when they practice the skills. For example, prepare charts or transparencies that list what the behavior "looks like" or "sounds like."
3. Have students identify why each skill is important.
4. Observe the skills during team study and discuss them following study time.
5. Focus on the same skill until there is class mastery.
6. Focus on only three or four skills a year.
7. Before class begins, prepare observation forms with names of group members and the skill to be practiced.
8. Copy the forms onto transparencies for recording observations during team study.
9. Walk around class and record observations of social skills. Write down everything that demonstrates the skill.
10. Write only positive words or behaviors and do not identify which individuals or groups demonstrated the behaviors.

11. Give feedback to groups privately.
12. Select words or comments from anecdotal notes and add to the "looks like–sounds like" charts.
13. Post each group's observation form near their station.
14. Listen to and record for more than one group on each occasion.
15. Write a processing statement on the board or on worksheets. For example, write, "We did well on (skill) by (three behaviors)." Always include specific behaviors for students to identify in their responses.
16. Process only one skill during each lesson.
17. Process after each lesson.
18. Process for only five minutes, using a timer.

## Addressing Special Problems During Cooperative Learning

Cooperative learning methods were developed for use in general education classrooms with little consideration for the special needs of students. It is possible that special educators will need to collaborate with general classroom teachers to make adaptations for individuals with special needs. When adaptations are made, consultants should be conscious to include the essential elements of effective cooperative learning lessons cited by Slavin (1986): 1) Rewards should be provided to teams rather than individuals; 2) each individual within a team must be held accountable for learning the material; and 3) individuals should have equal opportunities for success. For example, a consultant might suggest providing different material for a student with a learning problem to study with the help of teammates. However, the student's score, or improvement points, would be included in the team average. The team could be awarded bonus points for helping the disabled student. This type of adaptation would provide the individual with a learning problem the opportunity for success while assuring individual accountability and team rewards. A similar approach could be taken for a more able student who needs to be challenged.

Classroom teachers and consultants should engage in systematic problem-solving processes to address the needs of students who are not experiencing success in cooperative learning situations. (see Chapter 5 for more information about problem-solving processes). Some examples of common problems that can occur during cooperative learning activities and possible solutions are listed in figure 10–3.

## Classwide Peer Tutoring

The Classwide Peer Tutoring approach is a highly structured variation of cooperative learning that involves principles of applied behavior analysis. This approach has been recommended for use with students having special educational needs (Delquadri et al., 1986). Instead of working in heterogeneous teams,

## Learning Problems

*Student cannot read and/or write the material.*
Have a teammate read material to the student.
Have teammates read material aloud "round robin."
Highlight main ideas and important information.

*Student is hearing impaired.*
Have team work in area of room with most sound control.
Seat student where lips of team members can be seen.
Provide extra teacher prompting during team study.

*Student is visually impaired.*
Provide more time to completed assignment.
Seat student where team discussion can be heard easily.
Reinforce efforts of team to explain information.

*Student has difficulty making oral presentations.*
Have student write and a team member read the report.
Allow student to preplan comments by assigning issue.
Have student work closely with another to offer ideas.

*Student cannot do any of the group work.*
Give different material to study and different quiz.
Form teams by achievement levels (is hard to manage).
Give direct teacher instruction to provide head start.

## Behavior Problems

*Student cannot get along with other team members.*
Give team bonus points based on team cooperativeness.
Move from team to team, reinforcing right behavior.
Ignore the behavior (as team sometimes handles it well).

*Student is ostracized by team members.*
Use improvement points to provide equal opportunity.
Select the team for that student with care.
Place a sympathetic person on that student's team.

*Student refuses to become involved in team study.*
Use bonus points often to reinforce involvement.
Make every effort to involve student in the group.
Allow student to work alone, but keep door open.

*Student is frequently absent or tardy.*
On return, have student complete assignment or quiz.
Use late score for individual grade, but not for team score.
Give creativity bonus if team copes well with absence.

*Parents of high ability students disapprove of the strategy.*
Meet with parents to explain cooperative learning.
Stress universal need to learn cooperative strategies.
Promote the concept of developing leadership skills.

**FIGURE 10–3   Common Problems And Possible Solutions During
             Cooperative Learning**

students work in pairs in the classroom to monitor and provide feedback in academic tasks such as oral reading, reading comprehension, reading workbook practice, and practice with spelling word lists, math facts, and vocabulary word definitions. The approach requires specialized training in order to be implemented effectively.

Classwide Peer Tutoring is based on the principle of "opportunity to respond." When children are provided with systematic opportunities to respond, such as spelling words aloud, reading, or naming history facts, their achievement will increase. Parents, teachers, paraprofessionals, and peers who have used techniques based on the principle of opportunity to respond report significant gains in student achievement (Hall et al., 1982).

## Peer Tutoring

Peer tutoring, including same-age and cross-age tutoring, is receiving renewed attention within the mainstreaming movement. Peer tutoring is more cost-effective than other tutoring approaches such as the use of paraprofessionals, computer-assisted instruction, and reduced class size (Jenkins and Jenkins, 1985). The benefits of peer tutoring include improved achievement (for tutors as well as tutees), opportunities to learn responsibility, improved social skills, and enhanced self-esteem of tutors and tutees (Gerber and Kauffmann, 1981; Scruggs and Richter, 1986).

Classroom teachers occasionally are reluctant to implement peer-tutoring programs despite obvious benefits, because they must spend time and effort in gaining successful results. Since time, energy, and resources for establishing effective peer-tutoring programs are considerable, consulting teachers can collaborate with teachers to develop the programs. Peer-tutoring programs can be building-wide or limited to one or a few classrooms.

Jenkins and Jenkins (1985) identified the following critical components of a successful peer-tutoring program:

1. Provide highly structured lesson formats for tutors to use during the tutoring session, such as packaged programs with teacher instruction.

2. When possible, use content that correlates with the classroom content. Do not expect the tutor to teach material that has not already been presented by the teacher.

3. A mastery model of instruction is preferred because it provides satisfaction to tutor and tutee.

4. Schedule tutoring sessions frequently for moderate lengths of time (about one-half hour every day at the elementary level and daily one-hour sessions at the secondary level).

5. Provide tutor training and supervision, including feedback and reinforcement to tutors and classroom teachers.

6. Keep daily performance data on instructional objectives (as discussed in Chapter 8 concerning Curriculum-Based Assessment). Other types of informa-

tion can include a daily assignment record, monthly calendar, diary, or log book.

**7.** Carefully select and pair tutors with learners. The most important selection criteria are individual characteristics such as dependability, responsibility, and sensitivity.

Consideration should be given to personalities and compatibility of the tutor and tutee, congruence of schedules, gender differences (not a critical issue, but perhaps pertinent at the secondary level), tutor knowledge of content to be tutored, interests, and eagerness to participate. More highly skilled tutors are often placed with more difficult-to-teach students (Jenkins and Jenkins, 1985).

One of the most important elements of a good peer-tutoring program is tutor training. The amount and type of training will vary depending on the ages and abilities of the tutors and learners. Training usually addresses topics such as information about the program, tutor responsibilities, measurement procedures, lesson structure, teaching procedures, and personal behavior. The training should include personal relationship skills such as responsive listening, conversing, and praising good effort as described in Chapter 6.

It is important that the tutors be instructed in specific procedures that have been experimentally validated to assure maximum learning and minimum frustration. A systematic, low response-cost set of tutoring procedures for oral reading, math facts, and spelling was validated with parents as tutors (Thurston and Dasta, 1990). The procedures are listed in Figure 10–4.

An example of peer tutoring at the high school level is the H.E.L.P. room in a midwestern high school. The program (Here to Encourage the Learning Process) was developed for students who had difficulties keeping up in general education classrooms, but who did not qualify for special education programs. Although a teacher and a paraprofessional staffed the program, peer tutoring was the principal methodology. Tutors were trained over a period of several weeks in communication skills, study skills, observation skills, writing of behavioral objectives, and tutoring skills.

---

1. Select material to be used (book, flash cards . . .)
2. Sit in a quiet place.
3. Tell the child what response is wanted. ("Let's read this story. Start here." "Read this problem and give the answer.")
4. Praise correct responses.
5. For errors or pauses, tell the answer and ask child to say the answer. Then ask the question again, or restate the problem. For oral reading, have the child go to the beginning of the sentence and reread.
6. Praise correct responses.
7. Enter results on a graph or chart.
8. End on a pleasant note.

---

**FIGURE 10–4 Basic Tutoring Instructions**

Evaluations of the H.E.L.P. program show positive results. Parents report that their children are more interested in school, and teachers welcome the assistance. Students say they are less frustrated and more successful in the classroom (Thurston and Dover, 1990).

# Student-directed Approaches

Students with learning difficulties often show marked improvement in general education classrooms after they have been taught strategies for using information presented in the classroom. Many learning strategies resemble processes more commonly recognized as study skills. Some consultants and collaborators have taught learning strategies either in resource rooms or in general education classrooms. The Class-Within-a-Class approach described in Chapter 9 is one example in which learning strategies curriculum is used. Once students learn to use more efficient strategies, it is usually possible for the consultant or collaborator to step back and assist the classroom teacher in monitoring and reinforcing student use of the strategies.

## *Strategies Intervention Model*

The Strategies Intervention Model (Deshler and Schumaker, 1986) was designed to teach secondary-level students how to learn, rather than to teach specific content. The learning strategies are techniques, principles, or rules that enable students to learn, solve problems, and complete tasks independently. For example, one strategy involves making several "passes" through a text, each time focusing on a different element and building a cumulative information base for helping retain the content. The strategy is useful for anyone but particularly helpful for slow readers.

The Strategies Intervention Model requires a set of instructional packets that provide materials and procedures needed by a teacher for training the students in use of the strategies. One strand of materials includes strategies that help students acquire information from written materials, such as Word Identification Strategy, Visual Imagery Strategy, Self-Questioning Strategy, Paraphrasing Strategy, and Multipass Strategy. A second strand includes strategies that enable students to identify and store important information, such as Listening and Note-Taking Strategy, First-Letter Mnemonic Strategy, and Paired-Associates Strategy. The third strand includes strategies for facilitating written expression and demonstrating competency, such as Sentence-Writing Strategy, Paragraph-Writing Strategy, Theme-Writing Strategy, Error-Monitoring Strategy, Assignment Completion Strategy, and Test-Taking Strategy.

Deshler and Schumaker (1986) stress the importance of deliberately teaching for generalization across settings. If the special education teacher is collaborating with the classroom teacher, this generalization process will be much more effective than other delivery options. Perhaps the special education teacher will teach the strategies in the resource room, but the regular classroom teacher will want to take over monitoring the generalization. The classroom teacher provides explicit cues that will help the student know when to use a particular strategy and gives periodic probes to determine whether or not the student continues to use the strategy.

> *Central to the entire generalization process just described are regular cooperative planning efforts between the resource and regular classroom teacher. Regular communication is essential to determine the degree to which the newly-acquired learning strategies are being used in the regular classroom. In addition, in such meetings classroom teachers can be encouraged to cue students to use the strategy at the appropriate time (Deshler and Schumaker, 1986, p. 586).*

The significant student gains in academic achievement reported by Deshler and Schumaker (1986) seem to correlate highly with the level of staff training. For more information about becoming certified to use the Strategies Intervention Model, contact:

> *Kansas Institute for Research in Learning Disabilities*
> *Department of Special Education*
> *University of Kansas*
> *Lawrence, Kansas 66045*

## Classroom Survival Skills

The essential strategies for success in elementary schools differ to some extent from those needed at the secondary level, although many strategies can be adapted to serve elementary-age students. Archer and Gleason (1989) provide a set of materials for teaching elementary and middle school students in grades three through six the skills needed for classroom success. The skills included in the materials are based on a survey of five hundred middle school teachers.

Skills for school survival identified by this teacher survey include:

- school behaviors and organization skills such as before-class behaviors, during-class behaviors, organization of notebooks, keeping an assignment calendar, getting ready and completing homework, organizing assignments or papers, and organizing desks;
- learning strategies such as completing assignments with directions, memorizing and studying information, answering chapter questions, proofreading written assignments, previewing chapter content, reading expository chapters, taking notes on written material and lectures, and test-taking strategies;
- textbook reference skills such as using the table of contents, glossary, index, and reference lists;
- interpretation skills such as using graphs and tables; and
- reference skills such as using the dictionary and encyclopedia.

The materials also contain a "Teacher Checklist of Critical School Behaviors" which can be a helpful resource for consultants and collaborating teachers, even if the instructional materials are not used. The checklist identifies school behaviors that must be consistently demonstrated by students as well as teachers in order for learning to take place. For example, one school behavior desired of students is "gets ready for class (sits down and clears desk of unnecessary materials)" (Archer and Gleason, 1989, p. 157). The parallel item for teaching practices promoting that behavior is listed as "provides appropriate places for students to store personal belongings, directly teaches students how to prepare for class, communicates the expectation that students will get ready for class" (Archer and Gleason, 1989, p. 157)."

## Group and Individual Programs for Managing Behavior

Behavior problems prevent a number of students from being successful academically and accepted by their peers. Special education teachers and consultants are called on often to consult and collaborate with teachers, parents, administrators, work-study supervisors, and others about modifying social and learning behaviors that are disruptive to the student's progress as well as to that of the people around them.

As discussed in Chapter 9, behavior management procedures are complex and require specific training in order to be implemented productively and ethically. Teachers and parents who feel the need to use behavior management strategies with individual students or groups of students should consult with special education teachers and work as a team to select the most promising approaches, implement them, and evaluate the results.

### Behavior Management Strategies

The next section briefly describes a number of well-known behavior management strategies. They can be helpful to special education personnel and classroom teachers as they collaborate to develop programs for students at risk with behavioral and learning disorders.

**1.** *Turtle Technique* This procedure is effective with children who have temper tantrums and experience difficulty in coping with failure. The steps include (Robin, Schneider, and Dolnick, 1976):

* responding to the cue word *turtle* by pulling arms, legs, and head close to the body;
* combining this response with relaxation; and
* using problem-solving techniques by having the student imagine the consequences of the various behaviors she or he might use in a difficult situation.

The teacher tells a story about a turtle who wanted to think about a problem quietly. So the turtle worked it out by pulling into his shell where nobody could bother him. The teacher explains to the children that they can be like the turtle by pulling in the arms and legs and tucking down the head. This technique is demonstrated and practiced. Children are taught to relax in this position by counting backward, or tensing and then relaxing muscles, or taking big, slow breaths. They are taught to think through the problem and various consequences that might occur. For example, If I tear up my paper and yell, then this will happen. If I raise my hand and ask for another worksheet, then this will happen. Students are praised for learning the steps of the Turtle Technique and encouraged to use it when the teacher says "turtle" or when they say "turtle" to themselves in a difficult situation.

**2.** *Good Behavior Game* The Good Behavior game, a system of contingent reinforcement, is used with the entire class (Barrish, Saunders, and Wolf, 1969). Students are divided into two or more groups, and the rules of appropriate behavior are established. Each inappropriate behavior or rule infraction is recorded for the groups. If a group's total infractions are fewer than a previously specified number, the group earns special privileges. In this game all of the subgroups can "win."

**3.** *Differential Reinforcements of Low Rates of Behavior* Dietz and Repp (1973) used this procedure with a group of high school students in an office procedures class. Because the students continually discussed personal issues rather than class topics, the teacher requested the class to "stay on topic." The students earned a free talk day (Friday) if, during the four preceding days, they strayed from the topic fewer than six times. This technique could be used with one student or a group of students.

**4.** *Rules, Praise, and Ignoring* Madsen and colleagues (Madsen, Becker, and Thomas, 1968) demonstrate the effects of Rules, Praise, and Ignoring procedures with two classrooms of young students who display inappropriate behaviors, such as not finishing work, swearing, fighting, refusing to pay attention, and roaming around the room. The teachers establish a few rules with these guidelines:

4.1 Make rules short and to the point, so they can be memorized easily.
4.2 Set only five or six rules.
4.3 Phrase rules positively when possible.
4.4 Remind students about the rule throughout the day.
4.5 Follow through with the consequences.

After rules are established, students are praised when they behave appropriately or follow the rules. Praise statements are immediate, natural, and accompanied with smiles, nods, and other affirming behaviors.

The third step is to ignore inappropriate behaviors such as breaking rules. Students who also ignore inappropriate behavior are praised. Of course, a time-out or punishment procedure is used for any dangerous behavior.

**5.** *Contingency Contracting* In this strategy, students are involved in setting up their own behavior management programs (Homme, 1977). Target behaviors are identified, as are reinforcers for the student. There are two parts to a contingency contract:

listing the student's obligations in the contract; and
listing the reinforcers that can be earned for performing the obligations.

For example, the student may earn credits or points for completing household chores, for studying two hours a day, or for not smoking in school and at home. Credits may be exchanged for extra privileges such as more allowance, use of the family car on weekends, or extension of curfew. The student and the adult both have obligations under the contract. All parties must agree with the terms of the contract and sign it. A contract also may contain penalties for specific infractions of rules. Contracts are effective for all ages of students, and for many types of behavior.

**6.** *Private Reprimands* O'Leary, Kaufman, Kass, and Drabman (1970) suggest a punishment strategy for disruptive behaviors in classroom settings. First the teacher defines target behaviors such as being out of chair, making noise, being aggressive, and touching others' property. When a student displays one of the target behaviors, the teacher moves to the child quickly without fuss, tells the student in a low voice what he or she did, and asks the student to stop. The teacher needs to avoid letting others see this approach to the student and should take care that others do not hear the reprimand.

**7.** *LISTEN* Reducing inattention and improving listening skills are important goals of most teachers. Bauwens and Hourcade (1989) suggest teaching students a mnemonic device to help them learn to pay attention. LISTEN is written on a card on each student's desk, as well as on a poster in the front of the room. Teachers can prompt listening and paying attention by pointing to the card or the poster or by saying quietly, "Listen, please." Students learn that LISTEN means:

- *L* ook at the teacher.
- *I* dle your motor.
- *S* it up straight.
- *T* urn toward the teacher.
- *E* ngage your brain.
- *N* ow . . . (follow instructions, etc.).

**8.** *Daily Report Card* Fairchild (1987) suggests that a Daily Report Card is effective with students from kindergarten through ninth grade. The steps in developing and implementing a Daily Report Card system are:

8.1 Identify behaviors of concern.
8.2 Collect baseline data.
8.3 Design a report card format.

    8.4  Select reinforcers.
    8.5  Talk with student and others.
    8.6  Implement the system.
    8.7  Follow up with parents.
    8.8  Phase out the system.

The system involves working with parents, because the report card is sent home. It should be sent also to the special education teacher by general educators of students in the mainstream. The card format would vary with the age of the student and the behaviors of concern. For example, a young student might have happy faces on blocks representing "follows direction," "avoids disrupting," "finishes all assignments," and "sits up in seat." An older child might have several grades posted that represent behavior and effort in all mainstreamed subject areas.

## Evaluating Results of Behavior Management Strategies

As discussed in Chapter 8, consultants need to assess the efficacy of their collaborative efforts. Defining behavior and collecting and graphing data, discussed in Chapter 9, are important in demonstrating success of behavior management programs and usefulness of collaborative efforts. When consultants gather baseline data as described earlier, they can present a clearer picture of pre-intervention behavior and post-intervention outcomes.

    Data should be recorded and graphed continuously during the intervention. These data tell how well the program is meeting the goals of changing student behavior, and they provide positive feedback to the adults who are working together. Consultants will want to share data on child behavior changes with parents, teachers, and appropriate others. The entire team should be credited with program success.

## Classroom Modifications

One frequently used technique for fostering academic achievement of very able as well as mildly handicapped students is to modify general classroom settings or task demands. Ten general areas most amenable to classroom modification (Munson, 1987) are:

- instructional level,
- curricular content,
- instructional materials,
- format of directions and assignments,
- instructional strategies,
- teacher input mode,

- student response mode,
- individual instruction,
- test administration, and
- grading policies.

While classroom modifications may seem to be the most logical way of addressing special learning needs, the consultant should be aware that classroom teachers may resist suggestions for modifying their classrooms and curriculum (Ammer, 1984; Zigmond, Levin, and Laurie, 1985). Teachers seem to be most receptive to adapting the format of directions and assignments and to making test modifications (Munson, 1987.) Consultants and collaborators must consider whether or not their suggestions for classroom modifications are reasonable and feasible for the situation. (See Chapter 6 for information about dealing with consultee resistance.)

Many of the resources available for helping teachers make classroom modifications represent the views of special educators rather than the collaborative views of classroom teachers and special education teachers. However, Figure 10–5 contains a list of modifications taken from materials prepared collaboratively by elementary classroom teachers and special education teachers (Munson, 1987; Riegel, 1981). The list is a helpful resource to share with classroom teachers during consultations.

*Instructional Level*

Let student work at success rate level of about 80 percent.
Break task down into sequential steps.
Sequence the work with easiest problems first.
Base instruction on cognitive need (concrete, abstract).

*Curricular Content*

Select content that addresses student's interest.
Adapt content to student's future goals (job, college. . . )

*Instructional Materials*

Fold or line paper to help student with spatial problem.
Use graph paper or lined paper turned vertically.
Draw arrows on text or worksheet to show related ideas.
Highlight or colorcode on worksheets, texts, tests.
Mark the material that must be mastered.
Reduce the amount of material on a page.
Use a word processor for writing and editing.
Provide a calculator or computer to check work.
Tape reference materials to student's work area.
Have student follow text while listening to taped version.

**FIGURE 10–5  Suggestions for Classroom Modifications**

*Format of Directions and Assignments*

Make instructions as brief as possible.
Introduce multiple long-term assignments in small steps.
Read written directions or assignments aloud.
Leave directions on chalkboard during study time.
Write cues at top of work page (noun = . . . ) .
Ask student to restate or paraphrase directions.
Have student complete first example with teacher prompt.
Provide folders for unfinished work and finished work.

*Instructional Strategies*

Use concrete objects to demonstrate concepts,
Provide outlines, semantic organizers, or webbings.
Use voice changes to stress points.
Point out relationships between ideas or concepts.
Repeat important information often.

*Teacher Input Mode*

Use multisensory approach for presenting materials.
Provide a written copy of material on chalkboard.
Demonstrate skills before student does seatwork.

*Student Response Mode*

Accept alternate forms of information sharing.
Allow taped or written report instead of oral.
Allow students to dictate information to another.
Allow oral report instead of written report.
Have student practice speaking to small group first.

*Test Administration*

Allow students to have sample tests to practice.
Teach test-taking skills.
Test orally.
Supply recognition items and not just total recall.
Allow take-home test.
Ask questions requiring short answers.

*Grading Policies*

Grade on pass/fail basis.
Grade on individual progress or effort.
Change the percentage required to pass.
Do not penalize for handwriting or spelling on tests.

*Modifications of Classroom Environment*

Seat students according to attention or sensory need.
Remove student from distractions.
Keep extra supplies on hand.

**FIGURE 10–5**  *(Continued)*

### Textbook Selection and Adaptation

Very few teachers use modified or adapted texts to accommodate the needs of mainstreamed students (Munson, 1987), although many would agree that most texts written for classroom use are not well suited to serve mainstreamed students with learning difficulties. The need for modified texts in mainstream classrooms was addressed by the Office of Special Education Programs in the U.S. Department of Education, which sponsored a series of projects to adapt widely used texts (Burnette, 1987). The adapted textbook materials are described in a document available from the Council for Exceptional Children. Tape-recorded textbooks can be used on occasion for blind and learning-disabled students. If the student qualifies, tape-recorded texts are available from:

*Recordings for the Blind*
*214 East 58th Street*
*New York, NY 10022*

Some consultants have arranged for volunteers to record textbooks on tape. If consultants and collaborators choose to have volunteer readers tape-record texts, they should instruct the readers to provide advance organizers for the student, to call attention to visual aids, charts, and graphs, and to periodically remind the student to review material just read. Other helpful hints for preparing tape-recorded texts are provided by Mercer and Mercer (1989).

Students with high ability also are served poorly by conventional textbooks. The Educational Products Information Exchange, a nonprofit educational consumer agency, revealed in 1980–81 that 60 percent of the fourth-graders in some of the school districts studied could achieve a score of 80 percent or higher on a test on the content of their math text before opening the books in September. Similar findings were reported for tenth-grade science texts and social studies texts (Reis and Renzulli, 1986). Efforts to locate more appropriate, challenging texts were met with discouraging reports from textbook publishers, who acknowledged that text difficulty had dropped two grade levels during the past decade. When concerned Californians tried to reserve room on the statewide adoption list for textbooks that could challenge the top one-third of students, no publisher had any such textbooks to present (Kirst, 1982).

Part of the role and responsibility of consultants and consulting teachers is serving on textbook selection committees, in order to provide information that will increase the probability of selecting textbooks appropriate for students with special learning needs. Readability formulas (Fry, 1977) are often used by these committees, to determine whether or not students will be able to comprehend the texts. However, this practice has been questioned by some researchers (Armbruster and Anderson, 1988).

Readability formulas typically measure factors such as sentence complexity, word difficulty, or word length. But there are other, perhaps more important, factors to consider. The readability formulas do not take into account student characteristics such as background knowledge, motivation, interest or purpose, or characteristics of the text that research has shown to facilitate comprehension (Armbruster and Anderson, 1988).

Other elements to be noted when selecting textbooks are:

**1.** *Organization.* The text should have a logical, easily identifiable organization using a clearly distinguishable outline; informative headings and sub-headings; format clues such as marginal notations, graphic aids, or boldface italics, and signal words and phrases that designate particular patterns of organization.

**2.** *Coherence.* The ideas in the text should stick together, as indicated by use of elements such as connectives or conjunctions, clear references, transition statements, chronological sequences that are easy to follow, and graphic aids clearly related to the text.

**3.** *Content.* Content should be well-suited to the reader's level of knowledge and skills, as shown by factors such as building carefully on student's prior knowledge, providing substantive explanations of topics about which students are likely to know very little, providing the first sentence in a paragraph as a topic sentence, including preview or summary statements of main ideas, and highlighting main ideas by using underlining and boldface print or color cues (Armbruster and Anderson, 1988).

## Modified Testing

Many students with learning and behavior problems have difficulty taking tests on subject matter they have learned. As a student progresses to higher grade levels, the ability to demonstrate knowledge through tests becomes more and more important. Many consultants at upper grade levels will need to give careful attention to the test-taking skills of mainstreamed students with learning and behavior difficulties.

When students have difficulty taking teacher-made tests in content subjects, consultants should give attention to a number of elements about the nature of the tests and ways to either help students take the tests as written, or collaborate with the teacher to make test adaptations. Lieberman (1984) suggests the first week of each school year, beginning at about the seventh-grade level, should be devoted to teaching study skills and test-taking strategies.

Other suggestions to consider when consulting with classroom teachers about alternative test construction and administration include:

- Give frequent, timed mini-tests;
- Give practice tests;
- Have students test one another and discuss answers;
- Use alternative response forms (for example, multiple choice rather than essay);
- Back up the written tests with taped tests;

- Provide extra spacing between discussion of short-answer items;
- Underline key words in test directions as well as test items;
- Provide test-study guides featuring a variety of answer formats;
- Provide additional time for students who write slowly;
- Administer tests orally (Mercer and Mercer, 1989).

Curriculum-Based Assessment (CBA), discussed in Chapter 8, is an appropriate testing tool for use at any grade level. It has the most direct application in monitoring growth in basic skill areas such as reading, writing, and mathematics. Standardized test scores and commercially-made criterion-referenced tests usually do not give appropriate information to determine how the student is performing in a particular classroom or whether or not the modification was effective. The consultant or classroom teacher should take frequent measures using the actual materials or content from the classroom.

## Assigning Grades

Consultants will need to discuss with the teacher the matter of assigning grades based on modified curriculum or tests. Teachers often hesitate to adapt their grading methods because they fear the adjustments will lower academic standards, deviate from established policy, or become unfair to other students (Carpenter, 1985). Yet it is unfair to mainstreamed students if they are graded in the same manner as other students in the classroom. Grading is an essential part of the educational experience; therefore, eliminating grades for mainstreamed students is unrealistic.

Assigning grades to daily work is a way of providing feedback to students. Grade cards and transcripts communicate messages about the student's progress to parents, prospective employers, or other consumers, as well as to students. If grading policies are not clear, the grades may communicate inaccurately. For example, an interviewed parent said, "I have three children. One is gifted, one is average, and the third is mentally retarded. Which one do you think made the honor roll this quarter? The mentally retarded child! That's hard for me to understand and even harder for my other two children to understand." The mentally retarded child was being graded on progress toward the IEP goals, while the other two children were being graded on performance compared with other students in their classes. Grading policies in the school these three students attended were not made clear to teachers, parents, or students.

Grading policies can vary from one school to another. It is important that teachers, parents, administrators, and students consult and collaborate to establish clear guidelines.

*In order to grade mainstreamed handicapped pupils fairly and without ambiguities, a fair and clear grading system for all pupils must be operating. If the basic system lacks merit, adjustments for handicapped pupils will suffer the same problem.*

*Particularly where secondary pupils are concerned, educators must be vigilant so that the messages that are sent are clear, accurate, and meaningful (Carpenter, 1988, p. 58).*

Carpenter (1985) reviewed the literature addressing the assignment of grades for mainstreamed remedial and handicapped pupils and found many practical suggestions, including:

basing grades on progress toward IEP goals;
using lowered grading standards;
grading process and product separately;
basing grades on contracts;
weighting grades, based on difficulty of class or assignments; and
considering effort in assigning grades.

Some teachers use pass/fail systems, mastery checklists, narrative reports, or a combination of these feedback mechanisms instead of grades. Carpenter (1985) made several recommendations, based on a literature review:

**1.** The school should adopt a reasonable policy for assigning grades to pupils with disabilities. Deviations from standard grading practices should only be used when the pupil's disability is a mitigating factor.

**2.** When a pupil's disability interferes with learning and performance, a multicategory grading system should be used employing criterion-referenced and self-referenced methods. Number or letter grades should be based on progress toward, or mastery of, clearly stated objectives. Pass/fail systems should not be used.

**3.** If the teachers wish to report more than one message, such as both progress and effort, two or more grades should be used.

**4.** Involve students in grading by including them in setting goals and predetermining how the students' performances will be evaluated in relation to progress toward the goals.

**5.** Grade frequently. Weekly grades should be considered a minimum time between grade reports to the student.

**6.** Supplement letter or number grades with narrative reports that invite two-way communication.

**7.** Consultation and collaboration between teachers is essential when instruction is shared. One purpose of the collaboration is to obtain a broader view of the pupil's overall performance.

**8.** Separate judgments about effort, attitude, and similar factors from the grading process. In most cases, a grade for effort is appropriate only when a specific objective to that end is clearly stated. For example, if a goal of working alone for twenty minutes has been stated, then progress toward that goal should be reported.

## Curriculum Modifications for Very Able Students

Consultants who endeavor to enhance the academic achievement of all students in the classroom must not overlook the needs of very able students. Stimulating learning experiences for gifted students within the general classroom program cannot be provided without extensive modifications to curriculum content, tests, textbooks, and other learning resources.

Several strategies presented in this chapter as effective practices for mainstreamed students with learning and behavioral disorders are identified as less appropriate for gifted students (Schatz, 1990; Robinson, 1990). For example, mastery learning could be a promising approach for developing remarkable talent (Howley, Howley, and Pendarvis, 1986), but to ensure that this occurs, it will be necessary to provide exemplary instruction and truly challenging enrichment. As another example, cooperative learning is an effective instructional strategy for a variety of reasons. However, it should not be justified for gifted students by inferring that they require remediation in social skills. Nor should it be used to make gifted students available as handy tutors (Robinson, 1990). While peer tutoring can be challenging and rewarding for the gifted student, it should not be used to set very able students up as surrogate teachers in lieu of modifying the curriculum appropriately for both tutor and tutee.

When gifted students are mainstreamed into general classrooms, as the majority are, their needs as well as the needs of students with learning problems must be considered when any strategy is employed for the entire classroom. These cautions and concerns underscore the need for intensive collaboration and consultation among gifted program facilitators, classroom teachers, and resource personnel, so that classroom modifications and resource adaptations help mainstreamed gifted students develop their learning potential.

### Classroom Enrichment

Since most gifted children in elementary schools spend more time with their classroom teachers than with specially trained resource teachers (Gallagher, 1985), the general classroom curriculum should be enriched and adapted to meet their needs. Classroom teachers are responsible for a wide range of student needs and often do not have the time, resources, and facilities to challenge students who can function two, four, or more grade levels beyond their age peers. They want bright students to master the basic skills without falling victim to learning gaps that will impede their progress later. They feel the brunt of parent pressures to provide advanced opportunities, and they wince when their most able students describe lessons as "boring." Some do not feel prepared to teach children who may be as knowledgeable, or more so, in subjects than they.

VanTassel-Baska (1989) notes four mistaken beliefs that need to be overturned regarding educational programs for gifted students. First, consultants and consultees should not assume that differentiated curriculum must always be different from what all learners receive. Neither do all learning experiences need to be product oriented. One curriculum package or a single learning strategy will *not* provide all that is needed.

Acceleration of content for gifted students is *not* harmful as a general rule. VanTassel-Baska promotes a content-based, accelerative curriculum, which contains a process/product/research dimension for in-depth learning, and involves exploration of issues, themes, and ideas across curriculum areas. Activities that can be provided through collaborative efforts of consultants, teachers, parents, and resource personnel include:

- flexible pacing (appropriate acceleration in content);
- meaningful enrichment (not busywork or enrichment that is irrelevant to their strong abilities and interests;
- group activities (seminars, special classes); and
- individual arrangements (independent study, acquisition of skills in areas needed for pursuing major interests and talents, mentorships, and internships).

## *Curriculum Compacting*

Curriculum compacting (Renzulli and Reis, 1985) is a strategy that consulting teacher and classroom teacher can plan and implement productively for very able students. Just as teachers condense daily lessons and assignments for children returning to school after an absence, they can compact curriculum for students who learn more quickly and easily than the majority of students. This "buys time" for students to pursue individual interests and independent study in complex areas of regular or accelerated curriculum.

Gifted students need not always accelerate at a fast pace through the curriculum. On occasion they may welcome the opportunity to slow down and study a subject in depth and detail, catching up with the class by completing regular assignments on a compacted basis at a later date.

Some arrangements needed by gifted and talented students are accessible only outside the school setting. When students leave their school campus for enrichment or for accelerated coursework, learning effectiveness, group, or individual arrangements, special educators and classroom teachers must assume responsibility for collaborating and communicating often, to ensure the students master basic skills and continue to be involved in the life of the school. A list of learning options and alternatives for gifted students is provided in Figure 10–6.

## Computer-assisted Instruction (CAI)

A discussion of approaches for improving learning experiences for students with special needs would not be complete without considering the powerful potential of personal computers in the classroom. Computer-assisted instruction (CAI) provides individually paced programming for students who have attention problems or who need more practice or examples in order to under

Exciting, challenging learning activities for gifted and talented students can be provided in the classroom. Collaborators can shop among these basic enrichment options when working together to plan alternatives for very able students.

- Allow students to test out of already-mastered material.
- Compact curriculum to "buy time" for enrichment activity.
- Acquire advanced texts and references for students to use.
- Allow students to study a subject longer than usual.
- Arrange cross-age tutoring between very able students with similar interests and learning styles.
- Facilitate independent study.
- Encourage investigations by a small group of able students working as a team.
- Provide learning packs, modules, minicourses, and task cards on topics of interest to gifted students.
- Bring in resource speakers to discuss special issues.
- Cultivate and facilitate mentorships.
- Allow dual coursework for dual credit.
- Permit extended library or laboratory time.
- Schedule time each day for concentrated, uninterrupted work on a project or reflection on an idea.
- Conduct discussions about complex, appealing topics.
- Prepare resource files of community members who could help in the classroom or behind the scenes.
- Provide instruction to students on learning taxonomies and principles.
- Set up mini-seminars for groups of students who share similar interests and abilities.
- Use biographies of exemplary persons to model for and motivate students.
- Set aside an area where student research projects and creative products are showcased and discussed.
- Introduce the world's wisdom through use of quotes, credos, maxims, fables.
- Conduct problem-solving sessions, using real and hypothetical problems.
- Provide discussion time for moral dilemmas, logic, and ethics.
- Make career information and resource persons available.
- Encourage students to keep idea journals, sketchbooks, and idea files.
- Cultivate student self-assessment of learning habits and self-evaluation of learning products.
- Use feedback, grading, and reporting alternatives that do not penalize students for selecting harder curriculum.
- Seek outlets for displaying and publishing exemplary student work.
- Arrange for student participation in appropriate competitive activities.
- Provide instruction in "life tools" such as parliamentary procedure, orienteering, interviewing, research.
- Provide opportunities for developing global awareness.
- Arrange independent study or tutorial in a foreign language.
- Provide "how-to" books on various areas of human endeavor.
- Encourage students to read something from each subject area in the library.
- Recognize and respect unusual, creative questions and ideas.
- Provide liberal, in-depth critiques and comments on work.
- Use intrinsic rewards and appeals to reasoning as much as possible for reinforcement.

**FIGURE 10–6  Appropriate Learning Programs for Gifted Students**

stand the lesson. The computer can be an effective tool for students with behavior and learning problems because it provides an objective, neutral response to student responses, regardless of how the student behaves.

Carman and Kosberg (1981) studied the use of a computer program ifor behavior-disordered students who were at least two years behind grade level in math. When compared to a control group, the CAI students demonstrated learning rate gains and also paid significantly more attention to the tasks at hand. Woolfolk (1990) lists several examples of using computers for instruction. They can provide a wide variety of ways for students with special needs to develop different skills at different times, such as:

- drill and practice programs;
- word processing;
- learning a programming language;
- assistance with collaborative and cooperative learning experiences;
- data recording for self-assessment and self-monitoring; and
- motivation, through games and sensory involvement.

Computer-based instruction will provide many options and alternatives for the learning programs of students with special needs. Computers will soon offer great interactivity, present information from many different perspectives, provide simulations that portray and test conflicting theories, and promote reflectivity (Kay, 1991). All teachers and students can expect to benefit from these learning enhancements, while those with special needs may respond to the particular innovations that deliver stronger representations of the world than traditional approaches to learning now provide.

## Selecting Instructional Approaches

This chapter includes a menu of ideas and program options shown to be effective for encouraging academic achievement in classroom settings. Which should consultants and consultees select when collaborating to provide service for students with special needs? Any of them, of course, that promise to serve one student, or a group of students, well.

The options and alternatives should be tested against a number of practical considerations. Idol, West, and Lloyd (1988) suggest a decision-making framework based on the concept of Levels of Intensity of Intervention. The first dimension of the framework addresses the type(s), extent, and content of specialized instruction needed for each student. The second dimension examines the relative responsibilities of the classroom, remedial, and/or special education teacher for implementing the level of instructional modifications needed.

An intervention should address both the instructional needs of students with special needs and compatibility with current knowledge regarding effective instruction (Reisberg and Wolf, 1986). Interventions with the best chances for successful adoption by classroom teachers are direct, benefit other children in the classroom, make reasonable time demands on the teacher, and are easy to implement and maintain (Reisberg and Wolf, 1986). Several principles need to be considered when selecting interventions:

1. First, be sure the technique can be applied in the type of classroom organization where the application is needed. For example, individualized instruction in which children are provided extensive one-on-one instruction by classroom teachers, as is often done in special education settings, is not stressed here because it is a difficult approach for an overburdened classroom teacher to implement effectively. One of the peer-assisted approaches may be much more appropriate when one-on-one instruction is needed.

2. Select strategies that are based on research demonstrating general classroom effectiveness. Information about some of the more promising research-based approaches is included in this chapter.

3. Give priority to techniques and strategies that do not require extensive reorganization of the classroom or special equipment and materials. The research on classroom modification convincingly argues for this point. Teachers are not likely to follow through on an idea if it requires too much that is incompatible with their normal organizational structure. Select the "least invasive" technique (Idol, West, and Lloyd, 1988; Reisberg and Wolf, 1988) and, whenever possible, use the general classroom curriculum.

4. Give priority to ideas that are cost-effective. For example, the use of computers has great potential but might not be cost-effective if the school does not own enough computers. Some other possibilities, such as special books and materials, might also be prohibitive due to cost. Time and effort are other aspects of cost that should not be overlooked.

5. Choose techniques for which you feel competent or can gain the necessary competency. Many of the approaches, such as cooperative learning, Classwide Peer Tutoring, or Strategies Intervention Model, require extensive training beyond the information presented here.

6. Choose techniques and procedures the teacher feels competent to implement or can learn to implement in a reasonable amount of time. (Staff development for teachers will be discussed in Chapter 12.) Until a teacher has had training for use of the approaches, they should not be looked on as viable alternatives.

7. Choose approaches that can benefit many children in the classroom. Although the consultation may be precipitated by the needs of one particular student, there are likely to be several more students that could benefit from the same assistance. If the strategies selected can be used with several students at once, the effectiveness of the consultation efforts will be multiplied, and the need for consultation about other students at a later time may be reduced. In addition, these interventions are more likely than others to be accepted by classroom teachers (Reisberg and Wolf, 1988).

8. Be realistic. Consider all aspects of the classroom and select the best approaches for the situation at that particular time.

## Tips for Consulting and Collaborating

**1.** Rather than just telling classroom teachers about materials modification, *show* them. Give examples or do one for them.

**2.** Have a consultant/consultee discussion about individual styles and preferred resources for teaching.

**3.** Request demonstration lessons from classroom teachers featuring *their* most outstanding teaching techniques.

**4.** Offer to retype a test for a teacher (to space it out, type in large print, or organize it differently) for use with a student who has a learning problem.

**5.** Before ordering computer software, have students try it out first. This gives them an opportunity to be consultants for teachers and cultivates student ownership in educational planning and evaluation.

**6.** When preparing and distributing materials for classroom use, don't just drop them off and run. Help the teacher or student get started, and stay awhile to see how it goes.

**7.** Keep a supply of materials to send to classrooms for students who need reinforcement, even those with whom you don't work that could use the practice.

**8.** Have a favorite dozen of successful strategies available for demonstration teaching or sharing.

**9.** Have students assist in helping make up tests. It teaches them to focus on important things, and perhaps they will study more, too.

**10.** Compile a list of summer activities, programs, camps, and other opportunities for students. Send it along with the last communication of the year to teachers and/or parents.

**11.** Be understanding of classroom teachers' daily trials with some mainstreamed students. Celebrate with classroom teachers even the smallest progress by students.

**12.** Use observation and data-recording time effectively, so that overworked classroom teachers do not think it is being misused and flaunted.

**13.** Have parents observe their child working in the school setting, and then consult with them about behavior management programs in the home.

**14.** Have a student calendar with assignments listed and stickers to mark off their completions. Have the student earn daily rewards that can be accumulated into a larger reward.

**15.** Make it a point to give a verbal compliment or send a note to each teacher in recognition of contribution to the behavior management program for a particular student.

**16.** When approaching a difficult discussion, sandwich the complaint in between two compliments. First practice saying something positive to a colleague who has been difficult or noncooperative toward consultation, and then *say* it to that person.

**17.** Use "compliment papers" for selected secondary-level students. While a few might be embarrassed, some like it very much. (You helped a classmate appropriately. You ignored a "set-up"—great. You did your homework. You handled frustration well.)

**18.** Remind yourself often that when children are the least lovable, that is when they need love the most.

## Chapter Review

**1.** Teachers who are skilled in using effective teacher-directed instruction practices and mastery learning approaches are helpful to students who risk school failure. Consultants and collaborators should be knowledgeable about effective instructional procedures, in order to provide assistance and meaningful consultation. Skilled teachers and knowledgeable consultants make a powerful educational team.

**2.** Cooperative learning techniques and peer tutoring programs provide a means of extending one-on-one assistance so badly needed by low-achieving students. Improved social relationships are added benefits that accompany academic improvement for all students, both tutors and tutees. Consultants can provide valuable assistance to classroom teachers who wish to use one or both of these instructional approaches. Gifted learners have special needs. In order to develop their potential, they need compacted and accelerated content, appropriate enrichment, nurturant group activities, and opportunities for independent study and production. Many of the effective programs for gifted students require collaboration between teachers, institutions of higher education, and school districts or other community agencies.

**3.** The techniques with potential for the most long-lasting benefit to students are those that help students develop learning strategies and study skills that are generalizable from one classroom setting to another. When special education teachers collaborate with general classroom teachers in teaching and monitoring student use of learning strategies and study skills, the benefits to student learning will be enhanced.

**4.** Several strategies are available for classroom use to improve individual or group behavior. Team effort by general classroom teachers, special education teachers, and related services and support personnel can compound the benefits of any behavioral technique. A behavior management program must be designed so that it does not infringe on rights of any student or rules of the school. It is important that the success of the intervention is shared by all concerned.

**5.** The most widely used consultation approach to fostering student achievement in general classrooms is modification of tasks or setting of variables to match student learning styles or other special needs. Consultants should develop a set of guidelines to help in selecting the classroom modifications and suggested techniques. Modified textbooks are not used often enough, although they are very much needed by mainstreamed students. Modified work format and test modifications are more frequently used. Modifications that can benefit large groups and more children in the classroom usually are well received by teachers. Part of consultation should involve developing plans for testing and grading students with special learning needs. Modifying the test format and extending testing time are common practices. Assigning grades, however, is a problem for many teachers, due to concern about fairness, school policy, or lowered academic standards. Consultants should be sensitive to these concerns and help develop grading policies that are fair and reasonable to all students.

**6.** When consultants work collaboratively with others in planning, implementing, and evaluating programs and tactics to manage child behavior, all are winners—school personnel, parents, and most of all, students.

## Activities

**1.** Prepare a list of innovative teaching techniques teachers in your school, or a hypothetical school, would be interested in using for students at risk. How might you share some of these techniques through consultation and collaboration?

**2.** Brainstorm possibilities for using collaborative consultation to enhance or modify an activity or lesson you have previously taught or from which you have learned. Talk over your ideas with others to expand and refine them.

**3.** Develop a plan for implementing a peer tutoring program that could be used in your school.

**4.** Write sources listed in this book to get more information about the strategies discussed in the chapter. Work with teachers to determine which of these strategies or skills are most needed by the students in your school. Develop a comprehensive plan for including the strategies in a systematic way, and include plans for obtaining training in their use.

**5.** Select a real or hypothetical situation in which you would be consulting about a student with severe learning disabilities. Draft ideas that might come up for discussion regarding testing and grading. The ideas should be consistent with school policy and fair and honest for the student.

## For Further Reading

To obtain information about training in the use of procedures discussed in this chapter, contact the following sources.

On the topic of student team learning:

Robert Slavin
Center for Research on Elementary and
   Middle Schools
Johns Hopkins University
3505 North Charles Street
Baltimore, MD 21218

On the topic of learning together:

David Johnson and Roger Johnson
Cooperative Learning Center
7208 Cornelia Drive
Edina, MN 55435

On the topic of classwide peer tutoring:

Joe Delquadri
Juniper Gardens Children's Project
1614 Washington Boulevard
Kansas City, KS, 66102

On adapting textbooks for special needs of students:

*Adapting Instructional Materials for Mainstreamed Students,* by Jane Burnett, 1987.
Council for Exceptional Children
1920 Association Drive
Reston, VA 22091-1589

On the topic of classroom survival skills:

Skills for School Success
Curriculum Associates
5 Esquire Road
North Billerica, MA 01862-2589

On instructional strategies to challenge gifted and talented students:

*Instructional Strategies for Teaching the Gifted,* by Jeanette Plauche Parker, 1989
Allyn and Bacon
160 Gould Street
Needham Heights, MA 02194

# References

Archer, A., and Gleason, M. (1989). *Skills for School Success, Book Three, Teacher Guide.* North Billerica, MA: Curriculum Associates.

Ammer, (1984). The mechanics of mainstreaming: Consider the regular educators' perspective. *Remedial and Special Education, 5*(6): 15-20.

Armbruster, B. B., and Anderson, T. H. (1988). On selecting "considerate" content area textbooks. *Remedial and Special Education, 9*(1):47–52.

Barrish, H. H., Saunders, M., and Wolf, M. M. (1969). Good behavior game: Effects of individual contingencies for group consequences on disruptive behavior in a classroom. *Journal of Applied Behavior Analysis,* 2:119–24.

Bauwens, J., and Hourcade, J. J. (1989). Hey would you just listen. *Teaching Exceptional Children, 21,* 61.

Bloom, B. S. (1984). The search for methods of group instruction as effective as one–to–one tutoring. *Educational Leadership, 41*(8):4–18.

Britt, S. (1985). Our high priests of process. *Newsweek,* November 18, p. 30.

Burnette, J. (1987). Issue brief 1: Adapting instructional materials for mainstreamed students. Reston, VA: Council for Exceptional Children. The ERIC/SEP Special Project on Interagency Information Dissemination, the ERIC Clearinghouse on Handicapped and Gifted Children.

Carman, G., and Kosberg. B. (1981). Educational technology research: Computer technology and the education of emotionally handicapped children. *Educational Technology, 22,* 22–30.

Carpenter, D. (1985) Grading handicapped pupils: Review and position statement. *Remedial and Special Education, 6*(4):54–59.

Delquadri, J., Greenwood, C. R., Whorton, D., Carta, J. J., and Hall, R. V. (1986). Classwide Peer Tutoring. *Exceptional Children,* 52:535–42.

Deshler, D. D., and Schumaker, J. B. (1986). Learning strategies: An instructional alternative for low–achieving adolescents. *Exceptional Children,* 52:583–90.

Dietz, S. M. and Repp, A. C. (1973). Decreasing classroom misbehavior through the use of DRL schedules of reinforcement. *Journal of Applied Behavior Analysis,* 6:457–63.

Dishon, D. and O'Leary, P. W. (1989). Tips for teachers: Time saver options. *Cooperaative Learning, 10*(2):30.

Dishon, D. and O'Leary, P. W. (1990). Social skills and processing. *Cooperative Learning, 10*(2):35–36.

Fry, E. (1977). Fry's readability graph: Clarifications, validity, and extension to level 17. *Journal of Reading, 21:24–52.*

Gallagher, J. J. (1985). *Teaching the Gifted Child* (3d ed.). Boston: Allyn and Bacon.(1985).

Gerber, M., and Kauffmann, J. (1981). Peer tutoring in academic settings. In P. Strain (ed.):*Utilization of Classroom Peers as Behavior Change Agents*, pp. 155–87. New York: Plenum Publishing.

Guskey, T. R. (1988). Mastery learning and mastery teaching: How they complement each other. *Principal, 68*(1):6–8.

Guskey, T. R. (1990). Integrating innovations. *Educational Leadership, 47,* 5, 11–15.

Hall, R. V., Delquadri, J., Greenwood, C. R., and Thurston, L. (1982). The importance of opportunity to respond in children's academic success. In E. Edgar, N. Haring, J. Jenkins, and C. Pious (eds.):*Mentally Handicapped Children: Education and Training*, pp. 107–40. Baltimore, MD: University Park Press.

Homme, L. (1977). *How to use contingency contracting in the classroom.* Champaign, IL: Research Press.

Howley, A., Howley, C. B., and Pendarvis, E. (1986). *Teaching Gifted Children: Principles and Strategies.* Boston: Little, Brown, and Co.

Idol, L., West, J. F., and Lloyd, S. R. (1988). Organizing and implementing specialized reading programs: A collaborative approach involving classroom, remedial, and special education teachers. *Remedial and Special Education, 9*(2):54–61.

Jenkins, J., and Jenkins, L. (1985). Peer tutoring in elementary and secondary programs. *Focus on Exceptional Children, 17*(6):1–12.

Johnson, D. W., and Johnson, R. T. (1987). *Learning Together and Alone: Cooperative, Competitive, and Individualistic Learning* (2d ed). Englewood Cliffs, NJ: Prentice Hall.

Kagan, S. (1989). *Cooperative Learning: Resources for Teachers.* San Juan Capistrano, CA: Resources for Teachers.

Kay, A. (1991). Computers, networks, and education. *Scientific American,* September 1991, 138–48.

Kirst, M. W. (1982). How to improve schools without spending more money. *Phi Delta Kappan, 64*(1):6–8.

Lieberman, L. M. (1984). *Preventing special education: For those who don't need it.* Newton, MA: GloWorm.

Lloyd, J. W., Crowley, E. P., Kohler, F. W., and Strain, P. S. (1988). Redefining the applied research agenda: Cooperative learning, prereferral, teacher consultation, and peer–mediated interventions. *Journal of Learning Disabilities, 21*:43–52.

Madden, N. A., and Slavin, R. E. (1983). Cooperative learning and social acceptance of mainstreamed academically handicapped students. *Journal of Special Education, 17:*171–82.

Madsen, C. H., Jr., Becker, W. C., and Thomas, D. R. (1968). Rules. praise, and ignoring: Elements of elementary classroom control. *Journal of Applied Behavior Analysis, 1*:139–150.

Mercer, C. D., and Mercer, A. R. (1989). *Teaching Students with Learning Problems* (3d ed.). Columbus, OH: Merrill.

Munson, S. M. (1987). Regular education teacher modifications for mainstreamed mildly handicapped students. *Journal of Special Education, 20*(4):489–502.

O'Leary, K. D., Kaufman, K. F., Kass, R. E., and Drabman, R. S. (1970). The effects of loud and soft reprimands on the behavior of disruptive studnets. *Exceptional Children, 37,* 145–55.

Parker, J.P. (1989). Instructional Strategies for Teaching the Gifted. Needham Heights, MA: Allyn and Bacon.

Reis, S. M., and Renzulli, J. S. (1986). The secondary triad model. In J. S. Renzulli (ed.). *Systems and Models for Developing Programs for the Gifted and Talented* (pp. 267–305). Mansfield Center, CT: Creative Learning Press.

Renzulli, J.S., and Reis, S.M. (1985). The Schoolwide Enrichment Model: A comprehensive plan for educational excellence. Mansfield Center, CT: Creative Learning Press.

Reisberg, L., and Wolf, R. (1986). Developing a consulting program in special education: Implementation and interventions. *Focus on Exceptional Children, 19*(3):1–14.

Reisberg, L., and Wolf, R. (1988). Instructional strategies for special education consultants. *Remedial and Special Education, 9*(6):29–40.

Riegel, R. H. (1981). *Making Modifications in the Mainstream: A Consultant's Guide to Cooperative Planning.* Unpublished manuscript. Plymouth, MI: Model Resource Room Project.

Robin, A., Schneider, M., and Dolnick, M. (1976). The turtle technique: An extended case study of self-control in the classroom. *Psychology in Schools, 13*(4):449–53.

Robinson, A. (1990). Cooperation of exploitaation? The argument against cooperative learning for talented students. *Journal for the Education of the Gifted, 14*(1):9–27.

Rosenshine, B. V., and Berliner, D. C. (1978). Academic engaged time. *British Journal of Teacher Education,* 4:3–16.

Schatz, E. (1990). Ability grouping for gifted learners. *Educating Able Learners.* 15(3)3, 5, 15. Denton, TX: Gifted Students Institute.

Scruggs, T. E., and Richter, L. (1986). Tutoring learning disabled student: A critical review. *Learning Disability Quarterly,* 9(1):2–14.

Slavin, R. E. (1990). Research on cooperative training: consensus and controversy. *Educational Leadership,* 47(4):52–54.

Slavin, R. E. (1986). *Using student team learning* (3rd ed.). Baltimore, MD: Center for Research on Elementary and Middle Schools, The Johns Hopkins University.

Slavin, R. E., and Madden, N. A. (1989). What works for students at risk: A research synthesis. *Educational Leadership,* pp. 4–13.

Thurston, L. P., and Dasta, K. (1990). An analysis of in-home parent tutoring procedures: Effects on children's academic behavior at home and in school and on parents' tutoring behaviors. *Remedial and Special Education,* 11 (4), 41–52.

Thurston, L. P., and Dover, W. (October, 1990). *Rural at-risk students.* Paper presented at the 12th annual Rural and Small Schools Conference, Manhattan, KS.

VanTassel–Baska, J. (1989). Appropriate curriculum for gifted learners. *Educational Leadership,* 46 (6), 13–15.

Wang, M. C. (1987). Toward achieving educational excellence for all students: Program design and student outcomes. *Remedial and Special Education,* 8:25–34.

Zigmond, N., Levin, E., and Laurie, T. E. (1985). Managing the mainstream: An analysis of teacher attitudes and student performance in mainstream high school programs. *Journal of Learning Disabilities,* 18(9):535–41.

# 11

# CONSULTING AND COLLABORATING IN PARTNERSHIPS WITH PARENTS

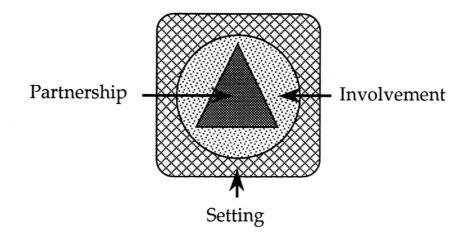

Partnership ——— Involvement

Setting

## To Think About

Interacting with parents of students who have special needs can be one of the most rewarding aspects of an educator's work. It also can be frustrating and discouraging at times. Whether parents are supportive and cooperative or antagonistic and uncooperative, educators must include them in planning, implementing, and evaluating the student's individual education program.

Parent involvement is mandated by Public Law 94–142. However, the necessity for parent involvement and support is much more than just meeting a mandate. Parents are the child's first and most influential educators. Up to 87 percent of a child's waking hours from birth to age eighteen are spent under the control of the home environment, leaving only thirteen percent of the time under the supervision of schools (Bevevino, 1988). The family setting is critical to a student's performance in school.

While much of the responsibility for a child's learning has been turned over to schools in recent years, it is now time to cultivate home-school collaboration that will allow both school educators and parent educators to fulfill their commitments to develop each child's potential. Home-school partnerships provide students the best opportunity for overcoming risks and disabilities, and for becoming all that they can be in a complex, challenging world.

## Focusing Questions

1. How does involvement by parents in partnerships and collaboration with school personnel benefit students and their families?
2. What does parent collaboration require?
3. What are barriers to home-school collaboration?
4. How can educators examine their values and attitudes toward parents?
5. How can educators build collaborative relationships with parents?
6. How should educators initiate home-school interactions?
7. How should educators individualize parent involvement?
8. How can parent-school collaboration be evaluated?

## Key Terms

home-school collaboration          Kroth Mirror Model
home-school partnerships          parent involvement

---

### Scenario

The setting is a junior high school. The learning disabilities itinerant teacher has just arrived at the building, hoping to make some contacts with classroom teachers before classes begin, when the principal walks out of her office briskly, with a harried look.

*PRINCIPAL*: Oh, I'm glad you're here. I believe Barry is part of your caseload this year, right? His mother is in my office. She's crying, and says that everybody's picking on her son.

*LD CONSULTANT*: What happened?

*PRINCIPAL*: He got into an argument with his English teacher yesterday, and she sent him to me. After he cooled down and we had a talk, it was time for classes to change, so I sent him on to his next class. But he skipped out. The secretary called and left word with the babysitter to inform the mother about his absence. He must have really unloaded on her, because she's here, quite upset, and saying that the teachers do not care about her son and his problems. Could you join us for a talk?

*LD CONSULTANT*: O.K., sure. (enters the principal's office and greets Barry's mother)

*MOTHER*: I am just about at my wit's end. It has not been a good week at home, but we've made an effort to keep track of Barry's work. Now this problem with his English teacher has him refusing to come to school. Sometimes I feel that we are at cross purposes—us at home and you at school.

*LD CONSULTANT*: We certainly do not want this to happen. I would like to hear more about your concerns and the problems Barry and his teachers are having. Is this a good time, or may we arrange for one that is more convenient for you?

*MOTHER*: The sooner, the better. I don't want Barry missing school, but with the attitude he has right now, it wouldn't do him any good to be here.

*LD CONSULTANT*: Let's discuss some strategies we can work on. We are all concerned about Barry, and we need for him to know that.

## Mandate for Parent Involvement

Parent involvement was mandated by the Education for All Handicapped Children's Act, or Public Law 94–142. Parent involvement requirements included in P.L. 94–142 are listed in Figure 11–1.

Strong home-school relationships support student development and learning (Hansen, Himes, and Meier, 1990; Reynolds and Birch, 1988). Extensive research about the effects of parent involvement demonstrates that involvement with the school by a student's parents enhances the student's chances for success in school (Epstein, 1989) and significantly improves student achievement (Henderson, 1987; Rich, 1987; Kroth and Scholl, 1978). Students improve in terms of both academic behavior and social behavior, with higher attendance rates and lower suspension rates. They have higher test scores, more positive attitudes toward school, and higher completion rates for homework (Christenson and Cleary, 1990).

Children are not the only beneficiaries of parent involvement. Parents benefit from improved feelings of self-worth and self-satisfaction and increased incentive to enhance the educational environment of the home (Murphy, 1981). They have the opportunity to learn skills that help with their child's needs, such as behavior management techniques and communication

1. Parents are to participate in the development, approval, and evaluation of the Individualized Education Program (IEP).
2. All notifications to parents must be sent in the parents' language.
3. Parents are to participate in assessments of child progress, to contribute to placement decisions, and to participate in program evaluation.
4. Parents have the right to look at their children's records, and those records are to be confidential.
5. Parents are allowed "due process" to resolve disagreements with the school system.
6. Parent counseling and training qualify as related educational services.

In addition:

7. P.L. 99–457 involves parents of children aged three through five, in a written individualized Family Service Plan developed jointly with parents.

**FIGURE 11–1 Parental Rights Established By P.L. 94–142**

(modified from Abeson and Weintraub, 1977 and Shea and Bauer, 1991.)

strategies. As parents work with teachers, they find ways of altering their own behaviors, if necessary (Murphy, 1981). They perceive teachers as allies and a readily available source of help (Shea and Bauer, 1985).

Teachers also benefit from parent involvement by learning more about their students' backgrounds. They receive support from parents who are valuable sources of information about their children's interests and needs.

School systems benefit from home-school collaboration through improved parental attitudes toward schools and advocacy for school programs. A positive home-school relationship helps others in the schools and the community. Parent involvement increases positive communication among all who are involved on the education team. It augments opportunity for school program success (Shea and Bauer, 1985) and enhances school and community accountability for serving special needs (Turnbull, Turnbull, and Wheat, 1982). These points all provide strong evidence that "reaching the family is as important as reaching the child" (Rich, 1987, p. 64).

## Moving Beyond Parent Involvement to Parent Collaboration

It is possible for parents to be involved in educational activities without being collaborative. Although the two terms—*collaboration* and *parent involvement*—have been used interchangeably in the literature, collaboration goes beyond involvement. Educators too often regard parent involvement as giving parents information, conducting parenting classes, and developing parent advocacy committees. However, this kind of involvement does not assure that parent needs and interests are being heard and understood. It does not signify that educators are setting program goals based on parent concerns and input. It might involve parents in a narrow sense, but not in *working together* to form a home-school partnership.

It is important to distinguish between parent involvement and parent collaboration in this way:

- Parent involvement is parent participation in activities that are part of their children's education—for example, conferences, meetings, newsletters, tutoring, and volunteer services.
- Collaboration is the development and maintenance of positive, respectful, egalitarian relationships. It includes mutual problem solving and shared decision-making.

Consultation and collaboration with parents add a dimension to school personnel involvement with parents, for not only should parents be involved with schools for their child's education; educators must be involved with parents. Metaphorically speaking, a one-way street becomes a two-way boulevard to provide an easier road to "Success City" for students.

James Comer (1989), at the Yale Child Study Center, reports a decline in school failure after parents and community members from diverse areas of expertise contribute in the schools, and after parents and school personnel collaborate. Comer also documents improvement in educational achievement of parents as well as their children (Morsink, Thomas, and Correa, 1991). Parent involvement *can* create possibilities for collaboration and development of relationships essential to student achievement (Christenson and Cleary, 1990).

## Barriers to Collaboration with Parents

The success of parent involvement activities is based on partnerships developed and maintained by using the relationship and communication skills described in Chapter 6. However, other barriers overshadow the need for effective communication. They surface as formidable challenges to educators even before lines of communication with parents are established. Such barriers can be classified as perceptual, attitudinal, or historical. Examples are time limitations, anticipation of negative or punishing interactions, denial of problems, blaming, or a personal sense of failure in parenting and teaching (Swap, 1987).

Parents of children with learning and behavior problems can be effective change agents for their children; therefore, the question is not whether or not to involve these parents, but how to do it (Shea and Bauer, 1985). Although parents may want very much to play a key role in encouraging their children to succeed in school, they may be inhibited by their own attitudes or circumstances. Many parents, while very concerned about their child's education, are fearful and suspicious of schools, teachers, and education in general (Hansen, Himes, and Meier (1990). They may fear or mistrust school personnel because of their own negative experiences as students. Or they may have experienced an unfortunate history of unpleasant experiences with other professionals, with current school personnel falling heir to that history.

Parents of children with special needs face many economic and personal hardships. Work schedules and health concerns prevent some parents from participating in school activities (Leitch and Tangri, 1988). Low-income parents may have difficulty with transportation and child care, making it difficult to attend meetings or volunteer in school, even when they would like to do so.

The single parent, already burdened with great responsibilities, is particularly stressed in parenting a child with special needs. The role can be overwhelming at times. When working with the single parent, school personnel will need to tailor their requests for conferences and home interventions and to provide additional emotional support when needed (Conoley, 1989).

Many types of disability are very expensive for families, and the impact on the family budget created by the special needs of a child may produce new and formidable hardships. Sometimes parents arrive at a point where they feel their other children are being neglected by all the attention to the special needs child. This adds to their frustration and stress. In addition, children with special needs and their parents are vulnerable to stereotypes about physical, learning, or behavioral disabilities. They feel the impact of their family's dependence on others for services (Schulz, 1987). The ways in which parents cope with the frustrations and stress influence their interaction with school personnel.

Parents may avoid school interactions because they fear being blamed as the cause of their children's problems. Sometimes teachers do blame parents for exacerbating learning and behavior problems—"I can't do anything here at school because it gets undone when they go home!" But blaming does not facilitate development of mutually supportive relationships. Parents are very sensitive to blaming words and attitudes by school personnel.

Judging attitudes, stereotypes, false expectations, and basic differences in values also act as barriers to diminish the collaborative efforts among teachers and parents. It is difficult to feel comfortable with people who have very different attitudes and values. Parents and teachers should make every effort not to reproach each other, but work together as partners on the child's team. Educators, including teachers and parents, must abandon any posture of blaming or criticism, and move on to collaboration and problem-solving. It is important to remember that it does not matter where a "fault" lies. What matters is who steps up to address the problem.

Collaboration requires respect, trust, and cooperation. However, as discussed in Chapter 4 on individual differences and Chapter 6 on rapport-building, collaboration need not require total agreement. Educators cope with value differences in positive ways when they:

1. Remember that a teacher's place is on the parent's side as a team member working for a common goal—the child's success.
2. Become aware of their own feelings of defensiveness. Taking a deep breath and putting the feelings aside will help them continue building positive relationships. If that is not possible, they should postpone interactions until the defensiveness can be handled.
3. Remember that the focus must be on the needs and interests of parents and their children, not on their values. It is important to attack the problem, not the person.
4. Accept people as they are and stop wishing they were different. This applies to parents as well as to their children.
5. Remember that most parents are doing the best they can. Parents do not wake up in the morning and decide, "I think today I will be a poor parent."
6. Respect parents' rights to have their own values and opinions. Different values do not mean better or poorer values. It is not possible to argue parents out of their values, and teachers do not have the right to do so.

## Developing Home-School Partnerships

The crucial issues in successful learning are not between home *or* school, and parent *or* teacher, but in the relationship between each pair of variables (Seeley, 1985). When school personnel collaborate with parents, they nurture and maintain partnerships that facilitate shared efforts to promote student achievement. The more parents become partners with teachers and related services personnel, the smoother and more consistent the delivery of instruction to the student can be (Reynolds and Birch, 1988). As parents and teachers plan together and implement plans of action, they find that working as a team is more effective than working alone (Shea and Bauer, 1985). Each can be reassured that the other is doing the best for the child (Stewart, 1978).

### *Five Steps for Collaborating with Parents*

Five basic steps will assist school personnel in developing successful home-school partnerships:

> Step 1: Examining Your Own Values
> Step 2: Building Collaborative Relationships
> Step 3: Initiating Home-School Interactions
> Step 4: Individualizing for Parents
> Step 5: Evaluating Parent-School Collaboration

*Step 1: Examining Your Own Values*  Value systems are individualistic and complex. They are the result of nature and the impact of experiences on nature. People need to apply information and logic to situations that present values different from their own. Kroth (1985) provides an example. He notes that a significant amount of research indicates a positive effect on children's academic and social growth when teachers use a daily or weekly report card system to communicate with parents or guardians. This information provides logical support for interaction among teachers and parents on a regular, planned basis. However, in spite of the evidence, many teachers do not use the system.

School personnel must guard against setting up a climate of unequal relationships. It is vital to recognize parents as the experts when it comes to knowing about their children, no matter how many tests educators have administered to students, or how many hours they have observed students in the classroom. If professional educators are perceived as *the* experts, and the *only* experts, false expectations may create unrealistic pressure on them. Some parents find it difficult to relate to experts. So a beautiful boulevard of progress becomes a one-way street of judging, advising, and sending solutions (refer to communication roadblocks in Chapter 6).

The first step in collaborating with parents is to examine your own values. Figure 11–2 is a checklist for examining values and attitudes toward parents.

A parent of a student with special learning needs spoke with candor and insight to a teacher about school and her child:

> *When you don't have an education and you're poor, it's easy for those school people to look at you and not ever see you. It's like a wall or an invisible shield or something. People talk nice and you know they're nice, and you know they care about your kids, even though the kids have some problems. But sometimes they talk like they know more than I know about my own kids, and when they talk I hardly know it's my kids they're speaking about. I want to say, 'Hey, wait a minute. Who are we talking about?' They don't listen to me, though. I can't use their education words, and I can't always say things I want to say. So, you know, I quit going to those meetings. It didn't really do any good. I feel bad about some of the things my kids do. I decided I didn't want to just sit listening to those people talk about my kids and not listen to me.*

Communicating messages of equality, flexibility, and a sharing attitude will facilitate effective home-school collaboration. The message that should be given to parents of students with special needs is, "I know a lot about this, and *you* know a lot about that. Let's put our information and ideas together to help the child."

The checklist in Figure 11–3 serves as a brief self-assessment to test congruency of attitudes and perceptions with the two-way parent involvement discussed earlier. Inventorying and adjusting your own attitudes and perceptions about parents are the hardest parts of consulting with them. Attitudes and perceptions about parents and their roles in partnerships greatly influence implementation of the consulting process. School personnel also must keep in mind that parents are not a homogeneous group; therefore,

*Instructions*: Rate belief or comfort level, from 1 (very comfortable or very strong) to 5 (very uncomfortable or not strong at all).

*How comfortable do you feel with each?*

_____ Parents who are over protective
_____ Teachers who think they are never wrong
_____ Parents who send their children to school without breakfast
_____ Teachers who get emotional at conferences
_____ Teachers who do not want mainstreamed students
_____ Open discussions as parent meetings
_____ Parents who have lost control of their children
_____ Volunteers in the classroom
_____ Conflict
_____ Being invited to your students' homes
_____ Using grades as a behavior management tool
_____ Parents who call every day
_____ Teachers who do not follow through
_____ Students attending conferences
_____ Principals attending conferences
_____ Parents who do not allow their children to be tested
_____ Different racial or ethnic groups
_____ Parents who do not speak English
_____ Others who think special needs children should be kept in self-contained classrooms
_____ Teachers who think modifying curriculum materials or tests is watering down the lessons
_____ Parents who drink excessively
_____ Administrators who do not know your name
_____ Criticism

*How strongly do you believe the following?*

_____ Parents should be able to call you at home.
_____ Newsletters are an important communication tool.
_____ Parents should volunteer in the classroom.
_____ General classroom teachers can teach students with special needs.
_____ All children can learn.
_____ Parents should come to conferences.
_____ Resistance is normal and to be expected in educational settings.
_____ Children in divorced families have special problems.

*(Continued)*

**FIGURE 11–2 Examining Own Values**

_____ Parent resistance is often justified.

_____ Teacher resistance is often justified.

_____ Family influence is more important than school influence.

_____ Medical treatment should never be withheld from children.

_____ Children with severe disabilities are part of a Supreme Being's plan.

_____ Sometimes consultants should just tell others the best thing to do.

_____ Consultants are advocates for children.

_____ Teachers should modify their classrooms for children with special needs.

_____ It is a teacher's fault when children fail.

_____ Consultants are experts in educating special needs children.

_____ Some people do not want children with special needs to succeed.

Do you think all teachers, administrators, counselors, psychologists, parents, grandparents, social workers, and students would have responded as you did? What happens when members of the same educator team have different views?

**FIGURE 11–2** *(Continued)*

experiences with one parent or family cannot be generalized to all other parents and families. There is evidence that mothers and fathers react differently to their exceptional children (Levy-Shiff, 1986). Furthermore, parental stress seems to be related to the child's developmental age and parental coping strengths (Wikler, Wasow, and Hatfield, 1981).

*Step 2: Building Collaborative Relationships* The second step in collaborating with parents is building collaborative relationships. As emphasized in Chapter 6, basic communication and rapport-building skills are essential for establishing healthy, successful relationships with parents. To briefly review, these are the most important skills for educators in interacting with parents:

- responsive listening;
- assertive responding; and
- mutual problem solving.

Prudent teachers avoid words and phrases that may give undesirable impressions of the children or the special needs with which they are concerned (Shea and Bauer, 1985). They listen for the messages given by parents and respond to their verbal and nonverbal cues, as discussed in Chapter 6.

In communicating with parents, school personnel must avoid jargon that can be misunderstood or misinterpreted. Some professional educators seem unable, or unwilling, to use jargon-free language (Schuck, 1979).

Choices of words can ease or inhibit communication with parents, and professional educators must respect language variations created by differences in culture, education, occupation, age, and place of origin (Morsink, Thomas, and Correa, 1991).

|  | No | 1 | 2 | 3 | 4 | 5 | Yes |
|---|---|---|---|---|---|---|---|

1. I understand the importance of parent involvement.

2. I recognize the concerns parents may have about working with me.

3. I recognize that parents of students with special needs may have emotional and social needs I may not understand.

4. I recognize and respect parents' expertise.

5. I feel comfortable working with parents whose values and attitudes differ from mine.

6. I am persistent and patient as I develop relationships with parents.

7. I am comfortable with my skills for communicating with parents.

8. I am realistic about the barriers for me in working with parents.

9. I find it difficult to understand why some parents have the attitudes they have.

10. I recognize that some parents will have problems interacting with me because of their experience with other teachers.

**FIGURE 11–3 Self-Assessment Of Attitudes And Perceptions Concerning Parents And Parent Involvement**

Teachers and administrators often find one of the most important but difficult aspects of developing relationships with parents is listening to them. The challenge lies in listening to parents' messages even though they might disagree strongly with the parents, and their attitudes and values might differ significantly from those of the parents. Although the quality of the interaction should be a primary focus in parent relationships, the number and variety of initiated communications are important as well. Hughes and Ruhl (1987) found that most teachers averaged fewer than five parent contacts per week, but 27 percent averaged from eleven to twenty parent contacts per week. Phone calls, introductory and welcoming letters, newsletters, parent-to-parent calendars, and notepads with identifying logos all have been used effectively by educators to initiate partnerships. Each note, phone call, conversation, or conference, whether taking place in a formal setting or on the spur of the moment at the grocery store, should reflect willingness and commitment of school personnel to work with parents as they face immense responsibilities in providing for the special needs of their child.

An effective partner-educator provides support and reinforcement for parents in their parent roles. In addition to listening to parents and recognizing their expertise, it is crucial to support parents by giving them positive feedback about their efforts toward the child's education. Many parents spend more time with their children who have disabilities than with those who do not (Cantwell, Baker, and Rutter, 1979). Parents often get very little reinforcement for parenting, particularly for the extra efforts they may expend in caring for children with special needs.

Too many parents hear very few positive comments about their children. They may feel guilty or confused because of their children's problems. Examples of support and reinforcement that teachers use include thank-you notes for helping with field trips, VIP (Very Important Parent) buttons given to classroom volunteers, supporting phone calls when homework has been turned in, and Happygrams when a class project is completed. It is important for teachers to arrange and encourage more regular, informal contacts with parents. Parents often report being put off by the formality inherent in some scheduled conferences, particularly when they are limited to ten minutes, as they often are, with another child's parents waiting just outside (Lindle, 1989).

One innovative program is the Trans*Parent* Model (Baush, 1989), in which teachers use a computer-based system called Compu-Call that stores messages in a computer. It directs the autodialer to place calls either to all parents or to specific groups of parents. The purpose of these calls can be to describe learning activities, explain homework assignments, or suggest ways

---

**Guidelines for Communicating with Parents**

When communicating with parents, try using these suggestions by parents and teachers for guidelines:

- Be aware of your voice tone and your body language.
- Be specific.
- Give your point of view as information, not *law*.
- Be honest and direct about what you expect.
- Don't monopolize the conversation.
- Show respect for the other's dignity.
- Don't assume your message is clear.
- Focus on positive or informational aspects of the problem.
- Attack the problem, not the person.
- Stay away from educational or psychological jargon.
- Try to have five positive contacts for every negative contact.
- Always be honest. Don't "softpedal" reality.

that parents can support the child's home study. Parents call any time from anywhere and get the information they need. The system enables parents of children who are having problems or have an extended absence from school to help them keep up.

Parents often become frustrated when they do not understand the subjects their children are attempting to master. A program of Family Math encourages parents and children to work together as a team in evening sessions involving a hands-on approach to learning math concepts and logical thinking (Lueder, 1989). Family literacy programs that are established in some communities enable parents to help children with their schoolwork (Nuckolls, 1991). Some schools have set up an evening computer literacy program in which parents and students can learn together and reinforce each other as they gain skills in educational technology.

Parents are not the only ones who put energy and time into such programs. The programs require a level of school personnel involvement that challenges the staff and pushes them to the limit. But the positive ripple effect of having parents play more active roles in their child's education makes the effort worthwhile.

Teachers use interviews, checklists, and more complex assessment instruments to solicit information about parent needs. Planning workshops, booklets, and classes without first assessing parent interest in such activities communicates a message that educators know more about their needs than they do, and parent involvement is not a true partnership. An example of a needs and interests assessment is included in Figure 11–4. Schoor (1988) notes that in a study of twenty-five successful interventions programs, all are facilitated by professionals who respond to the needs of those they serve, rather than to the perceptions and demands of professional educators and bureaucrats.

*Step 3: Initiating Home-School Interactions*  Parents, regardless of their educational background and socio-economic status, want their children to be successful in school (Epstein, 1987). Even parents who are considered "hard to reach," such as nontraditional, low-income, and low status families, usually want to be more involved (Davies, 1988). Most parents, however, wait to be invited before becoming involved as a partner in their children's education. Unfortunately, many parents have to wait for years before someone opens the door and provides them the *opportunity* to become a team member with others who care about the educational and social successes of their children.

Parent satisfaction with their involvement is directly related to perceived opportunities for involvement (Salisbury and Evans, 1988). They are more motivated to carry on when they are aware that the results of their time and energy are helping their child learn. School personnel who are in a position to observe these results can provide the kind of reinforcement that parents need so much.

Parents! We want to learn more about you so we can work together helping your child learn. Please take a few minutes to respond to these questions so your voice can be heard. It will help the Home-School Advisory Team develop programs for parents, teachers, and children.

*Check those items you are most interested in.*

1.  Family resource libraries or information centers
2.  Helping my child learn
3.  Support programs for my child's siblings
4.  Talking with my child about sex
5.  Helping with language and social skills
6.  Mental health services
7.  Talking with another parent about common problems
8.  Respite care or babysitters
9.  Parent education—my role as a parent
10.  Parent education—managing behavior problems
11.  Making my child happy
12.  Managing my time and resources
13.  Making toys and educational materials
14.  Reducing time spent watching television
15.  What happens when my child grows up
16.  Recreation and camps for my child
17.  Statewide parent meetings
18.  Vocational opportunities for my child
19.  Talking to my child's teacher
20.  Talking with other families
21.  Learning about child development
22.  Things parents can do to support teachers
23.  Home activities that support school learning
24.  Information about the school and my child's classes
25.  Helping my child become more independent
26.  Others _____

_____

_____

Thanks for your help!

Name of Parent or Guardian Responding to This Form:

_____

Child's Name: _____

**FIGURE 11–4  Parent Needs Assessment**

**Student Collaboration.** The child has the greatest investment and the most important involvement in a planning conference (Hogan, 1975). It seems counterproductive to engage in plan sessions for the child's development without involving him or her as a member of the team. Shea and Bauer (1985) stress several benefits from having students participate in conferences for their individualized programs:

- Awareness that parents and teachers are interested in them and working cooperatively;
- Information about teacher and parent evaluation of their progress;
- Feeling of involvement in the efforts toward personal achievement; and
- A task-oriented view of improving their performance.

Shea and Bauer recommend discussing advantages of the child's participation with parents and encouraging their support, but not including the child if there are strenuous parental objections.

**Kroth Mirror Model.** The Kroth Mirror Model (Kroth, 1985) of parent involvement reminds educators that it is important to recognize the strengths parents have to contribute as well as their needs in parenting exceptional children. One side of the Mirror Model represents parent "wants" and school "strengths". There are four levels of parent wants/school strengths: What all parents need (such as information about their children's right to a free, appropriate public education); what most parents need (such as information about school functions); what some parents need (such as parent training); and what few parents need (such as intensive therapy). These wants and needs of parents are met by the skills and strengths of the school. Care must be taken not to stereotype parents by assuming that all will need more information about community resources, parenting classes, or life-planning workshops. By asking parents about their needs and interests, educators can plan activities and programs that will be helpful to them, and can communicate to parents that their needs and interests are important to the school.

The complementary side of the model reflects the same four levels concerning what the school wants and needs from parents and parental strengths at meeting those needs. For example, all teachers need information about family medical history from parents. The next level represents what most schools need and parents could provide in the home-school partnership, such as support of educational programs. The third level, what some educators need from parents and what some parents have the strengths and skills to provide, is exemplified by volunteers for the classroom. The fourth level is what few parents have skills to provide and what is required of only a few parents, such as leading parent support groups.

Kroth's Mirror Model stresses the importance of providing opportunities for parents to use their strengths and utilize their commitment and skills to contribute as full partners to the education of their children. Parent involvement is not based on a deficit model of blame and inequality. Parents appreciate having their special efforts recognized, just as teachers do.

Tools for assessing parent strengths are similar to those used for assessing needs. Interviews and checklists are useful in determining what types of contributions parents can bring to the partnership. Again, these assets can be conceptualized along four levels of involvement, from strengths all parents have to skills only a few parents are willing and able to contribute. For example, all parents have information about their children that schools need. At more intensive levels of involvement, some parents are willing and able to tutor their children at home, come to meetings, help make bulletin boards, and volunteer to help at school. At highest levels of involvement, only a few parents can be expected to lobby for special education, serve on advisory boards, or conduct parent-to-parent programs.

A number of parent advocates of children with learning and behavioral disorders have made impressive gains in recent decades toward state and national focus on the rights of children with special needs. They have formed organizations, identified needs, encouraged legislation, spoken for improved facilities, and supported each other through crises. In many instances they have involved pediatricians, community agency leaders, and businesses in special projects for children with special needs.

Sometimes school personnel can involve parents without being collaborative. By considering parent strengths as well as needs and interests, educators will be focusing on the collaborative nature of parent involvement. An example of a strengths assessment form is provided in Figure 11–5.

As stated earlier, involvement is not synonymous with collaboration. Developing a workshop on discipline or a parent volunteer program without consulting with parents to assess strengths, needs, and goals demonstrates a failure to respect the partnership between school and home. A true partnership will feature mutual collaboration and show respect for the expertise of both parties in the partnership. Activities for involvement include:

- parent conferences, reflecting parent needs and school strengths;
- parent tutoring, reflecting parent strengths and school needs; and
- parent advocacy groups, reflecting parent strengths and school needs.

**Parent Involvement in IEP Development.** The Individual Education Plan conference can be a productive time or a frustrating experience. Parents may be emotional about their child's problems, and teachers apprehensive about meeting with the parents (Reynolds and Birch, 1988). A number of researchers have found that minimal parent involvement in team decisionmaking, particularly relating to IEP development and ITP (Individual Transition Planning), is a major problem in special education programs (Pfeiffer, 1980; Boone, 1989).

Parents! We need your help. Many of you have asked how you can help provide a high-quality educational program for your children. You have many talents, interests, and skills you can contribute to help children learn better and enjoy school more. Please let us know what you are interested in doing.

1. I would like to volunteer in school.
2. I would like to help with special events or projects.
3. I have a hobby or talent I could share with the class.
4. I would be glad to talk about travel or jobs, or interesting experiences I have had.
5. I could teach the class how to _____ .
6. I could help with bulletin boards and art projects.
7. I could read to children.
8. I would like to help my child at home.
9. I would like to tutor a child.
10. I would like to work on a buddy or parent-to-parent system with other parents whose children have problems.
11. I would like to teach a workshop.
12. I can do typing, word-processing, phoning, making materials, or preparing resources at home.
13. I would like to assist with student clubs.
14. I would like to help organize a parent group.
15. I want to help organize and plan parent partnership programs.
16. I would like to help with these kinds of activities:

    at school _____

    at home. _____

    in the community. _____

17. I am:

    _____ a mom parent, or guardian.

    _____ a dad parent, or guardian.

    _____ a grandmother

    _____ a grandfather

    _____ other _____ .

Your comments, concerns, and questions are welcomed. THANKS!

Name:_____

Child's Name:_____

Home Phone: _____ Work Phone:_____

**FIGURE 11–5 Parent Strengths Assessment**

School consultants will improve parent involvement in these areas if they provide parents with information and preparation for the meeting. They can communicate with parents by phone, letter, or informal interview to inform them about:

- names and roles of staff members who will attend;
- typical procedure for such meetings;
- ways they can prepare for the meeting;
- contributions they are encouraged to make; and
- ways in which follow-up to the meeting will be provided.

Figure 11–6 outlines ways parents can be involved in IEP development and implementation before, during, and after the IEP conference.

*Step 4: Individualizing for Parents* Special education professionals are trained to be competent at individualizing educational programs for students needs. Nevertheless, they may assume that all parents have the same strengths and needs, thereby overlooking the need to individualize parent involvement programs (Schulz, 1987; Turnbull and Turnbull, 1985). By using the assessments discussed earlier and taking care to avoid stereotypes and judgments, they will be more able to involve parents in individualizing their child's learning program.

Christenson and Cleary (1990) confirm that successful home-school consultation includes mutual problem identification, mutual monitoring of effects of involvement, and active sharing of relevant information. Successful work with parents calls for establishing respectful and trusting relationships, as well as responding to needs of all partners. The degree to which parents are placed in an egalitarian role, with a sense of choice, empowerment, and ownership in the education process, is a crucial variable in successful collaboration (Cochran, 1987; Peterson and Cooper, 1989).

When school consultants and collaborators solicit information from parents, they should use the communication skills discussed in Chapter 6. Interviews must not seem like interrogations. The types of questions consultants ask are important in preserving respectful relationships. Inappropriate types of questions would be yes-or-no questions, "why" questions, forced-choice questions, double-binds that result in no-win responses, and questions that solicit agreement with the educator.

On the other hand, questions that are appropriate for parent interviews explore feelings and focus on the what, when, where, and how dimensions of child learning and behavior. Only questions that provide essential information and nurture the collaborative spirit should be asked. Figure 11–7 demonstrates inappropriate questions that have been restated in a more appropriate manner.

*Throughout the year,* parents will want to:

Read about local, state, and national educational issues and concerns.

Learn about the structure of the local school system.

Observe their child, noting in particular the child's work habits, play patterns, and social interactions.

Record information regarding special interests, talents, and accomplishments, as well as areas of concern.

*Before the IEP conference,* parents should:

Visit the child's school.

Discuss school life with the child.

Talk with other parents who have participated in conferences to find out what goes on during the conference.

Write down questions and points they would like to address.

Review notes from any previous conferences or other meetings with school staff.

Prepare a summary file of information, observations, and products that would further explain the child's needs.

Arrange to take along any other persons they feel would be helpful in planning the child's educational program.

*During the IEP conference,* parents should:

Be an active participant.

Ask questions about anything that is unclear.

Insist that educational jargon and "alphabet soup" acronyms not be used.

Contribute information, ideas, and recommendations.

Let the school personnel know about the positive things school has provided for the child.

Ask for a copy of the IEP or other plan made, if it is not offered.

Ask to have a follow-up contact time to compare notes about the child's progress.

*After the IEP conference,* parents will want to:

Discuss the conference proceedings with the child.

Continue to monitor the child's progress and follow up as agreed on.

Continue to reinforce school staff for positive effects of the planned program.

Keep adding to the notebook of information, observations, and products.

Serve as an active participant in efforts to improve schools.

Say supportive things about the schools whenever possible.

**FIGURE 11–6 Parent Partnership In Developing IEPS**

**Parents From Culturally Diverse Populations.** At times the consultant's communication and collaboration skills are challenged by ethnic and cultural differences between teachers and parents. It is important that parents from diverse populations become involved with school decisions and evaluation (Williams and Chavkin, 1987). Language and cultural differences can be barriers that must be overcome by understanding the knowledge and skills needed to provide "culturally competent services" (Cross, 1988). Cross (1988) lists five keys to services that school personnel should use when interacting and consulting with parents from culturally diverse groups:

1. Acknowledge cultural differences and become aware of how they affect parent-teacher interactions.
2. Examine your own personal culture, such as how you define family, desirable life goals, and behavior problems.
3. Recognize the dynamics of group interactions such as etiquette and patterns of communication.
4. Explore the significance of the child's behavior in relationship to his or her culture.
5. Adjust collaboration to legitimize and include culturally specific activities.

| *Appropriate* | *Inappropriate* |
| --- | --- |
| I'd like to hear your thoughts on Ramona's progress. | I think Ramona is doing much better, don't you? |
| What problems do you have with Jim's teacher? | Why don't you like Jim's teacher? |
| What thoughts have you had about you and Kay talking with a counselor? | When are you and Kay going to see a counselor? |
| What are some strategies we can work on to make sure Sherry gets to her first hour class? | Don't you think you should curtail Sherry's late nights on weekdays? |
| What is the history of Lionel's hearing problems? | Didn't you take Lionel to the doctor about his persistent earaches? |
| What kinds of concerns do you have? | Do you have any questions? |
| What are the behaviors that you worry about? What does the scene look like when it happens? | What do you mean, he is always in trouble? |

FIGURE 11–7 Appropriate/Inappropriate Questions To Ask Parents

Well-publicized policies at the district level encouraging home-school collaboration are vital in providing opportunities for minority parents to become full partners with teachers, but effective structures and strategies often do not exist (Chavkin, 1989; Lynch and Stein, 1987). Lightfoot (1981) suggests that traditional methods of parent involvement such as PTA meetings, open house, or newsletters permit little or no true collaboration, constructing instead a "territory" of education that minority parents are hesitant to invade. Concern, awareness, and commitment on the part of individuals in the educational system are a beginning in challenging the limitations that inhibit collaboration between teachers and parents who have language, cultural, or other basic differences.

*Step 5: Evaluating Parent-School Collaboration* Evaluation of efforts to provide opportunities for parent involvement in schools can indicate whether or not parents' needs are being met and parent strengths are being utilized. Evaluation also shows whether or not needs and strengths of educational personnel are being met. Assessment tools used after a workshop or conference, or at the conclusion of the school year, allow school personnel to ask parents, "How did we do in facilitating your learning of the new information or accessing the new services?" Some teachers use a quick questionnaire, to be completed anonymously, to see if the activity or program fulfilled the goals of the parent involvement. If the data show that the activity gave parents the information they needed, provided them with the resources they wanted, and offered them the opportunities they requested, educators know whether or not to continue with the program, offer the activity again, or modify the plans.

Educators also should evaluate their own involvement with parents. This means assessing the use of parent strengths and skills to facilitate educational programs with children who have special needs. Did teachers get the information they needed from parents? How many volunteer hours did parents contribute? What were the effects of parent tutoring on the achievement of the resource room students? What changes in parent attitudes about the school district were measured? Chapter 8 contains information about procedures for evaluating collaboration efforts. Note again the purpose of parent collaboration is to utilize the unique and vital partnership on behalf of their children.

Teacher belief in the importance of parent involvement (Epstein and Becker, 1982) and teacher ability to communicate effectively with parents (Hulsebusch, 1989) are key variables in the success of the partnership. Translating commitment for this partnership into action is essential for ensuring student success. Epstein (1991) recommends a full-time staff at state, district, and school levels, for cultivating parent involvement. School consultants should consider themselves leaders of a team. As such, they are responsible for involving all the appropriate people in planning and implementation of programs for children with special learning and behavior needs.

## Tips for Consulting and Collaborating

**1.** Establish rapport with parents early in the year. Call right away, before problems develop, so that the first parent contact is a positive one.

**2.** Invite parents to talk about their traditions, experiences, hobbies, or occupations.

**3.** Send "up slips" to parents, as opposed to "down slips," making sure they are a different color from the more negative types of communication that parents sometimes receive. Have a parent conference because the student is *performing well* in the classroom.

**4.** When sharing information with parents, sandwich any necessary comments about problems or deficits between two very positive ones.

**5.** During interaction with parents, notice how your actions are received, and adapt to that.

**6.** When interacting with parents, never assume anything.

**7.** When several staff members will be meeting with parents, make sure each is introduced by role and purpose for being included in the meeting.

**8.** Introduce parents to all support personnel working with the child.

**9.** Some parents shy away from being handed sample work, preferring to have the work laid out on a surface to view without forced attention. Do not continue talking when parents are reading their child's work.

**10.** Send out monthly newsletters to parents, describing the kinds of things the class is doing, and school news or events coming up. Attach articles parents would be interested in. Have a "Parents' Corner" occasionally, for which parents provide comments or ideas.

**11.** Encourage parents to volunteer in the classroom: to read stories, help with art lessons, listen to book reports, or give a lesson on an area of expertise such as their job or a hobby.

**12.** Invite parents to help students find resource materials and reference books on research topics in the library.

**13.** Send follow-up notes to parents after meetings. Put out a pamphlet about parent involvement in IEP planning conferences.

**14.** Provide classroom teachers with handouts that can be useful during parent conferences.

**15.** Have a "Home Book" notebook of pictures, activities, and stories about class that students take turns sharing with parents at home.

**16.** Put a "Parents Board" at the entrance of the building for posting ideas of interest to parents, examples of class activities, and pictures.

**17.** Invite parents and siblings, babysitters, and grandparents to all class parties.

**18.** Write thank-you notes for suggestions parents provide.

**19.** Have parents from other countries or culture groups talk to students about their customs and culture.

**20.** Ask parents what their family goals are, and respond with how those goals are being met by the classroom curriculum.

## Chapter Review

**1.** The variable with the most significant effect on children's development is parent involvement in their child's learning. Although educational professionals come and go in children's lives, and school settings change often for many students, parents are the link of continuity in the lives of most children. They are the decisionmakers for their children, whose futures are largely dependent on the continued ability of their parents to advocate for them.

**2.** Educators must be partners with parents of students with special needs. While this is a demanding and challenging responsibility, educators are committed to such a partnership because it fulfills a legal right of parents. Research confirms the benefits of the partnership for children, parents, and schools. Involvements mean teacher involvement as well as parent involvement. This becomes collaboration and mutually respectful, committed teamwork.

**3.** Educators and parents face barriers to home-school involvement, including differing attitudes, history, values, culture, and language. Examining their own culture and values as potential barriers to understanding will enable them to address diversity they encounter during collaboration.

**4.** Educators must clarify their own values in order to respect the values of others. Checklists, structured value clarification activities, or thoughtful consideration helps educators identify their specific values about education, school, and parent involvement.

**5.** Using rapport-building and communication skills such as responsive listening, assertive responding, and mutual problem solving will convey respect for parents and willingness to collaborate with them. Patience and quiet, calm persistence are needed.

**6.** Educators should provide a variety of opportunities for parents to become involved with the school. These opportunities should be based on parent strengths, expertise, and needs. Parent strengths represent contributions that parents can make to the partnership. The needs of parents are those interests and needs they have concerning their children.

**7.** Educators must assess both needs and strengths, then work cooperatively with parents to utilize their strengths and fulfill their needs. In this manner, programs can be individualized for parents and educators.

**8.** Parent-school collaboration can be evaluated using informal or formal assessment methods to determine the effects of the program on children's learning and behavior, as well as on the attitudes and behavior of parents and school personnel.

# Activities

1. Brainstorm to identify parent characteristics that would be encouraging to a consultant or teacher who has students with learning and behavioral disorders. Then develop plans for interaction and involvement with parents that would cultivate those characteristics.

2. Identify roadblocks in these three interactions. Then suggest what could and should have been said differently by the teacher in Scene A, by the parent in Scene B, and by the consultant in Scene C.

**Scene A.**
*PARENT*: What's this about suspending my child from your class for three days? I thought you people were supposed to be teaching kids instead of letting them sit and waste time in the principal's office.

*TEACHER*: You're being unreasonable. You don't understand our rules and neither does your child. Your child needs to learn some manners and plain, old-fashioned respect!

**Scene B.**
*TEACHER*: I'm calling to tell you that your son caused a disturbance again in my class. I would like you to meet with me and his counselor.

*PARENT*: He's always been an active kid. Can't you people learn to handle active, curious children without always dragging us parents into it?

**Scene C.**
*PARENT*: How can I get Bobby to settle down and do his homework without a battle every night? It's driving us crazy.

*CONSULTANT*: I'm glad you're concerned, but I think he will be O.K. if you just keep on him. Don't worry, he's a bright kid and he'll snap out of this phase soon. Just be glad your other three aren't dreamers like he is.

3. Plan a booklet that could be used by consultants to improve parent-teacher communication and collaboration. Report on what will be included, how it can be used, and how it will be helpful.

4. Reflect on the often-told story about three bricklayers being interviewed by a reporter to find out what they were doing. The first retorted, "I'm laying bricks, so don't bother me." The second elaborated a bit, "I'm making a wall, that's what." But the third, with purpose gleaming in his eyes, responded, "Why, we're building a cathedral." In what ways can educators build functional but beautiful relationships with parents, and not just go through the required motions?

# For Further Reading

*Educational Leadership*, *47*(2). Several articles on parent involvement and parent partnerships.

Kroth, R. (1975). *Communicating with Parents of Exceptional Children.* Denver: Love.

Stewart, J. (1978). *Counseling Parents of Exceptional Children.* Columbus, OH: Merrill.

Sue. D. W., and Sue, D. (1990). *Counseling the Culturally Different: Theory and Practice* (2d ed.). New York: Wiley.

Turnbull, H.R., III and Turnbull, A.P., (1985). *Parents Speak Out., Then and Now* (2d ed.). Columbus, OH: Merrill. Stories written by parents of children with disabilities, with follow-up comments several years later.

# References

Abeson, A., and Weintraub, F. (1977). Understanding the individualized education program. In S. Torres (Ed.), *A Primer on Individualized Education Programs for Handicapped Children.* Reston, VA: Council for Exceptional Children.

Baush, J. P. (1989). The transParent school model: New technology for parent involvement." *Educational Leadership, 47*(2): 32-35.

Bevevino, M. (1988). The 87 percent factor. *Delta Kappa Gamma Bulletin, 54*(3); 9–16.

Boone, H. A. (1989). Preparing family specialists in early childhood special education. *Teacher Education and Special Education, 12*(3):96–102.

Cantwell, D. P., Baker, L., and Rutter, M. (1979). Families of autistic and dysphasic children: Family life and interaction patterns. *Archives of General Psychiatry, 36*:682–87.

Chavkin, N. F. (1989). Debunking the myth about minority parents. *Educational Horizons, 67*:119–23.

Christenson, S. L., and Cleary, M. (1990). Consultation and the parent-educator partnership: A perspective. *Journal of Educational and Psychological Consultation, 1*:219–41.

Cochran, M. (1987). The parent empowerment process: Building on family strengths. *Equality and Choice, 4*:9–22.

Comer, J. (1989). Children can: An address on school improvement. In R. Webb and F. Parkay (eds.), *Children Can: An Address on School Improvement by Dr. James Comer with Responses from Florida's Educational Community*, pp. 4–17. Gainesville, FL: University of Florida, College of Education Research and Development Center, in collaboration with the Alachua County Mental Health Association.

Conoley, J. C. (1989). Professional communication and collaboration among educators. In M. C. Reynolds (Ed.), *Knowledge Base for the Beginning Teacher* (pp. 245–253). Oxford, England: Pergamon Press.

Cross, T. (1988). Services to minority populations: What does it mean to be a culturally competent professional? *Focal Point:2*, 1–3.

Davies, D. (1988). Low-income parents and the schools: A research report and plan for action. *Equity and Choice:4*, 51–59.

Davis, W. E. (1989). The regular education initiative debate: Its promises and problems. *Exceptional Children, 55*(5):440–47.

Epstein, J. L. (1987). Parent involvement: What research says to administrators. *Education and Urban Society, 19*:119–36.

Epstein, J. L. (1989). Building parent-teacher partnerships in inner-city schools. *Family Resource Coalition Report, 8*:7.

Epstein, J. L., and Becker, J. H. (1982). Teacher practices of parent involvement. *The Elementary School Journal, 83:* 103–13.

Epstein, J. L. (1991). Paths to partnership: What we can learn from federal, state, district, and school initiatives. *Phi Delta Kappan, 75*(5):344–49.

Hansen, J. C., Himes, B. S., and Meier, S. (1990). *Consultation: Concepts and Practices.* Englewood Cliffs, NJ: Prentice Hall.

Henderson, A. T. (1987). *The evidence continues to grow: Parent Involvement Improves Student Achievement.* Silver Springs, MD: National Citizens Committee in Education.

Hogan, J. R. (1975). The three-way conference: Parent, teacher, child. *The Elementary School Journal, 75*(5):311–15.

Hughes, C. A., and Ruhl, K. L. (1987). The nature and extent of special educators' contacts with students' parents. *Teacher Education and Special Education, 10:*180–184.

Hulsebusch, P. L. (1989). *Significant Others: Teacher Perspectives of Relationships with Parents.* Paper presented at the annual meeting of the American Educational Research Association, San Francisco.

Kroth, R. L. (1985). *Communication With Parents of Exceptional Children: Improving Parent-Teacher Relationships.* Denver: Love.

Kroth, R. L., and Scholl, G. T. (1978). *Getting Schools Involved with Parents.* Arlington, VA: Council for Exceptional Children.

Leitch, M. L., and Tangri, S. S. (1988). Barriers to home-school collaboration. *Educational Horizons, 66:*70–75.

Levy-Shiff, R. (1986). Mother-father-child interactions in families with mentally retarded young child. *American Journal of Mental Deficiency, 91:*141–142.

Lightfoot, S. (1981). Toward conflict and resolution. Relationships between families and schools. *Theory into Practice, 20*(2), 97–104.

Lindle, Jane C. (1989). What do parents want from principals and educators? *Educational Leadership, 47*(2), 12–14.

Lueder, Donald C. (1989). Tennessee parents were invited to participate—and they did. *Educational Leadership, 47*(2), 15–17

Lynch, E. W., and Stein, R. C. (1987). Parent participation by ethnicity: A comparison of Hispanic, black, and Anglo families. *Exceptional Children, 54:*105–11.

Morsink, C. V., Thomas, C. C., and Correa, V. I. (1991). *Interactive Teaming: Consultation and Collaboration in Special Programs.* Columbus, OH: Merrill.

Murphy, A. T. (1981). *Special Children, Special Parents: Personal Issues with Handicapped Childlern.* Englewood Cliffs, NJ: Prentice Hall.

Nuckolls, C. W. (1991). Culture and causal thinking: Diagnosis and prediction in a South Indian fishing village. *Ethos, 19*(1):3–51.

Peterson, N. L., and Cooper, C. S. (1989). Parent education and involvement in early intervention programs for handicapped children: A different perspective on parent needs and parent-professional relationships. In M. J. Fine (ed.), *The Second Handbook on Parent Education,* pp. 197–234. New York: Academic Press.

Pfeiffer, S. (1980). The school-based interprofessional team: Recurring problems and some possible solutions. *Journal of School Psychology, 18*(4), 388–94.

Reynolds, M. C., and Birch, J. W. (1988). *Adaptive Mainstreaming: a Primer for Teachers and Principals* (3d ed.). New York: Longman.

Rich, D. (1987). *School and Families: Issues and Actions.* Washington, D. C.: National Education Association.

Salisbury, G., and Evans, I. M. (1988). Comparison of parental involvement in regular and special education. *Journal of the Association for Persons with Severe Handicaps, 13:*268–72.

Schoor, L. R. (1988). *Within Our Reach: Breaking the Cycle of Disadvantage.* New York: Anchor Books.

Schuck, J. (1979). The parent-professional partnership: Myth or reality? *Education Unlimited, 1*(4):26–28.

Schulz, J. B. (1987). *Parent and Professional in Special Education.* Newton, MA: Allyn and Bacon.

Seeley, D. S. (1985). *Education through Partnership.* Washington, D. C.: American Enterprise Institute for Public Policy Research.

Shea, T. M., and Bauer, A. M. (1985). *Parents and Teachers of Exceptional Students.* Boston: Allyn and Bacon.

Shea, T. M., and Bauer, A. M. (1991). Parents and teachers of children with exceptionalities: A handbook for collaboration. Needham Heights: Allyn and Bacon.

Stewart, J. C. (1978). *Counseling Parents of Exceptional Children.* Columbus, OH: Merrill.

Sue, D. W., and Sue, D. (1990). *Counseling the culturally different: Theory and practice* 2d ed.). New York: Wiley.

Swap, S. M. (1987). *Enhancing Parent Involvement in Schools.* New York: Teachers College Press.

Turnbull, H. R., III, and Turnbull, A. P. (1985). *Parents Speak Out: Then and Now* (2d ed.). Columbus, Oh: Merrill.

Turnbull, H. R., III, Turnbull, A. P., and Wheat, (1992). Assumptions about parental participation: A legislative history. *Exceptional Education Quarterly, 3* (2), 1–8.

Wikler, L., Wasow, M., and Hatfield, E. (1981). Chronic sorrow revisited: Parent vs. professional depiction of the adjustment of parents of mentally retarded children. *American Journal of Orthopsychiatry, 51* :63–70.

Williams, D. L., and Chavkin, N. F. (1987). *Final Report of the Parent Involvement in Education Project.* Washington, D. C.: National Institute of Education.

# 12

# IN-SERVICE AND STAFF DEVELOPMENT FOR ENHANCING CONSULTATION,COLLABORATION, AND TEAMWORK

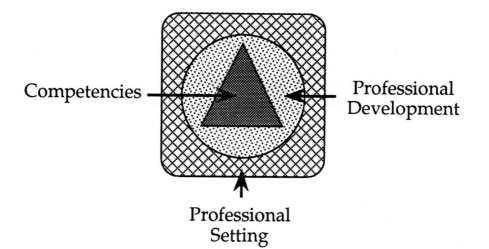

Competencies ———— Professional Development

Professional Setting

## To Think About

Consultants serve as stimuli for change and help develop the context within which change can be launched (Pugach and Johnson, 1990). School reform efforts require close collaboration among educators, parents, and others outside the schools as well. The consultant is a likely catalyst for developing collaborative structure within the school context. However, educational researchers find that the reform literature is silent on the topic of preparing teachers to participate in a collaborative profession (Friend and Cook, 1990).

Preservice students majoring in teacher education do not receive sufficient training and modeling for learning how to collaborate. Nor have many experienced teachers developed the consultation and collaboration skills they must have to adapt to new roles initiated by school reform. School personnel now teaching also need in-service and staff development (ISD) for enhancing their ability to engage productively in collaborative endeavors. Consultation, collaboration, and teamwork can be cultivated through carefully designed and well-conducted in-service and staff development experiences.

## Focusing Questions

1. What are the roles, responsibilities, and opportunities for consultants in providing in-service and staff development?
2. How do in-service and staff development differ?
3. What characteristics of adult learners are important for planning in-service and staff development?
4. How should school personnel needs for consultation, collaboration, and teamwork be assessed?
5. What formats are useful for consultants in implementing in-service and staff development?
6. What techniques facilitate productive in-service and staff development?
7. How should in-service and staff development be evaluated?

## Key Terms

| | |
|---|---|
| follow-through | needs assessment |
| follow-up | needs sensing |
| incentives | simulation |
| in-service | staff development |

---

**Scenario (adapted from Dettmer, 1990)**

Several teachers at a middle school are conversing in the teachers' workroom on Friday afternoon.

*SOCIAL STUDIES TEACHER:* What a week! I feel like I've attended to everything this week but my students and the curriculum. Maybe things will slow down a bit next week.

*MATH TEACHER:* Guess you didn't look at your office memo yet, hmmm? There's a reminder about the staff development sessions next Tuesday and Thursday mornings before school. Something about working with consultants.

*SOCIAL STUDIES TEACHER*: Consultants? You mean people who drive over from the central office to borrow your clock and tell you what time it is? Or imported experts from more than fifty miles away?

*MATH TEACHER*: I believe this group involves our own special education staff. We're supposed to find out about school consultation service and get ready to collaborate with staff who will be consulting teachers.

*ART TEACHER:* Oh, great. How does that involve me? I had my required course in special education. What I really need is a bigger room and more supplies.

*SOCIAL STUDIES TEACHER*: And if we are supposed to collaborate with these people, where will we find the time?

*PHYSICAL EDUCATION TEACHER*: Uh-huh. It will be hard enough just carving out the time to go to the *meeting* about it.

*MATH TEACHER*: Now you know you'll just *love* sitting in that stuffy room trying to act interested when you'd rather be in your classroom getting set for the day.

*SOCIAL STUDIES TEACHER*: Well, let me put it this way. If they don't dismiss by 8:20 sharp, I'm leaving!

## Roles, Responsibilities, and Opportunities for In-service and Staff Development

Educators are caught up in demands for school reform and restructuring efforts that emphasize consultation, collaboration, and teamwork as goals. However, they receive little coaching and preparation for the new roles. Teacher education programs may eventually incorporate consultation training into preservice and degree programs, but it will be too late for those just completing teacher requirements and those already on the job. Teachers now practicing in the field have not been prepared, for the most part, to deliver this kind of service (White and Pryzwansky, 1982).

In more and more schools in-service and staff development (ISD) is being organized on a total school or district basis and tailored for specific groups of personnel who are engaged in institutional change processes (Reynolds and Birch,1988). Consultants and consulting teachers should assume an active role in providing leadership for professional development of all school personnel. Their roles are ideal for orchestrating awareness experiences and training activities in a variety of content and process areas, including skills for collaboration and teamwork.

Unfortunately, attitudes toward in-service and staff development are not generally positive. They range from indifference to resentment to disdain. Criticisms cited by Davis (1985) and others in regard to in-service and staff development are the lack of:

clear purpose,
relevance,
meaningful objectives,
structure and organization,
practicality and long-term applicability,
flexibility and choices,
interest and intrigue,
attention to adult learner characteristics,
and most of all, follow-up activities.

In order to provide the most constructive in-service and staff development experiences possible, planners and presenters need to address several points:

- What are the characteristics of school personnel as adult learners?
- What are the needs of school personnel in serving students with learning and behavior problems?
- What kind of material is most helpful for them?
- How might the material be presented effectively and efficiently?
- How can follow-up and support be provided after the in-service and staff development experiences?

## Differentiating In-service from Staff Development

In-service and staff development are two necessary but distinctly different structures for professional growth. In-service is ordinarily a single event or a series of short sessions on a topic of educational interest or school need. School personnel attend in-services on assertive discipline, critical thinking skills, cooperative learning, drug awareness, student motivation, and a host of other content and process topics. They participate in in-service days as orientation for the new school year, or as refresher sessions during the school term. These one-shot sessions, on a topic of general appeal, are most often provided by an expert on a topic, who might be a state official, university professor, professional consultant, corporate leader, or educator from another district. In-service goals generally are directed toward awareness and information.

Staff development, on the other hand, is a process of long-term commitment to professional growth across a broad range of school goals. It should involve all school personnel and usually includes local leadership in place of, or at least in addition to, service by outside consultants. Goals are directed toward involvement, commitment, and renewal. School personnel determine their own needs, develop steps to address those needs, and evaluate their professional growth.

Under ideal circumstances in-service is one useful component of a long-range, ongoing staff development program to serve the professional needs of teachers, administrators, and support personnel in the school system. Staff development is a fundamental part of the general plan for improving education for all students.

## Characteristics of the Adult Learner

First and foremost, participants in ISD must be approached as the adult learners and professionals they are. Participants in in-service and staff development demonstrate several basic characteristics as adult learners. They have (Knowles, 1978):

a desire and need to be self-directed in the learning;
a wide experience base upon which to draw;
a time perspective for the learning that is oriented to the here and now;
a problem-centered focus on the learning.

Recent research (Feuer and Geber, 1988) indicates that the most definitive of these four characteristics for educators is the wide experience base they bring to the ISD. Those who provide ISD for school personnel must recognize that the recipients will be self-directed, experienced, and interested primarily in material they can use at the present for real problems. They desire ownership in the ISD process, and they will resist aspects of staff development that are perceived as attacks on their competence. They can and should serve as resources for their colleagues during professional development activities. And although some fun and reward are refreshing and necessary, adult learners respond best to intrinsic motivations rather than extrinsic motivations.

With these adult learner characteristics in mind, staff developers will need to:

arrange for participant comfort;
provide participants with options and choices;
manage participants' time well;
deliver practical, focused help; and
follow up on the effectiveness of the experience.

Adult learners value in-service and staff development activities in which they work toward realistic, job-related, useful goals. They need to see results for their efforts with follow-through and feedback experiences, and most of all, with success in using the activities within their school context.

Guskey (1985) stresses that ISD for busy school personnel must illustrate clearly ways in which new practices can improve student performance, and how these practices can be implemented without too much disruption or extra work. This is particularly important for ISD that focuses on consultation and collaboration, because this kind of professional activity often involves more time and effort initially. In Guskey's model of teacher change, staff develop-ment should be designed for the purpose of modifying classroom teaching practices. This change cause changes in student learning outcomes, which result in altered teacher beliefs and attitudes. This is a promising concept for promoting collaboration to help students with special needs.

## Planning In-service and Staff Development

Many professional growth activities can—particularly activities designed to improve teacher ability in meeting needs of students at risk—and should take place among practicing teachers right at the school site. However, the experiences will need to have specific personnel assigned to the task of preparing the activity and coordinating it (Howey, Bents, and Corrigan, 1981). "Staff development will never have its intended impact as long as it is grafted onto schools in the form of discrete, unconnected projects" (Joyce, 1990, p. 21). Those who conduct staff development should be selected carefully. They have a much more important role in teacher readiness than has been accorded to them (Joyce, 1990; Dettmer, 1986). In-service and staff development planners and presenters need expertise in content, process, and understanding of the school context.

The consultant role is ideal for coordinating useful in-service and staff development activities. Special education personnel often inherit these responsibilities either as a part of a plan or by default. There are disadvantages as well as advantages in being a "prophet in your own land" to conduct professional development activities, but one of the biggest advantages is knowledge of the school context.

### Determining In-service and Staff Development Needs

The consultant or consulting teacher who provides staff development will want to assess the needs of other school personnel for the ISD. What do they know about a topic at this point? What do they want to learn? How can they be involved in planning, conducting, and evaluating the staff development for their individual needs? This information should be solicited through needs assessment instruments. Before conducting needs assessment, however, the staff developer should engage in *needs-sensing* activities. What do participants *need* to *want* to know? This radar-reading of what the participants-to-be need to know is a subtle but vital precursor to assessing needs. After all, if educators knew what they wanted or needed in every case, they probably would be doing it.

*Needs Sensing* Needs-sensing information allows planners to design formal needs assessment procedures that will reflect the true needs of all involved. For example, if a needs assessment questionnaire asks, "Which of the five topics do you want to know more about?" and the list includes discipline, motivation, computer literacy, alternative grouping structures, and mainstreaming, the ranked results will be somewhat predictable in a typical district. Alternative grouping structures probably would rank low, with discipline and motivation high.

Prior to the needs sensing activity, an interviewer or investigator might ask teachers if they would like to explore possibilities for structuring their classrooms to promote better discipline and stimulate student interest. If the answer is affirmative, staff development on modified grouping structures could be offered as an area of interest that facilitates discipline as well as student motivation. As another example of needs sensing, teachers could be asked if they wish to explore ways in which children can work together, learn from each other, and share in the results of the learning. If the answer is yes, staff development on cooperative learning could be implemented. For a third example, it would be less helpful to assess needs with the question, "Do you want to know more about advanced placement possibilities at your high school?" than to *sense* where needs lie by first asking, "How might we extend learning of very able students beyond courses that cover grade-level material they have already mastered?"

Needs sensing is a very important precursor to needs assessment. It can be carried out best through:

classroom observations;

visits to successful programs, followed by a comparative analysis;

dialogues and interviews with students, parents, support personnel, and others in the community;

task force investigations; and

buzz group outcomes.

Staff developers should develop instruments that allow target groups to feel able and willing to contribute information.

---

**Application for**
*Conducting Needs Sensing*

Conduct a needs-sensing study by interviewing school personnel to obtain information on these concerns:

1. What do we need to know to help students in our schools feel good about themselves?
2. How important are test formats, designs, and reporting procedures in helping students learn to the best of their ability?
3. How can we determine which reinforcers work best for different ages and developmental levels and interests?
4. Do we use ancillary and support personnel to the greatest advantage for our students?
5. Does our current material develop critical thinking, or do we need more effort in this area?
6. Do we have the resources for adapting materials to the needs of low-achieving students?

**Application for**
*Conducting Needs Assessment*

As a needs assessment procedure, ask teachers to check the topics that interest them most:

___ Assertive Discipline—creating a positive atmosphere in the classroom

___ Critical Thinking—developing effective skills of analysis and evaluation through course materials

___ Behavior Management—techniques for assimilating behavioral-disordered students into the mainstream

___ Beyond the Basals—guiding very able students in using library and supplementary texts as basals

___ Working Smarter, not Harder—using consulting teachers and resource personnel to meet the needs of all students more effectively

It is important to leave space on the instrument for open-ended responses, and to encourage them. After the needs assessments have been returned, summarize the information and use it to plan ISD activities that will be meaningful for participants and relevant to the needs they specified.

*Needs Assessment*  After needs sensing has been conducted, needs assessment instruments and procedures can be developed from the data. Most school personnel have had experience with completing needs assessments. Formats for needs assessments include:

- checklists;
- questionnaires and surveys;
- open-ended surveys of areas of concern;
- interviews; and
- brainstorm session records.

Needs assessment might ask personnel to check topics of need, or to describe their concerns, which can be developed into a staff development activity.

## Presenting In-service and Staff Development

Presenting an in-service session or a staff development activity to adult learners might be compared to giving presents (Garmston, 1988). Garmston says the "present" should be something participants (presentees) want or can utilize, personalized to individual taste as much as possible, attractively wrapped, and a bit suspenseful. The presenter should:

- know audience needs and interests;
- conduct the ISD in interesting, efficient, pleasant manner;

- package the ISD material attractively;
- provide an element of surprise and intrigue; and
- deliver follow-up help, support, and additional information.

## Target Groups for In-service and Staff Development

Target groups for school-related in-service and staff development include a wide variety of roles: classroom teachers; administrators; librarians and media specialists; food-service, custodial, and secretarial staff; school board members; paraprofessionals, social workers and health workers; mentors, talent instructors, and youth directors; pediatricians and dentists; legislators, community leaders, and university personnel for teacher education.

## Formal and Informal In-service and Staff Development

Just as there are formal and informal approaches to consultation, as discussed in Chapter 3, there are formal and informal approaches to ISD. Formal ISD can be conducted through scheduled sessions, conferences, programs, press releases, presentations, modules, courses, brochures, retreats, and other planned activities. Informal ISD occurs through conversations, observations, reports about one topic that include another aspect of education, memos, references to media productions, software programs and reading material. One very informal, convenient, and particularly effective in-service technique is to display information, explanations of procedures, invitations to collaborate, and morale boosters on bulletin boards located in places school personnel frequent (see Figures 12–1 through 12–3 for examples).The possibilities for both formal and informal ISD activities are limited only by the imagination of the personnel who provide them. Some special education consultants prepare bulletin boards

---

**Application For**
*Planning Professional Development for*
*Related Services and Support Personnel*

Related services and support personnel were discussed in Chapter 7 as important partners in programs for students with learning and behavior problems. Think of at least two reasons for including each of the target groups named above in awareness and information sessions about an educational topic. For example, pediatricians and dentists may wish to learn more about characteristics of exceptional children, in order to diagnose problems that are brought to their attention. They also may need to know about referral systems in the schools and the possibilities for arrangements such as sheltered workshops for educable mentally handicapped individuals.

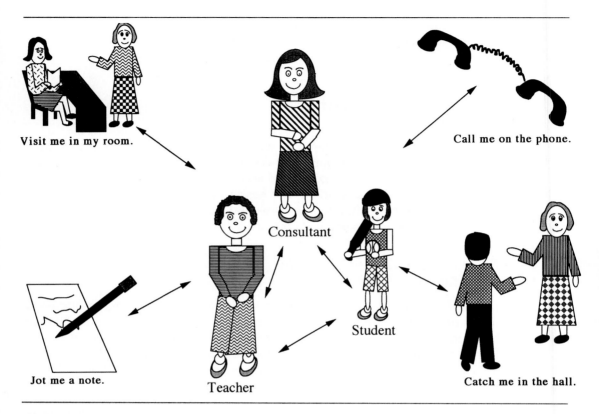

Visit me in my room.

Call me on the phone.

Consultant

Jot me a note.

Student

Teacher

Catch me in the hall.

**FIGURE 12–1** "Let's Communicate!"

of information about pertinent topics. Others provide staff members with newsletters or columns within existing newsletters. Some request ten minutes in which to talk to the teachers at faculty meetings.

One enterprising group of teachers organized a series of sessions called "THT—Teachers Helping Teachers," in which they took turns delivering short sessions on topics in their area of expertise. Soon the idea caught on among other teachers. A teacher who had a school-related skill to share was excused, with the endorsement of the administration, for one-half day, to prepare for and present to teachers in another school within the district. Teachers truly collaborated and consulted to help other teachers.

A popular practice with some gifted program consultants is to provide calendars of enrichment activities for classroom teachers. As these are used, they become vehicles for carrying out goals of the gifted program, such as creative thinking, independent study, research, and small-group investigations. A productive inservice could be a brief session to explain the consultant role and what the consultant will be doing. Such endeavors often increase interest in consultation and collaboration dramatically. Consultants also might prepare information sheets of "Questions Frequently Asked About . . . " and suggest

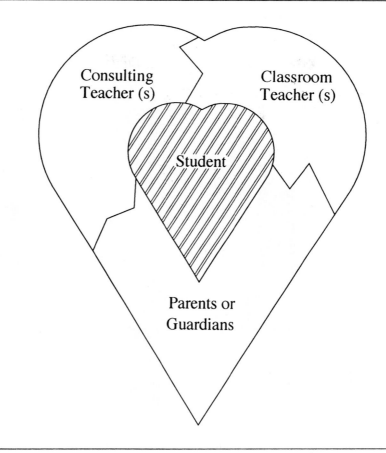

**FIGURE 12–2 "Let's Collaborate"**

by Kay Wright

answers for the questions. A bagged treat or a package of peanuts could be stapled on as a friendly, caring gesture.

When consultants work with one key teacher and their colleagues observe the results, that is informal staff development. As they ask what they can do to help teachers, then discuss their needs, and finally deliver on their promises to the best of their ability and the resources of their area, they are cultivating professional development among school personnel.

Learning is often a spontaneous event, occurring as a synergy of learner interest and need, teacher insight, and a supportive environment. This is the ideal "teachable moment." It is not stretching the comparison too much to suggest that there is an ideal "professional development moment." Perceptive consultants who seek ways of meeting students' special needs will find that

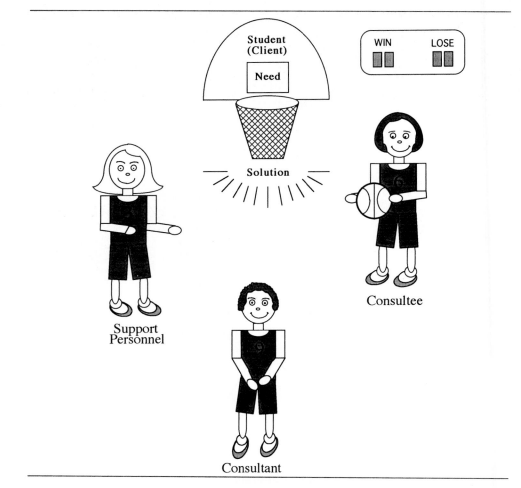

**FIGURE 12–3** "Let's Talk!" Helping Every Students Win

by H. Chestnut and P. Dettmer

in-service and staff development are appropriate tools. They need not expect all ISD experiences to be formal and planned. Both formal staff development and the informal, or "teachable moment for teachers" approaches, are needed.

## The Teachers' Workroom as ISD Forum

Very little has been written about the teachers' workroom. This is surprising, because so many teachers spend time there on a fairly regular basis. Of course, some go there quite frequently, and others hardly ever do. Visits usually fall within one of three purposes—physical, social, or personal. There are physical benefits of refreshment, a quick nap, or a restroom break. Social benefits of interaction with adults are important to some. Personal benefits include attending to professional tasks such as grading papers or reading materials; it is a personal decision to accomplish these tasks in the workroom rather than in the classroom or at home (Dettmer, 1989).

Elementary teachers, in particular, often seek the opportunity to have interaction with colleagues and share reflections about teaching practices. Occasionally this is problematic because the discourse can become quite negative and cynical. When workroom talk affects your morale negatively, going there becomes iatrogenic and should probably be avoided. Nevertheless, the teachers' workroom has long been recognized by special education teachers as a useful hub of interaction. They recognize the opportunity to develop rapport with consultees and learn more about their teaching approaches and student needs.

It is important that consultants spend enough time in the teachers' workroom ("Don't the special ed people want to be a part of our faculty?"), but not

---

**Application For**
*Differentiating Between Formal and Informal ISD*

Determine which of the following staff development activities might be formal and which might be informal. (If two or more people engage in this application exercise, it is not likely there will be complete agreement on the classifications.)

Study groups and problem-solving sessions

Planned interactions between classroom and special education teachers

Demonstration teaching by a consulting teacher

Packets containing program information for administrators

County fair exhibits on handicaps

Seminar programs involving scientists, business leaders, engineers, military personnel, environmental leaders, physicians

Saturday programs for parents

Exchange programs for teachers (from rural to urban and urban to rural)

Grant-writing workshops

Educational television programs

Summer workshops

Interactive video programs

Satellite discussions with leading educational figures

Teaching strategy books and software

A "share fair" in which each staff member brings a favorite idea to share

---

**Thought Problem**

*In your thoughts, or on sketch paper, create a "dream workroom" that would serve school personnel in their physical, social, and personal needs. What would it look like? What would it sound like? How might a consultant nurture the collaborative spirit there? What would it take to construct and appoint such a room? Could some of your suggestions be made right away, with little cost or disruption?*

---

too much ("Don't those special ed people have anything to do?"). Of course, care must be taken to keep professional conversation general in nature. Confidentiality and ethical treatment of information are necessary behaviors for all teachers, and special education teachers in particular. But in this room that is provided for relaxation, reflection, and refreshment, a collaborative spirit can be nurtured and then carried out the door to classrooms and offices beyond.

Suggestions for improving the workroom/lounge in general, and for making it more conducive to collegial interaction,in particular, include (Dettmer, 1989):

- having a suggestion box in which staff could put ideas for time-savers, student pleasers, or budget easers.
- having salad luncheon potluck once a month, perhaps on payday. (Set out different salads every half hour or so, if there are many people.) Simpson (1990) describes a "Tuesday Luncheon" concept that has been in effect for nine years and supports teachers' efforts to reflect on their instruction.
- holding a Friday afternoon snack time to encourage teachers to recap the week and think ahead to the next.
- posting a "Brag Board" on which commendations could be displayed involving anyone and everyone connected with the school, from students to bus drivers to parents of students.
- providing an "Orientation to Special Education" folder on an accessible table, changing its contents often.

More research is needed on the problems and possibilities of this important facet of school life. However, the consultant will find many opportunities in the workroom for developing rapport with consultees and initiating constructive interactions. This school place must be used wisely and judiciously.

## Format for In-service and Staff Development

In-service and staff development plans can be classified as an economy package, a conventional package, or a deluxe package of experiences. For example, a gifted program consultant generated three sets of plans for gifted program staff development to serve the differentiated needs of his six assigned schools. He offered:

*The Economy Model, featuring*

- characteristics of gifted students;
- curricular needs of gifted students; and
- activities to serve the curricular needs.

*The Conventional Model, featuring*

- characteristics and needs of gifted students;
- curricular implications of those needs;
- program differentiation to meet the needs;
- strategies and activities for serving the needs; and
- community resources for gifted students.

*The Deluxe Model, featuring*

- characteristics and needs of gifted students;
- curricular implications of those needs;
- gifted program goals and objectives;
- learning theories and teaching models suited to gifted students' needs;
- learning styles and student interests;
- curricular planning for gifted students;
- community resources for gifted students; and
- parental involvement in gifted programs.

There is no single pattern for in-service and staff development format that will be appropriate for every school context. However, the following outline is one that can be adapted to a variety of schools and staff needs.

1. Engage in needs sensing.
2. Conduct needs assessment.
3. Select the topic to be featured.
4. Determine the audience to be targeted.
5. Choose a catchy, upbeat title for the activity.
6. Determine presenters who will contribute.
7. Decide on incentives, promotion, and publicity.
8. Outline the presentation.
9. List the equipment and room arrangement needed.
10. Plan carefully the content to be covered.
11. Prepare handouts and visual materials.
12. Rehearse the presentation.
13. Determine an evaluation procedure for the activity.
14. Plan for the follow-up activity.

Examples of sessions that follow this format are included in Figures 12–4 and 12–5.

*Needs Sensing*: Interviews with support staff

*Needs Assessment*: Survey form of questions participants would like to have answered

*Topic*: Students with special needs

*Audience*: Paraprofessionals, social and health workers, food service and custodial staff, secretary staff, bus drivers, librarians and media specialists

*Title*: "Helping All Kids Succeed in Our School"

*Presenters*: Consulting teachers for learning disabilities, behavioral disorders, mental handicaps, and physical handicaps

*Incentives*: Door prize, refreshments

*Publicity*: A basket of treats and an announcement about the meeting, placed in the school office, workroom, and bus barn

*Format*: A thirty-minute overview of exceptionalities, followed by a short videotape of exceptional children. Then a refreshment break, and a thirty-minute small-group discussion of ways in which each school role contributes to the learning of students with special needs. At the conclusion, a five-minute whole group summary of goals for all school staff

*Equipment and room*: Videotape player, overhead projector and screen, table for refreshments, semicircles for whole-group, and tables in corners of the room for small-group discussion.

*Content*: To be planned by the consulting teachers, speaking to needs identified in the needs sensing and needs assessment data, goals of special education programs, student needs, curricular modifications that teachers make that affect such school conditions as schedules and rewards, strategies that support personnel can use to help students, and an individual plan by each participant for giving support to meet special needs of students

*Handouts*: None

*Visuals*: A high-quality, overview type of videotape on exceptionalities. Basic transparencies for describing exceptional student characteristics and needs

*Rehearsal and preparation*: At a time all presenters can be there

*Evaluation procedure*: Modified version of Evaluation Form in Figure 12–10

*Follow-up*: Brief interviews with participants to check on individual plan progress and any further questions

**FIGURE 12-4   ISD Module for Support Personnel**

## Time for In-service and Staff Development

Time is the enemy when planning in-service and staff development activities. There is not enough of it readily available at student-free times when teachers can concentrate and reflect. Before-school hours and after-school hours might seem workable because participants are coming to school anyway or are required to stay after school for a specific length of time. But teachers find it hard to focus on their own learning at an early hour, when their thoughts are

*Needs Sensing*: Information gained during regularly scheduled observations in classrooms

*Needs Assessment:* Questionnaires asking teachers to check major areas of interest and add others if they wish

*Topic*: Mainstreamed students with special needs

*Audience*: Elementary-level classroom teachers

*Title*: "Teamwork Makes Every Child a Winner"

*Presenters*: Consultants for learning disabilities, behavioral disorders, gifted students, and students with mental and physical handicaps

*Incentives*: Released time, attendance by administrator, credit on professional growth plan, refreshments

*Publicity*: School newsletter, personal written invitations

*Format*: Two one-hour sessions after school. During the first one, held on Tuesday, five-minute presentations by each consulting teacher, and five-minute presentations by key elementary teachers, describing the need to mainstream. Refreshment break. Small-group problem-solving sessions to identify major problems of mainstreaming. The following Thursday, again the five-minute presentations but this time focusing on on modifications and alternatives teachers can use to overcome the problems identified during Tuesday's session. Small-group problem-solving sessions to determine best approaches for trying some of the ideas

*Equipment*: Overhead and screen, samples of materials, table for refreshments. Theater-in-the-round arrangement for total group, and small work tables for the break-out groups

*Content*: Prepared specific to the exceptionalities discussed, and including information on student characteristics, learning and behavior needs, curricular implications, and possibilities for collaboration and teamwork among special and general education personnel to meet those needs

*Handouts*: Color coded, to accompany content

*Visuals:* Transparencies, samples of student work when using the curricular modifications

*Rehearsal*: All presenters during the week before the ISD

*Evaluation*: An instrument similar to Figure 12–10

*Follow-up*: Individual consultations with each teacher by consulting teachers who have mainstreamed students in those classrooms

**FIGURE 12-5   ISD Module for Classroom Teachers**

centered on beginning the school day efficiently. By day's end, energy and emotions may be lagging and other responsibilities beckon. Saturday sessions are no more popular and encroach on the family and community life so necessary for sustaining teacher vitality and support.

The arrangement preferred by most teachers is released time. This means that their responsibilities with students will be assumed by others. Loucks-

Horsley et al. (1987) recommend providing released time for ISD participants by using:

- substitute teachers;
- a substitute cadre that conducts planned enrichment activities;
- roving substitute teachers; or
- teacher triads where one teacher teaches two classes to free up the second teacher.

The substitute cadre eliminates the necessity for detailed lesson planning by the teacher, because the enrichment activities are planned and provided by the cadre. Roving substitutes allow released teachers to have short periods of time for observing, coaching, gathering research data, or assisting in another classroom. Loucks-Horsley et al. (1987) counsel that the time issue is a "red herring," because the problem often lies in the constructive use of time, not its availability.

Released time to attend professional development activities away from the school district must be supported strongly by school administrators. Permission to attend may be granted more readily if you are slated to make presentation. If that is not possible, you might volunteer to facilitate or chair a session, or to work a few hours in some capacity at the conference. Administrators may respond favorably to a plan for attending and bringing back information in the form of a written report or a summarized presentation to be shared with colleagues. If none of these possibilities is viable, professional or personal leave days will have to be used.

### Incentives for Participation in ISD

Incentives for attendance and enthusiastic participation at in-service and staff development sessions need to feature interest, humor, and intrigue. They should include both extrinsic and intrinsic reinforcement for adult learners. Intrinsic incentives for long-range staff development are, of course, personal and professional growth, benefits for students, and advancement in the profession. But there are good reasons for providing pleasurable, extrinsic rewards as well. For example, a drawing could be held in which the lucky winner receives a free class period during which the principal substitutes. Teacher aide time could be provided. Participants could be treated to a gala affair upon "graduation" from a program. They might be transported to this gala affair in a limousine provided by local businesses (Robert, 1973). Recognition for their participation could be publicized in local papers and professional magazines. Released time from playground or lunch duty for specified period could be provided. The best parking spot in the lot (perhaps the superintendent's!) could be awarded, for a week or so, as a door prize. A starter list of incentives is provided in Figure 12–6.

Prospective participants should receive information about the ISD through school newsletters, memos, bulletin boards, and public announcements.

Publicity spots that are run on radio and T.V. provide the added benefit of calling attention of the community to professional development efforts by the school district. They are a natural prelude for follow-up work to build awareness and support among the public for school improvement issues.

## Techniques for Conducting ISD

Consultants who deliver in-service and staff development on their own professional turf may face some difficulty in being accepted as "prophets in their own land" (Smith-Westberry and Job, 1986). They will want to scrutinize their own capabilities and deficits first. Practice sessions can help presenters gain confidence and skill. Smith-Westberry and Job recommend videotaping the practice sessions, discomforting though that may be, and critiquing them carefully to correct deficiencies.

### *Presenter and Participant Responsibilities*

Presenters have a responsibility to know their participants well. They should be experienced and confident with the content they are presenting. After assessing participant needs, they should develop the format and content carefully, rehearse for the presentation, plan the closing segment even more carefully, arrange for feedback and evaluation, and form ideas for follow-up to the presentation.

| | |
|---|---|
| Released time | Child care during the ISD |
| Paid college credit | Many options and choices |
| Progress on professional plan | Reduced teaching load |
| Stipend | Hair stylist demonstrations |
| Door prize | Badges and buttons |
| Sabbatical for long-term ISD | Demonstrations of materials |
| Free food | Free teacher supplies |
| A plush site for the session | Endorsement by community leaders |
| Choice parking lot spaces | Drawing for resort weekend |
| A note on yearly evaluation | Free material from merchants |
| Have a famous person there | Ticket giveaway (dinner, a banquet |
| Faculty performances | theater, sports) |
| Have a theme party | Lively entertainment |
| Lots of useful handouts | Funny fashion show |
| Retreat at a resort | Progressive format—moving from place |
| Grab bags | to place for parts of the session |
| Publicity in local paper | A share fair |
| Recognition for attending | Controversial topic |
| Make-and-take products | Assurance of follow-up support |
| Attendance by administrators | Bring one idea, take home many |
| Free xeroxing of materials | |

**FIGURE 12-6   Incentives for Participating in ISD**

Participants, as presentees, have the responsibility to participate whole-heartedly in the ISD, collaborate and cooperate with the activities and evaluation, and commit themselves to the follow-up activities. One of the most helpful contributions on their part is to defer any negative attitudes toward in-service and staff development and anticipate good experiences from the ISD to come.

### Delivery of ISD Content

The ISD may follow one of two basic formats—lecture format, or interactive style (Smith-Westberry and Job, 1986). Lectures should include real-life examples and practical approaches. For lectures, the room arrangement might be configured as semicircles, a theater-in-the-round, or chairs in small semicircles to allow for periodic subgrouping. Stiff formats of straight rows generally should be avoided. For interactive sessions, chairs can be placed in a circle or around individual tables in octagon form. Larger tables might be arranged in a diamond shape. A "maple leaf" format of chairs allows for subgrouping (Knowles, 1970).

Presenters should have with them all supplies that they anticipate needing:

chalk, eraser, pointer;

overhead transparency markers, extra bulb, extension cord, blank transparencies, three-prong adapter;

pens, pencils, writing paper, pad for sign-up requests;

masking tape, thumbtacks, scissors, strong tape for securing cords, clip-on light to read notes in the dark;

other emergency items (tissues, hose, cup for water, stick-on notes, mints or cough drops, string, screwdriver and pliers).

A good way to begin an ISD is to use an icebreaker, particularly if participants do not know one another. However, the icebreaker must not encroach on presentation time. Early arrivers could begin the brief activity, and time could be called when the hour to begin is at hand. An example of a well-known icebreaker technique is provided in Figure 12–7.

It is vital for the presentation to *begin on time.* Also, presenters will want to "begin with a bang." The opening remarks in a presentation should be snappy and to the point. They should "hook" the participants into being interested. Now is the time to stress that the session has been developed from data on needs assessments that participants completed. Presenters should state the goal(s), the procedures to be followed, a *brief* overview of the issue(s) to be addressed, and the range of probable avenues the ISD will take, while remaining somewhat flexible for any circumstances that arise.

ISD content should be presented through more than one sensory channel, just as good teachers present materials for learners. Handouts, visuals, brief

---

# ICEBREAKER ACTIVITY

### Let's Get Acquainted

Move about the room and get a signature from a person who fits each category. Use a person's name only once.

1. Someone who loves chocolate. _____

2. One who has swum in both the Atlantic and Pacific. _____

3. Someone who knows who won the Super Bowl last year. _____

4. Someone who doesn't *care* who won the Super Bowl. _____

5. A person with a birthday in the same season as yours. __ _____

6. Someone who plays a musical instrument. _____

7. One who loves cats. _____

8. An elementary level teacher/student. _____

9. A high school level teacher/student. _____

10. One who traveled more than twenty miles to be here. _____

When your list is complete, sit down and interact with those around you.

---

**FIGURE 12-7  Ice Breaker Activity**

tape-recorded messages, and frequent changes in presenter position and style will be appreciated by adult learners, just as they are welcomed by students in the classroom. A new activity should occur approximately every fifteen to twenty minutes (Britton, 1989). And, of course, presenters do need to be prepared for inevitable contingencies and emergencies—burned-out bulbs, too few handouts, loud noises, a rude question, or a tornado alert! Presenters can use small-group activities intermittently to encourage involvement and sustain interest. Huddle groups of six people conferring for six minutes, circle response groups in which each person speaks in turn around the small circle, and buzz groups of dyads or triads work well.

Some presenters dread speaking to groups. Would-be presenters may be inexperienced or feel terrified to stand before groups, particularly of their peers.

It is a good idea to practice the presentation before the event. A script of remarks can be typed (triple spaced for easy reading) and rehearsed in front of the mirror or a kindly compatriot. Holding private practice sessions before a mirror will allow you to critique gestures and body language. It may help to watch other performers, or to practice with dramatic readings.

Engaging in relaxation exercises before the event has helped some nervous speakers to be at ease. During the presentation the speaker might locate supporters in the audience and key in on them for assurance. If a tense time arises, a cartoon or joke might be brought out to ease the tension, but this must be used with care. The humorous piece must be inoffensive and related to the topic. That is a tall order. At any rate, presenters will find it comforting to remember that most audiences are more interested in the usefulness of the content than in the skills of the presenters; therefore, the key is to provide useful, timely information.

Garmston (1990) stresses that presenters can make or break the success of the session in its last few minutes. Final impressions should encourage participants to sort and store the material. The last comments should stimulate inquiry and support commitment and collegiality. Closing activities need to be planned carefully and calculated precisely. Perhaps the most important criterion of all is to *end on time.* Figure 12–8 contains a brief list of do's and don'ts for conducting successful ISD activities.

*Visuals for the Presentation* Many presenters use visuals during presentations—transparencies, films, videotapes, charts, and posters. The visuals should be simple, clear, and visible. They must not be cluttered with infinite detail, but represent the "bottom line" about the topic. The audience will attend more to color graphics than to black-and-white. An effective transparency presents one main idea per sheet, with a maximum of seven words per line and seven lines per visual, and does not contain technical language or jargon. A rule of thumb for the display of figures and graphs is to present only information that the audience could sketch freehand with accurate representation of the main idea. The type on transparencies must be BIG! It should be tested for legibility from the back of the room by a person who has never seen it before.

Presenters should not read from the transparency material, but wait until the audience has time to peruse it. When noting information, speakers should point to the transparency, not to the screen. Expeditious use of the on/off switch allows the presenter to control the audience's attention. It is best to leave room lights on unless the visual is a film. After a point is made, turning off the machine and standing away from it directs attention back to the presenter. Clip-on microphones allow presenter mobility. Imaginative use and variation of space, location, volume, and graphics will enliven the presentation and focus participant attention.

A dramatic effect can be achieved with the use of two overhead machines and screens. The main point might be presented on one screen while subpoints

## Do's and Don'ts for In-service and Staff Development

| | |
|---|---|
| Do assess needs. | Don't lecture exclusively. |
| Do set goals. | Don't use jargon. |
| Do arrive early and prepared. | Don't schedule at poor times. |
| Do be flexible. | Don't read to participants. |
| Do provide incentives. | Don't assume all have same needs and |
| Do keep on task. | interests. |
| Do follow up. | Don't try to do too much. |
| Do start on time. | Don't run overtime. |
| Do carry a "survival box." | Don't demean efforts and competencies |
| Do provide good handouts. | of others. |
| Do be enthusiastic. | Don't allow one participant to dominate. |
| Do summarize often. | Don't be afraid to say, "I don't know." |
| Do make eye contact often. | Don't get unnecessarily technical. |
| Do encourage administrators to attend. | Don't rush through material. |
| Do be prepared to modify. | Don't overuse the overhead. |
| Do follow through on promises. | Don't be discouraged. |
| Do involve the audience. | |
| Do use evaluation data to plan better ISD. | |

**FIGURE 12-8  Dos's and Don'ts for Inservice and Staff Development**

or illustrations are flashed on the other. As a variation, two presenters could collaborate, one at each machine, to dialogue about the material. This technique needs to be rehearsed before it is used.

*Handouts for the Presentation*  Presentees appreciate good handouts. Handouts are more widely read and better remembered when they are in color. They should be practical, usable, and attractive. There should not be too many nor too few. Unless the handout is needed as a component of participation involvement, it should be distributed at the close of the session. If handed out during the session, an orderly procedure must be preplanned, so that distribution does not consume valuable session time and make the audience restless.

Participants tend to become annoyed when there are not enough handouts to go around. Even with the best planning, this does happen occasionally. Presenters should have a sign-up paper available for those who were shortchanged; and must follow through right away by sending the material. It is best not to distribute handouts before the session begins. In order to minimize requests and avoid having to refuse, presenters will want to keep printed material out of sight until it is needed.

## Follow-Up Activities

Follow-up to in-service and staff development is the breeze that fans any fires of change that were sparked by the activity (Dettmer, 1990). Educators sometimes avoid trying new concepts and techniques because they are uncomfortable with them or uncertain about the outcomes. It is easy to revert to business as usual, once the ISD activity is over. So follow-up to ISD is vital, just as it is with the consultation process. Follow-up should be a long-term practice of support for the innovation, and as such, might more appropriately be described as *follow-through* (Dettmer, 1990). The possibilities include peer coaching, discussion groups, visits to sites where the innovation is occurring, newsletters, and interviews. Data gathered during follow-up and follow-through can be used to plan future in-services and staff development projects.

One caution must be noted regarding ISD outcomes. When educators are introduced to new concepts and challenged to try new approaches, some discomfort is inevitable. Learning new skills involves greater effort than continuing to use old ones (Joyce and Showers, 1983). The adage that training may make you worse before it makes you better is an important point to consider. This accents the need for follow-through efforts and perseverance on the part of the consultant.

## Evaluation of the In-service and Staff Development

The tool used most often for in-service and staff development evaluation is a questionnaire participants complete immediately following the activity. The evaluation should include both objective responses and an invitation for open-ended responses. A Likert scale of five to seven values is preferable to a Yes-or-No format. The evaluation data should be used to design more meaningful activities as well as to improve presentation skills. (see Figure 12–9 for an example of an ISD evaluation tool, and consult Chapter 8 for additional information on evaluation.)

Presenters may want to evaluate the participants as well. By doing so, consultants ascertain participant preparedness and responsiveness to the topic. This provides information that can help them and their host schools plan further consultation and collaboration directed to the participants' needs.

---

**Application For**
*Preparing a Staff Development Outline*

Prepare an outline of a staff development activity that might be used by special education consultants to cultivate a spirit of collaboration and teamwork among general classroom teachers, special education personnel, and related services and support personnel. Include a list of do's and don'ts that would be pertinent to this ISD activity.

---

---

### In-service/Staff Development Evaluation

Date _____

Name (optional) _____ Teaching Area and Level (s) _____

Site of the In-service/Staff Development _____ Topic _____

Rate the following with a value from 1 through 5:
1 = None     2 = A little     3 = Somewhat     4 = Considerably     5 = Much

1. The event increased my understanding of the topic. _____

2. The goals and objectives of the event addressed needs I had identified. _____

3. The content was well developed and organized. _____

4. The material was presented effectively. _____

5. The environment was satisfactory. _____

6. I gained ideas to use in my own situation. _____

7. I will use at least one idea from this event. _____

8. Strengths of the event: _____

9. Ways the event could be improved: _____

10. I would like to know more about: _____

---

**FIGURE 12–9  Inservice/Staff Development Evaluation**

## Benefits of In-service and Staff Development

In-service and staff development for consultation, collaboration, and special needs of students have the potential to create positive ripple effects that have no bounds. They encourage:

- increased respect for individual differences, creative approaches, and educational excellence;
- teacher proficiency in innovative curriculum and teacher strategies;
- staff and parent involvement, and satisfaction with the educational system;
- collegiality and collaboration among all school personnel as well as community and parents.

In order to attain these positive outcomes, in-service and staff development must be planned, conducted, and evaluated thoroughly.

# Tips for Consulting and Collaborating

1. If an opportunity arises, suggest certain activities to certain teachers who might want them. Don't force. Sometimes, although not often, the distribution of material to teachers backfires because they resent the inference that they need it, so let them decide. Instead of stuffing teachers' mailboxes with things they may not want, lay out new books or activities on tables in the teachers' workroom.

2. Have an in-service on parent-teacher conferences for students with special needs. Ask teachers to submit "stumper" problems. Then use them to determine how to react and deal with those situations. Have lots of ideas to distribute.

3. Do your very best to get administrators to *attend* and *participate* in the ISD activities.

4. About two months after in-service, send teachers a checklist of outcomes derived from the in-service, with a place for them to comment before returning the lists.

5. In the teachers' workroom, have treats and note cards with the directions, "Take a treat and take a sheet," meaning to take a sheet that has tips concerning student needs. A variation is "Take a treat and leave a sheet" in which the sheet is a needs assessment or evaluation you wish to collect.

6. Travel with others to workshops and conferences. The trip provides opportunities for conversation and rapport building.

7. Hand out your school's business cards at conferences, writing your name, educational area, and shared interest on them. This opens up possibilities for future interaction and collaboration.

8. After attending a convention, conference, or other helpful meeting, or after reading an informative piece, write a short note describing it and put a copy in teachers' boxes, spreading the news on things learned.

9. Organize a system so you will know all teachers have been reached through informal or formal ISD.

10. Develop calendars and time lines of program activities to post in teacher areas or to distribute among school personnel. Do not overlook secretaries, for whom such information is particularly important.

11. Prepare teaching videotapes that demonstrate activities appropriate for students with special needs.

12. Bring in the expertise of other school personnel to assist with consultations, especially for specific content areas.

13. Make a personal pledge to read at least one article a week from a professional journal.

14. Join a dynamic professional organization and become actively involved in it.

15. Conduct workshops on topics teachers request. If a topic is outside your line of expertise, find someone who can present it.

**16.** After each informal or formal ISD, check back to see how the ideas were used, and if there were difficulties, assist in overcoming them.

**17.** Learn a new technique and infect others with your enthusiasm for using it. Don't just "drop off "learning centers and activities you have prepared. Ask teachers if you can help get them started.

**18.** Become acquainted with people in businesses and organizations who are field-testing products, materials, and processes.

**19.** Observe programs in other schools and share observations with key people in your own school context.

**20.** Remember that knowing how to consult does not guarantee you the opportunity to do it! Create the opportunity.

## Chapter Review

**1.** Consultants and consulting teachers have ideal roles for planning and implementing in-service and staff development. Through their involvement with ISD activities, they can share content and help build processes that facilitate learning by students with special needs. They also will have the opportunity to develop consultation and collaboration networks in their local school context.

**2.** In-service is one specialized component within long-range, ongoing staff development programs involving all school personnel.

**3.** Adult learners have a need to be self-directed in their learning. A group of adult learners represents a wide experience base on which consultants can draw and build. Adult learners want learning that is oriented to the present and that helps them deal with problems they are now facing.

**4.** In-service and staff development must be designed to address assessed needs of the participants. Before needs assessment is conducted, needs sensing should be undertaken. Teachers may not always know, or verbalize, what they need to know about helping students with special needs.

**5.** In-service and staff development for facilitating learning by students with special needs should be presented to a wide range of target groups— teachers, administrators, support personnel, policymakers, teacher educators, and others who are involved with learning programs and materials. ISD can be informal or formal. The teachers' workroom/lounge should not be overlooked as an important area for informal ISD. Finding time, arranging incentives and publicity, and developing the format are important points in planning ISD.

**6.** Successful ISD activities are created by effective delivery styles, appropriate visuals, helpful handouts, careful evaluation, and commitment to follow-up after the ISD.

**7.** In-service and staff development can create positive ripple effects for the entire school, through development of teacher proficiency, greater staff involvement, and cultivation of collegiality and collaboration.

# Activities

1.  Propose several ways a consulting teacher might serve the special needs of students through in-service and staff development activities.

2.  Reflect on concerns a classroom teacher might express through needs sensing and needs assessment in regard to learning and behavior needs of students in the classroom.

3.  Suppose that an in-service session on alternative grouping techniques is scheduled for an elementary school, with attendance by all building teachers required. The one-hour session is scheduled for Thursday after school, in the kindergarten room. A methods instructor from a nearby university will lecture to the group. Later this evening there is a high-school play performance, and the next day is the end of term before the grading period. How do the in-service topic, time, location, and format violate the principles of good adult learning experiences?

4.  Design a teachers' workroom bulletin board that could be considered an informal in-service concerning a handicap or an example of students at risk.

5.  In a brainstorm session, think up a list of "Things I Don't Want to Happen" with regard to in-service and staff development activities. After having fun with this, it may be a good idea to countermand these "ISD Horrors" with a list of preventives.

6.  In a teacher's guide for a particular subject, locate instances where collaboration and use of a consultant are referred to, or better still, encouraged.

7.  How might in-service and staff development activities promoted by the special education consulting teachers activate positive ripple effects throughout the school for all students?

8.  Talk about the following quotations as they might relate to in-service and staff development:

> "It is easier to produce ten volumes of philosophical writing than to put one principle into practice" (unknown).

> "Doors can open on tiny hinges" (Eliot Wigginton, *Sometimes A Shining Moment*, p. 240).

# For Further Reading

Caldwell, S. D. (Ed.). (1989). *Staff Development:Handbook of Effective Practices*. Oxford, OH: National Staff Development Council.

*Journal for Staff Development*. Manhattan, KS; Kansas State University. All issues.

Joyce, B. (ed.). (1990). *Changing School Culture through Staff Development*. Alexandria, VA: Association for Supervision and Curriculum Development.

Joyce, B., and Showers, B. (1988). *Student Achievement through Staff Development*. New York: Longman.

Morsink, C. V., Thomas, C. C., and Correa, V. I. (1991). *Interactive Teaming: Consultation and Collaboration in Special Programs*. Columbus, OH: Merrill. Chapter 8, on empowering team members through staff development.

# References

Britton, N. (May, 1989). Training the trainer in Richardson, Texas. *The Developer*, pp. 1, 3.

Caldwell, S. D. (Ed.). (1989). *Staff Development:Handbook of Effective Practices*. Oxford, OH: National Staff Development Council.

Davis, W. E. (1985). *The Special Educator: Meeting the Cchallenge for Professional Growth*. Austin, TX: PRO–ED.

Dettmer, P. (1986). Gifted program inservice and staff development: Pragmatics and possibilities. *Gifted Child Quarterly, 30*(3):99–102.

Dettmer, P. (1989). The teachers' lounge: Professional asset or liability? *The Master Teacher State-of-the-Art Papers, 20*(25):1–4.

Dettmer, P. (Ed.). (1990). *Staff Development for Gifted Programs: Putting it Together and Making it Work*. Washington, D.C.: National Association for Gifted Children.

Feuer, D., and Geber, B. (1988). Uh-Oh . . . second thoughts about adult learning theory. *Training*, December 1988.

Friend, M., and Cook, L. (1990). Collaboration as a predictor for success in school reform. *Journal of Educational and Psychological Consultation, I*(1):69–86.

Garmston, R. (October, 1988). Giving gifts. *Developer*, pp. 3, 6.

Garmston, R. (February, 1990). Maintaining momentum, Part II: Keeping the train rolling. *The Developer*, pp. 3, 7.

Guskey, T. (1985). Staff development and teacher change. *Educational Leadership, 42*(7):57–60.

Howey, K. R., Bents, R., and Corrigan, D. (eds.). (1981). *School–focused Inservice: Descriptions and Discussions*. Reston, VA: Association of Teacher Educators.

Joyce, B. (Ed.). (1990). *Changing School Culture through Staff Development*. Alexandria, VA: The Association for Supervision and Curriculum Development.

Joyce, B. R., and Showers, B. (1983). *Power in Staff Development through Research on Training*. Alexandria, VA: The Association for Supervision and Curriculum Development.

Knowles, M. (1970). *The Modern Practice of Adult Education*. New York: Association Press.

Knowles, M. (1978). *The Adult Learner: A Neglected Species*. Houston, TX: Gulf Publishing.

Loucks–Horsley, S., Harding, C. K., Arbuckle, M. A., Murray, L. B., Dubea, C., and Williams, M. K. (1987). *Continuing to Learn: A Guidebook for Teacher Development*. Andover, MA: The Regional Laboratory for Educational Improvement of the Northeast and Islands.

Morsink, C. V., Thomas, C. C., and Correa, V. I. (1991). *Interactive Teaming: Consultation and Collaboration in Special Programs*. Columbus, OH: Merrill. Chapter 8, on empowering team members through staff development.

Pugach, M. C., and Johnson, L. J. (1990). Fostering the continued democratization of consultation through action research. *Teacher Education and Special Education, 13*(3–4):240–45.

Reynolds, M. C., and Birch, J. W. (1988). *Adaptive Mainstreaming: A Primer for Teachers and Principals* (3d ed.). White Plains, NY: Longman.

Robert, M. (1973). *Loneliness in the Schools (What to Do about It)*. Niles, IL: Argus Communication.

Simpson, G. W. (1990). Keeping it alive: Elements of school culture that sustain innovation. *Educational Leadership, 47*(8):34–37.

Smith-Westberry, J., and Job, R. L. (1986). How to be a prophet in your own land: Providing gifted program inservice for the local district. *Gifted Child Quarterly, 30*(3):135–137.

Staff. (April, 1989). Staff development in the journals. *Developer*, p. 6.

White, G. W., and Pryzwansky, W. B. (1982). Consultation outcome as a result of in–service resource teacher training. *Psychology in Schools, 19*:495–502.

Wigginton, E. (1985). *Sometimes a Shining Moment: The Foxfire Experience*. New York: Anchor.

# EPILOGUE

## CONSULTATION, COLLABORATION, AND TEAMWORK FOR SCHOOLS IN A CHANGING WORLD

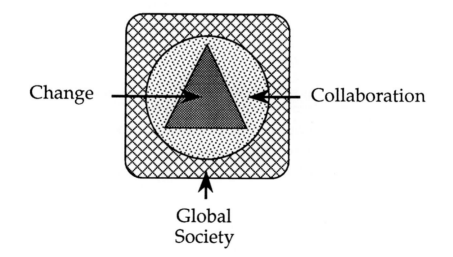

*To Think About*

Never before in history have so many elements of people's lives changed so quickly. No one knows for certain where these changes will lead, but trends that have been set into motion should help futurists predict with considerable insight what the world will be like in the twenty-first century. The predictions by these futurists will help educators determine the changes that must occur in schools if they are to meet the demands of the future.

School reform and restructuring movements are addressing the ever-increasing demands for a responsive, responsible educational system. However, schools cannot function as the sole provider of all services needed and still meet their substantial academic responsibilities. Interrelationships must be developed with other public and private sector agencies.

Social and economic trends will place even further demands on schools. These social and economic trends reach around the globe and are reflected in the profound changes of political and cultural structures that erupted in the early 1990s. Changes of such magnitude will ripple throughout social institutions, including schools and the families they serve.

Schools must change dramatically to prepare students for their future. Students who are at risk now because of special learning and behavior difficulties will be placed in even greater jeopardy by ever-accelerating demands on them to keep pace. It is clear that consultation, collaboration, and teamwork among professional and parent educators are keys to increasing the opportunities for all students to be successful learners, happy individuals, and productive members of society. This final chapter summarizes key trends that are likely to affect changes in schools and other societal institutions, and that signal the need for extensive consultation, collaboration, and teamwork among educators.

## Focusing Questions

1. What changes are predicted in society, and how do these predictions relate to the future of students with special needs?

2. What changes are occurring that will affect schools of the future?

3. How is the nature of student needs changing?

4. What role will educators play in serving the needs of students and families in the future?

5. Why are new metaphors needed for education?

6. What are the demands and challenges for consultive and collaborative efforts in schools of the future?

## Key Terms

advocacy
change agent
demographic data
futurist

global village
metaphor
reification
Zeitgeist

---

**Scenario**

Another school day is over. The events of the past week are history. What remains beyond the moment is the future. As the teachers in the Chapter 12 scenario conclude their discussion about next week's staff development sessions and head for their rooms to pick up schoolwork they will take home for the weekend, their glances fall on a poster that hangs beside the door:

*"The Future Is Now!"*

Below the poster in smaller type is an often-quoted maxim—"If we do what we have been doing, we will continue to get what we have been getting." And below that in firm, bold letters, is the question, "Can we do better?" It is a good question to ponder over the weekend. . .

---

## World Trends and Social Concerns Affecting Education

A host of world trends and social concerns is mandating changes in school and home education. Populations are shifting and becoming more diverse. Complex social and health issues affect people of all ages. Critical shortages of skilled, competent workers exist in a variety of business and service areas. The structure of the family and home has undergone tremendous pressures that affect all members deeply, especially children. Resolutions of these concerns are vital, in order to help children and youth become productive, fulfilled individuals. Although these children and youth are only about one-third of the population, they are 100 percent of the future.

Futurists contribute a wealth of information and ideas to help guide decision making as the twentieth century settles into the history books and the twenty-first century emerges. Their ideas tend to fall into one of four main themes:

- changes in society;
- economic trends;
- family structure changes; and
- demographic trends.

These trends and changes will have a major impact on all aspects of society, including schools.

### Changes in Society

The next three decades promise to bring as much change to the world as the previous two hundred years produced. Change is the decisive factor in the structure of the modern world (Benjamin, 1989). Many of the trends point to the need for cooperation, collaboration, and teamwork in making decisions. One of the more obvious trends is the global village concept. Societies have become more and more interdependent. It is no longer possible to limit your concerns to the immediate area in which you lives. Technology connects individuals, schools, and governments around the world. In this global village of interdependent societies, a decision on one side of the globe can dramatically affect the other side.

In order to survive in the global village, each society must learn to cooperate, collaborate, and communicate with all others. A responsible global citizenry is an expected outcome of the educational system. Tye (1990) suggests that global education can serve as a vehicle for bringing about school improvement. Global education focuses on the importance of involving communities and creating partnerships.

Technology will bring about complex changes at a rapid pace. The capability to store and retrieve information using computer data bases will force businesses, governments, and institutions such as schools to restructure. Toffler (1990b) suggests information networks will allow nonhierarchical communications to pass up and down the corporate ladder. Young employees on the bottom rung of the career ladder will be able to communicate directly with top-level executives working on the same problem. Employees who cannot collaborate within this process are not likely to survive in the workplace. Workers of the future will need to assess critically the information gathered across many cultures.

Knowledge is mushrooming at a pace no one individual can master. Statistics show that, in this country, some two thousand new titles appear on the bookshelves *every* month. It would require reading sixty-six books per day in order to stay abreast of new information in just this one information format. How, then, are you to deal with the overwhelming barrage of new information?

In the future, requirements for knowledge and responsibilities for decision making will be redistributed. In a continual cycle of learning, unlearning, and relearning, workers will master new technologies, adapt to new organizational forms, and generate new ideas. Technology that enhances team decision making will replace old hierarchical and bureaucratic structures. "Five-year-olds today experience more information in one year than their grandparents did in a lifetime" (Gayle, 1990, p. 12). It will be impossible for any one person to know everything needed for making good decisions.

If a student is having difficulty in today's learning environment, what will be the prognosis for that student's survival in tomorrow's world? What will it take for students with special learning needs to be successful lifelong learners? How can students with behavioral disorders be constructive, productive members in increasingly complex social environments? In what ways can the potential of those with special gifts and talents be developed?

It will become more and more necessary for individuals to work in teams and share their knowledge and skills, in order to be effective decision makers.

Schools will need to de-emphasize coverage of facts, stressing instead access to information and synthesis of that information. Consultation with others in their areas of expertise, and collaboration to pool the ideas and resources of all, will be key tools for human survival.

## Economic Trends

The pool of available labor is growing more slowly as fewer young people enter the job market (Gayle, 1990; Szabo, 1991).With the United States and other western nations shifting from an industrial and manufacturing economic base to a service, information, and high-technology base, there is a decline in work for unskilled laborers. There is also a growing mismatch between the skills needed in the workplace and the skills workers learn in school (Szabo, 1991).

In the near future, fewer than forty out of one hundred high school graduates will complete a college education, and the other sixty will be employed in vocations that require knowledge in technology. Some 73 percent of jobs today require information-processing skills at some level (Gayle, 1990), and this is likely to increase. Just as the industrial and agricultural economies diminished decades and centuries ago, as the service sector becomes automated, vocations in this sector will diminish as well. The cost of labor in the United States has enticed American industry to transport work requiring unskilled labor to third-world countries for completion.

In order to compete in the future world economy, a country must prepare its young people in basic concepts, principles, and systems of technology (Daggett, 1989). The future will provide few employment opportunities for those unable to read, write, and speak English easily, understand and perform basic mathematical computations, or apply learning to new situations. The future work force will need competence in problem solving and team effort (Gayle, 1990). Employers are depending on schools to prepare young people for this demand. However, nearly 20 percent of companies report difficulties in finding applicants who can read well enough to qualify for entry-level jobs (Szabo, 1991). Schools have a long way to go to meet the demands of the business, industry, and professional world for competent, qualified workers.

## Family Structure Changes

Another profound societal change can be found within the family unit. The stereotypical family of a mother, father, and two children constitutes only 7 percent of the families in the United States. Changes in family structure will significantly influence the way schools are structured in the future. The number of single-parent families will increase to about one in four among minority families and one in seven among white families. Single parents are predominantly women, many with no major job skills and little access to training. These families make up the majority of the poor in this country, so that ". . . the 'new poverty' among youth is primarily the result of having a single parent"

(Hodgkinson, 1988, p. 11). Collaboration will be required in order for public and private sector agencies, including schools, to help many of these families survive.

## Demographic Trends

Cultural diversity within ethnic groups is vast, and ethnic diversity in the United States is increasing. Two-thirds of the world's immigrants are coming to the United States. The increase in immigration will continue for the foreseeable future (Hodgkinson, 1988). Ethnic minorities soon will be the ethnic majority in the United States.

The median age of the population of the United States will rise from 30.6 years of age to 36.3 years of age by the year 2000, while the proportion of population over 65 years of age will rise from about 12 percent to about 17 percent. It is likely there will be competition for resources needed to provide expensive programs for dependent youth and services for the elderly (Hodgkinson, 1988).

Each of the issues in every summary group of trends that follows has implications for schools, and for educators as consultants, collaborators, team members, and partners in schools.

*In world trends:*

There will be greater interdependence among nations, diverse ethnic groups, and complex systems (Benjamin, 1989).

Technology will bring about complex changes at a rapid pace.

The capability to store and retrieve information, using computer data bases, will force businesses, government, and other institutions such as schools to restructure.

Society will demand a more convenient life style, expecting institutions to deliver their services with ease and speed.

*In economic trends:*

The pool of available labor is growing more slowly as fewer young people enter the job market (Gayle, 1990; Szabo, 1991).

Minorities and women will comprise 82 percent of the new entrants into the work force by the year 2000.

Although many people will use technology in the future, a relatively small percentage of the total work force will require sophisticated technical knowledge (Benjamin, 1989).

Just as the agricultural and industrial economies have diminished, the service sector is about to become automatized, and vocations in that semiskilled sector will diminish.

*In family structure changes:*

The American family will continue to be diverse, with no single family type representing the majority of Americans.

"People will change jobs or careers five or more times, which will require lifelong training and learning"(Gayle, 1990, p. 12).

Work at home will increase as office automation becomes more portable and powerful.

*In demographic trends:*

The proportion of the population over age 65 will rise from 12 percent to about 17 percent by the year 2000. This "graying of America" means that the future will require better understanding of the implications of lifelong learning (Benjamin, 1989; Gayle, 1990).

Minority populations will increase faster than majority populations and will become the majority populations in large urban areas, the South, and western sections of the country. ". . . a majority of today's California elementary school students are minorities; therefore, we can predict a 'minority majority' in California adults by 2010" (Hodgkinson, 1988, p. 11).

## Changes Affecting Schools of the Future

In Chapter 1, current school reform movements were related to the need for consultation and collaboration among educators. Reform and restructuring movements are a response to societal changes that have placed increased demands on schools to meet the changing needs of students and their families. According to Newmann (1991), the call for drastic changes is related to two issues:

- large numbers of students, especially low-income students of color, who fail in school and score poorly on national tests; and
- students who succeed in school and score well, but are not fully prepared to cope successfully with the demands of contemporary life.

Many key leaders in education are trying to predict and forecast for schools of the future. Thoughtful educators recognize schools will need to be very different from the way they are now, but they do not always agree about changes needed. It is clear that more choices must be available for young people during their high school years, in order to prepare the work force needed for the future. Without an educated work force, the economy will suffer and decline in productivity. Educational changes will be needed in school governance, reform of curriculum and instruction, accountability, and roles of educators (Newmann, 1991). Although there is considerable debate on the meaning of reform and restructuring initiatives, there is agreement on two issues:

- The purpose of changes called for is to provide a quality education for all children, especially those with learning and behavior problems.
- There will be considerable role change, including increased collaboration and consultation (Jenkins, Pious, and Jewell, 1990).

Reform and restructuring call for collaboration in planning and problem solving, and this will require enhanced collegial relationships (West, 1990). Educational collaboration can be an effective catalyst for bringing about needed changes in complex educational systems.

> *The greatest challenge facing education is not technology, not resources, not accountability—it is the need to discover with our students a new way of thinking. This quest does not require merely different information, but rather a whole new way of viewing the world. (Crowell, 1989, p. 60)*

This new way of thinking is happening whether we are immediately aware of it or not. There is a shift away from the Newtonian ideas of simplicity, hierarchy, mechanics, assembly, and objectivity that have nourished our current view of the world. The new view is more integrative, holistic, collective, cooperative, and organizational. These changes are occurring in scientific thought, but they have implications for education as well (Crowell, 1989; Meyen and Skrtic, 1988).

This new way of thinking will profoundly affect the structure of schools in the future. The school cannot separate itself from teaching and learning. It *is* teaching and learning.

> *Our new world view suggests that isolation cannot lead to meaningful learning within any organization. But schools isolate kids from experience. Teachers are isolated in classrooms. Principals are isolated from students, teachers, and other principals. Staff evaluation is isolated from professional growth. Schools are isolated from each other. . . .We must ask, 'How can the school and all its constituent parts become more integrated, more cohesive?'. . . For me, the concept of 'embeddedness' is a useful metaphor. For example, embedded in teaching is learning; the two cannot really be talked about separately. Embedded in the teacher is the student, for one is incomplete without the other. Embedded in history is art, science, literature, and music. Embedded in humans is nature; we are part of our environment, and it is part of us. (Crowell, 1989, p. 61)*

Crowell (1989) stresses that we do need to appreciate where we are and how we got here. The challenge of new ways of thinking is not a call to abandon our cherished values that have provided meaning and direction. Instead, it is a challenge to participate in creating a new vision of the human role and educating students to achieve their potential.

Schaps (1990) asserts the public is seeing the necessity of changing the overall *system* for education, while realizing that the efforts will not work if they focus *only* on improved teaching processes, *or* content of the curriculum, *or*

**Application For**
*Matching Predictions to Consultation and Collaboration Roles*

Consider the following changes in school some educators are predicting for the next century. How do these changes match your ideas? What will be the role of consultation, collaboration, and teamwork in education from "birth to death" if these predictions come to pass?

Total integration for many special education students who are currently served in pull-out programs will continue well into the next century (Wiederholt, 1989).

As the reform efforts bring about restructuring of schools to include integration of academic and technical skills for changing society, vocational education will become more valued in secondary schools (Gayle, 1990).

More emphasis will be given to early childhood education as a preventive measure and, if this is successful, remedial programs will be decreased (Benjamin, 1989). There will be a need for more collaboration among preschool teachers, school psychologists, parents, health service providers, and other personnel within and outside the school.

The Back-to-Basics movement will become Forward-to-Emerging Basics, which will include the use of telecommunications technology in problem solving and other advanced technical skills (Gayle, 1990).

Increased student learning times will result from flexible school scheduling (Gayle, 1990).

Students will be taught to expect change and use it to advantage, while more emphasis will be given to preparing students to think like generalists rather than specialists (Benjamin, 1989).

Individual differences will be acknowledged through personalized goals without adherence to arbitrary time schedules, grade levels, and classification systems; there will be an emphasis on "learning how to learn" rather than on learning facts (Benjamin, 1990). There will be a new collaborative role for teachers and students in which students accept an active senior partnership role in the learning enterprise (Benjamin, 1989).

Professions are products of the Zeitgeist, or the general intellectual and ethical climate and needs of a particular time in history (McGaghie, 1991). This is an important consideration in assessing the competence of educators for performing their roles. Data from educator evaluations will be interpreted in a broader framework, encouraging expanded roles for teachers and support personnel.

"Education will be respected as a valuable and prestigious profession by the 21st century" (Gayle, 1990, p. 13).

goals and policies of schools. Instead, process, content, and policy are strongly tied to one another so that change in any one necessitates change in all three.

## The Future for Students with Special Needs

Family status, ethnicity, and economic level of students in schools of the future will be different from those today. It is necessary to speculate about the nature of the problems students in special education programs for learning and behavioral disorders will have if the dual system of regular education and special education survives. Schools will enroll an increased number of children with severe impairments—for example, cerebral palsy and such syndromes as Trisomy 13 and 18—who will need special services. Medical problems that used to result in death during the first year of life are now being treated; children with these complications are living long enough to become students in public schools. Increasing numbers of premature infants are being saved at even earlier stages of their development. The rapidly increasing group of children whose parents ingested alcohol and other drugs before conception or during pregnancy, or who transferred complications through sexually transmitted diseases will have an alarming impact on education. For example, one of the fastest growing populations at risk for AIDS is young children. These children will greatly tax the physical, emotional, and economic resources of schools and school personnel. The burgeoning population of senior citizens will vie for the same resources that children need.

These problems require up-to-date knowledge on the part of school personnel and ongoing collaboration with professionals in the medical field. In addition to this challenge, schools will face the increasing financial demands made by students with such types of problems.

## Changes in Teaching Practices for the Future

"Many concepts in special education are proving increasingly unworkable. Nowhere is this more evident than in our attempts to reify the 'conditions' we decided were evidenced by individuals who failed in school" (Ysseldyke, 1986, p. 22). Reification (converting an abstraction into a concrete thing) of categories, labels, delivery systems based on test scores, and the like, too often has diverted the attention of educators away from improving instruction. As stressed in an earlier chapter, a growing number of special education leaders contend that students at risk of school failure in conventional settings are not disabled and deficient students. The problem lies in the misfit between their abilities and the demands made on them in an inflexible school situation. Teachers would do well to examine their teaching practices, curricular requirements, and learning environment structure as a first alternative, if students are not learning and behaving acceptably.

With school consultation and collaboration as an integral part of the educational program, there is hope for creating the flexibility students need, and for enhancing the repertoire of teaching practices that will enable them to succeed. The best teachers have always been those who expand, change, modify, and compact the requirements so that the important material is taught, but in a way and to the extent that serves each student's individual, special needs.

In their book that is widely used in special education courses, Hallahan and Kauffman (1991) include several descriptions of collaborative efforts between a classroom teacher and a special education teacher. For example, when an itinerant teacher for the visually impaired and a third-grade teacher work together to adapt material and team up to provide services, there are three beneficiaries of their efforts: consultant, consultee, and client. Even the roles are somewhat interchangeable, depending on who provides the direct service to whom. When a teacher of emotionally disturbed students and a fifth-grade teacher collaborate on procedures and reinforcements for a seriously disturbed student, all three roles again benefit. Additionally, the student's improved behavior creates a positive ripple effect for other school personnel and students in the school.

Literature on change and the future is evolving from viewing teachers as recalcitrant and resistant to change, toward examining the structure of the school context and the personal attributes of teachers that affect whether or not they implement changes (Richardson, 1990). Hoyt (1991) identifies two kinds of educational change as:

- process, or people change; and
- structural, or system, change.

Structural changes will work only after the "people change" creates an attitude of readiness for structural change (Hoyt, 1991).

In a study sponsored by the Association for Supervision and Curriculum Development, concerning changes needed in high school curriculum, high school principals who were surveyed identified six new roles or needs emerging in high schools (Cawelti and Adkisson, 1986):

- instructional processes specialist;
- technology specialist;
- parent advisory group specialist;
- school/private sector liaison;
- minority affairs specialist; and
- change facilitator.

Unfortunately, the existence of these roles in schools of the mid-1980s was reported by the principals as minimal.

It will be important for school personnel in the future to participate actively in school improvement projects. Keys to the success of organizational development projects are a genuine investment in the process by the top administrator and skillful involvement of the staff (Conoley, 1989). Conoley emphasizes teachers will need to take some responsibility for achieving the quality of outcomes they desire. However, they must also feel the extra effort they give to committee work, problem identification, or problem-solving teams is not just added to their load of responsibilities. They need to perceive this effort as having a positive effect on their daily lives.

## School Changes Requiring Collaboration and Teamwork

In their commentary on the necessary restructuring of special and regular education, Reynolds, Wang, and Walberg (1987) propose that unless major structural changes are made in the field of special education, special education will become more a problem, and not so much a solution, in providing education for children with special needs. Disjointedness and proceduralism are twin facets of the overall problem these researchers identify as inefficiency in using costly resources. Increasing numbers of students who qualify for special education and an increasingly negative climate for funding to support special projects add to the problems and trends that signal the need for change.

Collaborative consultation is recommended by Phillips and McCullough (1990) as a viable tool for educators to use in coping with a rapidly changing, increasingly complex society. They also suggest that correlates of collaboration

---

**Application For**
*Making Changes Through Consultation, Collaboration, and Teamwork*

Consider the following typical school needs, and ways that consultation and the collaborative ethic might assist in making school changes:

- Create opportunities to interface special education programs with the general program.
- Institute communication networks among school staff, parents, advocacy groups.
- Contribute to text selections, curriculum revisions, general school reform.
- Identify exemplary, successful teaching practices.
- Coordinate use of community resources for students' needs.
- Help parents identify ways to contribute to school programs.
- Help other educators and parents set realistic goals for students with learning and behavioral problems.
- Contribute to planning and conducting in-service and staff development.
- Conduct formative and summative evaluation to improve school programs.

such as group morale, cohesion, and increased knowledge of processes and alternatives are important to success in meeting student needs. However, they note:

> *Administrative, teaching and support personnel must address matters of conceptual dissonance and reach a consensus regarding the nature and importance of collaborative relations. In short, educational leaders and advocates of consultation-based programming must develop ways to effectively institute a collaborative ethic in schools. (Phillips and McCullough, 1990, p. 295)*

This collaborative ethic is a means of empowering professionals to assist each other in solving problems. Teacher empowerment is threatened when teachers are asked to make changes without the opportunity to reflect on the theoretical frameworks. Opportunities should be provided that allow teachers to interact and have conversations about their work (Richardson, 1990). Richardson cautions that this process must be implemented in an atmosphere of trust.

Hoyt (1991) stresses that collaboration involving school personnel must involve not only shared responsibility, but shared authority and shared accountability as well. As Hoyt puts it, this three-way sharing will help ensure the concept of collaboration fares better in the 1990s than the concept of partnerships did during the 1980s.

## Coordination of Health, Education, and Social Services

Schools alone are not responsible for solving all the problems that keep students from succeeding in the adult world. Numerous other public and private sector agencies combine to make up the current system of services for families and children. Mental health, employment and training, child development, recreation, health, and welfare services, as well as education, have a vital interest in promoting school success of all students. The Education and Human Services Consortium (Melaville and Blank, 1991) proposes that education, health, and human service agencies join each other as coequals in orchestrating the delivery of services, instead of each struggling on its own and succeeding imperfectly. Too often these agencies operate like ships that pass in the night, seldom perceiving each other as allies. Joint efforts are needed to bring together the assortment of services needed by the one-in-three children and youths who are most at risk. Practitioners, policymakers, parents, and taxpayers are concurring that finding ways of keeping children in school is a shared responsibility (William T. Grant Foundation, 1988).

Improved relationships, interagency partnerships, and the creation of new roles are keys to developing high-quality comprehensive services and delivery systems, so children receive the services they need. Collaborative strategies are essential; therefore, education agencies and others must modify "business as usual" attitudes and approaches, in order to collaborate for the needs of students. Collaboration requires commitment, trust, and cooperation, to expedite and sustain needed changes. Structures and mechanisms must be created that enable providers to get as much mileage as possible out of available resources, while improving the quality and range of services (Melaville and Blank, 1991). Communication and problem solving will be needed to achieve a future in which students become successful, contributing members of society. Comprehensive solutions to complex social and economic problems will require the highest and best collaboration skills educators can provide. Although specialization is the trend, partnerships are the means of assuring a successful future for students.

## New Metaphors for Education

The very essence of thinking about issues and attributes can be revealed by metaphor (Pollio, 1987). Metaphors are mental maps that permit the connection of different meanings through some shared similarity. They appear often in spoken and written communication. For example, "Life is a loom," "The fog swallowed the ship," and "The flower garden is a paintbox of colors" are metaphors. They connect, in order to explain. People use metaphors to sort out their perceptions, evaluate, express feelings, and reflect on the purpose of things, in order to make better sense of their world (Deshler, 1985).

Belth (1977) suggests that as we create or reject particular metaphors, we form problems. The world's problems become what we form them to be. So, through metaphors, we can imagine the world as we wish it to be, and can fashion it accordingly.

Even though metaphors are good tools for explaining ideas and achieving new perspectives on both the unfamiliar and the very familiar, they can imprison thinking if they are simplistic or outdated (von Oech, 1983). Schools and education have generated a variety of metaphors, but some of them are now viewed as uninspiring and somewhat demoralizing to the human spirit. Dobson, Dobson, and Koetting (1985) assert that education is imprisoned today within three unfortunate metaphors:

- A military metaphor—characterized by concepts and vocabulary such as target population, strategy, objectives, training, standardized, discipline, schedule, and information systems;
- An industrial metaphor—revealed by language such as cost-effectiveness, product, feedback, efficiency, quality control, and management; and
- A disease metaphor—reflected in words and practices such as diagnostic, prescriptive, treatment, remediation, label, impaired, monitor, deviant, and referral.

These metaphors may be counterproductive, and perhaps iatrogenic, for educators, parents, and most of all, students. Now more than ever before, we need good metaphors in education. One promising metaphor is gardening, assimilating concepts and vocabulary that reflect budding potential, special needs, and productive outcomes.

For example, a gardening/cultivator metaphor might focus on :

- seeds—students;
- climate—learning environment;
- soil—curriculum;
- gardener—teacher, parent, support personnel;
- light—ideas;
- rain—materials, resources, opportunity for learning;
- shade—incubation, protection;
- fertilizer—stimulation, interest, curiosity, fun;
- weeds—irrelevancies;
- pruning/grafting—deficits, talents;
- predators/disease—learning and behavior problems;
- seasons—time, rhythm and cycle of development; and
- harvest—achievement, fulfillment;

Development of a powerful new metaphor that features school consultation, collaboration, and teamwork just might intrigue resistant, reluctant colleagues and entice them to try these complex interactive processes (see Figure E–1). Stimuli for creating new metaphors can come from many sources:

- thinking about important student outcomes;
- finding ways parents, support personnel, and other community members can be involved in learning;
- engaging in collegial interactions among school educators and parent educators;
- highlighting examples of teacher satisfaction;
- carrying out school reform; and
- acknowledging today's students as society's future.

---

*Thought Problem*

*Create a new metaphor for learning, teaching, consulting, or collaborating. Make it more positive than the conventional military, industrial, and disease metaphors. Decide on a way to express your new metaphor. For example, you might use a paragraph, poem, drawing, song, or physical movement that releases it from your own inner thoughts into a form that can be shared with others. Share it with colleagues. What new vocabulary does your metaphor contribute to the profession?*

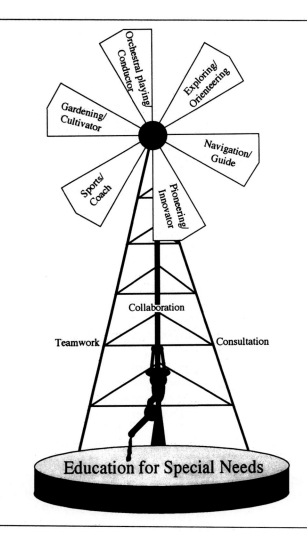

**Figure   E–1**

by L. Katzer

## Challenges for Consultation, Collaboration, and Teamwork in the Future

As educational consultants struggle to establish themselves in school class-rooms and buildings, they often find they are pioneers in modeling consulta-tion, collaboration, and teamwork. They must serve as consultants and advo-cates of children with learning and behavior needs when the nature of those needs is changing quickly. They will be collaborating with professionals in

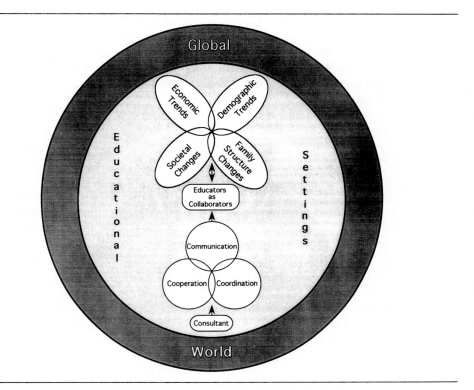

**Figure E–2**

by P. Dettmer and L. Katzer

fields focusing on problems as varied and alarming as alcohol and other drug abuse, neonatal health, sexually transmitted diseases, disintegration of the family, psychological disorders, poverty, child abuse, English-as-second-language concerns, geographic isolation, environmental hazards, and a host of unresolved or not-yet-recognized needs.

Struggles to establish new collaborative roles for educators will be stressful and time-consuming (Newmann, 1991). No simple solution exists for the complex issues and concerns of the future. Now is the time to develop skills of consultation, collaboration, and teamwork on behalf of students with special needs and the society in which they live (see Figure E–2).

Collaboration is the future. It is intrinsic to school reform and restructuring, interagency cooperation, responses to changing student needs, and future global, economic, demographic, and technological trends. As consultants facilitate collaboration and teamwork within the school context, to serve special needs each school day, they provide a basis and a framework for continued collaboration throughout the global village. This framework provides help and hope for our students of today, who will be the citizens of tomorrow.

## Tips for Consulting and Collaborating

1. Don't try to do it all by yourself.
2. Advertise successes, both yours and those of classroom teachers. Sometimes teachers are amazed that a student or a situation has shown *any* progress whatsoever.
3. Give talks at community clubs and service organizations—about schools, student needs, consultation and collaboration endeavors.
4. Develop a networking system for support and delivery of positive "strokes" to school personnel and parents.
5. Inform teachers of legislative and litigative activity.
6. Host sessions at conferences for policy makers and administrators.
7. Have open house and extend invitations to school board members.
8. Follow up open house with-thank you notes to visitors for their interest and attendance.
9 During the summer, send postcards to teachers saying, "I'm looking forward to working with you this year."
10. Don't appear *too* dedicated—so much so that your involvement is intimidating to others who are still unsure and a bit reluctant.
11. Write a proposal and receive resources for sharing with the schools.
12. Do not expect the same levels of involvement and commitment from everyone.
13. Do not try to "go it alone." Look to colleagues for support and counsel.
14. Be an advocate through serving as officer and committee member of organizations whose goals support your consultation goals and role.
15. Never give up!

## Chapter Review

1. World trends and societal changes in economics, family structure, and demographics will affect students with special needs in a number of significant ways.
2. Schools of the future will house large numbers of students who are failing and performing poorly on national tests, as well as students who perform better on tests but are not prepared adequately for the demands of the workplace.
3. There will be increasingly large populations of students who have profound learning and behavior problems brought on by social problems, medical problems, and economic hardships.
4. Successful schools of the future will require educators to make changes in role functions and school personnel, and will encourage parents to be actively involved in school reform and restructuring.

**5.** New metaphors are needed for education. Metaphors help define problems and clarify thinking. Visions for the future of learning and teaching that focus on traditional metaphors for education, such as military, industrial, and disease, are myopic and somewhat demoralizing.

**6.** Bringing about needed school change requires greater emphasis on collaboration and teamwork. School consultation will be an important tool for coordinating health, social, and educational services to help all students, particularly those with special needs.

## Activities

**1.** Discuss three to five major concerns regarding social, economic, and environmental issues of the future that will have a major impact on school learning and teaching. How can consultation, collaboration, and teamwork help students with special needs succeed in spite of the pressures they face from these issues?

**2** What are the major conditions within school contexts and competencies of school personnel that are needed for successful consultation, collaboration, and teamwork by educators?

**3.** Select one or more of the issues and concerns discussed in this chapter. Have a panel of four or five members read more about these issues and reflect on them. Then conduct a panel forum, directing questions from the whole group to panel members for their comments.

As a variation, have a roundtable discussion in which each participant reads about one issue presented in the chapter, and a moderator asks each, in turn, questions having a common denominator of focus—in this case, school consultation and collaboration. (A seating arrangement around tables forming a U shape, with the moderator moving about inside the U shaped space, works well.)

**4.** Generate a list of possibilities for inclusion in a newsletter to parents, community leaders, or school personnel that reflects consulting teacher roles and the contributions these roles can make to students, school programs, and communities for the future.

**5.** Create a list of school reform research questions needed for the future that might be explored within the context of strong school consultation programs and competent consulting personnel.

**6.** Develop a personal plan for using concepts of school consultation, collaboration, and consultation within the school context, and in the role responsibilities you anticipate for the future.

**7.** Find a forum in which to promote your new metaphor for education.

**8.** Create a motivational bumper sticker that will proclaim the importance of professional and parent educators during the 1990's and into the next millennium.

# For Further Reading

Naisbitt, J., and Aburdene, J. (1990). *Megatrends 2000.* New York: Morrow.

Toffler, A. (1990). *Powershift.* New York: Bantam.

William T. Grant Foundation Commission on Work, Family, and Citizenship. (1988). *The Forgotten Half: Pathways to success for America's Youth and Young Families.* Washington, D.C.: Author.

# References

Belth, M. (1977). *The Process of Thinking.* New York: McKay.

Benjamin, S. (1989). An ideascape for education: What futurists recommend. *Educational Leadership, 47*(1):9–14.

Cawelti, G., and Adkisson, J. (August, 1986). ASCD study documents changes needed in high school curriculum. *Curriculum Update,* pp. 1–10.

Conoley, J. C. (1989). Professional communication and collaboration among educators. In M. C. Reynolds (ed.), *Knowledge Base for the Beginning Teacher.* Oxford, England: Pergamon Press.

Crowell, S. (1989). A new way of thinking: The challenge of the future. *Educational Leadership, 47*(1):60–63.

Daggett, W. R. (1989). The changing nature of work—A challenge to education. Unpublished speech delivered to the Kansas Legislative and Educational Leaders.

Deshler, D. (November–December, 1985). Metaphors and values in higher education. *Academe,* p. 22–29.

Dobson, R. L., Dobson, J. E., and Koetting, J. R. (1985). *Looking at, Talking About, and Living with Children: Reflections on the Process of Schooling.* Lanham, MD: University Press of America.

Gayle, M. (1990). Toward the 21st century. *Adult Learning, l*(4):10–14.

Hallahan, D. P., and Kauffman, J. M. (1991). *Exceptional Children: Introduction to Special Education.* Englewood Cliffs, NJ: Prentice Hall.

Hodgkinson, H. (1988). The right schools for the right kids. *Educational Leadership, 45*(6):10–14.

Hoyt, K. (1991). Education reform and relationships between the private sector and education: A call for integration. *Phi Delta Kappan, 72*(6):450–53.

Jenkins, J. R., Pious, C. G., and Jewell, M. (1990). Special education and the regular education initiative: Basic assumptions. *Exceptional Children, 56*:479–91.

McGaghie, W. C. (1991). Professional competence evaluation. *Educational Researcher, 20*(1):3–9.

Melaville, A. I., and Blank, M. J. (1991). *What it Takes: Structuring Interagency Partnerships to Connect Children and Families with Comprehensive Services.* Washington, D.C.: Education and Human Resources Consortium.

Meyen, E. L., and Skrtic, T. (eds.). (1988). *Exceptional Children and Youth: an Introduction* (3d ed.). Denver: Love.

Naisbitt, J., and Aburdene, J. (1990). Megatrends 2000. New York: Morrow.

Newmann, F. M. (1991). Linking restructuring to authentic student achievement. *Phi Delta Kappan, 72,* 458–64.

Phillips, V., and McCullough, L. (1990). Consultation–based programming: Instituting the collaborative ethic in schools. *Exceptional Children, 56*(4):291–304.

Pollio, H. (Fall, 1987). Practical poetry: Metaphoric thinking in science, art, literature, and nearly everywhere else. *Teaching–Learning Issues,* pp. 3–17.

Reynolds, M. C., Wang, M. C., and Walberg, H. J. (1987). The necessary restructuring of special and regular education. *Exceptional Children, 53*(5):391–98.

Richardson, V. (1990). Significant and worthwhile change in teaching practice. *Educational Researcher, 19*(7):10–18.

Schaps, E. (1990). Cooperative learning: The challenge in the 90s. *Cooperative Learning, 10*(4): 5–8.

Szabo, J. C. (February, 1991). Finding the right workers. *Nation's Business,* pp. 16–22.

Toffler, A. (1990) *Powershift.* New York: Bantam.

Toffler, A. (1990b). Power shift: Knowledge, wealth and violence at the edge of the 21st century. *Newsweek,* October 15, pp. 86–92.

Tye, K. A. (ed.). (1990). *Global Education: from Thought to Action.* Alexandria, VA: Association for Supervision and Curriculum Development.

von Oech, R. (1983). *A Whack on the Side of the Head.* New York: Warner Books.

West, J. F. (1990). Educational collaboration in the restructuring of schools. *Journal of Educational and Psychological Consultation,* 1:23–41.

Wiederholt, L. L. (1989). Restructuring special education services: The past, the present, the future. *Learning Disability Quarterly,* 12:181–91.

William T. Grant Foundation Commission on Work, Family, and Citizenship. (1988). *The forgotten half: Pathways to Success for America's Youth and Young Families.* Washington, D.C.: Author.

Ysseldyke, J. E. (1986). The use of assessment information to make decisions about students. In R. J. Morris and B. Blatt (eds.), *Special Education: Research and Trends.* New York: Pergamon Press.

# AUTHOR INDEX

# SUBJECT INDEX